THE
NATURE
OF
CRIME

HAROLD J. VETTER

IRA J. SILVERMAN

Department of Criminal Justice,
University of South Florida,
Tampa, Florida

1978

W. B. SAUNDERS COMPANY / Philadelphia / London / Toronto

W. B. Saunders Company: West Washington Square
Philadelphia, PA 19105

1 St. Anne's Road
Eastbourne, East Sussex BN21 3UN, England

1 Goldthorne Avenue
Toronto, Ontario M8Z 5T9, Canada

Library of Congress Cataloging in Publication Data

Vetter, Harold J

The nature of crime.

Includes index.

1. Crime and criminals.   I. Silverman, Ira J., joint author.
   II. Title.

HV6025.V49   364   76-20092

ISBN 0-7216-9017-3

Cover photography by John Shearer, Bill Eppridge, Margaret Bourke-White
for Life Magazine, courtesy Time, Inc., and by Fred Conrad, Mickey
Osterreicher, for Time Magazine, courtesy Time, Inc.

The Nature of Crime   ISBN 0-7216-9017-3

Last digit is the print number: 9 8 7 6 5 4 3 2 1

TO GINA AND HAPPY —

with all our love

PREFACE

The main purpose of this book is to acquaint the student and general reader with the characteristics of some of the major types of personal and property crimes and their perpetrators. In preparing this account, our principal sources have been official statistics on the frequency and distribution of crimes, such as the *Uniform Crime Reports* published annually by the Federal Bureau of Investigation, and research on offenses and offenders reported in the professional literature of criminal justice and criminology. Invaluable additional help has been received from our colleagues, to whom we owe our sincere gratitude and appreciation.

Our account does not purport to be exhaustive. We have excluded specific consideration of the so-called "consensual," or "victimless," crimes, such as gambling and prostitution, most of which are currently the target of intense efforts by various groups to bring about decriminalization.

Our primary focus has been on crimes against the person — murder, forcible rape, robbery, and aggravated assault — and conventional property crimes, including larceny, burglary, and motor vehicle theft. We have also dealt in some detail with organized crime, examining its structure and history and its range of illegitimate and legitimate enterprises. We are very much in debt to Ralph Salerno, who was kind enough to share with us his insights on organized criminal activity.

Another category of crime we have explored is economic, or "white-collar," crimes, which includes a broad spectrum of offenses involving frauds directed against individuals and groups. The United States Chamber of Commerce has estimated that economic crimes cost the public more than $40 billion each year.

We have touched briefly on a number of "special category offenders" — persons who pose unique problems for the criminal justice system and process. Included here are juveniles, women, narcotics and alcohol addicts, the mentally disturbed and the mentally retarded, and antisocial (psychopathic) offenders. In each instance, we have tried to indicate the nature of the problems these offenders create for a crininal justice system that is oriented primarily toward adult male criminals.

Theoretical attempts to account for crime causation have generated a large and controversial body of professional literature. To do justice to this topic would require a book that would at least equal — and probably exceed — the size of the present volume. Nevertheless, we considered it important to provide the reader with a sampling of the major contemporary theories of crime causation.

In one of the concluding chapters, we have devoted attention to a subject that has been of increasing concern to both criminologists and criminal justice professionals: the crime victim. We are heavily indebted to Dr. John Dussich, presently on the faculty of the Department of Criminal Justice at the University of Southern Mississippi, for his critical comments on victimology. Dr. Dussich's contributions to the professional literature on victim services and their delivery were a significant source of information on this important topic.

The closing chapter of this book is concerned with the impact of crime on American society. More debilitating than mere economic losses, however grievous these may be to victims who are poor, elderly, or in ill health, is the social and psychological toll exacted by crime depredations. As long as people fear the streets of their own cities and feel compelled to barricade themselves behind deadbolts and electronic security systems, no amount of official reassurance is likely to shake their belief that the criminals, not the forces of law and order, have been the victors in the war against crime.

The senior author wishes to acknowledge his indebtedness to those from whom he has received assistance, support, and counsel in the development of this book: Reed Adams, theoretician and researcher in the criminogenic process; Harry Allen, internationally recognized criminologist and administrator; Peter Lewis, an indefatigable legal scholar and Supreme Court watcher; Cliff Simonsen, criminal justice educator and author; and Jack Wright, Jr., friend and accomplice in a variety of endeavors, some of which have relevance for the criminal justice system.

The junior author would like to express his gratitude to several persons who have contributed directly or indirectly to this project. First, he would like to recognize a debt to two former teachers: Professor Simon Dinitz — mentor, scholar, and friend — whose tutelage, support, and inspiration contributed significantly to the author's development during his graduate education; and Professor Walter C. Reckless, teacher and scholar, who also made major contributions to the author's growth during his graduate career. Finally, to Happy Silverman, his wife, for her patience, forbearance, and assistance throughout the preparation of this text he wishes to acknowledge his deepest and most heartfelt appreciation.

Both authors are grateful for the encouragement they received from Jack Snyder, Criminal Justice Editor at W. B. Saunders Company. They also appreciate the expert and imaginative work that was expended on this manuscript by Ellen Murray, Lorraine Battista, and the rest of the capable Saunders production staff. Special thanks are due to Maggie Deutsch and Mae Ogle for their yeoman services in reducing our often indecipherable hieroglyphics to a coherent manuscript. We cannot say enough on their behalf.

H.J.V.

I.J.S.

Tampa, Florida

CONTENTS

1 DEVIANCE, SOCIAL CONTROL, AND CRIMINALITY

In Tallahassee, Florida, an official of the state government accepts a "gift" of $10,000 from a land developer in return for a favorable zoning decision. In Toronto, Ontario, a teenager arms himself with two rifles and engages in a shooting spree at a local high school, leaving three people dead and thirteen wounded. In New Orleans, Louisiana, two men and a woman are taken into custody by federal officers when they land a plane loaded with two tons of marijuana. An exasperated taxi driver in Newark, New Jersey, deliberately rams the back of another cab that has taken his space at the curb outside the air terminal building.

All of these acts are *crimes*; in each instance, some law or statute has been violated. These actions have the additional common property that they are all *deviant* acts. According to Webster's Dictionary, to deviate is to "turn aside from a course, direction, standard, doctrine, etc." Used in the more specific context of sociological analysis, deviance involves behavior that varies or diverges from social norms which regulate conduct within a group or society. Most people tend to be "socially invisible" within their community. Deviance means, among other things, that an individual or group becomes visible to the majority.

A crime is defined legally as the violation of one or more criminal statutes. The implication is that such behavior is harmful to the public and an offense against the community, state, or nation. However, for those who wish to pursue the systematic study of crime, criminals, criminal behavior, and the criminal justice system, this legal definition is unduly restrictive because it

1

limits the study of criminal behavior to only those persons who have been officially adjudicated or labeled "criminal" or "delinquent." Consequently, a great deal of behavior that is of interest and concern to the student of criminal justice would remain unexamined. Criminologists and other criminal justice professionals tend to consider criminal behavior as simply a part of the much more extensive spectrum of *deviant* behavior.

NORMS AND SANCTIONS

Every society has adopted rules to regulate the behavior of its members. These consensually agreed-upon rules, designed to protect society against disruption and to safeguard its basic structure and values, are called *norms*. Norms may contain both *proscriptive* and *prescriptive* elements. *Proscriptions* are statements of behavior that is forbidden (e.g., murder, rape, kidnapping, treason, and other forms of rebellion against group authority). *Prescriptions* are statements of behavior that is encouraged or reinforced (e.g., getting married, raising children, holding down a steady job, paying taxes, and other behavior that appears to foster the common welfare). Norms specify a variety of *social sanctions* (rewards and punishments) that serve to encourage "proper" behavior. Perhaps it will help us to understand the operation of social sanctions if we conceive of social behavior *as a continuum*, as shown in Figure 1–1.

Behavior toward the center of the continuum is controlled by social norms which the anthropologist or sociologist calls *folkways*. Enforcement of these social rules is usually accomplished by mild disapproval (a cold stare, raised eyebrows, a reproving glance) or by mild encouragement (a smile, applause, an approving glance). Behavior which threatens the existence of the group or is

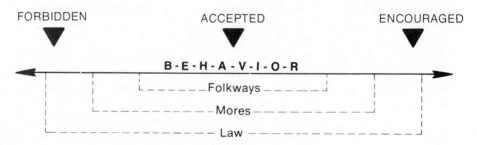

Figure 1–1. Continuum of social behavior.

seen as necessary to the perpetuation of the group is controlled by a stronger set of norms called *mores*. Mores are enforced by more vigorous or severe expressions of social disapproval (verbal abuse, beatings, temporary ostracism) or by stronger encouragement (monetary rewards, praise, testimonials, promotions). Norms can evolve into formal statements of proper behavior called *laws*. These formal statements will most likely represent the more important social values of a society at a given time. (Things having social value include objects, conditions, or states which are considered desirable and good and which people are willing to expend time and energy to own or achieve.) In early tribal societies, laws were statements of strong social rules that were perpetuated by word of mouth and passed from leader to leader; only later were they codified and put into written form. Laws now have been written to cover the entire spectrum of behavior.

Law evolves as an expression of the moral sentiments of a society and, in turn, reinforces these same mores. Those persons who flout legal norms may find themselves fined, imprisoned, exiled, or executed. Laws are most effective when supported by the existing mores. For example, the legal requirement that citizens of the United States wear appropriate clothing in public seldom needs enforcement. The American people have so internalized this norm that its breach is a relative rarity.

However, the United States is not a monolithic culture; it is an aggregation of diverse subcultures with varying religious and social values, held together by a common belief in the democratic processes of decision-making. The values which bind the people of the United States together are stronger than the forces which divide them. Given a pluralistic society, seldom would any national legislation be in complete harmony with the mores of all the groups in the society. When the Supreme Court decided in 1954 that "separate but equal" was a misnomer, the order to integrate public schools was an attempt to change mores and laws, especially of the southern United States. Later, the North was to discover that it had practiced a more subtle form of segregation, and the changing of these norms would at times prove more difficult than changing the visible legal system of the South. When a law is backed by no clear consensus (e.g., the implementation of court decisions requiring integration in the South), only over-whelming force can bring about its application. It took an army to enroll one black student in the University of Mississippi.

If the mores are so powerful, can one legislate against them? If effective law enforcement is dependent upon community support, how can legislation succeed if it is contrary to the mores of the group? The law cannot change subjective attitudes directly. But the law can change interaction patterns, and in time new social relations will come to seem as natural and desirable as the old ones whose preservation was once so diligently defended. Indeed, in the United States the law has been the principal agent in creating both segregation and integration of the races. A large body of law developed around the turn of the century which accelerated the trend toward the segregation of the races. A new social order evolved in the South to replace the old one destroyed by the Civil War. Laws were passed which prohibited members of different races from using the same lavatories and drinking from the same water fountains. Institutions for the aged, orphans, and the blind were segregated. In 1909, Mobile, Alabama, passed a curfew law applying exclusively to black people, requiring them to be off the streets by 10:00 P.M. In 1915, the Oklahoma legislature saw fit to provide segregated telephone booths. New Orleans, Louisiana, with a logic fathomed only by those who drafted the ordinance, segregated white and black prostitutes.

For the law to be effective in social change, it must operate with, and not against, the forces of change in society. "Nothing is so powerful as an idea whose time has come." When the law is in harmony with the processes of change, it accelerates that change. Since 1954, the entire trend of national legislation, and judicial decrees, has been to speed the process of undoing the normative system of segregation which the law had helped to create around 1900.

NORMS AND SOCIALIZATION

From the very beginning we are made aware of norms as expected ways of behaving, and through the socialization process, we internalize these norms and adopt them as our personal guidelines for behavior. In fact, internalization and habit are the major reasons why people do not violate norms.

The principal agency of socialization, and society's basic unit, is the family. Generally, children adopt the norms, folkways, values, and speech patterns of their parents. Through a series of rewards and punishments, parents prepare their children for life and society. It is inevitable that this training would produce an ethnocentric attitude on the part of the child. Ethnocentrism is the belief that one's own culture or normative system is the criterion by which all other cultural norms should be judged as appropriate, moral, eccentric, or sinful.

FUNCTIONAL AND DYSFUNCTIONAL PROPERTIES OF NORMS

Ethnocentrism is functional to social groups; it ties the members to their normative system. No social group or society can remain cohesive if its members are divided in their commitment to the normative system. For individuals to be able to predict the responses of their fellows, agreement on norms is necessary. The society envisioned by George Orwell in his social science-fiction novel *1984* was highly cohesive and tolerated little deviation. Such societies stifle the imagination necessary for creativity and may become dysfunctional. In Orwell's novel, police patrol helicopters snooped into people's windows. Telescreens received and transmitted simultaneously, and there was no way of knowing whether you were being watched or overheard at a given moment. Children were trained to inform on their parents. The family had become, in effect, an extension of the "Thought Police." The essential crime was "thought crime," and for this treasonous act, one could be "vaporized." The totalitarian system attempted to control the individual entirely; to wear an improper expression on one's face was a punishable offense called "facecrime."

Deviance can be functional and can reinforce social solidarity by enabling social groups to more adequately define their social norms. The rising crime rate in the United States created a situation in which the speeches of the three major presidential candidates in 1968 all sounded like paraphrases of each other in their call for law and order. Riots caused this country to reaffirm its commitment to change through orderly processes.

Groups who rigidly reject deviants and lack the ability to tolerate dissent may find that this posture leads to dysfunctional consequences. Disputes over church doctrines have led to the creation of more than three hundred Protestant denominations and sects in this country, fragmenting the group's influence in the larger society.

While the strengthening of the group norms may be functional for the group immediately, the long-run consequences may be detrimental to the group's relations to out-groups or the larger social world. When Rosa Parks deviated from the seating norms of the Montgomery, Alabama, bus system by refusing to move to the rear, the South reacted by reaffirming its belief in segregation of the races. In turn, the nation as a whole responded by reaffirming its belief in democracy by passing national legislation to force southern states to conform to national norms. This national reaffirmation, however, brought to light *de facto* segregation in the

North and spawned movements to make the ideal culture normative all over the United States.

Deviance may be functional; it affords a safety valve for discontent. In American culture, there is no socially approved outlet for the sex drive except in marriage. Young persons reach puberty as early as twelve years of age yet must wait six or seven years before they can economically afford to be in the societally approved marital state. Widows, bachelors, and married persons separated for long periods are expected to remain as chaste as monks chained to a vow of celibacy. Kinsey's* research in this area revealed an enormous difference between the conformity society expects and the deviance it gets.

DEVIANCE

A Definition of Deviance

"Human behavior is deviant to the extent that it comes to be viewed as involving a personally discreditable departure from a group's normative expectations, and elicits interpersonal or collective reactions that serve to isolate, treat, correct, or punish individuals engaged in such behavior" (Schur, 1971, p. 24). This definition reflects the multifaceted nature of deviant behavior. First, it points to the fact that deviance encompasses quite diverse types of departures from normative expectations, ranging from violations of the law to minor departures from customary ways of behaving in informal situations. Thus, both the murderer and the individual failing to dress properly for a formal occasion may both be labeled deviant. In addition, it recognizes that deviance is a function of the extent to which behavior is condemned, punished, or ignored. For example, although individuals who use either marijuana or heroin are both viewed as deviant, those who use the latter substance are more likely to be condemned and punished. In addition, the phrase "behavior is deviant to the extent that it is personally discreditable" points to the fact that violations do not equally reflect on or affect the individual's identity. Hence, despite the fact that occasional marijuana use is defined as deviant, this is not likely to affect an individual's self-concept or the way in which he is viewed by society, because large sectors of our population do not consider this to be reprehensible behavior. On

---

*The results of Kinsey's research into American sexual norms and mores are reported in *Sexual Behavior in the Human Male* (1948) and *Sexual Behavior in the Human Female* (1953), Philadelphia, W. B. Saunders Co.

the other hand, the perpetration of a robbery, if discovered, is likely to materially affect an individual's identity because this behavior is viewed as an extremely serious breach of norms. In fact, an individual convicted of robbery is likely to be scarred for the rest of his life. Furthermore, this definition also specifies some of the possible reactions that are elicited from individuals or groups against those who engage in deviant behavior. The types of reactions elicited depend upon such factors as the degree to which the behavior threatens basic social values; the degree to which it is viewed as volitional; and current beliefs regarding punishment versus rehabilitation. For example, during the 1960's, we began to see a move to decriminalize a variety of behaviors, including homosexuality, alcoholism, and drug addiction, because they came to be viewed as being beyond the control of the individuals involved. In effect, this moved these individuals from the ranks of the criminal to the ranks of the sick, which permitted them to be treated rather than punished. Finally, this definition alludes to the fact that deviance may vary with time and place. This suggests that over a period of time, acts can move along a continuum from criminality-sinfulness, to behavior eliciting disapproval, to behavior tolerated without approval, to normal behavior. Examples of behavior that have moved along this continuum include: homosexuality, participation in labor unions, divorce, and doing business on Sundays. In short, then, the deviance of an act or of an individual is always relative, changeable, and a matter of degree.

Societal Reaction: Labeling the Deviant

A knowledge of how society will react to the deviant act and of how the individual involved may be labeled is extremely important in understanding the nature of deviant behavior. All individuals engage in deviant behavior, some of which violates basic social values. However, there is ample evidence to indicate that many people are not officially labeled for their violative behavior. It is this act of censure by society that affixes the deviant label and results in changes in the way in which individuals are viewed by society and by themselves.

Lemert (1967) has used the term *primary deviance* to refer to deviant behavior that has not materially affected an individual's self-concept and social status. Included in this category are (1) those repeatedly arrested for drunkenness, but who are still accepted by their families and employers; (2) drug users who are able to conceal their drug use from those who might take action against them; (3) juveniles who engage in delinquency but have not been arrested and/or adjudicated for their aberrant acts; (4) individuals who temporarily manifest some symptoms associated with mental illness; (5) adults who engage in occasional criminal acts such as shoplifting. What all these behaviors have in common is that they are normalized and dealt with as functions of a socially acceptable role by an individual's associates or the individual restricts his involvement to situations which will not result in the imposition of a deviant label. The latter circumstance is illustrated by men who engage in occasional impersonal homosexual relations in public lavatories or with male prostitutes.

Lemert (1967) used the term *secondary deviance* to refer to "the importance of societal reaction in the etiology of deviance, the forms it takes and its stabilization in deviant social roles or behavior systems" (p. 40). First and foremost, this concept distinguishes between those who are viewed as deviant and those whose deviance does not affect their social identities. The decision on the part of the community to take action against those who are deviant is not a simple act of censure. It is, as Erickson (1964) suggests:

> . . . *a sharp rite of transition at once moving him out of his normal position in society and transferring him into a distinct deviant role. The ceremonies which accomplish this change of status ordinarily have three related phases. They provide a formal* confrontation *between the deviant suspect and representatives of his community (as in the criminal trial or psychiatric case conference). They announce some* judgement *about the nature of his deviancy (a verdict or diagnosis) and they perform an act of social* placement *assigning him to a special role (like that of prisoner or patient) which redefines his position in society* (p. 16).

Following these "status degradation ceremonies" there is a shift from viewing the individual's acts as deviant to viewing the individual as a deviant character. Labeling an individual as generally deviant, rather than his specific acts as deviant, may produce a self-fulfilling prophecy. For example, once a youngster is labeled a delinquent, teachers, parents, store owners, and others tend to expect the youngster to engage in further delinquency. In fact, this youngster is generally the first to be accused when property is missing, damaged, or destroyed. Furthermore, other parents are likely to forbid their children to play with him for fear that he will influence them to engage in delinquency. Therefore, this younster is likely to be excluded from his peer group and also from adult-sponsored activities, such as church groups, scouts, and so forth. Moreover, his ability to obtain after-school jobs is also likely to be restricted. Denied participation in conventional groups and activities, this youngster is likely to graduate to delinquent groups and further delinquent activity. Movement into a juvenile gang can be viewed as the final step in the stabilization of the youngster's delinquency because it involves acceptance of a deviant identity. Gangs also provide members with a system of rationalization that serves to neutralize and justify their deviant identities and delinquent behavior. In addition, gang participation results in the development of more skillful means of carrying on delinquent activities.

In short, the likely result of the imposition of a deviant label is that an individual will (1) be regarded as a deviant and expected to engage in further deviant activity; (2) be denied participation in conventional groups; and (3) participate in deviant groups which provide rationales for neutralizing deviant identities and behavior and better techniques for carrying on deviant activities.

Once labeled, an individual will have an extremely difficult time disavowing his deviance and moving back into the mainstream of social life. Erickson suggested that part of the problem faced by deviants wishing to "shake off" their deviant identities results from the lack of any kind of terminal ceremony which marks the individual's relinquishment of his deviant status: "He is ushered into the deviant position by a decisive and dramatic ceremony [e.g., a trial], yet, is returned from it with hardly a word of public notice. And as a result, the deviant often returns home with no proper license to resume a normal life in the community. Nothing has happened to cancel out the stigmas imposed upon him by earlier commitment ceremonies; from a formal point of view, the original verdict or diagnosis is still in effect" (Erickson, 1964, pp. 16–17). Disavowal of deviancy is also difficult because people believe that it is difficult, if not impossible, for an individual to change his character (e.g., "once a con always a con").

A study conducted by Schwartz and Skolnick (1964) illustrates one problem faced by individuals who attempt to move back into the mainstream of social life following contact with the criminal justice system. Their experiment was designed to test the effect of a police record on gaining employment as a dishwasher in a resort area. To accomplish this objective, four folders were prepared which were the same in all respects except for the criminal record of the applicant. In all the folders he was described as a thirty-two year old single male of unspecified race, with high school training in the mechanical trades and a record of successive short-term jobs as a kitchen helper, maintenance worker, and handyman. The folders varied as follows: (1) the first folder indicated that the prospective employee had been convicted and sentenced for assault; (2) in the second, he had been tried for assault and acquitted; (3) in the third, he was tried for assault and acquitted with a letter from the judge certifying the finding of not guilty and reaffirming the legal presumption of innocence; and (4) in the fourth, no mention was made of a criminal record. Each of these folders was presented to twenty-five potential employers. The percentage of employers indicating a willingness to employ the applicant declined as his involvement with the criminal justice system increased. Thirty-six per cent of the prospective employers presented with the application of the man with no record indicated a willingness to employ him; twenty-four per cent would employ the acquitted man with the letter from the judge; twelve per cent would employ the acquitted man without the letter; and four per cent would employ the convicted man. Thus, this study shows that an individual's chances for employment, even in the most menial of occupations, is affected by his involvement as a subject of formal labeling ceremonies. It is this very type of response that prompts a deviant to abandon his efforts to achieve a conventional status and return to his deviant activities. For example, if an ex-convict cannot obtain legitimate employment, he will be compelled to return to a life of crime in order to support himself.

LAW AS A MEANS OF SOCIAL CONTROL

Social control, as Kerper (1974) observes, is "the process by which subgroups and persons are influenced to conduct themselves in conformity to group expectations" (p. 525). The means of this control vary with the behavioral situation; religion, custom, public opinion, and law all control or limit our behavior in varying degrees and in differing circumstances. Law, as the formal means of social control, "involves the use of rules that are interpreted, and are enforceable, by the courts of a political community" (Kerper, 1974, p. 518).

Howard and Summers (1965) list five conditions necessary for law to accomplish its stated ends.

1. The rules of law must set forth a clearly understandable standard of conduct so that citizens can know what is expected of them.

2. Laws are more effective when they prohibit certain actions rather than when they require duties (such as the "Good Samaritan" law requiring a motorist to stop and give aid at the scene of an accident).

3. The punishment must fit the crime and be in proportion to the "damage" to society. The stringent penalties against marijuana possession have been under attack as the public becomes aware that this "narcotic" is not physically habituating.

4. Law should be in concert with the prevailing moral sentiments of the community it is intended to serve. Compulsory school attendance laws have always been difficult to enforce in Amish communities as these persons do not "believe" in education beyond the eighth grade.

5. Laws must be administered uniformly and with consistent interpretation. Due process of law is an ideal not always adhered to.

ORIGINS OF THE CRIMINAL LAW

Law originates in the growth and development of the concept of private property and in the societal institutions of marriage and government. Primitive societies are generally ruled by custom rather than by law. But the absence of law does not mean an idyllic society totally free of social control, for custom can be as binding on individual and social behavior as any law. The bedrock of society is custom. The natural selection of custom retains those modes of action which grant to society some measure of order and stability. Should a supernatural sanction be added to the demands of custom, flouting the norm becomes a sacrilege, for one thus violates the will of the gods. Even with the arrival of law, custom remains the last "magistrate of men's lives." Only with the coming of private property, which gave the owner economic authority, and of the state, which gave the individual a legally defined status, did the concept of the "individual" begin to emerge.

Durant (1954) has identified four stages in the development of law: (1) the seeking of personal revenge; (2) the imposition of fines; (3) the establishment of courts; and (4) the assumption by the state of the obligation to prevent and punish wrongs. In primitive societies, vengence is personal, and every man is his own "sheriff," meting out "justice" according to his ability to enforce it. In the early days of the American West, as is regularly portrayed in films, a cowboy walked into the local saloon, called out the killer of his brother, dispensed "justice" with his Colt .45, and rode off into the sunset. The dead man's brother was then obligated to get revenge for the murder (presumably by locating the killer in another saloon), and so on *ad infinitum*. Indeed, Theodore White (1969) believed that the glorification on television of this primitive philosophy of personal revenge was partly responsible for the rising crime rate in the United States.

This concept of revenge is expressed in the ancient principle of *Lex Talionis*—the law of equivalent retaliation. Durant (1954) claims that the Abyssinians were so painstaking in measuring out this form of justice that when a boy fell from a tree upon his companion and killed him, the judges decided that the requirements of justice would be satisfied only by having the bereaved mother send another of her sons into the same tree to fall upon the offender's neck. This concept of retaliation has been incorporated in our modern practice of making penalties proportionate to the gravity of the offense, i.e. "making the punishment fit the crime."

The second stage in the development of law was the substitution of damages (fines) for revenge. A demand for the equivalent of the damages in gold replaced the demand for "an eye for an eye." This ancient principle persists today in *tort** actions as well as in criminal cases. Melvin Belli (dubbed the "King of Torts" by his colleagues) once presented a jury with an artificial leg and asked the members how much money they would take in exchange for a limb.

As fines began to supplant personal revenge, the need arose for some means of apportioning blame and assessing damages, and in response to this need came the third natural development of the law, the formation of courts. For many centuries, resort to courts remained optional; should the offended party remain dissatisfied with the verdict, he was still free to seek personal revenge. These courts were not always judgement seats as we know them today but were more often boards of voluntary conciliation.

In many cases, disputes were settled by trial by ordeal. Primitives were practical criminologists and established the rite not on the theory that some metaphysical jurist would reveal the guilty party but on the practical grounds that a long-standing feud would disrupt the tribe for generations. This early adversary system of justice presaged our own system in which the state marshals all its forces against the accused, the defense parries these attacks with all the resources at its command, and out of this conflict truth is supposed to emerge. The contemporary legal duel

---

*Black's Law Dictionary defines a tort as "a private or civil wrong or injury. A wrong independent of contract." You would commit a tort if you knowingly left a banana peel on your front step, and the mailman slipped on it and broke his leg.

is in some ways a remnant of this ancient practice of trial by ordeal.

The fourth advance in the development of law was the assumption by the state of the obligation to prevent and punish wrongs. The state thus enlarged its area of responsibility from merely settling disputes to making an effort to prevent them. To the general body of "common law," derived from the customs of the group, was now added "positive law," derived from judicial and governmental decrees. Laws, then, "grow up" from custom and are "handed down" from the government.

Other theorists have attributed the genesis of law to the rational processes of a unified society trying to eradicate some wrong, to the crystallization of mores, and to the conflict of interests between different groups. Part of the reason for our lack of knowledge about the origins of criminal law is the law schools' preoccupation with what the law is and neglect of the social origins of law. This situation is being rectified somewhat by the trend among modern schools of law to adopt a "law-science" model.

DEFINITION OF CRIME

Crime is defined by Perkins (1966) as "any social harm defined and made punishable by law." Crimes are regarded as offenses against the state because their perpetration in some way adversely affects the community. As a result, the state assumes responsibility for both protecting individuals from being victimized and apprehending and punishing those who transgress. Finally, no act or omission to act, no matter how reprehensible, is regarded as a crime unless a specific statute forbids or requires it. Sutherland and Cressey (1970) have identified four characteristics which distinguish the criminal law from other rules regarding human conduct: *politicality*, *specificity*, *uniformity*, and *penal sanction*.

Politicality. Criminal laws are enacted, modified, and repealed by duly constituted legislative bodies. In a pluralistic society such as ours in which there is no common value system, what is defined as criminal behavior during any period of time depends to a large degree on what behavior certain politically powerful and influential groups view as threatening to their value system. Thus, since the turn of the century we have seen the Eighteenth Amendment (establishing Prohibition) enacted and repealed, the liberalization of our abortion laws, gambling laws, and pornography laws, and the enactment and subsequent modification of laws concerning the sale and possession of narcotics and marijuana.

Specificity. If people are to follow the law, it must be stated in terms that clearly indicate what conduct is expected of them. A statute which punishes a commonly understood offense, such as "robbery" or "rape," is not too indefinite, but a statute which forbids "immoral acts" would not be sufficiently clear. Any statute which requires or prohibits the doing of an act in terms so vague that men of normal intelligence must guess at its meaning violates the first essential of due process of law, which is that the law as stated must be understandable to anyone who is not a legal expert. One of the objections to statutes covering juvenile offenses is that they contain ambiguous terms like "ungovernability" without specifying what the term means.

Uniformity. Justice is depicted as blindfolded as she weighs the evidence for the guilt or innocence of those who stand before her. This represents the ideal of American jurisprudence: all persons who are adjudged by the law will be treated equally, regardless of social standing. In practice, of course, some persons are "more equal" than others.

Penal Sanction. *Nullum crimen sine lege* (no crime without law) is a guiding principle in the field of criminal law. Not only must criminal statutes give citizens "fair warning" of what behavior to avoid, but they should also give an indication of the penalties which may accrue upon violation of the criminal law. The goal of punishment is the protection of society, for the first duty of the government is to protect the lives and property of its citizens. No civilized society can long endure that tolerates unrestrained lawlessness. Given the propensities of human beings toward unruly or aggressive behavior, laws without penalties would be more honored in the breach than in the observance.

BASIC PREMISES OF CRIMINAL LAW

Anglo-American criminal law is founded upon certain basic premises which have been more or less strictly observed by courts in applying, and by legislatures in formulating, the substantive criminal law (LaFave and Scott, 1972, p. 175). From these basic premises comes the requirement that a criminal law incorporate the following elements: an act; mental state; concurrence; harm; causation; legality; and punishment.

First, before behavior can be defined as criminal, there must be a voluntary affirmative act or an omission where there is a lawful duty to act. Thus, mere thoughts alone cannot constitute a crime. One can with impunity wish an enemy dead, contemplate robbing a bank, or think about avoiding the payment of income taxes, so long as these thoughts produce no action to bring about the desired results. However, it is necessary to distinguish mere thoughts from speech, since under our legal system a crime can be committed by an act of speech. For example, since we consider individuals acting in concert to represent a greater threat to society than does a lone offender, we deem an agreement by two or more persons to commit a crime a criminal conspiracy, which is a misdemeanor at common law. Nevertheless, it is important to note that about half of the states have added by statute the additional requirement of an act in furtherance of the conspiracy (LaFave and Scott, 1972, pp. 476–478). Other crimes that can be committed by acts of speech include perjury, solicitation, and false pretenses.

Secondly, in order for conduct to be considered criminal there must be something more than mere action or inaction; some bad state of mind or fault (*mens rea*) is also required. To demonstrate *mens rea* it must be proven that an individual intentionally (purposely), knowingly, recklessly, or negligently behaved in a given manner or caused a given result. A crime is not committed when an individual has not intentionally brought about a given result. Similarly, if a man buys goods from a local merchant not knowing they are stolen, he is not guilty of the crime of receiving stolen property. On the other hand, a man who drives 80 miles per hour through a residential area and kills a young child is likely to be convicted of manslaughter because his behavior constituted a reckless disregard of the risks associated with that type of behavior. Finally, a nightclub owner was deemed "criminally negligent" and convicted of manslaughter because he did not provide proper fire escapes, and this caused the death of many patrons during a fire. In affirming the owner's conviction, the court stated the principle underlying convictions in criminal negligence cases: "even if a particular defendant is so stupid (or) heedless . . . that in fact he did not realize the grave danger, he is guilty of manslaughter if an ordinary normal man under the same circumstances would have realized the gravity of the danger" (LaFave and Scott, 1972, p. 212).

There are, however, offenses which involve no specific mental state element but consist only of forbidden acts or omissions of acts. These are classified as *strict liability offenses*. Thus, a statute may simply indicate that whoever does (or omits doing) so and so or (whoever) brings about such and such a result is guilty of a crime. These statutes are justified on the grounds that there is a need to control the behavior in question, yet convictions would be difficult if the prosecution were required to prove fault. Examples of laws imposing liability without fault include liquor and narcotics laws, pure food laws, and traffic laws.

The law recognizes that there are certain people who are not able to entertain the requisite mental state. Children, mental defectives, and in some cases the mentally ill are excused from criminal responsibility on the grounds that they cannot appreciate the nature and quality of their behavior. In addition, mens rea is also considered lacking when persons are acting under coercion, defending themselves or others, or acting under statutory authority as a police officer would.

Third, the physical conduct and the mental state must concur. In essence, this requires that the mental state of the perpetrator activate the act or omission. For example, concurrence can be demonstrated when A, who planned to kill B, finds his victim and kills him. On the other hand, let us suppose that Sue Ann is angry with Mary for having stolen the affections of Lou, her boss. She plans to kill both of them with a poisoned lemon meringue pie. But when she searches for them in the newsroom, she finds that they have eloped to Winnipeg. Ten years later, at an intersection in Denver, Lou (who suffers from color blindness) runs a red light, and both he and Mary are killed instantly when their VW Rabbit is totaled in a collision with a customized Econoline Van driven by none other than Sue Ann. Is she guilty of murder? No, because there was no concurrence between the intent and the harmful conduct. Fate had delivered the couple into her hands.

Fourth, the law is premised on the idea that only harmful conduct can be considered criminal. This concept is reflected in the substantive due process notion that a criminal statute is unconstitutional if it bears no reasonable relationship to injury to the public. However, it is important to recognize that criminal harm is not restricted to physical injury. For example, in cases of libel, perjury, and treason, there is no physical injury, and in still other cases, physical injury may be minimal, as in robbery without assault. Therefore, the criminal law must be seen to deal with intangibles, such as harm to institutions, public safety, autonomy of women, reputation and the like. In essence, criminal harm signifies loss of value because an individual who commits a crime does something contrary to community values (Hall, 1960, p. 217).

The fifth basic element, causation, is involved in those crimes that require that the defendant's conduct produce a given result. On the other hand, some crimes such as perjury and forgery are so defined that the conduct, accompanied by an intention to cause the harmful result, constitutes the crime without regard to whether that result actually occurs. On the other hand, offenses such as the intent-to-kill type of murder and intent-to-injure type of battery require a given result. In these cases, it must be demonstrated that the defendant's conduct is the "but for" cause of the forbidden result and that the forbidden result which actually occurs is similar enough to the intended result that the defendant can be held responsible for it. In most cases, there is no difficulty in proving this causal connection. For example, if F with intent to kill G drives a knife into G's heart, a prosecutor would have no difficulty demonstrating that F caused G's death. However, in a small number of cases, the intended harm varies as to person, manner, and type. For example, A shoots B and, believing B dead, leaves his body on an interstate highway. However B is still alive when F runs over B and kills him. Will A be convicted of B's murder? A will be convicted if it can be demonstrated that his conduct was a substantial factor in bringing about B's death or if B's death was a foreseeable consequence of A's behavior.

The rule of causation has also been said to generally apply to cases of felony murder. At issue is the question of whether an offender can be held responsible for the unintended deaths that result from his perpetration of a felony. For example, A sets out to rob B and in the course of the robbery B, in order to protect his property, fires at A and accidentally kills a bystander. Furthermore, after the robbery, a policeman shoots at B in order to stop him and by accident kills an innocent bystander. Would A be liable for these deaths? In general, the courts have ruled that if the death is a natural and foreseeable consequence of the offense, the offender is liable (LaFave and Scott, 1972, pp. 263–264).

Sixth, in order for conduct to be criminal, it must be forbidden by a law or laws which give advance warning that such conduct is criminal. This idea, which is sometimes labeled the principle of legality, is reflected in the prohibition against ex post facto laws that seek to make legal conduct illegal after its occurrence and in the requirement that laws be precise enough that an individual can determine in advance what conduct is prohibited or required.

Finally, there must be a legally prescribed penalty associated with each offense. This premise is derived from the ancient legal maxim, *No crime without punishment*. Under our legal system, citizens not only must be forewarned as to what conduct is forbidden but must also know the consequences of such conduct.

CLASSIFICATION OF CRIMES

Crimes are typically classified as either felonies or misdemeanors. The more serious crimes are termed *felonies* and are punished by a year or more in the state penitentiary. Less serious offenses are regarded as *misdemeanors* and are generally punished by a year or less in the city or county jail. Exceptions exist, as in the case of North Carolina where the misdemeanants are confined by the state department of corrections. The implication of this system of classification for the study of crime is that petty acts indicate a petty offender. But an act which would be regarded as a misdemeanor in one state can be a felony in another state. In some states, for example, first-offense marijuana possession is punished as a misdemeanor. In other states, the same offense is classified as a felony and can bring the offender a heavy prison sentence.

Originally, the common law distinguished between those crimes that are "wrong in themselves" (*mala in se*) and those that are "wrong because they are prohibited" (*mala prohibita*), i.e., any act that is forbidden by statute but that otherwise would not seem to shock the conscience of the community. Such a classification finds little support among contemporary legal authorities or criminologists, who tend to regard the distinction as naive.

Other classifications of crime include "crimes against nature" (Nice, 1965), which in its broadest sense includes carnal knowledge of an animal, and when applied to sex between humans, generally includes sodomy, cunnilingus, fellatio, and intercourse (even between legally married persons) in any but the vis-a-vis position. The reference to these acts as "crimes against nature" does not, of course, represent an indictment from Nature herself but rather a value judgement on the part of some legislative body as to what is "natural." If we can repose any confidence in a lengthy series of investigations of sexual behavior, from Kinsey to Masters and Johnson, a type of sexual experience that is regarded as "unnatural" in one segment of our society may be the norm in another social group.

One of the most recent crime classifications, developed during the World War II war crimes trials at Nuremberg, is that of "crimes against humanity." The offenses were seen as being of such magnitude that the offenders were to answer to humanity in general and not just to a specific individual country or jurisdiction.

European peace groups applied this concept to President Johnson and his staff and tried them in absentia for alleged war crimes in Viet Nam; Johnson et al. were found guilty.

Offenses may be classified as a private wrong, called a "civil injury" or *tort*, or a public wrong, which would be covered by the criminal law. A public wrong is a violation of public peace for which the community may take action. The punishment imposed is for the protection of the community and not for redress of the injury to the individual. Individuals must seek redress in a civil action. When an individual or organization sues another to obtain a remedy for an alleged injury, the case is a civil case. When the state prosecutes an individual or organization for a violation of a statute, the case is normally a criminal one. The same offense may give rise to both civil and criminal actions. Assault and battery may result in a civil action by the victim to obtain damages for the injuries received and also in criminal charges filed by the state to punish the guilty party by fine or imprisonment.

SUMMARY

In order to clearly understand the problem of crime, it is necessary to grasp the wider problem of deviance from societal norms. Societies attempt to contain deviance through controls ranging from informal disapproval to the police powers of the state. Antisocial attitudes, conduct norms, eccentricities, and odd behaviors may all be studied and are useful in shedding light on criminal conduct. All criminal acts are deviant, but not all deviants are criminals. Therefore, only those deviant acts which legislative bodies have defined by statute as criminal may legitimately be considered as crimes. The more serious crimes are classified as felonies; less serious crimes are classified as misdemeanors. These categories also reflect a difference in the severity of sanctions that society sees fit to impose in the punishment of such crimes.

REVIEW

Find the answers to the following questions in the text:

1. Why do the authors maintain that the study of deviant behavior is more appropriate for the beginning student of criminal justice and criminology than the more specific study of criminal and delinquent behavior?

2. How do we distinguish between proscriptions and prescriptions as forms of social sanction?

3. Explain the difference between functional and dysfunctional properties of norms and give examples of each.

4. Discuss the distinction between primary and secondary deviance. What are some of the principal consequences of being labeled deviant?

5. Identify four characteristics of criminal law that distinguish it from other rules governing human conduct.

6. What are felonies and how do they differ from misdemeanors?

7. How do crimes differ from torts?

TERMS TO IDENTIFY AND REMEMBER

proscription
social sanction
secondary deviance
mores
Lex Talionis
politicality
uniformity

felony
strict liability offense
mala prohibita
"crimes against nature"
prescription
primary deviance
norms

folkways
mens rea
specificity
penal sanction
misdemeanor
mala in se
tort

REFERENCES

Durant, W.: *Our Oriental Heritage.* New York, Simon and Schuster, Inc., 1954.

Erickson, K. T.: Notes on the sociology of deviance. *In* Becker, H. S. (ed.): *The Other Side: Perspectives on Deviance.* New York, The Free Press, 1964.

Hall, J.: *General Principles of Criminal Law.* Indianapolis, The Bobbs-Merrill Co., Inc. 1960.

Howard, G. G., and Summers, R. S.: *Law: Its Nature, Functions, and Limits.* Englewood Cliffs, N. J., Prentice-Hall, Inc., 1965.

Kerper, H. B.: *Introduction to the Criminal Justice System.* St. Paul, West Publishing Co., 1974.

LaFave, W. R., and Scott, A. W.: *Criminal Law.* St. Paul, West Publishing Co., 1972.

Lemert, E. M.: *Human Deviance, Social Problems, and Social Control.* Englewood Cliffs, N. J., Prentice-Hall, Inc., 1967.

Nice, R.: *Dictionary of Criminology.* New York, Philosophical Library, Inc., 1965.

Perkins, R. M.: *Criminal Law and Procedure.* New York, The Foundation Press, Inc., 1966.

Schur, E. M.: *Labeling Deviant Behavior: Its Sociological Implications.* New York, Harper & Row, Publishers, 1971.

Schwartz, R., and Skolnick, J. H.: Two studies of legal stigma. *In* Becker, H. S. (ed.): *The Other Side: Perspectives on Deviance.* New York, The Free Press, 1964.

Sutherland, E. H., and Cressey, D. R.: *Criminology.* Philadelphia, J. B. Lippincott Co., 1970.

White, T. H.: *The Making of the President: 1968.* New York, Atheneum Publishers, 1969.

2 EPIDEMIOLOGY OF CRIME IN THE UNITED STATES

Epidemiology is the medical specialty that deals with the frequency and distribution of diseases within a given population. In his efforts to maintain an up-to-date assessment of reported cases of various diseases and their location, the epidemiologist employs many of the survey and sampling methods that are familiar to the social scientist. He is especially concerned with *changes* in reported rates for contagious diseases, because such changes may signal a serious outbreak of rapidly spreading disease, i.e., an *epidemic*.

With regard to the study of crime and criminals, the epidemiological approach seeks to relate the frequency and distribution of criminal behavior to such variables as age, sex, race, and residence. The analyst attempts to find answers to such questions as: What is the comparative rate of violent crimes among first offenders and repeaters? Research of this kind leads to the formulation of predictive statements about crime, e.g., violent offenders are poor risks for probation or parole.

Epidemiological studies distinguish between two types of statistical surveys. The first, called *incidence rates*, refers to the *known* number of cases occurring within a specified time interval. A second type, *prevalence rates*, refers to the *total* number of crimes committed or criminals present in a given population during a specified time interval. (This type of survey includes both first offenders and repeaters.) While we can measure the incidence of various kinds of criminal behavior by means of indices of arrest or conviction, we have no way of accurately gauging the true

21

prevalence of crime in the United States. Crime by its very nature is not easily measurable, for secrecy is its essential characteristic. To the extent that criminals are successful—that is, able to conceal their actions or identities—our statistical measures are not accurate. For some categories of crime, especially those "victimless crimes" in which the "victim" is a satisfied customer, our measures fall absurdly short of reality. As Geis (1965) points out, there are only about 20 convictions for every 60 million homosexual acts performed. (Homosexuality may or may not be an "illness," but in many states it is a crime.)

THE UNIFORM CRIME REPORTS

Many crimes go undetected, others are detected but unreported, while others are reported but unrecorded. Thus any attempt to measure the absolute number of crimes committed in a particular locale by such yardsticks as "crimes known to the police," "arrests," "convictions," or "commitments to prison" can only be viewed as providing a rough approximation at best since these figures represent only a portion, and probably a small portion in some categories, of the total crime rate. Police records, however, are compiled by persons who are in close relation to the actual crime and so are a more accurate measure of the actual number of crimes committed than are arrest rates, court records, or prison statistics.

Since 1930, the Federal Bureau of Investigation has published statistics on "crimes known to the police" in its annual *Uniform Crime Reports (UCR)*. This information is voluntarily submitted by law enforcement agencies from all parts of the country. Despite their limitations, which we shall discuss later in some detail, these statistical summaries are considered the most authoritative source of information available on the frequency and distribution of crime in the United States.

Seven categories of crime are used in the *UCR* as an index to measure the trends and distribution of criminality in the United States. These seven crimes—murder, forcible rape, aggravated assault, robbery, burglary, larceny-theft, and motor vehicle theft—represent the most serious offenses and the crimes which are most consistently reported to the police. They are referred to as index, or Part I, offenses.

Part II offenses include: simple assault; arson; forgery and counterfeiting; fraud; embezzlement; buying, receiving, or possessing stolen property; vandalism; unlawful carrying or possession of weapons; prostitution and commercialized vice; sex offenses (excluding forcible rape, prostitution, and commercialized vice); offenses against narcotic drug laws; gambling; offenses against the family and children; driving under the influence; offenses against state liquor laws; drunkenness; disorderly conduct; vagrancy; suspicion*; curfew and loitering law violations (juveniles); running away (juveniles); and all other violations of state or local laws.

During calendar year 1975, the compilers of the *UCR* received data from law enforcement agencies representing more than 12,000 city, county, and state jurisdictions covering 97 per cent of the total United States population in cities (other than Washington, D. C.) and 83 per cent of the rural population. The combined average accounts for 95 per cent of the population of the entire nation (Federal Bureau of Investigation, 1976, p. 3). The offenses reported are violations of the criminal law of the separate states; no violations of the federal law are included in the *UCR*.

Since 1958, crimes have been reported by geographical area following as closely as practicable the definitions used by the Bureau of the Budget and Census. Standard metropolitan statistical areas (SMSA's) are generally made up of an entire county or counties having at least one core city of 50,000 or more inhabitants. "Other cities" are urban places outside standard metropolitan statistical areas, most of which are incorporated communities of 2500 or more inhabitants. "Rural areas" are defined as unincorporated portions of counties outside of urban places or SMSA's.

Data for the *UCR* is collected from law enforcement agencies in all 50 states. Since there are variations in the definitions of the various crimes, an arbitrary set of crime classifications has been adopted in an attempt to remove this barrier to uniformity. However, it should be kept in mind that such a system cannot distinguish between "felonies" and "misdemeanors," because these categories vary from state to state. Not only does the definition of what constitutes a felony vary by state statute, but whether a crime is a felony also depends upon the subjective evaluation of the seriousness of the offense made by the arresting officer. Brief definitions of the crime classifications utilized in the *UCR* are as follows:

Criminal Homicide. Criminal homicide includes two sub-

---

*"Suspicion" covers a very broad range of behavior that provides the police officer with cues (probable cause) to take a closer look at the individual or individuals involved.

categories: (1) Murder and non-negligent manslaughter: all willful felonious homicides as distinguished from deaths caused by negligence. Excluded are attempts to kill, suicides, accidental deaths, or justifiable homicides. Justifiable homicides are limited to: (a) the killing of a person by a peace officer in the line of duty; (b) the killing of a person in the act of committing a felony by a private citizen. (2) Manslaughter by negligence: any death that the police investigation establishes to be primarily attributable to the gross negligence of some individual other than the victim.

Aggravated Assault. This is an unlawful attack by one person upon another for the purpose of inflicting severe bodily injury, usually accompanied by the use of a weapon or other means likely to produce death or serious bodily harm. Attempts are included since it is not necessary that an injury result when a gun, knife, or other weapon is used which could, and probably would, result in serious personal injury if the crime were successfully completed.

Forcible Rape. Forcible rape is the carnal knowledge of a female through the use of force or the threat of force. Assaults to commit forcible rape are also included; however, statutory rape (without force) is not included in this category. Crime counts in this offense classification are broken down into actual forcible rapes and attempted forcible rapes.

Robbery. This is a crime which takes place in the presence of the victim. Robbery takes place when a person obtains property or a thing of value from another person by use of force or threat of force. Assault to commit robbery and attempts are included. Beginning in 1974, information concerning robbery was collected to show the type of weapon used, as well as strong-arm robbery in which no weapon other than a part of the body is used. The latter category includes crimes such as mugging, yoking, etc.

Burglary. Burglary is the unlawful entry of a structure to commit a felony or theft. The use of force to gain entry is not required for the crime to be classified as a burglary. The offense of burglary is broken down into three subclassifications: forcible entry, unlawful entry where no force is used, and attempted forcible entry.

Larceny-Theft. This is the unlawful taking or stealing of property or articles without the use of force, violence, or fraud. It includes crimes such as shoplifting, pocket-picking, purse-snatching, thefts from motor vehicles, thefts of motor vehicle parts and accessories, bicycle thefts, etc. In the *UCR*, this crime category does not include embezzlement, "con" games, forgery, or the passing of worthless checks.

Motor Vehicle Theft. This is the unlawful taking or stealing of a motor vehicle, including attempts. Excluded is a taking for temporary use by any person having lawful access to the vehicle.

The factors which cause variations in crime rates are numerous, and readers of the *UCR* are cautioned against drawing conclusions from direct comparisons of crime figures of individual communities. Among the conditions which are listed in the *UCR* (Federal Bureau of Investigation, 1976, p. 2) as affecting the amount and type of crime that occurs in a given locale are:

1. Density and size of community population and the metropolitan area of which it is a part.
2. Composition of the population with reference particularly to age, sex, and race.
3. Economic status and mores of the population.
4. Stability of population, including commuters, seasonal, and other transient types.
5. Climate, including seasonal weather conditions.
6. Educational, recreational, and religious characteristics.
7. Effective strength of the police force.
8. Standards of appointments to the police force.
9. Policies of the prosecuting officials.
10. Attitudes and policies of the courts and corrections.
11. Relationships and attitudes of law enforcement and the community.
12. Administrative and investigative efficiency of law enforcement, including degree of adherence to crime reporting standards.
13. Organization and cooperation of adjoining and overlapping police jurisdictions.

THE EXTENT OF KNOWN CRIME

As mentioned earlier, the FBI Crime Index is made up of statistics for seven major felonies. These crimes were chosen because they are the types of offenses most likely to be reported to the police. From these statistics a crime "rate" is constructed.

A crime rate can be considered a victim risk rate. According to the *UCR*, the crime index rate for the United States in 1975 was 5281 offenses per 100,000 inhabitants, as compared with a crime index rate of 4821 offenses per 100,000 inhabitants in 1974—a 9 per cent increase. The risk of being a victim of one of the seven crimes in the index has increased 39 per cent since 1970, and this increase cannot be explained by population growth alone.

CRIME AND POPULATION

1970 - 1975
PERCENT CHANGE OVER 1970

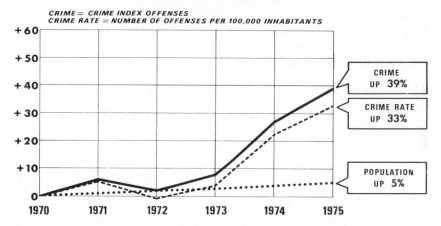

CRIME= CRIME INDEX OFFENSES
CRIME RATE = NUMBER OF OFFENSES PER 100,000 INHABITANTS

CRIME
UP 39%

CRIME RATE
UP 33%

POPULATION
UP 5%

Figure 2–1. Increase in the crime rate over the period 1969 to 1974, based on the number of Crime Index offenses committed. (From Federal Bureau of Investigation: *Uniform Crime Reports: 1974.* Washington, D. C., U. S. Government Printing Office, 1975, p. 12. Reproduced by permission of the U. S. Department of Justice.)

Murder

In 1975, there were an estimated 20,510 murders committed in the United States; this crime comprises approximately 2 per cent of the crimes of violence and represents less than ½ of 1 per cent of all Crime Index offenses. Since 1970, the murder rate has increased 28 per cent. Geographically, the number of murder victims in proportion to population was highest in the southern states, with Georgia possessing the highest murder rate in the nation. Males outnumber females as murder victims by more than 3 to 1, and the ratio of arrests for murder was more than 5 males to each female in 1975. Fifty-one of every 100 murder victims were white and 47 were black.

Firearms continue to be the predominant weapon used in murder (66%). As in prior years, handguns were the principal instrument used, accounting for 51 per cent of murders. Since 1964, murder through the use of a firearm has more than doubled. Federal legislation has attempted to restrict the sale of cheap foreign-made weapons, the famous "Saturday Night Specials," but foreign distributors effectively evade the spirit of the law by shipping to the United States parts which may be readily assembled.

Murders tend to be committed by relatives or acquaintances of the victim. Along with our concern for "crime in the street" we need to focus attention on "crime in the home." In 1975, killings within the family accounted for approximately one fourth of all murders. Of this 25 per cent, over half involved spouse killing spouse (the wife was the victim in 52 per cent of the cases, and the husband in the remaining 48 per cent.) Lovers' quarrels were the cause of 7 per cent of homicides. "Trouble in paradise" resulted in females being the victims in 55 per cent of such murders, but when a third party entered the scene to complicate a romantic setting, a male was the victim in 93 per cent of the confrontations. In 1975, 78 per cent of the criminal homicides were "solved" by arrests—the highest percentage of clearance by arrest of any Crime Index offense. Since 1970, the nationwide clearance rate has decreased from 86 per 100 offenses to 78 per 100 offenses in 1975.

Aggravated Assault

In 1975, there was an estimated total of 484,710 aggravated assaults in the United States. This figure represents an increase of 45 per cent in the rate per 100,000 inhabitants since 1970. The southern states had the highest aggravated assault rate in the country. As with murder, this offense tends to increase in the warm summer months.

Most aggravated assaults occur within the family unit or among neighbors or acquaintances. Because of these close relationships, victims are frequently unwilling to testify for the prosecution. Consequently, acquittals and dismissals account for nearly half of the dispositions in assault cases. This type of disturbance is hazardous to the police as well; since 1966, 157 officers have lost their lives responding to this kind of call.

Forcible Rape

Forcible rape made up less than 1 per cent of the Crime Index total and nearly 6 per cent of the crimes of violence in 1975. The rate of rape per 100,000 female inhabitants of the United States has increased 41 per cent since 1970. Women living in large core cities are four times more likely to become the victims of rape than are women living in rural areas. Regionally, females living in the western states, where the male-female ratio is weighted on the male side, were most often the victims of forcible rape. This imbalance, however, does not constitute the sole explanation for the rate of forcible rape being highest in this area.

Fifty-eight per cent of the arrests for forcible rape during the year 1975 were of persons under the age of 25. This offense is probably one of the most underreported crimes owing to the potential for publicity and embarrassment and the psychological rigors of being interrogated by detectives and defense attorneys. However, on a national average, 15 per cent of all forcible rapes reported to the police in 1975 were determined by investigation to be unfounded, i.e., no forcible rape or attempt had occurred.

Robbery

Robbery takes place in the presence of the victim, and money or other items of value are obtained by use of force or intimidation. In 1975 an estimated 464,970 robberies were committed in the United States. This represents an increase of 27 per cent in the robbery rate since 1970. Cities with over 250,000 inhabitants accounted for nearly 3 out of every 4 robberies which occurred during 1975. Robbery rates tend to increase in proportion to density of population. Larger cities reported robbery rates about ten times greater than those reported in the suburban areas. Geographically, this crime tended to occur most frequently in the heavily populated regions of the northeastern United States. During the period from 1970 to 1974, service station holdups *decreased* by 20 per cent—a reflection, perhaps, of the widespread adoption by station owners of security measures such as refusing to accept cash payments for gas and services after dark and keeping money in a safe for which the station attendant has no key. In 1975, however, gas station holdups *rose* by 7 per cent over 1974. By contrast, during the 1970 to 1975 period, chain store robberies increased 112 per cent and bank robberies rose by 79 per cent. Three out of every four persons arrested for robbery in 1975 were under 25 years of age, and 59 per cent of those arrested were black. Of the adults prosecuted for robbery in 1975, 55 per cent were convicted of the substantive charge.

Burglary

An estimated 3,252,100 burglaries occurred during 1975, with the peak month being December. This figure represents an increase of 41 per cent in the burglary rate since 1970. Burglary is a crime of stealth and opportunity, and the increase in the number of daytime residential burglaries reflects the increasing number of apartments and houses that are left unattended as both husband and wife are employed.

Victims suffered an economic loss of $1.4 billion to burglars in 1975. Police were able to solve less than 1 of every 5 of these reported burglaries. Arrests tend to be concentrated among young persons—85 per cent of all arrests for burglary in 1975 were of persons under the age of 25.

Larceny-Theft

Larceny-theft refers to crimes such as shoplifting and purse-snatching—any theft without the use of force or fraud. There were 5,977,700 larcenies in 1975, an increase of 14 per cent from the previous year. This figure may be somewhat unrealistic as an inflationary economy exerts an effect on the value of goods; thefts which would not have been included in these figures in former years may suddenly become translated into felonies through inflation. (Whether an act of larceny is a felony or misdemeanor depends on the value of what is taken; statutes set an arbitrary dollar amount as the dividing point.) Adding further to the tentative character of these figures is the variability of the police estimate of the worth of goods. Further, victims who are insured tend to overestimate their losses. (If this is intentional, it is itself an offense.)

Larceny is a crime of opportunity. Shoplifting rates are similar in the city and suburban areas but there is a decided drop in the rural area. A lack of witnesses and the tremendous volume of these cases make clearance by the police difficult. Only 20 per cent of the larceny offenses brought to police attention in 1975 were solved. Another characteristic of this crime is that females are often the perpetrators. They account for one fourth of all arrests for larceny-theft; in fact, women were arrested more often for larceny than for any other offense in 1975. In absolute numbers, twice as many persons were charged for larceny-theft as for any other serious offense, with 73 per cent being found guilty.

Motor Vehicle Theft

In 1975, over one million motor vehicles were reported stolen. From 1970 through 1975, the percentage increase in motor vehicle theft was four times greater than the percentage increase in motor vehicle registrations and four times greater than the percentage increase in the youthful population between the ages of 15 and 24 years.

Motor vehicle theft is primarily a big city problem, with five times as many vehicles stolen in cities with more than 250,000 inhabitants as in the suburbs, and 100 times as many stolen as in rural areas. Motor vehicle theft, like larceny, is a crime of opportunity. Two thirds of all thefts occur at night and over one half are from private residences, apartment buildings, or streets in residential districts.

Law enforcement agencies were successful in solving only 14 per cent of these thefts in 1975 by arrest of the offender. They were, however, successful in recovering 84 per cent of the stolen vehicles, but the remaining unrecovered 16 per cent represented a loss to owners of $140 million.

Arrests for motor vehicle theft come primarily from the age group under 21 (73 per cent). Of all adults prosecuted, 53 per cent were found guilty. Sixty-three per cent of persons processed for auto theft were referred to juvenile court jurisdiction.

Characteristics of Known Offenders

Age

Persons under 18 were arrested for 26 per cent of all crimes reported by police agencies in 1975. However, for the seven index offenses, youths under 18 accounted for 43 per cent of these serious offenses. Persons under 25 were arrested for 57 per cent of all crimes and 75.3 per cent of the seven most serious offenses. The crimes most frequently committed by persons under 25 include forcible rape (58 per cent of all arrests for that offense), robbery (77 per cent), vandalism (86 per cent), violation of liquor laws (80.8 per cent). The crimes for which persons over 25 are most likely to be arrested include criminal homicide, embezzlement, gambling, drunkenness and drunk driving. The most dramatic increase in arrests of young persons has been for violation of narcotic drug laws. The percentage of persons under 18 arrested for this offense is four times what it was in 1963, for persons under 21 the increase is two and one half times the 1963 figure, and for persons under 25 arrests for drug law violations have increased 54 per cent. Four out of every five persons arrested for violation of narcotics laws are under 25 years of age. The increase in the number of arrests for drug violations is due, in part, to the increased sophistication and interest of police departments in making drug arrests.

Sex

Analysis of 8,013,645 arrests from law enforcement agencies representing 179,191,000 people in 1974 reveals that 1,262,100

(15.7 per cent) involved females. Females accounted for only 10.3 per cent of all arrests for violent crimes but the female arrest rate is approximately 21 per cent in the area of property crime. The percentage of women arrested for each of the following offenses is higher than the overall arrest average for females for all crimes: for forgery and counterfeiting, women accounted for 28.9 per cent of all arrests; for fraud, 34.2 per cent; for embezzlement, 31.1 per cent; for prostitution and commercialized vice, 74.3 per cent; for narcotics, 13.8 per cent; for curfew and loitering law violations, 20.3 per cent.

In 1973, there was a total of 6,684 sentenced female prisoners confined in state and federal institutions (U. S. Department of Justice, 1976, p. 16), representing an increase since 1971 of 3.4 per cent in the number of women incarcerated in state institutions and of 21.4 per cent in the number of females incarcerated in federal institutions. At the same time (1973), there were 197,665 males confined in all institutions in the United States. The estimated civilian population of the United States in July, 1973, was 209,860,000 (U.S. Bureau of the Census, 1975). Females accounted for 16.1 per cent of all arrests in 1973 but comprised only 3 per cent of prisoners in state and federal institutions. In 1973, approximately 30 times as many men as women were confined in penal institutions. The states of New Hampshire and North Dakota had no women incarcerated; South Dakota had 3; Montana, 5; Delaware, 6; and Rhode Island, 7. California had the largest female inmate population in the country—627 (U. S. Department of Justice, 1976, pp. 16–17).

Race

Police statistics gathered from 7,993 agencies in 1974 revealed that blacks were arrested for 26.4 per cent of all crimes committed in the United States and for 32.8 per cent of the seven major offenses (Federal Bureau of Investigation, 1976, p. 192). Blacks accounted for 54.4 per cent of all murder and non-negligent manslaughter arrests, 45.4 per cent of arrests for rape, 58.8 per cent of arrests for robbery, 39.5 per cent of arrests for aggravated assault, and 26.4 per cent of arrests for motor vehicle theft. In the less serious offenses, 41.4 per cent of arrests for "carrying concealed weapons" were of blacks, 53.6 per cent of the prostitution and commercialized vice arrests were of blacks, and 72 per cent of arrests for gambling were of blacks. When an Indian is arrested, two thirds of the time it is for drunkenness.

Blacks are arrested at a disproportionately high rate for "suspicion" (arrest for no specific offense and release without formal charges being filed), but police investigatory practices may result in the underreporting of certain crimes by blacks (Skolnick, 1966). A stabbing by a white woman of her husband would probably be classified as attempted homicide, while a black stabbing or "cutting" is often written off as what Skolnick terms a "North Westfield battery."

The high black arrest rate may be explained in part by the social experiences to which many black people are subjected. In recent years, blacks have migrated to the inner city in increasing numbers (U. S. Bureau of the Census, 1975). For the United States as a whole, blacks comprise 11 per cent of the population, but in 1969, 21 per cent of the central city population was black—an increase from 16 per cent in 1960. Within metropolitan areas, most whites reside in suburban rings, while the overwhelming majority of blacks are central city residents. In metropolitan areas of 1,000,000 or more, blacks comprise 26 per cent of the central city population. The city is characterized by speed and tension, anonymity, impersonality, regimentation, and heterogeneity. These conditions generate more pressure toward deviance. Blacks accounted for 28 per cent of arrests in cities but only 15.6 per cent of all suburban arrests and 11.4 per cent of arrests in rural jurisdictions (Federal Bureau of Investigation, 1976, pp. 201–217).

Relating poverty to crime, especially property crimes, would help explain the over-representation of blacks in criminal statistics, but this factor fails to explain the relatively low criminality rate among black women who share the same socioeconomic conditions. The role expectations and socialization experiences of women differ from those of men, so it would not be unreasonable to expect a different response to the same environmental stimuli. Obviously, it would be gross error to infer from the high black crime rates that black people have some genetic predisposition toward crime. We must emphasize that black crime rates vary by sex, socioeconomic status, and geographic region. General theories of criminality will be discussed in a later chapter; suffice it to say here that race is related to crime only insofar as it affects the nature of social experiences and social interactions.

LIMITATIONS OF OFFICIAL STATISTICS

The method of reporting utilized by the *Uniform Crime Reports* has been the subject of analyses by a number of sociologists since its inception in 1930 (Beattie, 1960; Cressey, 1957; Newman, 1962; Sellin, 1961; Wolfgang, 1963). The following criticisms will be discussed: (1) the difficulty of determining the true volume of crime; (2) the fact that statistics are not compiled for all offenses; (3) the emphasis on per cent changes in the total volume of index offenses; (4) the practice of defining a crime as cleared when a suspect has been charged, regardless of the verdict; (5) the failure to base crime rates on a population of only those persons legally capable of committing crimes; (6) the expression of crime rates without taking into account the relative seriousness of the crime; (7) the inability to relate statistics to various phases of the criminal justice process; (8) the differential enforcement of criminal statutes; (9) the failure to devise a system that would take into consideration "accommodations which distort present figures"; and (10) the voluntary nature of primary data collection.

First, official statistics only reflect "offenses known to the police." As we noted earlier, many crimes go undiscovered, while others when discovered are not reported, or when reported are not recorded. Offenses are not recorded because: (1) some victims feel that the offense is a private matter and do not want to harm the offender; (2) some victims do not want to take the time to report the offense; (3) the victim or witness may fear reprisal; (4) some victims are too confused to know how to report the offense; (5) some victims feel that the police could not be effective in or would not want to be bothered with dealing with the offense; (6) some victims are too embarrassed about the circumstances of their victimization; e.g., a man who was robbed by a prostitute; (7) some victims are not aware that they have been victimized; e.g., in cases of shoplifting.

Second, the FBI does not routinely compile statistics for the *UCR* for some offenses, such as white-collar crimes. These are offenses committed by persons of "respectability" and high social status in the course of their employment. Embezzlement and fraud are common white-collar crimes. Such offenses are extremely widespread, yet an index of their frequency is not found in police reports (Sutherland and Cressey, 1974). Cressey suggests that "prosecution for this kind of crime can often be avoided because of the political or financial importance of the individuals involved, because of the difficulty in securing evidence, or because of the apparent triviality of the crimes" (Sutherland and Cressey, 1974, p. 40). Moreover, although these offenses are often punishable under our law, the perpetrators are often tried by administrative agencies or in civil courts and are not subjected to regular criminal court procedures. Commenting on the frequency of such offenses as misrepresentation in advertising, Sutherland (1941) said:

> *The manufacturers of practically every class of articles used by human beings have been involved in legal difficulties . . . with more or less frequency during the last 30 years, including the manufacturers of surgical instruments with which an infant may be assisted into the world, the bottle and nipple from which he may secure his food, the milk in his bottle, the blanket in which he is wrapped, the flag which his father displays in celebration of the event, and so on throughout life, until he is finally laid away in a casket which was manufactured and sold under conditions which violated the law (p. 111).*

Third, although the *UCR* has been reporting crime rates based on population changes since 1958, another misrepresentation still remains. The *UCR* continues to express changes in the volume of crime from one year to another in graphic "crime calendars," "crime capsules," "crime clocks," and "crime counts" without sufficient reference to the importance of population increases. The use of what Wolfgang calls the "tricky alliteration" of summarizing data in these forms tends, however, to highlight the absolute number of crimes, while the crime rate (i.e., the number of crimes per unit of population) is the more important measure. Moreover, the public receives a distorted picture of the crime problem because newspapers, local police, and civic groups interested in crime used data from these charts to portray the crime picture.

The crime clock expresses the number of serious crimes which occur each minute in the United States. For example, in 1975, 21 serious crimes occurred each minute, one forcible rape every 9 minutes, one murder every 26 minutes, one burglary every 10 seconds, and one larceny every 5 seconds (Federal Bureau of Investigation, 1976, p. 9). Unfortunately, this crime clock presents a distorted view of the crime picture because even if the number of crimes per unit of population remained constant, the crime clock would move more rapidly owing to increasing population. Conversely, if the population were to decrease and the volume of crime remain constant, the crime rate would have actually increased, yet the crime clock would show no change.

As an example, consider the presentation of the fact that there were 20,510 murders in the United States in 1975. The crime clock tells us that one murder is committed every 26 minutes, a rather startling figure. Yet if one divides the number of murders, 20,510, by 365 days, one finds that a person's chances of being murdered on a given day in a nation of over two hundred million

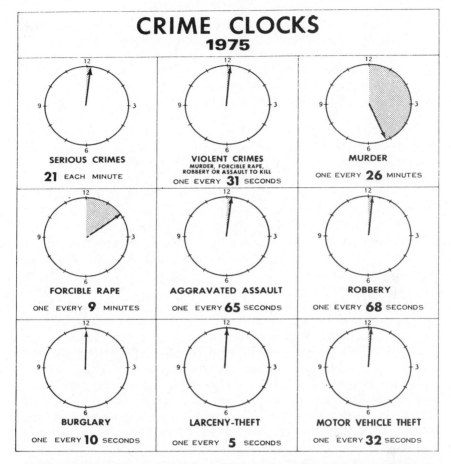

Figure 2–2. Crime clock used in the FBI's *Uniform Crime Reports* to graphically demonstrate increases in the rate of crime. (From Federal Bureau of Investigation: *Uniform Crime Reports: 1974.* Washington, D. C., U. S. Government Printing Office, 1975, p. 9. Reproduced by permission of the U. S. Department of Justice.)

people is approximately one in five million, a considerably less alarming state of affairs. Furthermore, this figure assumes that all persons in the United States stand the same chance of being murdered. However, when refinements are made with regard to the murder rate in terms of social class, rural-urban residence, and other pertinent factors, an average citizen's risk of being murdered is seen to be quite negligible. Thus, the crime clock method of presentation of crime rates gives us a caricature in place of an accurate picture of crime. Of this method Wolfgang (1963) writes:

> *If the purpose of this "crime clock" is to frighten consumers of the UCR, the statements probably succeed, for they are*

reproduced in scores of newspapers and read by millions, including congressmen, state legislators, and city councilmen who appropriate funds for police budgets. But some other documents should be used for this purpose, not a responsible publication that disseminates official statistics for use by social scientists and other analysts in scholarly research (p. 410).

Fourth, the police define a crime as "cleared" when they have enough evidence to take a suspect into custody and charge him with the crime. "Charge," then, bears the same relationship to police statistics as "guilty" does to court records. A crime remains "unsolved" until charges are filed. In effect, the suspect is "innocent" until "charged." The purely juristic view holds that a crime is not validly known to have taken place until a court finds someone guilty of that offense. In England, even today, police statistics are considered less reliable than judicial statistics, reflecting somewhat the lower social prestige of the police as compared with the judiciary.

Fifth, the crime rates presented in the *UCR* are based on the assumption that each person in the United States has the capacity to commit a crime. Legally, however, there are segments of the population who are not considered capable of forming criminal intent, e.g., children under the age of seven and persons in mental hospitals. Behaviorally, crime is rare in children under the age of twelve and among persons over age fifty. To allow for this, some foreign countries compute crime rates using as a population base those of "punishable age" or those "capable of committing a crime."

Sixth, the *UCR* does not provide an index of the gravity of the volume of crime committed, either as a whole or within specific legal categories. For example, if a community which did not experience any population increases for a decade reports that the volume of crime remained the same during that period, the crime index would also remain the same, and this would lead to the assumption that the crime picture in this community was constant for ten years. However, criminality in this community may well have grown worse during this decade owing to an increase in the relative proportion of serious personal offenses and a decrease in the relative proportion of petty property offenses, which would not be reflected by this method of compiling data on crime. In addition, the legal classifications used in reporting crime statistics also fail to adequately reflect the seriousness of offenses. For example, an offense is considered grand larceny if the amount stolen is $500 or $50,000. Likewise, robbery may mean the holdup of a bank by an adult with a gun, or the threat by one boy to beat up another if the latter fails to hand over his candy money.

Seventh, the *UCR* presents different sets of criminal statistics in a fashion which does not permit analysis of their relationships. Data are presented on "offenses known to police," "offenses cleared by arrest," "persons charged," and "persons found guilty," but it is impossible to move directly from one set of statistics to another due to the fact that not all of them are computed using the same population units. Further, it is not possible to analyze the relationship of "offenses" to "offenders"; the arrest of one person can clear several crimes, or several persons may be arrested in the process of clearing one crime.

Eighth, while statutes define the outer limits of criminal conduct beyond which criminal justice agencies cannot go, it does not follow that these agencies will fully enforce such statutes to their limits. As Newman (1962, p. 146) suggests, "Statutes may be enacted as expressions of desirable morality but with no intention of full and relentless enforcement (adultery), or may be retained due to legislative oversight or consciously as strengthening the 'arsenal' of prosecutors but without an expectation of general enforcement ('blue laws'), or will be vague and not clearly limited either inadvertently, deliberately, or as a necessary limitation of all attempts to write generalizable word formulas (gambling)." Moreover, public opinion in no way favors full enforcement of all statutes. Furthermore, police budgets and resources do not permit the full enforcement of all statutes, and therefore departments must make decisions regarding which laws will receive primary enforcement attention. For example, if a police department in a medium-sized city has a six-member vice squad, some decisions will have to be made as to whether the squad will focus primarily on the enforcement of the narcotics, gambling, or prostitution laws.

Ninth, "accommodation" (the routine and systematic practice on the part of police, prosecutors, and the judiciary of not requiring full implementation of the conviction process in spite of the legal evidence to do so) has an important effect on crime statistics. The prosecutor uses wide discretionary powers in deciding when and what to charge and may invoke his power of *nolle prosequi* (which means to decline to prosecute). Thus, some persons clearly guilty of crimes may never appear in conviction statistics. Further discretionary powers are invested in the judge with regard to sentencing. A judge may accept a "plea bargain," i.e., a plea of guilty in return for a reduced charge and sentence. The judge may even refuse to convict. Newman (1962) refers to the practice of a Detroit judge who routinely acquitted both prostitutes and homosexuals when, in his opinion, members of the vice squad had enticed them into criminal conduct. Offenders who turn state's evidence, as in the case of some of the Watergate defendants, may be granted immunity and acquitted. The reduction process modifies the label and the sentence of the person convicted; therefore, any generalizations about the crime problem based on conviction statistics are of limited value. While the two accommodations, acquittal and reduction, do affect the validity of crime statistics, the process is a necessary and wise one if the law is to function in a flexible and realistic manner.

Finally, the difficulty in producing crime statistics on a national scale to some degree relates to the fact that the FBI must depend on the voluntary cooperation of over 9000 state and local law enforcement agencies to provide the basic data from which national crime statistics are compiled. The FBI has no authority to compel state and local governments to cooperate in reporting crime data (Lejins, 1966). Only an organization with the prestige among law enforcement personnel that the FBI enjoys could obtain their voluntary cooperation. Moreover, since the FBI only gathers these statistics from other agencies, their reliability is dependent upon the reporting and recording procedures of those agencies. Despite the FBI's efforts to establish uniform reporting procedures, the reliability of criminal records varies with the reporting department. The Crime Index gains status from the FBI's reputation as a superior crime-fighting agency, but in fact it is only a measure of how many crimes are reported and is not an accurate measure of how many crimes are committed. A high "total crime index" may reflect a "reporting wave" rather than a "crime wave." For example, in 1970, California's total crime index (nation's highest) was five times that of Mississippi (nation's lowest), but this was probably due in part to the better reporting system in California. Lejins reminds those who criticize the *UCR* as a statistical series that it is intended to be a statistical organ of the police, and he feels it is unfair to fault it for failing to be something it was never intended to be.

"House organ" or not, there remains considerable evidence to support the view of some criminologists that the United States has the worst criminal statistics of any major country in the Western world. The *UCR* is the only compilation of crime statistics on a national scale. In the United States there are no national comprehensive judicial criminal statistics, no national probation or parole statistics, no national statistics on the dispositions of grand juries. In short, we have national statistics covering only one step of the criminal process, the arrest stage.

Finally, the President's Commission on Law Enforcement and Administration of Justice (1967) pointed out that at least four major governmental studies of national criminal statistics were made between the years 1934 and 1965 and each concluded that there was a critical need for a strong, effective federal statistical program. The commission recommended the establishment of a National Criminal Justice Statistics Center either within the Bureau of the Census or as an independent agency. Such an agency would be responsible for bringing about improvements in the gathering, compilation, and interpretation of national crime data. Until such a recommendation becomes a reality and until crime statistics can be tabulated on a national scale with the efficiency and clarity now achieved by the California system, the scientific study of crime will be seriously impaired.

A big step toward the creation of such a national system was taken in June, 1969, when six states (Arizona, California, Maryland, Michigan, Minnesota, and New York) were selected by the Law Enforcement Assistance Administration as participants in project SEARCH, an acronym for "system for electronic analysis and retrieval of criminal histories." The subsequent addition of five states has raised the total number of participants to eleven. The project is designed to give criminal justice agencies needed information on offenders in a matter of seconds. Each participating state has its own computer system which includes a file of 10,000 representative offender criminal histories. A national central index containing limited criminal history summaries of all state files is maintained by the Michigan State Police, in Lansing, Michigan. Long-range plans call for the creation of a national system, and if this is accomplished, SEARCH would provide a basis for a complete statistical system on every component of the criminal justice system, both within each state and nationally.

Prevalence Studies: The Extent of Unreported Crime

It has long been recognized that the *UCR* provides only a rough indication of the amount of crime that actually occurs because it reports only on "crimes known to the police." As the previous section indicated, many crimes go undiscovered, while others when discovered are not reported, or when reported are not recorded. Researchers have developed a number of different strategies to gain some indication of the amount of unreported-unrecorded crime and delinquency. These include the examination of social agency and juvenile court records and the use of self-reporting instruments and victim surveys.

Hidden Delinquency: Focus on the Offender

An early study by Robison (1936) in New York City found that over one third of the cases of delinquency that were known to private agencies were not known to the juvenile court. Other studies made around this time confirmed these findings. For example, Schwartz (1945) found that only 43 per cent of the cases that came to the attention of other agencies were known to the juvenile court. The staff of the Cambridge-Somerville Project (Murphy, Shirley, and Witmer, 1946) conducted a study of the case records of the boys who had been participating in this project for over five years. They found that 101 of the 114 project boys committed a total of 6416 acts of delinquency during this five year period of which only 1.5 per cent ever resulted in official court action. While most of these offenses (5800) were violations of city ordinances or minor offenses, 616 were serious offenses of which only 11 per cent resulted in prosecution.

Another common method of assessing hidden delinquency is the use of self-reporting instruments. The first of these studies was conducted by Austin Porterfield in Fort Worth, Texas. Porterfield (1946) initially studied the court cases of 2049 juveniles in order to determine what offenses these youngsters had committed. He then prepared a questionnaire that included questions about these offenses and administered it to 337 college students. All the college students reported that they had committed one or more of the offenses that had brought the delinquents to the attention of the juvenile court. Moreover, a comparison of the frequency, on the average, with which the same offenses were committed by 100 male college students and the boys in the juvenile court showed that the college men committed far more offenses than the juvenile court boys had been charged with, yet traffic offenses were the only violations for which a significant number of charges were brought against the college men. In fact, data from this study showed that, on the average, these students could have been charged with delinquency on at least 11 different occasions.

Short and Nye (1958) conducted a study in which they compared the self-reported delinquent behavior of students in three midwestern high schools and three western high schools to that of juveniles in a midwestern training school (Tables 2–1 and 2–2).

These tables clearly show that at least a few of the high school students were involved in each of the offenses committed by the training school youngsters. However, higher percentages of training school boys and girls indicated that they had engaged in each of these acts and had done so with greater frequency than the high

TABLE 2–1. REPORTED DELINQUENT BEHAVIOR AMONG BOYS IN THREE SAMPLES*

TYPE OF OFFENSE	PER CENT ADMITTING COMMISSION OF OFFENSE			PER CENT ADMITTING COMMISSION OF OFFENSE MORE THAN ONCE OR TWICE		
	M.W.†	West	Tr.S.	M.W.	West	Tr.S.
Driven a car without a driver's license or permit	81.1	75.3	91.1	61.2	49.0	73.4
Skipped school	54.4	53.0	95.3	24.4	23.8	85.9
Had fist fight with one person	86.7	80.7	95.3	32.6	31.9	75.0
"Run away" from home	12.9	13.0	68.1	2.8	2.4	37.7
School probation or expulsion	15.3	11.3	67.8	2.1	2.9	31.3
Defied parents' authority	22.2	33.1	52.4	1.4	6.3	23.6
Driven too fast or recklessly	49.7	46.0	76.3	22.7	19.1	51.6
Taken little things (worth less than $2) that did not belong to you	62.7	60.6	91.8	18.5	12.9	65.1
Taken things of medium value $2–$50)	17.1	15.8	91.0	3.8	3.8	61.4
Taken things of large value ($50)	3.5	5.0	90.8	1.1	2.1	47.7
Used force (strong-arm methods) to get money from another person	6.3	—	67.7	2.4	—	35.5
Taken part in "gang fights"	24.3	22.5	67.4	6.7	5.2	47.4
Taken a car for a ride without the owner's knowledge	11.2	14.8	75.2	4.5	4.0	53.4
Bought or drank beer, wine, or liquor (include drinking at home)	67.7	57.2	89.7	35.8	29.5	79.4
Bought or drank beer, wine, or liquor (outside your home)	43.0	—	87.0	21.1	—	75.0
Drank beer, wine, or liquor in your own home	57.0	—	62.8	24.1	—	31.9
Deliberate property damage	60.7	44.8	84.3	17.5	8.2	49.7
Used or sold narcotic drugs	1.4	2.2	23.1	0.7	1.6	12.6
Had sex relations with another person of the same sex (not masturbation)	12.0	8.8	10.9	3.9	2.9	3.1
Had sex relations with a person of the opposite sex	38.8	40.4	87.5	20.3	19.9	73.4
Gone hunting or fishing without a license (or violated other game laws)	74.0	62.7	66.7	39.6	23.5	44.8
Taken things you didn't want	15.7	22.5	56.8	1.4	3.1	26.8
"Beat up" on kids who hadn't done anything to you	15.7	13.9	48.7	3.1	2.8	26.2
Hurt someone to see them squirm	22.7	15.8	33.4	2.8	3.2	17.5

*From Short, J. F., and Nye, F. I.: Extent of unrecorded delinquency: tentative conclusions. Journal of Criminal Law, Criminology, and Police Science 49:296–302, 1958. Reprinted by special permission of the Journal of Criminal Law, Criminology, and Police Science, Copyright © 1958 by Northwestern University School of Law, Vol. 49, 1958.

†M.W. denotes the responses of students from a midwestern high school; West, those from a western high school; and Tr.S., those from a midwestern training school.

TABLE 2–2. REPORTED DELINQUENT BEHAVIOR AMONG GIRLS IN THREE SAMPLES*

TYPE OF OFFENSE	PER CENT ADMITTING COMMISSION OF OFFENSE			PER CENT ADMITTING COMMISSION OF OFFENSE MORE THAN ONCE OR TWICE		
	M.W.†	West	Tr.S.	M.W.	West	Tr.S.
Driven a car without a driver's license or permit	60.1	58.2	68.3	33.6	29.9	54.4
Skipped school	40.3	41.0	94.0	10.1	12.2	66.3
Had fist fight with one person	32.7	28.2	72.3	7.4	5.7	44.6
"Run away" from home	9.8	11.3	85.5	1.0	1.0	51.8
School probation or expulsion	2.7	3.7	63.4	0.3	0.2	29.3
Defined parents' authority	33.0	30.6	68.3	3.7	5.0	39.0
Driven too fast or recklessly	20.9	16.3	47.5	5.7	5.4	35.0
Taken little things (worth less than $2) that did not belong to you	36.0	30.0	77.8	5.7	3.5	48.1
Taken things of medium value ($2–50)	3.4	3.9	58.0	1.0	0.6	29.6
Taken things of large value ($50)	2.0	1.3	30.4	1.7	0.9	10.1
Used force (strong-arm methods) to get money from another person	1.3	—	36.7	0.3	—	21.5
Taken part in "gang fights"	9.7	6.5	59.0	1.7	1.1	27.7
Taken a car for a ride without the owner's knowledge	5.4	4.5	36.6	1.0	0.6	20.7
Bought or drank beer, wine, or liquor (include drinking at home)	62.7	44.5	90.2	23.1	17.6	80.5
Bought or drank beer, wine, or liquor (outside your home)	28.7	—	83.9	10.8	—	75.3
Drank beer, wine, or liquor in your own home	54.2	—	71.1	16.4	—	42.2
Deliberate property damage	21.7	13.6	65.4	5.7	1.6	32.1
Used or sold narcotic drugs	1.3	0.5	36.9	0.3	0.3	23.8
Had sex relations with another person of the same sex (not masturbation)	5.4	3.6	25.0	1.7	0.5	12.5
Had sex relations with a person of the opposite sex	12.5	14.1	95.1	4.1	4.8	81.5
Gone hunting or fishing without a license (or violated other game laws)	20.6	20.3	27.5	5.7	3.9	21.3
Taken things you didn't want	6.4	3.6	43.0	0.7	0.6	13.9
"Beat up" on kids who hadn't done anything to you	5.7	3.1	37.8	1.0	0.9	18.3
Hurt someone to see them squirm	10.4	9.3	35.4	1.0	1.1	20.7

*From Short, J. F., and Nye, F. I.: Extent of unrecorded delinquency: tentative conclusions. Journal of Criminal Law, Criminology, and Police Science 49:296–302, 1958. Reprinted by special permission of the Journal of Criminal Law, Criminology, and Police Science, Copyright © 1958 by Northwestern University School of Law, Vol. 45, 1958.

†M.W. denotes the responses of students from a midwestern high school; West, those from a western high school; and Tr.S., those from a midwestern training school.

school students. Furthermore, the training school youngsters admitted involvement in serious forms of conduct, which was not common among the high school students. Thus, training school boys were more frequently involved in stealing and fighting than their high school counterparts, while training school girls exceeded high school girls in fighting and sex related offenses. It can be concluded that although almost all of the high school students had engaged in some acts of delinquency, those in training schools had been involved in more serious and more frequent delinquent conduct.

Gold did considerable research (Gold, 1970; Williams and Gold, 1972; Haney and Gold, 1973) on the issue of hidden delinquency. One study surveyed a representative sample of 552 teenagers from Flint, Michigan, in 1961; a second study used a sample of 847 teenagers representative of all Americans 13 to 16 years old. In both these studies, youngsters were questioned by interviewers about their delinquent behavior out of earshot of their parents. The respondents in both these studies had engaged in a wide variety of delinquent acts.

Table 2–3 shows that boys are significantly more delinquent than girls, as official records suggest. Information collected in these studies also indicates that running away, incorrigibility, and fornication account for only 11 per cent of girls' delinquency, which contradicts the assumption that these offenses account for a major part of delinquent behavior of this group.

A major question associated with the use of self-reporting instruments is the extent of concealment by respondents. To counter this problem, a special validation study was carried out as part of the Flint project. Information was obtained from informants concerning the delinquent activities of 125 teenagers. These youngsters were then interviewed regarding their delinquent activities without being told that the researchers had prior information of their activities. Seventy-two per cent of these youngsters were classified as "truth tellers"; that is, they confessed to everything the informants had reported or to more recent or more serious offenses. Seventeen per cent were outright liars and the remaining 11 per cent provided questionable information.

Both these studies also found that respondents admitted to a great deal more delinquency than was ever detected and recorded. For example, in the Flint study, 433 of the 522 respondents admitted to 2490 delinquent acts, yet only 3 per cent of these offenses (47) were ever detected by police, and parents were aware of only 25 per cent.

Data from the Flint study and another study conducted by

TABLE 2–3. PER CENT OF RESPONDENTS WHO
COMMITTED EACH OFFENSE AT LEAST ONCE IN
THE THREE YEARS PRIOR TO THE INTERVIEW*

OFFENSE	BOYS		GIRLS	
	Flint Sample	National Sample	Flint Sample	National Sample
Trespass	50	54	23	27
Drinking	55	43	43	29
Theft	60	54	30	31
Threatened assault	20	49	7	31
Truancy	30	43	17	34
Property destruction	27	48	6	25
Entering	38	42	23	33
Assault	11	39	2	15
False I.D.	10	31	2	27
Gang fight	23	34	5	14
Fraud	3	23	1	15
Concealed weapon	13	12	1	1
Hitting parents	2	9	2	11
UDAA†	10	7	3	3
Runaway	6	6	6	5
Drugs	‡	2	‡	2
Arson	§	1	0	0
Extortion	8	1	1	0
Armed robbery	6	0	0	0

*From Haney, B., and Gold, M.: The juvenile delinquent nobody knows.
Psychology Today 7:49–102, 1973.
†Unauthorized driving away of automobile.
‡Not asked of Flint sample.
§Less than 1 per cent.

Gold and Williams (Haney and Gold, 1973) cast serious doubt on
the common belief that apprehension acts as a deterrent to further
delinquency. In both studies the apprehended youngsters committed more offenses than the unapprehended group. For
example, Gold and Williams (Haney and Gold, 1973) compared a
group of apprehended youngsters with a group of unapprehended
youngsters; the groups were matched with respect to sex, race, and
number and kinds of offenses. They found that in 20 of the 35
pairs, the apprehended youngsters subsequently committed more
offenses than their unapprehended match. Five pairs subsequently
committed an equal number of delinquent acts and in only 10
pairs did the unapprehended commit more offenses. They concluded that getting caught encourages rather than deters further
delinquency.

The Flint study also disputed the assumption that gang boys

are responsible for most delinquent behavior. This study found that large groups did not regularly and frequently commit delinquent acts together. Instead, group delinquency typically involved two or three youngsters who hung around together and engaged in both delinquent and conventional activities. Thus, out of the 522 teenagers they found only 11 youngsters who were classified as gang delinquents, i.e., a frequent offender who had committed at least half of his five or more offenses with his most frequent companion. In addition, only 11 younsters in this sample were deemed to be "loners," i.e., they committed delinquent acts relatively frequently and at least half of these offenses were committed alone.

Finally, one of the most striking findings of this study contradicted the common assumption, supported by official data, that delinquent behavior is predominately a lower-class slum problem. Both this study and the national study found no strong relationship between social status and delinquent behavior. Most surprising was the fact that the national survey found that higher-status white boys reported somewhat more serious delinquent behavior than did their lower-status peers.

Clark and Tifft (1966) used the polygraph to assess the accuracy of responses on anonymous self-report questionnaires. In their study, 45 male college students were asked to respond anonymously to a series of questions regarding their delinquent behavior. Later, the students were given an opportunity to make any modifications they wished to make their responses 100 per cent accurate. Prior to proceeding, they were told that a polygraph examination would be given to assess the accuracy of their final responses. The major finding of this study was that self-reporting of delinquency is rather accurate. More specifically, they found that accuracy was between 90 and 100 per cent for serious offenses (e.g., breaking and entering, stealing of items worth $50 or more) with accuracy being lower for less serious delinquent behavior and behavior considered to be inconsistent with either individual personal norms or reference group norms.

It is obvious from these and other studies that official statistics do not provide an accurate measure of delinquency. Furthermore, these studies raise some interesting questions about current delinquency programs. Is the over-representation of lower-class youngsters in police records, court records, and training schools a result of different enforcement policies, or are these youngsters really more delinquent than their middle-class counterparts? If middle-class youngsters are as delinquent as lower-class youngsters are we misdirecting our prevention programs?

TABLE 2–4. INDICTABLE OFFENSES ADMITTED BY
ADULT NONCRIMINALS*

OFFENSE	PER CENT	
	Men	Women
Malicious mischief	84	82
Disorderly conduct	85	76
Assault	49	5
Auto misdemeanors	61	39
Indecency	77	74
Gambling	74	54
Larceny	89	83
Grand larceny (except auto)	13	11
Auto theft	26	8
Burglary	17	4
Robbery	11	1
Concealed weapons	35	3
Perjury	23	17
Falsification and fraud	46	34
Election frauds	7	4
Tax evasion	57	40
Coercion	26	6
Conspiracy	23	7
Criminal libel	36	29

*Data from Wallerstein, J. S., and Wyle, J.: Our law-abiding law-breakers. Probation 25:107–112, 1947. Table reproduced from *Criminology and Penology* by R. R. Korn and L. W. McCorkle. Copyright © 1961 by Holt, Rinehart and Winston, Inc. Reproduced by permission of the authors and Holt, Rinehart and Winston, Inc.

Adult Studies: Focus on the Offender

The study conducted by Wallerstein and Wyle (1947) provides some indication of the extent of hidden adult criminality. They asked 1698 adults if they had committed any one of 49 listed offenses. Ninety-one per cent of the sample admitted that they had committed one or more of these offenses after age 16, with a mean of 18 offenses for men and 11 offenses for women. Also, 64 per cent of the men and 29 per cent of the women admitted the commission of a felony. Table 2–4 presents the percentages of men and women who admitted committing certain offenses.

Focus on the Victim

Another method to assess "hidden criminality" is to ask individuals if they have been the victim of a crime and if so whether they reported it to the police. A national victim survey of 10,000 randomly selected households was conducted by the National Opinion Research Center (NORC) for the President's Crime Commission in 1965 (President's Commission, 1967). Interviewers asked each respondent (1) whether they or any member of their household had been a victim of a crime in the past year and if so what offense and (2) whether the crime had been reported and, if not, why not. As Table 2–5 shows, the amount of "crimes against the person" reported to NORC was almost twice the *UCR* rate and the amount of property offenses was more than twice the *UCR* rate. More specifically, data from this study showed that the rate for forcible rape was three and one half times the reported rate; that for burglaries, three times greater; that for aggravated assault, more than twice as great; that for larcenies of $50 or over, more than twice as great; and for

TABLE 2–5. COMPARISON OF NORC SURVEY AND UCR RATES (PER 100,000 POPULATION)*

INDEX CRIMES	NORC SURVEY 1965–66	UCR RATE FOR INDIVIDUALS 1965†	UCR RATE FOR INDIVIDUALS AND ORGANIZATIONS 1965†
Willful homicide	3.0	5.1	5.1
Forcible rape	42.5	11.6	11.6
Robbery	94.0	61.4	61.4
Aggravated assault	218.3	106.6	106.6
Burglary	949.1	299.6	605.3
Larceny ($50 and over)	606.5	267.4	393.3
Motor vehicle theft	206.2	226.0	251.0
Total violence	357.8	184.7	184.7
Total property	1,761.8	793.0	1,249.6

*From President's Commission on Law Enforcement and Administration of Justice. *The Challenge of Crime in a Free Society.* Washington, D. C., U. S. Government Printing Office, 1967, p. 21. Reproduced by permission of the U. S. Department of Justice.

†"Uniform Crime Reports," 1965, p. 51. The UCR national totals do not distinguish crimes committed against individuals or households from those committed against businesses or other organizations. The UCR rate for individuals is the published national rate adjusted to eliminate burglaries, larcenies, and vehicle thefts not committed against individuals or households. No adjustment was made for robbery.

robberies, more than 50 per cent greater. Only in the case of motor vehicle theft was the NORC rate lower than the UCR rate and then only by a small amount. (The single homicide reported is too small a number to be statistically useful).

Even though the NORC rates were generally much higher than the UCR rates, the President's Commission felt that they had probably underestimated the actual amount of crime. The NORC study gathered the victim experiences of every member of a household based on an interview with one member. However, if analysis is restricted to information concerning only the family member interviewed and not other household members, the amount of victimization for the same offenses will be considerably higher since it is likely that the family member interviewed would remember more of his own victimization than that of other members of his household. Data from a survey conducted in three Washington, D. C., precincts in which only the victim was interviewed provide some support for this position. As Figure 2–3 shows, the number of offenses reported per thousand residents 18 years and over ranged, depending on the offense, from 3 to 10 times more than the number contained in police statistics.

The NORC survey also tabulated the reasons given by victims for not reporting crimes to the police. The reason most frequently given to interviewers for all offenses was that the police could not do anything. Table 2–6 shows that this reason was offered by 68 per cent of those not reporting malicious mischief and by 60 per

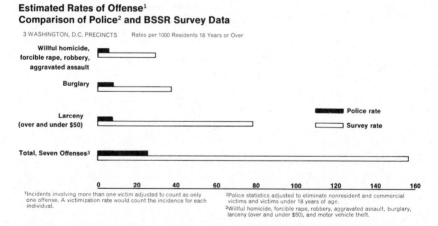

Estimated Rates of Offense[1]
Comparison of Police[2] and BSSR Survey Data

3 WASHINGTON, D.C. PRECINCTS   Rates per 1000 Residents 18 Years or Over

[1]Incidents involving more than one victim adjusted to count as only one offense. A victimization rate would count the incidence for each individual.

[2]Police statistics adjusted to eliminate nonresident and commercial victims and victims under 18 years of age.

[3]Willful homicide, forcible rape, robbery, aggravated assault, burglary, larceny (over and under $50), and motor vehicle theft.

Figure 2–3. Differences in the rate of crime based on victim interviews and police statistics. (From President's Commission on Law Enforcement and Administration of Justice: *Task Force Report: Crime and Its Impact—An Assessment.* Washington, D. C., U. S. Government Printing Office, 1967, p. 18. Reproduced by permission of the U. S. Department of Justice.)

TABLE 2–6. VICTIMS' MOST IMPORTANT REASON FOR NOT NOTIFYING POLICE*

| CRIMES‡ | PER CENT OF CASES IN WHICH POLICE NOT NOTIFIED | REASONS FOR NOT NOTIFYING POLICE | | | | |
		Felt it was private matter or did not want to harm offender (Per Cent)	Police could not be effec- tive or would not want to be bothered (Per Cent)	Did not want to take time (Per Cent)	Too con- fused or did not know how to report (Per Cent)	Fear of reprisal (Per Cent)
Robbery	35	27	45	9	18	0
Aggravated assault	35	50	25	4	8	13
Simple assault	54	50	35	4	4	7
Burglary	42	30	63	4	2	2
Larceny ($50 and over)	40	23	62	7	7	0
Larceny (under $50)	63	31	58	7	3	(†)
Auto theft	11	20 §	60 §	0 §	0 §	20 §
Malicious mischief	62	23	68	5	2	2
Consumer fraud	90	50	40	0	10	0
Other fraud (bad checks, swindling, etc.)	74	41	35	16	8	0
Sex offenses (other than forcible rape)	49	40	50	0	5	5
Family crimes (desertion, non- support, etc.)	50	65	17	10	0	7

*From President's Commission on Law Enforcement and Administration of Justice: *Task Force Report: Crime and Its Impact—An Assessment.* Washington, D.C., U.S. Government Printing Office, 1967, p. 18.
†Less than 0.5%.
‡Willful homicide, forcible rape, and a few other crimes had too few cases to be statistically useful, and they are therefore excluded.
§There were only 5 instances in which auto theft was not reported.

cent or more of those not reporting burglaries, larcenies of $50 and over, and auto theft.

The following two brief vignettes, taken by Bloch and Geis (1970, p. 117) from *The New York Times*, are typical of the types of situations in which people fail to report offenses:

> On Saturday, October 26, 1968, Robert Walters walked into the vestibule of an apartment building on West 75th Street, leaned over the buzzer and began searching for the name of a friend. Suddenly, two men appeared, placed a knife at his throat and demanded his money. Mr. Walters, a visitor from Washington,

did not report the armed robbery to the police. "It would have been a waste of my time and police time," Mr. Walters recalled recently, "They only took cash—which could not be traced, and the stick-up was so fast and professional that I really did not see their faces." On the same day that Mr. Walters was held up, Dr. Helen Mitchell, a sociologist and an anti-poverty official, was away from her apartment in the Southern Bronx from 7:00 P.M. to 9:00 P.M. During this two hour period, someone broke into her apartment and took her television set and radio. Dr. Mitchell did not report the burglary to the police. "I didn't bother calling them because there was nothing they could do," she said.

Glaser (1970) has formulated a hypothesis regarding the disparity between the number of victimizations for property offenses and the number of offenses reported to the police. He states that "the proportion of total crimes that are reported by victims to the police varies directly with the proportion of reported crimes on which the police act effectively." In short, people report those crimes they believe the police can or will solve. Improved police work leads to higher reported crimes statistics. In the area of assault and rape, these offenses tend not to be reported if the victims perceive these as "personal matters."

STATISTICS ON CRIME TRENDS

Public opinion polls, along with other indicators, suggest that crime is increasing at a rapid rate, and some people feel that crime has reached an all-time high. Certainly, it is important for us to know when crime has reached an all-time high, to know whether it is increasing or decreasing and by how much, and to be able to distinguish ups and downs from long-term trends. Citizens who run the risk of crime should have this information available to them, and officials must have it in order to plan and establish prevention and control programs. Unfortunately, our methods for measuring the trend of crime are even less reliable than those used for measuring the volume of crime, and the President's Commission on Law Enforcement and Administration of Justice (1967) has suggested some reasons for this:

Unlike some European countries which have maintained National statistics for more than a century and a quarter, the United States has maintained National crime statistics only since 1930. Because the rural areas were slow in coming into the system and reported poorly when they did, it was not until 1958 when other major changes were made in the UCR, that reporting of all crimes was sufficient to allow a total National estimate without special adjustments. Changes in overall estimating procedures and two offense categories—rape and larceny—were also made in 1958. Because of these problems, figures prior to 1958 and particularly those prior to 1940 must be viewed as neither fully comparable with nor nearly so reliable as later figures. (p. 23)

The President's Commission made some adjustments from unpublished figures in data collected prior to 1958 in an effort to provide some base line information on crime trends. Although these figures show that the crime rates (risk of being victimized) have fluctuated since 1933, rates at present are the highest for the period from 1933 to the present and appear to be rising. The upward trend for the period 1960 to 1975 has been faster than the long-term trend, up 199.3 per cent for violent crimes and 178.1 per cent for property crimes. During this period, rates of homicide nearly doubled, forcible rape rates increased more than one and one half times, robbery rates nearly tripled, and aggravated assault rates almost doubled. In the case of property offenses, burglary rates increased 200 per cent, larceny rates increased by 171.1 per cent, and auto theft rates went up 156.5 per cent. On the surface, these statistics would seem to indicate that the United States is experiencing an unprecedented crime wave. However, there are many good reasons for questioning this conclusion.

First, statistical information on crime has been collected only since 1930. It is quite possible that the rate of crime was much higher during other periods of our history. An analysis of early crime studies reveals that during the period immediately after the Civil War, the rate of violent crime in large cities was higher than at any other time in our history (Graham, 1969). Furthermore, Geis (1967) contends that, in comparison with frontier days, there has been a significant decrease in crimes of violence.

While the present rate of crime may appear to be high when compared with the crime rates of the past four decades, this may well reflect the fact that the crime rate was extremely low at the beginning of the reporting period and climbed steadily to a normal or slightly higher level in the following 47 years. Teeters and Matza (1966) provide some support for this position. They compared the number of delinquency complaints from Cuyahoga County, Ohio—which has within its bounds the city of Cleveland— for the years 1918 to 1957. They found that the delinquency rate was 65.9 per thousand children (12 to 17 years old) in 1918; 63.2 in 1919; and 52.0 in 1920. In 1925 the rate was 41.4; in 1932, 35.8; in 1939, 21; in 1943, 31.7; in 1945, 34.7; in 1950, 25.2; and in 1957, 33.5 (Teeters and Matza, 1966, p. 43).

Despite the fact that recording and detection methods were probably much better in 1957 than in 1918, delinquency rates were much higher in 1918 than in 1957 in at least one major metropolitan area. Since juveniles have always been responsible for a substantial amount of crime, these data show that it was quite possible that there were other times in our history when crime rates were much higher than they are today.

Second, it is also necessary to examine the reliability of the statistics upon which the conclusion that crime is at an all-time high is based. Most crime experts consider crime statistics to be the least reliable of all statistics available, and there are a number of good reasons why their accuracy is questioned. First, these statistics are based on crimes known to the police, and research has shown that these may represent only the tip of the iceberg. For example, when the President's Commission compared estimates of unreported crime obtained through a victimization study with officially reported statistics, they found that the amount of crime that actually occurred was between 50 and 350 per cent greater than official statistics had indicated. Since there is so much unreported crime, a "crime wave" can result merely from changes in citizen reporting. It is possible that part of our current crime wave may be the result of increased reporting by victims.

Recent official crime statistics are likely to have been affected by changes in the expectations of the poor and minority groups concerning civil rights and social protection. Not long ago, the police tended to ignore reports of all but the most serious crimes committed in the ghetto and other low-income areas. However, regardless of past practices, the studies made by the President's Commission indicate that residents in these areas now demand adequate police protection. Whereas in the past, these persons failed to report much of the crime in their area and police failed to record much of what was reported, now much more of this crime is likely to be reported and recorded. This alone explains a sizable part of the officially reported increase in crime because these areas have typically had high victimization rates.

Changes in police practices and in the make-up of police departments have resulted in more accurate reporting of the crime picture. Professionalization of police departments has led to a strong trend toward more formal action, more formal records, and less informal disposition of individual cases.

Changes in cities' recording procedures can also affect the crime picture. In the past, there have been numerous instances of deliberate under-reporting of crime by police departments so that they would appear efficient and local government would appear to have the crime situation well in hand. Just prior to the administration of Mayor John Lindsay, the New York City Police Department had been under-reporting the volume of crime in the city. When Mayor Lindsay took office he instructed the police department to begin presenting the true picture. Consequently, reported robberies rose from approximately 8000 in 1965 to about 23,000 in 1966 and burglaries leaped from 40,000 to 120,000. Although the President's Commission did not undertake an exhaustive study of changes in reporting procedures, data were presented on eleven jurisdictions to illustrate the impact of these changes on the crime picture: crime increases ranged from 34.4 per cent to 202.2 per cent as a result of improved reporting procedures (President's Commission, 1967).

There is certainly some question as to whether the crime rate now is really higher than it was in previous periods of our history. There is also some question as to whether the increases in crime since 1960 are actual or simply reflect changes in citizen reporting and police recording procedures. It would be unrealistic to attribute the dramatic increase in reported crime during this period solely to changes in reporting and recording procedures. In the last analysis, these factors must be viewed as affecting only the magnitude of the increase in volume over this period. However, it is impossible to accurately assess the magnitude of this increase.

FACTORS THAT CONTRIBUTE TO AN INCREASE IN CRIME

Changing Age Composition of Population

One of the most important factors that affect crime rate and volume is the age composition of the population. An examination of crime statistics reveals that young people contribute disproportionately to the crime problem. For example, in 1974, persons under 18 years of age accounted for 27 per cent of the total arrests, with those under 25 accounting for 57.8 per cent. Furthermore, when only index crimes are considered, 27.3 per cent of all arrests in 1974 were of persons 15 and under, and 52.3 per cent were of persons 18 and under (Federal Bureau of Investigation, 1975, p. 186). Thus, any expansion in the relative number of young people can be expected to lead to an increase in crime. During the 1960's and early 1970's, without taking into account any other factors that might affect the crime picture, the crime experts could have expected an increase in crime in the United States because during this period the postwar "baby boom" children became teenagers and young adults. However, while the population of this group has increased during this period, it has not increased in proportion to the volume of crime. For example, between 1960 and 1970 the number of persons between 10 and 17 years of age rose 29 per cent, but the arrests in this group more than doubled (Federal Bureau of Investigation, 1971). Thus, only part of the increase in crime during this period can be attributed to a relative increase in this population group.

Urbanization

Another factor that has contributed to the increased crime rate is a steady growth in our urban population and a decline in the proportion of the population living in rural areas and small towns. Between 1960 and 1970 our urban population increased by 19.2 per cent (U. S. Bureau of the Census, 1975).

Cities have traditionally had higher crime rates than small towns and rural areas. This can be attributed in part to the anonymity of city life which attracts deviants of all kinds because it allows them to carry on their deviant activities in relative obscurity. In addition, the anonymity of city life facilitates criminal activity because offenders can commit crimes and fade back into the crowd with the assurance that they will not come into contact with their victims. Furthermore, it also provides a greater number and variety of targets for criminal activities. Thus, as the urban population has increased, there has been a con- comitant increase in crime. For example, studies conducted by the President's Commission showed that if metropolitan, small city, and rural crime rates for 1960 had remained constant through 1965, we could have expected a 7 to 8 per cent increase in crime due to urbanization alone (President's Commission, 1967). There- fore, part of the increase in crime since 1960 can be attributed to increased urbanization.

Drug Addiction

An increase in the drug-using population would also account for a major portion of the increase in crime since 1960. The *Uniform Crime Reports* indicates that arrests for narcotic drug law violations increased 741 per cent between 1960 and 1970 and 174 per cent between 1968 and 1973.

In 1970 almost one third of these arrests involved users of heroin or cocaine, while in 1973 only 14 per cent of these arrests involved the users of these drugs.* The rather dramatic increases in drug arrests during this period indicate an increase in drug use in general.

Although there is no evidence to show that these drugs cause antisocial or violent behavior, the fact that they are illegal and costly causes most addicts to resort to crime in order to support their habits. The American Bar Association estimates that between one third and one half of all street crime in the United States can be attributed to addicts (Friedman, 1972). The estimates for New York City are even higher, with addict-related crime accounting for as much as 50 to 70 per cent of street crimes (Haskell and Yablonsky, 1970).

Addicts resort to crime because drugs are very expensive on the illegal market and the average addict cannot command a legal wage that would support his habit. Estimates of the cost of a daily drug habit vary from $10 to $67 per day (Haskell and Yablonsky, 1970; Levine, 1973; Williams, 1974). Between $3 and $5 a day in merchandise must be stolen to realize $1 in cash. Assuming that an average drug habit costs $30 per day (Levine, 1973), it is safe to say that an average addict needs to steal between $630 and $1,050 worth of merchandise a week to support this habit. Furthermore, estimates of the total number of addicts vary from 100,000 to 200,000. The amount of property stolen by addicts may reach several billion dollars per year. Thus, it is likely that a substantial proportion of the increase in crime since 1960 can be attributed to an increase in the addict population.

Changes in Business Practices

Some of the recent increases in property crime can be attributed to changes in business operations. Whereas in the past, most retail establishments kept the major part of their merchandise on shelves and closed counters, today most stores display their merchandise on open counters. This change has drastically reduced the need for large sales staffs, and in fact in some stores today, the only personnel present are those behind the cash registers. These new sales procedures encourage shoplifting and make detection difficult. Discount stores experience inventory

---

*The drop in the relative percentage of arrests for heroin and cocaine use between 1970 and 1973 may be related to an increase in marijuana use rather than a decrease in the population using hard drugs.

losses that are almost double those of conventional department stores. Unfortunately, exact estimates of the extent of shoplifting are not available because many businesses do not have inventory control or accounting systems to estimate the true amount of this loss. A survey made by the President's Commission reported that 65 per cent of the neighborhood wholesale and retail business surveyed in three cities experienced some shoplifting losses; estimates of median losses ranged from $100 to $500 annually (*Task Force Report: Crime and Its Impact—an Assessment*, 1967). The *Uniform Crime Reports* for 1970 revealed that shoplifting rose 221 per cent between 1960 and 1970 and 67 per cent between 1968 and 1973. Noteworthy is the fact that shoplifting figures are quite similar in metropolitan and suburban areas, while there is a decided drop in rural areas. The FBI attributes a large part of this difference to the absence of shopping centers in rural areas.

In addition, some businesses have become more vulnerable to victimization as a result of changes in security practices, interior design, and location. The recent increase in bank robberies seems to be related to the development of small, poorly protected branch banks in the suburbs (*Task Force Report: Crime and Its Impact—an Assessment*, 1967).

Minority Frustration

Some of the increase in crime can also be attributed to the fact that our economic system has not provided enough minority group members with opportunities to work at jobs that pay a living wage. Thus, these people take to crime as the only means available to them to get "a piece of the system" (Cook, 1971, p. 29).

SUMMARY

In this chapter, we attempted to relate the frequency and distribution of crime in the United States to such demographic variables as age, sex, race, and residence. Using incidence rates furnished by the FBI's *Uniform Crime Reports*, we noted that the crime rate showed an overall increase of 39 per cent during the period 1970 to 1975. Limitations of official statistics, both in regard to methods of gathering and presenting facts, were discussed and the hope expressed that eventually we may see the creation of a mandatory system of reporting to a national research agency.

An assessment of unreported crime using self-reporting instruments, victim surveys, and agency records revealed that there is much more crime than official statistics indicate. Although crime appears to be at an all-time high, there is good reason to question whether this is really the case, since official statistics have only been compiled since 1930. Furthermore, even the rather dramatic increase in crime that has occurred since 1960 is likely to reflect, at least in part, better citizen reporting and police recording procedures. It was suggested that a change in the age composition of the population, increased urbanization, increases in the drug addict population, changes in business practices, and minority frustrations account for some of the increase in crime since 1960.

REVIEW

Find the answers to the following questions in the text:

1. How do *incidence* rates differ from *prevalence* rates?

2. What are the sources of the data on crime published annually by the Federal Bureau of Investigation in its *Uniform Crime Reports*?

3. What are the seven crimes that make up the *UCR*'s Crime Index offenses?

4. Cite some of the factors listed by the *UCR* that affect the amount and type of crime that occurs in a particular locale.

5. What feature or features do homicide and aggravated assault have in common?

6. Identify some of the factors that might help account for the disproportionately high crime rate among blacks.

7. Cite and discuss at least five criticisms of the official statistics on crime in the United States.

8. What are some of the major criticisms of the FBI's use of the reporting device called the "crime clock"?

9. How do studies of so-called "hidden delinquency" help us to arrive at a more realistic assessment of the extent of crime?

10. What factors tend to support or refute the contention that crime is increasing in this country at the present time?

11. List some of the factors that might help to account for changes in the arrest rate for drug-related offenses.

TERMS TO IDENTIFY AND REMEMBER

epidemiology	*Uniform Crime Reports*
incidence rate	prevalence rate
Crime Index	SMSA (standard metropolitan statistical area)
SEARCH	"crime clock"
"hidden delinquency"	NORC victim survey

REFERENCES

Beattie, R. H.: Criminals and statistics in the United States: 1960. Journal of Criminal Law, Criminology, and Police Science 51:49–65, 1960.

Bloch, H. A., and Geis, G.: Man, Crime, and Society. New York, Random House, Inc., 1970.

Clark, J. C., and Tifft, L. L.: Polygraph and interview validation of self-reported deviant behavior. American Sociological Review 31:516-523, 1966.

Cook, F.: There's always a crime wave. In Cressey, D. R. (ed.): Crime and Criminal Justice. Chicago, Quadrangle Books, 1971.

Cressey, D. R.: The state of criminal statistics. National Probation and Parole Association Journal 3:230–241, 1957.

Federal Bureau of Investigation: Uniform Crime Reports: 1975. Washington, D. C., U. S. Government Printing Office, 1976.

Friedman, M.: Prohibition and drugs. Newsweek May 1, 1972.

Geis, G.: Statistics concerning race and crime. Crime and Delinquency 11:142–150, 1965.

Geis, G.: Violence in American society. Current History 52:354–358, 1967.

Glaser, D.: Victim survey research: theoretical implications. In·Guenther, A. L. (ed.): Criminal Behavior and Social Systems. New York, Harper & Row, Publishers, 1970.

Gold, M.: Delinquent Behavior in an American City. Monterey, California, Brooks/Cole Publishing Co., 1970.

Graham, P.: A contemporary history of American crime. In Graham, H. D., and Gurr, T. R. (eds.): The History of Violence in America. New York, Bantam Books, Inc., 1969.

Haney, B., and Gold, M.: The juvenile delinquent nobody knows. Psychology Today 7:49–102, 1973.

Haskell, M., and Yablonsky, L.: Crime and Delinquency. Chicago, Rand McNally & Co., 1970.

Lejins, P.: The Uniform Crime Reports. Michigan Law Review 64:1011–1030, 1966.

Levine, S. F.: Narcotics and Drug Abuse. Cincinnati, The W. H. Anderson Co., 1973.

Murphy, F. J., Shirley, M. M., and Witmer, H. L.: The incidence of hidden delinquency. American Journal of Orthopsychiatry 16:686–696, 1946.

Newman, D. J.: The effects of accommodations in justice administration on criminal statistics. Sociology and Social Research 46:144–155, 1962.

Porterfield, A.: Youth in Trouble. Fort Worth, The Leo Foundation, 1946.

President's Commission on Law Enforcement and Administration of Justice: Task Force Report: Crime and Its Impact—an Assessment. Washington, D. C., U. S. Government Printing Office, 1967.

President's Commission on Law Enforcement and Administration of Justice: The Challenge of Crime in a Free Society. Washington, D. C., U. S. Government Printing Office, 1967.

Robison, S. M.: Can Delinquency Be Measured? New York, Columbia University Press, 1936.

Schwartz, E.: A community experiment in the measurement of delinquency. Yearbook 1945, National Probation Association 1945, pp. 157–182.

Sellin, T.: The significance of records of crime. The Law Quarterly Review 67:489–504, 1961.

Short, J. F., and Nye, F. I.: Extent of unrecorded delinquency: tentative conclusions. Journal of Criminal Law, Criminology, and Police Science 49:296–302, 1958.

Skolnick, J. H.: Justice without Trial. New York, John Wiley & Sons, Inc., 1966.

Sutherland, E. H.: Crime and business. Annals of the American Academy of
Political and Social Science 1941, *217*:111–118.
Sutherland, E. H., and Cressey, D. R.: Introduction to criminology. Philadel-
phia, J. B. Lippincott Co., 1974.
Teeters, N. K., and Matza, D.: The extent of delinquency in the United States.
In Giallombardo, R. (ed.): *Juvenile Delinquency: A Book of Readings.*
New York, John Wiley and Sons, Inc., 1966.
United States Bureau of the Census. *Statistical abstracts of the United States:
1975,* Washington, D. C., U. S. Government Printing Office, 1975.
United States Department of Justice: Survey of Inmates of State Correctional
Facilities 1974 Advance Report. *In* National Prisoner Statistics Special
Report. Washington, D. C., U. S. Government Printing Office, 1976.
Wallerstein, J. S., and Wyle, J.: Our law-abiding law-breakers. Probation,
25:107–112, 1947.
Williams, J. B.: *Narcotics and Drug Dependence.* Beverly Hills, Glencoe Press,
1974.
Williams, J. R., and Gold, M.: From deliquent behavior to official delin-
quency. Social Problems *20*:209–229, 1972.
Wolfgang, M. E.: Uniform Crime Reports: a critical appraisal. University of
Pennsylvania Law Review *3*:408–438, 1963.

3 CRIMES OF VIOLENCE

It might be argued that there is a potential for violence in many criminal offenses that are not commonly thought of as crimes of violence. For example, an act of shoplifting can result in physical injury if a store employee attempts to restrain the shoplifter and is attacked in the process. While violence is an accidental feature of such criminal actions, there are other offenses in which bodily injury or the threat of bodily injury is the central element. As we observed in the preceding chapter, four of the seven index crimes reported by the Federal Bureau of Investigation — homicide, aggravated assault, robbery, and forcible rape — are defined as violent crimes or crimes against the person.

With regard to forcible rape, there has been an unfortunate tendency to emphasize the sexual component of this criminal offense and, consequently, to minimize the violence which is inflicted upon the victim. However, legislative changes in a number of states (e.g., Florida) have redressed this imbalance. In these states, forcible rape has been redefined to include "sexual battery" and carries with it a series of penal sanctions that are scaled in terms of the severity of violence to which the victim was subjected. For purposes of consistency in topical organization and to avoid an overly long chapter on crimes of violence, we have chosen to treat forcible rape in the following chapter on sexual offenses. We wish to make it clear that this arrangement of chapter contents does not reflect any endorsement on our part of earlier views on the nature of forcible rape. On the contrary, it is our belief that statutes which incorporate the language and concept of "sexual battery" provide a more accurate and realistic legal statement of the salient aspect of forcible rape — its violence.

TABLE 3–1. GEOGRAPHICAL BREAKDOWN OF REPORTED
CRIME IN THE UNITED STATES IN 1975*

CRIME	NORTH EASTERN STATES	NORTH CENTRAL STATES	WESTERN STATES	SOUTHERN STATES
Murder and non-negligent manslaughter	18%	23%	17%	42%
Aggravated assault	21%	21%	22%	36%
Forcible rape	19%	25%	25%	31%
Robbery	32%	26%	17%	25%

*Data from Federal Bureau of Investigation: *Uniform Crime Reports: 1975*, Washington, D. C., U. S. Government Printing Office, 1976, pp. 15–24.

FREQUENCY AND DISTRIBUTION OF VIOLENT CRIME IN THE UNITED STATES

The volume of violent crime in the United States has increased 199 per cent since 1960 and 39 per cent since 1970. In 1975 there were a total of 1,026,284 violent crimes reported to the police (*UCR*, 1976). These crimes were tallied as follows:

Murder and non-negligent manslaughter	20,510
Robbery	464,970
Aggravated assault	484,710
Forcible rape	56,090

With regard to geographic area, the South led the nation in 1975 in three of the four categories of violent crimes reported. Table 3–1 gives a geographical breakdown by percentages of the total number of reported crimes for the nation as a whole. Before we can evaluate the possible meaning and significance of these statistics, we must take a closer look at characteristics of violent offenses, the specific offenses themselves, and the offenders who perpetrate them.

THE CULTURAL CONTEXT OF VIOLENT CRIME

While violent crime is found among all population groups and within all areas of the country, there are heavier concentrations among certain groups and in certain areas. However, despite these heavy concentrations of crime, the overwhelming majority of individuals in these groups and areas are law abiding. The National Commission on the Causes and Prevention of Violence (1970) indicated that both the perpetrators and victims of violent crime live in sections of cities characterized by:

Low income
Physical deterioration
Dependency
Racial and ethnic concentrations
Broken homes
Working mothers
Low levels of education and vocational skills
High unemployment
High proportion of single males
Overcrowded and substandard housing
Low rates of home ownership or single-family dwellings
Mixed land use
High population density

After reviewing the available data on violent crimes and offenders, the commission sketched the following profile:

1. Violent crime in the United States is primarily a phenomenon of large cities.
2. Violent crime in the city is overwhelmingly committed by males.
3. Violent crime in the city is concentrated especially among youths between the ages of 15 and 24.
4. Violent crime in the city is committed primarily by individuals at the lower end of the occupational scale.
5. Violent crime in the city stems disproportionately from the ghetto slum where most blacks live.
6. The victims of assaultive violence in the cities generally have the same characteristics as the offenders; victimization rates are generally highest for males, youths, poor persons, and blacks.
7. Unlike robbery, the violent crimes of homicide, assault, and rape tend to be acts of passion among intimates and acquaintances.
8. By far the greatest proportion of serious violence is committed by repeaters.
9. Americans generally are no strangers to violent crime; the homicide rate for the United States is more than twice that of our nearest competitor, Finland.

Subculture of Violence

The existence of a subculture of violence, a social value system of a group or groups smaller than the total society, has been offered as an explanation of the variation in the rate of violent crime among different groups and in different regions and states in the United States (Wolfgang; 1967a; Wolfgang and Ferracuti, 1969). According to these authors, attitudes towards violence vary by ethnic and racial grouping, social class, and area. Rates of violence are high in those groups that subscribe to a subculture of violence. This subculture consists of a set of values, attitudes, and personality traits that have violence as their central focus. Violence is a potential theme in the lifestyle, socialization process, and social relations of these groups. While members of this subculture do not react violently to all situations, they do perceive a greater variety of situations as requiring a violent and physically aggressive response (Wolfgang, 1958, cited in Wolfgang and Ferracuti, 1969, p. 153).

> The significance of a jostle, a slightly derogatory remark or the appearance of a weapon in the hands of an adversary are stimuli differentially perceived and interpreted by Negroes and Whites, males and females. A male is usually expected to defend the name and honor of his mother, the virtue of womanhood, and to accept no derogation about his race (even from a member of his own race), his age, or his masculinity. Quick resort to physical combat as a measure of daring, courage, or defense of status appears to be a cultural expression, especially from lower socioeconomic class males of both races. When such a cultural norm response is elicited from an individual engaged in such social interplay with others who harbor the same response mechanism, physical assaults, altercations, and violent domestic quarrels that result in homicide are likely to be common. . . . (Wolfgang, 1958; cited in Wolfgang and Ferracuti, 1969, p. 153.)

Within these communities, ready access to weapons may become essential for protection against others who respond in similarly violent ways in certain situations. Thus, the carrying of knives or guns or other protective devices may become a common symbol of one's willingness to participate in violence, to expect violence, and to be ready to retaliate appropriately. Failure to respond appropriately in situations requiring a violent response may result in injury or social ostracism. Thus, the juvenile who fails to live up to the conflict gang's expectations will be pushed out of the group. Likewise, the adult male who does not defend his honor or that of his female companion will also be socially banished from the group.

Although all age groups adhere to this ethos of violence, there is evidence that it is most prominent during the years between late adolescence and middle age. This is attributed to the fact that this group values *machismo*, i.e., great masculinity often coupled with overt physical aggression, and the young male is better equipped to manifest this form of masculinity than are the very young, the middle-aged or the elderly. Once the young male has learned this value system, he needs no further education to employ the agents of physical aggression. Moreover, youth who have no other basis than violence upon which to validate their maleness will constantly seek violent encounters in order to reinforce their self-conceptions. The following case illustrates the operation of the subculture of violence:

> *Louis D. was a young, single, black man who grew up in a predominantly black neighborhood in San Francisco. Although poor, Louis and his four siblings were better off than many of their neighbors. His father was steadily employed and the family had never been on welfare. Louis graduated from high school with a B average even though he had been suspended once for repeated truancy. After graduating, he was arrested and convicted twice for possession of marijuana.*
>
> *When he was twenty, Louis and his family moved across the bay to Oakland. His new neighborhood was tougher than the old one. At a dance someone threatened him with a gun because he was dancing with another fellow's girlfriend; once three young men pulled guns on him and accused him of stealing; another time when he tried to collect a debt, the debtor struck him in the mouth. There were five robberies in the small apartment building where Louis and his family lived. He began carrying a .38 automatic.*
>
> *On a hot summer day, two years ago, Louis and his two cousins stood outside a local liquor store. An older man who was drunk walked up and accused Louis of throwing a pop bottle at him. Louis denied it and the two began to argue. The man pulled a knife and cut Louis on the hand. The next day Louis heard that the man's son, Fred, had accused him of jumping his father and was looking for him. Louis walked down to a corner where he knew Fred hung out. When Louis found him, he denied Fred's accusations, but insulted Fred's father. Fred threatened to kill Louis, and reached in his pocket. Louis pulled his gun out first, and while running backwards, fired three shots at Fred. Two shots hit and killed him. (Lunde, 1975, p. 37).*

A TYPOLOGY OF VIOLENT OFFENDERS

A number of different typologies of violent offenders, particularly murderers, have been developed (Guttmacher, 1960; MacDonald, 1961). The following typology, which was devised by criminologist John Conrad of Ohio State University and used by Spencer (1966), was chosen for discussion because it provides a fairly comprehensive picture of the distinctive types of violent offenders.

By means of an aggressive history profile (AHP) constructed by Conrad, violent offenders can be classified into groups hypothesized to differ in motivation, treatment needs, and parole outlook. Spencer employed the AHP to classify 704 offenders according to Conrad's typology for purposes of examining the criminal career, occupational history, and demographic characteristics of offenders in each category. The types of offenders studied, the criteria by which they are classified, and the results of Spencer's study are as follows:

1. The Culturally Violent Offenders grow up in a subculture where violence is an accepted way of life.

Distinguishing Characteristics

    A. *Aggression was perpetrated for its own sake as frequently seen in assault and battery and not for other ends as in robbery.*

    B. *The victim was a chance acquaintance or someone not well known to the offender.*

Background Dimensions

With slightly more than half belonging to racial minorities, the culturally violent tended to concentrate in urban areas where they had been exposed to their sub-culture for a relatively long time. Compared to other types of offenders, juvenile delinquency among the culturally violent has been high and tended more towards crimes of violence. Schooling was meager and the group did not perform well on pencil and paper tests of ability. The lack of skills to cope with society is reflected in their low occupational level, lack of employment and job instability.

They turned to alcohol, illegal drugs and petty crimes and vented their frustrations in aggressive assault and barroom brawls. There is a record of constant conflict with law enforcement with many arrests in misdemeanant convictions. A few came to institutions on charges of homicide, robbery and felonious assault but most of the present commitment offenses were non-violent. Their behavior can be characterized as a chaotic acting out of frustrations against society from which they are unable to gain normal satisfactions and rewards.

2. The Criminally Violent Offenders are those who commit violence if necessary to gain some end as in robbery.

Distinguishing Characteristics

    A. *Violence was used as a tool in carrying out some criminal act, typically robbery.*

    B. *The offender carries concealed weapons and is not classifiable under the other types.*

Background Dimensions

The criminally violent channel their aggressions into profitable avenues of robbery rather than into impulsive assaults. The criminally violent offender's lower percentage of arrests and higher percentage of prison terms suggest that his offenses are likely to be deliberate felonies. His high rate of escape attempts may be another indication of aptitude for planning a criminal act. Compared to the culturally violent, the criminally violent offender is better educated, has learned how to make better scores on group intelligence tests, and has worked often at white collar jobs. However, his talents generally serve illegal ends and his failure to assimilate himself into normal society is evident in his poor occupational record.

3. The Pathologically Violent Offenders are mentally ill or have suffered brain damage.

Distinguishing Characteristics

    A. *The offense is diagnostically related to a psychosis, brain damage including convulsive disorder, or other major psychological disability.*

    B. *The crime was a sex offense in which violence occurred, typically forcible rape.*

    C. *Harm inflicted was bizzare, sadistic or irrelevant.*

Background Characteristics

Characteristics of the pathologically violent form a distinct pattern — a relatively conservative offense frequency record and a favorable occupational history along with such indications of deviant instability as a comparatively high rate of homicide in present commitment offenses, excessive use of alcohol, suicidal tendencies, marked under-achievement in school and the tentative indication of the atypical recurrence of offenses in the higher range ages.

4. The Situationally Violent Offenders are those who under extreme provocation commit a rare act of violence.

Distinguishing Characteristics

    A. *The victim was related to the offender by blood or marriage, or [the victim was someone] with whom [the offender] has established [a] close personal relationship.*

Background Characteristics

The situationally violent type shows fewer offenses, a more socially conforming life pattern and better parole outlook than his fellow offenders. Compared to other types including the non-violent, he has less juvenile delinquency, fewer prison terms, less institutional violence, fewer escape attempts, high base expectancy scores, higher occupational level, greater job stability, better military record and a greater degree of schooling. The proportionately larger number of Mexican-Americans among the stiuationally violent suggests that possibly sub-culture influences in the Mexican-American society take a special turn leading to the Situationally Violent Offense. (Spencer, 1966; quoted in Reckless, 1973, pp. 205–206)

Criminal Homicide

Criminal homicide stands apart from other offenses because its results are not reversible, i.e., the victim is dead. In a culture such as ours that places a premium on human life, the seriousness of this offense is reflected in the fact that an offender may be subject to capital punishment if convicted.

Murderers, unlike other offenders, usually do not have a long history of criminal activities. Instead, for the most part, they are husbands, wives, neighbors, friends, and acquaintances; persons who no longer can endure chronic dissatisfaction and frustration. According to Lunde (1975):

Murderers are rarely colorful, careful or ingenious. Most kill on the spur of the moment, often during a heated quarrel. A victim's own relative, friend or acquaintance usually kills him. These killers rarely try to escape; they are easily caught and readily confess. It is not uncommon for such a killer to report himself to the police, then wait for them to arrive. In about two-thirds of all murders the suspect is in custody 24 hours after the crime. Also unlike fictional murderers, actual killers have little to gain from their crimes, financially or otherwise. The sensational publicity surrounding bizarre or mass murders leads us to believe the majority of killers are insane. Here again, not true, less than four percent of them are judged to be criminally insane. (p. 35)

As Lunde suggests, homicide is characterized by a strong victim-offender relationship. During 1974, murder in the family accounted for approximately one quarter of all murders, with over half of these killings involving spouse killing spouse. In these cases, the wife was the victim in 52 per cent of the incidents and the husband was the victim in the remaining 48 per cent. The remainder of the family killings involved parents killing children and other relative killings. In the case of spouse killing spouse, Lunde (1975) identifies one of the motives:

> *Typically, jealous slayers are husbands who, after more than five years of marriage, begin to suspect their wives no longer love them. They believe with or without evidence that their wives are unfaithful. Often they threaten to kill their wives or actually assault them sometime before the successful act. After the initial attack, the wife is genuinely frightened and may order her husband out of the house. But as weeks or months pass, her fear subsides and she reconciles with him.* (p. 36)

The following case illustrates the typical wife murderer:

> *Marvin C., a forty-five year old master machinist, is a typical wife murderer. He and Judy had been married eight years and had two children. He developed bleeding ulcers and had to have surgery. Because of his illness, he was out of work for extended periods, the family income fell, and they were saddled with huge medical bills. Judy went to work to support the family, first as a nurse's aide and then, to earn more money, as a cocktail waitress.*
>
> *Eventually, Marvin returned to work, but he began to drink too heavily on weekends. Because of his illness, his drinking, and her working, the couple's sexual activity declined. Marvin became increasingly critical of Judy. First, he accused her of spending too much money on the children, then he became convinced that she was having an affair.*
>
> *One week before the killing, he called her a "whore" and knocked her down. When she threw an ashtray at him and called the police he left the house and moved into a motel. But five days later, the couple reunited. They made love in his motel room "just like old times." Marvin moved back home.*
>
> *Two days later, on a Sunday afternoon, he went to a neighborhood bar; when he came home at five, Judy was not there. He went back to the bar and drank until eleven. By that time, Judy was home, and he accused her of drinking and having an affair with a divorced man who lived across the street. He stormed through the house, opening and slamming closet doors, shouting, "I know there's someone here." Judy reached for the telephone in the kitchen, but Marvin jerked it away. She grabbed a carving knife and ran into the bedroom. Marvin could not remember what happened after that but Judy died of internal bleeding caused by 15 stab wounds.* (Lunde, 1975, p. 36)

Lunde (1975) also provides an explanation of parents who kill their children:

> *Women who kill their infants or young children, usually are severely disturbed, suffer from extreme bouts of depression and*

may experience delusions. Before a woman kills her offspring, she is likely to go through a preliminary period when she thinks about how to commit the crime, visualizes the dead child and considers suicide. Fathers rarely kill their young children but when they do they also build up to the crime and often have a history of child abuse.

Fathers who murder are more likely to kill their teenage sons. These men are marginally adequate husbands and fathers who feel inferior and frustrated by life. Guns and alcohol play significant roles in their lives. Their criminal records, if any, usually involve drinking, drunk driving, and disorderly conduct. They rarely have any history of psychiatric illness. They simply are explosive individuals who kill impulsively. (p. 36)

In those instances when older children kill their younger sisters or brothers, Lunde suggests that the victim serves as a substitute for a parent who is the true object of the rage. The following case exemplifies this point:

One 15 year old boy wrote a letter to his father just before strangling his younger sister. The father had left the mother seven years earlier and rarely visited the children. The letter said, "Dad, I'm really sorry that I did this because I didn't know if you really love Mary (the victim) and me. You didn't come to her (grammar-school) graduation; that was a big thing to her, so now I am not even going to graduate . . . I wish all the kids would join the revolution and start killing off their parents." (p. 36)

Uniform Crime Reports for 1975 also indicates that 7 per cent of the homicides were the result of romantic triangles or lovers' quarrels. Other arguments were given as the cause of 37.9 per cent of the murders. This category would include killings by friends or acquaintances in barroom brawls, backyard arguments, stairwell confrontations, or the murderer's living room. Lunde states that "persons who kill casual acquaintances usually grow up in what some social scientists call a sub-culture of violence." The killer is often a young adult male who, like many of his friends, regularly carries a lethal weapon and is used to settling accounts by direct physical action.

Known and suspected felony type murders accounted for 32 per cent of the murders. Felony murders are defined in the *UCR* as "those killings resulting from robbery, burglary, sex motive, gangland and institutional slayings and all other felonies." Felony murders have increased dramatically in the last two decades. Twenty years ago, felony murder accounted for only 10 per cent of homicides as reported in the *UCR*. In 1975, 54 per cent of these killings occurred in connection with robbery offenses; prostitution, commercialized vice, rape, and sex offenses accounted for 8 per cent; and narcotic law offenses comprised 7 per cent. Lunde characterized felony murders as follows: "In felony murders, the killer, almost always a man, kills for money, sex, or drugs, or when he tries to escape detection for a crime." The following case typifies this pattern:

> *Frank E. was a 21 year old Mexican-American who was the oldest of eight children. His parents were divorced when he was 14. He ran away from home to be with his father who told him, "I'll show you how to be a real man." They lived a nomadic life, working in carnivals, on fishing boats, occasionally committing armed robbery. When the father was annoyed with his son he would beat him, kick him, or whip him with a belt. By the time Frank was 16, he had served two years in prison for armed robbery. Thereafter, he followed his father's example and roamed the country, supporting himself by stealing or working in odd jobs. At 21, he was drinking heavily and working with a traveling carnival. When he ran short of money, he and a buddy robbed a small town liquor store and pistol whipped the elderly owner. They sped away from the scene, but were stopped by a policeman. Frank got out of the car and with his gun behind his back approached the officer; when the policeman appeared to reach for his own gun, Frank shot and killed him.* (p. 38)

The FBI does not record the number of homicides that are a result of psychopathology (i.e., psychotic syndromes such as schizophrenia or manic-depressive reactions, psychopathy, and organic conditions of various kinds). However, data from other sources provide a perspective on this type of murder. A simple way to distinguish between homicides that are a product of some pathological condition and those that are not is to assess whether most individuals belonging to the murderer's same sex, ethnic group, social class, and age group would deem the offender's actions to be an appropriate reaction under the circumstances. In other words, would the offender be labeled as "crazy" by his peers or would they condone or at least understand his behavior under the circumstances? For example, people who are socialized to a subculture of violence can understand how a friendly exchange of insults between two men who are trying to assert their masculinity can, in the course of a night of drinking, escalate into murder. What occurs is that one of the participants may provoke the other to the point where he starts swinging or pulls a knife or a gun, and the result may be murder. The offender's behavior is not a product of any pathological condition but, instead, is merely a response based on his attachment to the subculture of violence. On the other hand, the following cases illustrate instances in which the offender's behavior is clearly a product of a pathological condition and would not be condoned or understood by members of his subculture:

> A 35 year old man charged with the murder of his wife claimed that she had been hypnotizing him for some months, and that he was in a hypnotic trance when he shot her. Indeed, he wondered whether his wife was really dead, as he did not hear the gun go off, and he thought that she might have hypnotized him into believing that he had killed her. He was arrested after he had driven his car with the body of his wife to the police station. A paranoid schizophrenic with delusions of grandeur and persecution, he boasted that he knew the location of all the gold mines in the country. He noted that his wife had tried to obtain this information from him through hypnosis, and that just prior to the shooting she accused him of sexual perversion with a Negro male. (MacDonald, 1961, p. 231)

> G. L. had served 14 years of a life sentence for the murder of an eight year old boy. Meeting the boy by accident, he took him to a barn where he wanted to put on some new clothes he had just gotten from the Salvation Army, and had a sudden impulse to choke the boy. He choked the boy into unconsciousness, took a beer can opener from his front pocket, stripped off the boy's pants, and with the can opener tore open the boy's rectum and slashed his testicles. He then sat down beside the mutilated body and masturbated. . . . At his trial for murder, psychiatrists for both the defense and the prosecution reported him to be a psychopathic personality, with ideas of of reference, paranoid tendencies, immature emotionality, marked deficiency of judgment and a deficient reasoning ability. . . . (Ellis and Gullo, 1971, p. 70)

In addition, most mass murderers are also included within this group because they are almost always psychotic. They also differ in several other respects from those who kill one person. These offenders are almost exclusively white, and alcohol is rarely a factor in the offenses. While the offender does not know the victim, they are also not total strangers; i.e., the murderer's relationship to the victim fits somewhere in between. Victims are typically members of a group (the rich) or a type (young girls) who torment the offender in his delusions. Of course, the victims themselves are unaware of their place in his scheme or sexual fantasies. With regard to pathological state, Lunde (1975) states:

> Most mass murderers are schizophrenics or sexual sadists. Paranoid schizophrenia is characterized by auditory hallucinations, delusions of grandeur or persecution, and a suspicious, hostile, aggressive manner. Sadists torture, kill, and mutilate their victims in order to reach sexual climax. (p. 39)

The following case provides an illustration of the schizophrenic mass murderer:

> On October 19, 1970, John Lindley Frazier killed a prominent eye surgeon, Victor M. Ohta, his wife, their two sons, and the doctor's secretary. He blindfolded, bound, and shot each one and threw their bodies into the swimming pool adjoining the Ohtas' $300,000 hilltop home. The bodies were discovered shortly after 8:00 PM when firemen responded to a report that the Ohta house was on fire. Under the windshield wiper of the Ohtas' red Rolls Royce was a bizzare note which read:
>
>> "Hallowe'en. . . 1970. Today World War III will begin as brought to you by the people of the free universe.
>> "From this day forward any one and/or company of persons who misuses the natural environment or destroys same will suffer the penalty of death by the people of the free universe.
>> "I with my comrades from this day forth will fight until death or freedom, against anything or anyone who does not support natural life on this planet, materialism must die or mankind will.
>>
>> NIGHT OF WANDS
>> NIGHT OF CUPS
>> NIGHT OF PENTICLES
>> NIGHT OF SWORDS."
>
> Down the hillside from the Ohta home was a grove of redwood trees, and beyond the trees a collection of ramshackle old sheds and a house trailer. Mrs. Pat Pascal lived in the trailer; her son by her first marriage, John Frazier, lived intermittently in a cowshed across the gulch. John was 24. He was separated from his wife.
> Frazier's own parents had separated when he was two. By the time he was five, he had been placed in a foster home because

his mother was unable to support herself and care for him. Throughout his adolescence he was in trouble for truancy, running away, and theft. He spent time in several California Youth Authority facilities.

At 21 John married. He worked off and on as an auto mechanic. Although his wife was aware of some unusual behavior, such as bedwetting, nightmares, and sleepwalking, she didn't find her husband strange or frightening until May 1970 when he was in a minor auto accident. Frazier was unhurt, but told his wife that he heard God's voice saying, "If you drive again, you will be killed."

From that point on he rapidly became more bizzare and unpredictable. He devoted himself to the implementation of God's special mission for him to save the world from the "materialism" that was polluting the planet Earth. He incorporated elements of occult philosophy, astrology, phrenology, and numerology into a confusing system of delusional beliefs that was reinforced by direct messages he received from God. Early that summer, he tried unsuccessfully to recruit 12 disciples to renounce all material possessions and to go out into the woods with him to live in union with nature. Then he began to speak of an impending revolution that was coming "on the 12th hour of the 12th day of the 12th year of the 12th century."

His wife and mother tried desperately to obtain psychiatric treatment for him, but Frazier was so paranoid that he viewed their efforts as part of a conspiracy. On July 4th, he left his wife and moved near his mother's house trailer. He was unusually agitated, pacing back and forth, constantly looking out the windows. He said the revolution was at hand and some materialists might have to die in the process.

On Monday, October 19th, Frazier carried out his "divine mission." Although he was found legally sane, there is no doubt in my mind that Frazier suffered from the most serious and most common psychosis — schizophrenia. (Lunde, 1975, pp. 39–40)

The following case illustrates the sadistic mass murderer:

Edmund Emil Kemper III was the second of three children. He bitterly recalls that his father was not around much when he was a young child, that his parents separated when he was seven years old, and that his mother moved the family to Montana. This meant Kemper had little contact with his father after the move, a fact he bitterly resented.

Kemper grew to be a hulk of a man, six feet nine inches, 280 pounds. He was a loner who escaped into the world of science fiction and the occult. He was fascinated with death; once he staged his own execution. His sister recalled teasing him about his second-grade teacher whom, she suspected, he admired. She taunted him by saying, "Why don't you go and kiss her," and was puzzled at his reply: "If I kiss her I would have to kill her first." Others recalled Ed's fascination with guns and knives.

Ed himself described recurring fantasies of killing women, his mother in particular. He admitted that several times he had actually entered her bedroom at night with a weapon in his hand.

But his first actual killings involved animals. He tortured and killed cats; one day his mother found the family cat decapitated, cut into pieces, and deposited in a garbage can.

Besides fantasies of killing his mother, Kemper also thought about having sexual relations with corpses, and killing everyone in town. As a young boy, he would sneak out of the house at night and stare at women walking down the street, fantasizing about loving them and being loved in return. Even then, however, he felt such a relationship would be impossible for him. The only kind of activity he could fantasize about with any hope of success was killing the women he saw.

Ed ran away from home when he was 13. He sought out his father, but his dad sent him back to his mother. She found the boy increasingly difficult to handle, so sent him to live with his grandparents on an isolated ranch. There Kemper transferred his fantasies about killing his mother to his domineering grandmother. In less than a year, when he was 15, he shot and killed both his grandparents and then called his mother, told her what he had done, sat down, and waited for the police to arrive.

Kemper spent four of the next five years in a maximum security mental hospital. At 21, the parole board discharged him to his mother, a disastrous solution for her and for Kemper. Repeated arguments with her made the old fantasies seem more and more attractive. Whereas animals and his grandparents had once been substitute victims, now he turned his wrath on young women.

Between May 7, 1972 and April 21, 1973, Kemper killed eight women by shooting, stabbing and strangulation. He acted out his childhood fantasies by cutting off the heads and hands of his victims, attempting sexual relations with the corpses, and eating flesh from some of the bodies. The first six victims all were young female hitchhikers. Then on April 21, 1973, Kemper killed his own mother and one of her friends. He cut off his mother's head, cut out her larynx, and put it down the garbage disposal. "This seemed appropriate," he said, "as much as she'd bitched, screamed and yelled at me over the years."

He fantasized there would be a nationwide manhunt for the "co-ed killer," and drove non-stop from Santa Cruz to Pueblo, Colorado, listening to the radio for an "all-points bulletin." After three days passed without a radio bulletin or a newspaper headline, Kemper called the Santa Cruz police to turn himself in. They told him to call back. He did, again and again, each time giving more details about the killings. Finally, he convinced them to arrest him, and the Pueblo police picked him up in front of a phone booth. Kemper was tried, convicted and sentenced to life imprisonment. (Lunde, 1975, pp. 40–42)

The Wolfgang Study

Marvin Wolfgang (1958) conducted one of the most comprehensive and detailed studies of criminal homicide ever reported and one from which a great many conclusions have been drawn by criminologists and other criminal justice specialists. His research covered 588 cases of criminal homicide which occurred during a five year period from 1948 to 1952 in Philadelphia. The major findings of this study were as follows:

1. Concerning race and sex, the proportion of blacks and males involved in homicide far exceeds their proportion in the general population, and they have rates of homicide many times greater than those of white females.

2. The age group 20 to 24 had the highest rate of homicides, while the age groups 25 to 29 and 30 to 34 had the highest rates of victimization.

3. Regarding the method of inflicting death, 39 per cent of the 588 criminal homicides were due to stabbings, 22 per cent to beatings, 3 per cent to shootings, and 6 per cent to other methods. Black males usually stab and are stabbed to death, while white males usually beat and are beaten to death. Females generally stab their victims with a kitchen knife, while as victims they are very often beaten to death.

4. Murder is most likely to be committed on the weekend. Sixty-five per cent of the homicides were committed between 8:00 P.M. Friday and midnight Sunday, while the period beginning Monday morning to 8:00 P.M. Friday accounted for the remaining 35 per cent of the homicides.

5. Regarding place, the most dangerous single place was the public highway (public street, alley, or field), although more slayings occurred inside than outside the home. Men kill and are most frequently killed in the street, while women most often kill in the kitchen but are slain in the bedroom.

6. In nearly two thirds of the cases, either the victim or the offender or both had been drinking immediately prior to the slaying.

7. Nearly two thirds of the total offenders had a previous arrest record and almost half of the victims had such a record. Offenders who have previous offense records are more likely to

have a record of offenses against the person than against property; and when an offender has a record of offenses against the person he is more likely than not to have a record of having committed a serious assault offense, e.g., aggravated assault or assault with intent to kill.

8. "Criminal homicide usually results from a vaguely defined altercation, domestic quarrel, jealousy, argument over money, and robbery. . . . Homicide appears, however, to be more personalized when directed against or by women. There are few important differences according to motive and the race of either victim or offender" (p. 23).

9. "Most of the 550 identified victim/offender relationships may be classified as primary group relationships or those that include intimate close frequent contact. Close friends and relatives accounted for over half of the contact" (p. 23).

10. "In 94 percent of the cases, the victim and the offender were members of the same race, but only in 64 percent were they of the same sex" (p. 23).

Wolfgang (1967b) has also focused on victim-precipitated homicide. A homicide is considered to be victim-precipitated when the victim made a direct, immediate, and positive contribution to his own death, manifested by his being the first to make a physical assault. The following cases, all of which resulted in the offender being tried in criminal court, illustrate this pattern of homicide:

> *A husband accused his wife of giving money to another man, and while she was making breakfast, he attacked her with a milk bottle, then a brick, and finally a piece of concrete block. Having had a butcher knife in hand, she stabbed him during the fight.*
>
> *A drunken husband, beating his wife in their kitchen, gave her a butcher knife and dared her to use it on him. She claimed that if he should strike her once more, she would use the knife, whereupon he slapped her in the face and she fatally stabbed him.*
>
> *A drunken victim with knife in hand approached his slayer during a quarrel. The slayer showed a gun, and the victim dared him to shoot him. He did.* (pp. 74–75)

Wolfgang (1967b) classified the 588 cases from the Philadelphia study just discussed. The 588 cases from the Philadelphia study were designated victim-precipitated and non–victim-precipitated based on the previously stated definition. Comparison of the victim-precipitated cases with the non–victim-precipitated cases revealed significantly higher proportions of the following characteristics among the victim-precipitated cases: (1) black victims; (2) black offenders; (3) male victims; (4) female offenders; (5) stabbings; (6) victim/offender relationships involving male victims of female offenders; (7) mate slayings; (8) husbands who are victims in mate slayings; (9) alcohol and the homicide situation; (10) alcohol and the victim; (11) victims with a previous arrest record; (12) victims with a previous arrest record of assault.

These data show that in many cases the victim has most of the major characteristics of the offenders. In addition, Wolfgang indicated that in some cases two potential offenders come together in a homicide situation and it is probably often only chance that causes one to become a victim and the other an offender.

Rate of Homicide

Although the FBI did not begin compiling data on crime in the United States until 1933, other sources indicate that the homicide rate in the United States moved steadily upward from 1900 until the mid 1930's (Bloch and Geis, 1970). *UCR* data show that homicide rates dropped sharply from the mid 1930's to the end of World War II, at which point there was an upswing for approximately three years followed by a drop in rates to pre-World War II levels. During the 1950's and into the mid 1960's, homicide rates remained relatively constant. However, beginning in the mid 1960's, homicide rates took an upswing and by 1974 had reached an all-time high of 9.7 per 100,000.

The decrease in homicide rates beginning in the 1930's and continuing into the 1960's can best be attributed to modern medical and surgical advances. As Bloch and Geis (1970, p. 226) suggest, "Many persons who formerly might have died from crimes of violence are now saved on operating tables, and their assailants are charged with assault with intent to kill rather than with murder or manslaughter." Regarding the increase in homicide rates in the mid 1960's, Barnett, Kleitman, and Larson (1975) indicate that the post-World War II baby boom can account for about 10 per cent of this increase since during this period post-World War II babies entered the age range of 20 to 30 when the risk of committing murder is the highest. On the basis of his examination of 40 cases of murder over the course of a five year period, Donald Lunde (1975) suggests some additional reasons for this sharp increase in murder rates. To begin with, he attributes part of the increase in homicide rates to economic dissatisfaction. In the past, during economic slumps such as the Great Depression, murder rates went down and suicide rates increased, whereas today just the reverse is occurring. He believes that this is due, at least in part, to the fact that Americans no longer hold themselves responsible for their material misfortune.

He further suggests:

> *The simple fact that Americans now own more than 50 million hand guns contributes to the likelihood of murder. Other factors add fuel to the fire: the return of thousands of Viet Nam war veterans who are proficient in the use of weapons, and who are psychologically attuned to doing so; the increased proportion of young adults in the population; the rise in expectations created by the Civil Rights Movement and the promise of a Great Society. Even changes in child rearing practices have contributed to the holocaust. Permissive parents are less likely to insist that children develop and use internal restraints. Organized religion, an institution that taught self-restraint and accountability, reaches fewer and fewer young people.*
>
> *Corruption in government makes it easier for people to blame external forces for hard times. Many have forgotten, and some have never realized, that "there is no free lunch."*
>
> *If we continue to place blame for our economic and other ills on others, to demand as rights what actually are privileges, we will continue to kill each other in frustration.* (p. 42)

Assault and Battery

Most offenses against the person that do not result in death, apart from some sex offenses, include as an element some form of assault and battery. Technically speaking, assault is only the threat, with or without physical gesture, to do bodily harm to another, while the actual injury is referred to as battery. Thus, if a person brandishes a two-by-four or a lead pipe against another, the former could be charged with assault even though no actual injury has occurred. Jurisdictions vary as to the inclusion of "battery" in the labeling of offenses falling within the category of assault. Typically, the more serious offenses, designated as felonies, are labeled as "aggravated assault," "assault with intent to commit murder," and "assault with a deadly weapon," while those designated as misdemeanors have such labels as "simple assault" and "fighting."

Little research has been conducted on the crime of assault, perhaps, as Bloch and Geis (1970) suggest, because it is a run-of-the-mill offense. With regard to threats, most people probably do not take these threats seriously, because most are uttered in anger with no real intention of carrying them out. Threats are only reported when the potential victim has reason to believe that the threats will be carried out as, for example in the case of an estranged wife. Assaults involving injuries are generally not reported unless there is serious injury or property damage, which may occur during bar fights.

Most assaults involving injuries occur in communities that subscribe to a subculture of violence. Within these communities, injuries are viewed as private matters. In addition, in these areas there is distrust of the police and a feeling that "they would not do anything" were the offenses reported. This view is widespread; the President's Commission on Law Enforcement and the Administration of Justice found in a national survey of households that 35 per cent of those who were victims of aggravated assault and 54 per cent of those who were victims of simple assault failed to report these offenses to the police. The reason given by 50 per cent of the victims who failed to report this offense was that they felt it was a private matter or did not want to harm the offender. Furthermore, 25 per cent of those who failed to report aggravated assault and 35 per cent of those who failed to report simple assault indicated that they did not notify the police because they felt that the police would not be effective or would not want to be bothered (President's Commission, 1967).

The Pittman and Handy Study

Pittman and Handy studied a random 25 per cent sample of 900 aggravated assault cases seen in 1961 by the St. Louis police. They analyzed their sample in terms of such variables as time and place of occurrence, relationship and kinship status of the offender and the victim, the type of force employed, and the disposition of the offender. The emergent pattern which characterized the modal, or "typical," case is described by the authors:

> An act of aggravated assault is more likely to occur on a weekend than during the week, specifically between 6:00 p.m. Friday and 6:00 a.m. Monday, with peak frequency on Saturday, between 10:00 p.m. and 11:00 p.m. While the event shows little likelihood of being more frequent in the four summer months considered together than in the winter, this type of assault peaks in the months of July and August.
>
> The crime will occur on a public street, or, secondly, in a residence. If a female is the offender, the act will occur indoors, if a male, outdoors. When offender and victim are related, the act will more likely occur in a residence than elsewhere. The general neighborhood context is one populated by lower socioeconomic groups — especially Negroes of this class.
>
> The weapon used by both men and women will in most cases be a knife, with a gun the second choice. In acts involving white offenders, personal force will be used more often than in those involving Negro offenders.
>
> Generally, the act will be reported to the police by the victim.

The victim will be wounded seriously enough to require hospitalization, but the offender will not. More than 75 percent of the aggravated assault cases will be cleared by arrest within one hour after the crime occurs. A Negro is more likely to be arrested for his crime than is a white.

These records indicate that neither the offender nor the victim will be under the influence of alcohol, nor will they have been drinking together, and neither will be a user of drugs.

The aggravated assault will be preceded by a verbal argument, most likely centering around a domestic quarrel.

The offender and victim will be of the same race and the same sex; there will be only one offender and one victim, and both will have been born outside the city in which the crime occurs. Both will be of the same age group, usually between the ages of 20 and 35, with the offender being older. The victim will more often be married than the offender, but both will be blue collar workers. A female is more likely to be related to her male victim than is the male offender to his female victim. Females assault males with whom they have had a previously close relationship (such as dating, sexual intimacy, or common-law marriage); but this is not the case with males assaulting females.

Negro offenders are no more likely than their white counterparts to have a prior arrest record. Offenders in the age bracket 20–34 will in the majority of cases have a prior arrest record. (Pittman and Handy, 1970, p. 98)

A further component of the Pittman and Handy study was a comparison of their findings on aggravated assault with those reported previously by Wolfgang (1958). Despite dissimilarities in time periods, cities, and police departments, the comparison reveals more similarities than differences:

1. *Time.* For both aggravated assault and homicide, occurrences were higher on Saturday, with the time of day being most frequently the late evening and early morning hours; for homicide, between 8:00 P.M. and 2:00 A.M., and for aggravated assault, between 4:00 P.M. and 3:00 A.M. The next highest time for both acts was the hours immediately following the highest period.

2. *Location.* Both crimes occurred more often on a public street than in any other location, with residences second. Summer months accounted for a higher percentage of crime in both cases, but to a greater extent for homicides. In winter these crimes occurred indoors. Females committed both acts more often indoors than outdoors. If the victim and offender were related, the crime most likely occurred in a residence. Both types of acts usually took place in a lower class, black neighborhood.

3. *Weapon.* The weapon most often used differed in homicide and aggravated assault; a pistol or revolver was most common in homicides, while a knife was common in assaults. White females used a revolver or pistol most often in homicide, while they used a knife most often in assault.

4. *Police Processing.* No other index crime was involved in the majority of both crimes, and there was a high clearance rate for both, although it was higher for homicides. The offender in both crimes was arrested within a short time of committing the act, and he was known to either witnesses or police. Clearance was higher for females and blacks than for males and whites, in both homicide and assault.

5. *Alcohol Involvement.* The ingestion of alcohol was more common in homicide than in assault, as was a drinking episode between offender and victim prior to the crime.

6. *Situational Context.* Verbal arguments preceded both crimes, but alcohol was involved in the arguments in homicide situations more often than in aggravated assault cases.

7. *Offender-Victim Relationship.* For both crimes, the victim and offender were typically of the same age, sex, and race. There were most often only one victim and one offender. Negro males were disproportionately involved in both types of crime. The participants in both acts were usually married, blue collar workers, and the victims of interracial assaults were white more often than Negroes. In acts of homicide, a wife attacked her husband more often than a husband attacked his wife, while the reverse was the case in aggravated assaults.

8. *Prior Arrest Records.* For both homicide and aggravated assault, the majority of the victims had no prior record, while the majority of the offenders did. For homicide offenders, two-thirds had a prior record of a crime against the person, while for aggravated assault the number of offenders having this type of record, if one excepts peace disturbance, was negligible. (pp. 98–99)

Further support for the Pittman and Handy findings was reported by Pokorny (1970), who compared homicide, aggravated assault, suicide, and attempted suicide. Pokorny concluded that homicide and aggravated assault "were similar in all aspects studied, which suggests that these are basically the same category of behavior" (p. 110).

Robbery

The President's Commission on Law Enforcement and the Administration of Justice (1967) termed robbery most representative of the crime which the public feared most, i.e., crimes in the street. In fact, the commission went on to say that robbery, along with burglary, is probably a significant if not major reason for America's alarm about crime. An examination of the nature of robbery will make it clear why most people are afraid of being the victims of this crime. First, this offense is almost always committed by a stranger in an unexpected and highly threatening way. Secondly, robbery evokes a stronger reaction than other crimes because it includes two threatening elements. Not only is the victim threatened with or actually subjected to bodily injury but the victim is also deprived of his property. By drawing from several recent studies of robbery, it is possible to provide a rough sketch of the major facets of this offense.

Characteristics of the Victims and Offenders

Based on a study of 1722 cases of robbery that occurred in Philadelphia, Pennsylvania, between January 1, 1960, and December 31, 1966, Normandeau (1968) found a strong association between this offense and the race and sex of both victim and offender. He found that blacks are disproportionately involved in robbery both as offenders and as victims; i.e., three times as many blacks were offenders and twice as many were victims relative to their proportion in the Philadelphia population. The UCR for 1974 indicated that 62 per cent of those arrested for this offense were black and 35 per cent were white, while all other races constituted the remainder. Regarding sex, Normandeau's data showed that males represented about three quarters of the victims and 95 per cent of the offenders, whereas they constituted only 45 per cent of the Philadelphia population. In addition, data from both the UCR reports and from Normandeau's study show that robbery is primarily a youthful offense. Normandeau found that for offenders, the age groups 15 to 19 and 20 to 24 predominated, while the highest rates for victims were in the age groups 20 to 24 and 25 to 29. National data parallel Normandeau's findings with respect to offenders. In 1974, the FBI indicated that 75 per cent of the persons arrested for robbery were under 25, 57 per cent were under 21, and 33 per cent were under 18. From these data it is clear that the typical robber is a young black male.

Motive

Typically, an individual commits robbery in order to obtain funds to carry on a particular activity, e.g., to maintain a hedonistic life style or to buy drugs. Conklin's (1972) study provides data on the monetary gain associated with this offense. While the information is somewhat dated, it does provide a relative indication of the monetary gain associated with the various types of robbery. Table 3–2 shows a comparison of the various types of robbery for the years 1964 and 1968 in Boston. The median gain from this crime is really quite low; in 1964 it was $35 and in 1968 it was $46. Data from Table 3–2 show further that there is considerable variation in the amount of loss by type of robbery. Cab robberies, purse snatches, and street robberies generally produce less than $50. These types of robberies are typically committed by youthful offenders and black offenders who are generally opportunistic and who steal from vulnerable victims. On the other hand, robberies from small and large commercial establishments and residential robberies generally net over $50 and typically are committed by older white offenders. Table 3–2 indicates that commercial robberies, particularly those involving large commercial establishments, net the largest amounts of money. Conklin found that in 1968, one commercial robbery in three resulted in a loss of more than $100 and only one in ten involved a loss of

TABLE 3–2. AMOUNT LOST IN TYPES OF ROBBERY IN BOSTON IN 1964 AND 1968*

Amount Lost	TYPE OF ROBBERY					
	Street	Pursesnatch	Residential	Cab	Small Commercial	Large Commercial
1964						
Under $10	37.5%	47.4%	5.6%	11.1%	1.8%	0.0%
$10–$49	36.4%	36.8%	33.4%	77.8%	31.5%	0.0%
$50–$99	14.6%	15.8%	22.2%	9.3%	29.8%	16.7%
Over $99	11.4%	0.0%	38.9%	1.9%	36.8%	83.3%
Total number	96	38	18	54	57	12
1968						
Under $10	28.7%	42.0%	19.4%	5.2%	5.0%	0.0%
$10–$49	29.5%	34.0%	29.1%	75.9%	25.6%	3.0%
$50–$99	19.3%	14.8%	21.0%	14.7%	19.3%	3.0%
Over $99	22.6%	9.1%	30.7%	4.3%	49.6%	94.0%
Total number	244	88	62	116	121	33

*From Conklin, J. E.: *Robbery and the Criminal Justice System*. Philadelphia, J. B. Lippincott Co., 1972. Reproduced by permission of the author and publishers.

more than $500. The truly big score is rare, as shown by the fact that in 1968 only 52 robberies netted more than $1000, of which only 13 involved $5000, with the largest score being $45,000. We feel that for a few offenders the money acquired from robberies may be worth the risk of apprehension; however, for the vast majority of offenders who net $50 and under, and certainly for those who net under $10, the risk would appear to outweigh the gain.

Selection of Victim

Conklin (1972) points out that most people who rob do so because they prefer to steal cash rather than property which has to be converted to cash. Furthermore, the conversion process may be time consuming, inconvenient, and sometimes risky. Robbery was also viewed by Conklin's subjects (robbers) as being less of a hassle than burglary in that burglary requires an individual to break into a house, search out the valuable goods, carry them out of the house, and exchange them for cash with a fence. In short, then, those who choose robbery as opposed to other offenses do so because they want a fast, direct means of obtaining cash.

Robbers choose their victims based on the amount of money they perceive the victim to have, the vulnerability of the victim, the risk faced during the robbery, and the likelihood that the victim will resist. Offenders usually have some idea of what they can get from a particular victim prior to committing the robbery. However, in some cases they will systematically calculate the amount of money they expect to obtain. For example, "one gang which specialized in jewelry store robberies always sent its 'straightest looking' member into the store to examine the store's most expensive jewelry. If the scout determined that the stock of the jewelry in the store was worth the effort and the risk of robbing the establishment, the gang would return a week later for the hold-up. As a result of casing the store, the gang had a good idea of how much it could expect to steal taking only the most expensive jewelry and fencing it at half of its retail value" (Conklin, 1972, p. 88).

With respect to the vulnerability of the victim, juveniles and blacks (opportunistic robbers) are more apt to consider this a more important factor than the size of the score. In this regard, this group is likely to rob victims whose age, sex, or solitariness makes them especially vulnerable (e.g., women, the elderly), even though such robberies rarely net much money. For the professional robber, on the other hand, a vulnerable victim is one he can rob after planning the crime, surveying the target, and neutralizing various risks. For example, a bank with a rear exit, a poor alarm system, and a nearby highway is a highly vulnerable target to the professional. Finally, a robber must also face the possibility that the victim will resist and even use force against him. For this reason, many offenders carry weapons in order to reduce the probability of resistance. Conklin states:

> Offenders also feel that individuals who give up money that is not their own are less apt to resist than those who are forced to part with their own money. For this reason, some robbers avoid small variety stores which are often owned and run by the clerk. Instead they prefer such establishments as department stores, banks, and gas stations. This reasoning is not typical of the professionals who take precautionary measures to reduce risks. (p. 92)

As part of his study of robbery, Conklin also interviewed 90 victims who were representative of all the victims of robbery that occurred in Boston in the first six months of 1968. These victims were asked why they thought they had been chosen as a target for robbery. Forty victims indicated that they felt they were chosen by pure chance, with an additional 15 indicating that they had been picked because they were alone or outnumbered by the robbers. Another 15 thought they looked like easy marks to the robber because they ran a store that was simple to rob, or were alone in a taxicab, or were elderly. Thirteen victims felt that they were victimized because the offender knew they had large sums of money in their possession. Four attributed their victimization to the racial hostility of blacks toward whites. The victims were also asked what factors they felt the offender considered before robbing them. A total of 174 responses were elicited to this question:

The victim was alone or outnumbered.	52
The victim appeared to have money.	49
The victim was in an isolated area.	30
The victim appeared to be "an easy mark."	14
The victim was elderly.	7
Other reasons.	22
Total	174

It is apparent that these reasons stress the vulnerability of the victim that results from their being alone, in an isolated area, elderly, or an easy mark. Conklin's data show that the only answer not directly related to vulnerability was that the victim appeared to the offender to have a large sum of money. Victims giving this response were most commonly employees of commercial establishments and cab drivers. With regard to victim vulnerability, Conklin concludes:

> *Certain roles are relatively high risk positions for individuals to occupy, such as cab driver, elderly person on the street alone at night, and a lone operator of a variety store. Since mobility from these roles is minimal, there tends to be a clustering of robberies on a relatively small number of individuals. Victims do not contribute to their own victimization in the sense that homicide victims and rape victims sometimes do, but they may contribute in the sense of continuing to occupy high risk roles.* (p. 97)

What Conklin's study has shown is that certain types of individuals are victim-prone in that they occupy certain positions that increase their probability of victimization.

The Planning of the Robbery

The planning associated with the commission of a robbery varies from those that involve a detailed blueprint of action to those that involve no planning at all, i.e., they just seem to happen. This latter type is illustrated by the following case: An inmate reported "that he and a friend were in a cab and his friend pulled a knife, grabbed the driver around the neck and demanded his money. The inmate did not know that any robbery had been considered until it was underway" (Conklin, 1972, p. 99).

There are several elements associated with those robberies that are planned. First, the offender must select a target. In conjunction with choosing a target, offenders will generally familiarize themselves with the areas in which the target is located. In the case of commercial robberies, the offender will survey the area near the target in order to be familiar with the possible obstacles in the area and for purposes of mapping out the best escape route and possibly a few alternate routes.

Secondly, robbers will try to learn what possible obstacles may be present during the robbery. For example, Conklin found that some robbers, particularly the opportunistic and addict robbers, prefer to rob people who are alone and in isolated areas because this minimizes the possibilities of resistance and interference. On the other hand, the professional robber who tends to have a preference for commercial establishments is likely to encounter such hazards as customers, guards, alarms, and cameras. The purpose of planning is to minimize or neutralize these obstacles. Robbers who victimize commercial establishments may spend considerable time estimating how many customers enter and leave the establishment during different periods of the day. They may also attempt to ascertain the movement of police in this particular area and the amount of traffic in the area during different periods of the day.

Role allocation represents a third element of the planning process. Conklin noted that three fifths of the 1964 and 1968 robberies in Boston involved more than one offender. In robberies involving more than one offender there may be an assignment of a particular task to one member of the group. Since the roles involved in committing this offense are not particularly difficult to perform, the assignment of an individual to a particular role generally serves the function of making sure that a particular job gets done. One man may be assigned the role of wheel man; his responsibilities may include stealing the getaway car, mapping the escape route, and driving to and from the scene of the robbery. "Look-out" represents a second role which may be assigned to the wheel man or to another member of the gang. An individual assigned to this role is supposed to maintain a watch and warn the other members of the gang of possible interruptions during the course of the robbery. Other assignments are specifically related to the target in question. In a bank robbery, one offender may be assigned the task of watching the customers while the others pick up the money from the tellers.

The Use of Force in Robbery

There is some confusion regarding whether robbery should be considered as a form of theft or as an assaultive crime, because it includes elements of both theft and force. Wolfgang and Ferracuti (1959) suggest that robbery, like homicide, rape, and aggravated assault, arises out of the "sub-culture of violence." Normandeau (1968), on the other hand, sees robbers as a group that is relatively nonviolent in their criminal activities. He views robbers as being primarily thieves who occasionally, though rather rarely, use force to achieve their objectives. "The display of violence in this context is on the whole an isolated episode." Thus, he contends that the label "'violent offender class' could not be applied to robbers without distorting the factual data to fit preconceived ideas" (p. 12). He concludes by stating that robbery arises more from a subculture of theft than from one of violence. These two contradictory positions raise an interesting question with respect to the crime of robbery: should robbery be classified as a violent offense or a property offense? This section will examine the role of force in robbery in order to provide a perspective on this question.

The Prior Offense Record of Suspects. One factor in determining whether robbers are "violent offenders" would be their prior offense records. Conklin (1972) found that in 1968 in Boston, 11.5 per cent of the juveniles and 26.6 per cent of the adults arrested for robbery had a prior record of crimes of violence excluding robbery. Spencer (1966) classified 225 of the 778 offenders she studied as criminally violent — a category which includes robbers — according to her criteria, which were presented previously in this chapter. Of these 225 offenders only 17 per cent had a prior record of convictions for actual violence. Finally, Normandeau found that 4 per cent of the 892 offenders that he studied had a past profile of assault, but that 45 per cent of this group had a pattern of robbery, larceny, or burglary. These studies show that robbers as a group do not have a past record of violent offenses.

The Use of Weapons. Conklin (1972) found that juveniles, blacks, and those who committed robbery with an accomplice are more likely to rob without a weapon, while adults, whites, and lone offenders are more apt to use firearms. Lone offenders feel the need to carry weapons in order to intimidate the intended victim, while this need is to some degree reduced in the case of those who rob with accomplices since the group serves as a functional equivalent of a weapon.

In interviews with robbers, Conklin found that weapons are primarily carried because of the instrumental function they serve. First, the weapon creates a buffer zone between the offender and the victim. In this regard, a firearm as opposed to a knife is most effective because it instills the greatest amount of fear in the victim. Many of the robbers he interviewed stated that "no one would try to take a gun away from you" and "it is easier to control people with a gun." The second function of a weapon is to intimidate the victim; i.e., the weapon is supposed to sufficiently frighten the victim so that he will give up his money or valuables without a struggle. Third, weapons are used by the offender to make good his threat to the victim to accomplish his objective; most often he will use the weapon to hit the victim on the side of the head or in the stomach in order to show him that he means business. Thus, in most instances, a weapon is used in a non-lethal manner to indicate to the victim that the offender will not hesitate to use force to complete the theft. Finally, weapons are used to ensure escape from the scene of the robbery. A robber knows that if he can successfully escape from the scene of the offense his chances of being arrested are greatly reduced. Thus, weapons will be used to keep victims, witnesses, and even police officers from blocking their escape. Conklin indicates that a robber is more likely to fire a gun to ensure escape than he is to use it to overcome his victim's resistance.

Injury to Victims. Contrary to popular belief, robbery does not usually involve injury to the victim. A survey of robbery cases in 17 cities conducted in 1967 for the National Commission on the Causes and Prevention of Violence found that injuries occurred in only 14 per cent of the armed robberies and 28 per cent of the strong arm robberies. Normandeau (1968) reported that 44 per cent of the robberies in Philadelphia resulted in no injury, while the remaining 56 per cent involved some injury; 26 per cent were minor, 25 per cent resulted in treatment and discharge, and 5 per cent resulted in hospitalization. Finally, Conklin (1972) found that in 1964, 32.1 per cent of the victims of robbery in Boston were injured, while in 1968 only 27.1 per cent were injured. Furthermore, these studies indicate that injuries are more likely in unarmed than in armed robberies and in noncommercial than in commercial robberies.

At the beginning of this discussion a question was raised regarding the appropriate classification of robbery as a violent or a property offense. Research presented in this section indicates that: (1) most robbers do not have a record of other violent crimes; (2) weapons are used primarily to intimidate rather than injure victims; and (3) victims are not injured in a majority of robberies. However, while violence is not the major objective of this offense, and injury appears to be relatively infrequent, there are some good reasons for classifying this as a violent offense. First, unlike the perpetrator of a property offense, the robber does threaten his victim with violence in order to achieve his objective. Secondly, the potential for injury is extremely high should the victim fail to comply with the robber's demand. In short, robbery is most accurately classified as a violent property offense. Classifying it as a property offense alone would tend to minimize the fact that this crime does involve a direct threat of injury to the person.

Types of Robbery Offenders

Conklin (1972) has identified four types of robbers based on interviews with inmates of Massachusetts prisons who were serving time for robbery. Admittedly, this is a small sample, but Conklin nevertheless feels that, although he was unable to assess the proportion of robbers falling within each of the four categories, he was able to delineate the types of offenders from his interviews. The four types of robbers he identified are: (1) the professional robber; (2) the opportunist robber; (3) the addict robber; and (4) the alcoholic robber.

The Professional Robber. Conklin defined professionals as "those who manifest a long-term commitment to crime as a source of livelihood, who plan and organize their crimes prior to committing them, and who seek money to support a particular lifestyle that may be called hedonistic" (1972, p. 64).

Conklin identified two types of professionals who commit robberies: (1) the professional robber, and (2) other types of professionals. The professional robber commits robbery almost exclusively. These offenders choose robbery because it is direct, fast, and often very profitable. Typically, these offenders do not hold a full-time job to supplement their income from their criminal activities. Their income is derived exclusively from four or five "big scores," each of which nets them over $500, and in some rare instances, as much as $10,000. They generally spend this money in a fairly short time on high living. However, while some do save some money for bail and to hire a good private lawyer, they do not as a rule save money in order to retire.

With regard to the execution of their crimes they exhibit considerable skill and engage in more planning than other offenders. This is necessitated in part by the fact that they usually steal from commercial establishments that have large sums of money. Although they tend to commit offenses with accomplices, these groups are not well organized and are generally formed only for a particular "score." Allocation of roles in these groups may involve assignment of one member to the position of wheel man, while another may be assigned the task of keeping customers from interfering with the successful completion of the robbery. These offenders are skilled in the use of guns and are less averse to using them to secure money or make a successful escape than are other offenders. Following a robbery, the professional will often leave the city for a few weeks, perhaps taking a trip to a resort area like Florida. He will not as a rule begin planning another offense until he has exhausted his existing supply of cash, though he is likely to be watching for possible scores all the time.

The "other types of professionals" manifest all of the characteristics of the professional robber except that they are committed to other forms of theft for their livelihood. Included within this group are burglars, pimps, and "paper hangers" (bad check writers). These offenders commit robbery out of necessity or because they find a good score. In some instances, these offenders are surprised by the victim, or by police, and thus what started out to be a property offense turns into a robbery. The pimp will sometimes rob one of his girl's customers because customers generally do not report the crime to the police, fearing either prosecution or public embarrassment.

The Opportunist Robber. Unlike the professional, the opportunist rarely manifests a long-term commitment to robbery; instead, these offenders are more apt to engage in property offenses such as larceny and shoplifting, engaging in robbery infrequently. In addition, in contrast to the professional who is typically white, in his mid twenties, and from a middle class or working class background, the opportunist is black, in his teens or early twenties, and from a lower class family. These factors, according to Conklin, may determine the level of achievement to which the opportunist robbers aspire and thus may explain why this group usually chooses a target which nets relatively small amounts of money, often less than $20. Preferred victims include elderly women with purses, drunks, cab drivers, and people who walk alone on dark streets. As their label might suggest, this group does not engage in elaborate planning prior to the commission of a robbery; for them, robberies "often just seem to happen." In addition, while most of these offenders commit robberies in groups, they do not allocate roles to different members of the gang. Also, they rarely carry guns or any other weapon. As Conklin suggests, "in a sense, the group itself becomes a weapon, for three or four young offenders are as threatening to a victim as one offender with a knife" (p. 70).

The Addict Robber. Conklin includes within this category both offenders who are addicted to opiates, particularly heroin, and those who make regular use of other drugs, such as amphetamines, other pills, and LSD. While these offenders have a high commitment to theft, their commitment to robbery is quite low. As a rule, these offenders prefer to shoplift or burglarize cars or homes rather than engage in robbery because the risk of apprehension is much less owing to the fact that the victim in most instances cannot identify the offender. The addict is concerned with apprehension because this often means cold turkey withdrawal from drugs, an experience the addict would rather avoid. With regard to planning, these offenders engage in less planning than the professional but plan more than the opportunist. In choosing a target, the addict tends not to be concerned with a large score but only with obtaining enough money to get the next fix. Targets are also chosen so as to minimize the risk of apprehension. In addition, addicts rarely carry loaded guns because they are afraid they may panic during the robbery, owing to their need for drugs, and seriously injure or kill the victim, which may lead to charges of aggravated assault or murder. However, by not using a weapon, the addict increases the likelihood that the victim will resist, thus requiring him to use force to accomplish his objective.

The Alcoholic Robber. A number of offenders in Conklin's sample robbed for reasons related to the excessive use of alcohol. He defined alcoholism as "excessive use of alcoholic beverages causing such negative consequences for the drinker as loss of employment, family discord, or criminal behavior" (pp. 75–76). Offenders included within this category were alcoholics according to this definition. In addition, they also indicated that they were drunk at the time of the offense and attributed their criminal behavior to intoxication. These offenders have no commitment to robbery as a way of life, nor are they committed to theft as a means of acquiring money. With regard to motivation, the alcoholic robber resembles both the opportunist, in that some rob to get "a little extra money," and the addict, in that others rob to get money to buy alcohol. Conklin (1972) characterizes their criminal activity as follows:

> *The alcoholic robber does not plan his crime in advance. As with the opportunist, the crime seems to happen randomly. Alcoholics do not even seek a vulnerable victim as do opportunists. Instead, they get involved in a situation which often leads to an assault, followed by a theft as an after thought. Because their crimes are not planned, alcoholic robbers usually do not employ a weapon, unless they are in the habit of carrying one. The alcoholic is less apt to take precautions and is therefore probably caught a higher proportion of the times he robs than other types of robbery offenders.* (p. 76)

SUMMARY

In this chapter we have examined the characteristics of the crimes of murder, assault, and robbery. Attention was drawn to some of the factors that are common to all violent offenses. In this regard, the subculture of violence was discussed as one factor that accounts for the differential distribution of violence among various segments of our society.

An examination of criminal homicide revealed that homicide

rates have reached an all-time high and there is no indication that they will decline in the future. Furthermore, traditional crime prevention procedures are not effective in reducing the number of homicides because most offenders victimize their friends, relatives, or acquaintances. Recent increases in homicide rates have been attributed to changes in the composition of the population, economic dissatisfaction, the presence of a large number of Viet Nam veterans who are proficient in and psychologically attuned to the use of weapons, and permissive child-rearing practices.

The discussion of assault and battery indicated that this offense is usually not reported unless there is serious injury. A comparison of aggravated assault and homicide showed that there were more similarities than differences between these offenses. This chapter also examined the patterns associated with robbery. Although robbery is classified as a crime against the person, its primary objective is financial gain. Injuries to victims are minimal; however, it still should be considered a crime against the person because it involves a direct threat of injury to the person. Four types of robbers were identified and discussed: the professional, the opportunist, the addict, and the alcoholic robber.

REVIEW

Find the answers to the following questions in the text:

1. List some of the factors that characterize the areas in which victims and perpretrators of violent offenses reside.

2. What features are common to both violent crimes and offenders?

3. Identify and briefly describe four types of violent offenders.

4. Whom do murderers primarily victimize?

5. What is felony murder? Which offenses are usually associated with felony murder?

6. Summarize the major characteristics of homicide victims and offenders.

7. Cite the factors that have been advanced to explain our spiraling homicide rate.

8. Discuss some of the reasons why people fail to report aggravated assault.

9. Should robbery be classified as a crime against the person?

10. Identify and briefly describe four types of robbers.

TERMS TO IDENTIFY AND REMEMBER

subculture of violence
victim-precipitated homicide
battery
criminally violent offender
situationally violent offender
opportunist robber
alcoholic robber

felony murder
assault
culturally violent offender
pathologically violent offender
professional robber
addict robber

REFERENCES

Barnett, A., Kleitman, D. J., and Larson, R. C.: On urban homicide: a statistical analysis. Journal of Criminal Justice 3:85—110, 1975.

Bloch, H. A., and Geis, G.: *Man, Crime, and Society*. New York, Random House, Inc., 1970.

Conklin, J. E.: *Robbery and the Criminal Justice System*. Philadelphia, J. B. Lippincott Co., 1972.

Ellis, A., and Gullo, J. M.: *Murder and Assassination*. New York, Lyle Stewart, Inc., 1971.

Federal Bureau of Investigation: *Uniform Crime Reports: 1975*. Washington, D. C., U. S. Government Printing Office, 1976.

Guttmacher, M. S.: *Mind of the Murderer*. New York, Farrar, Straus, and Cudahy, 1960.

Lunde, D. T.: Hot blood's record month: our murder boom. Psychology Today 9:35—42, 1975.

MacDonald, J. M.: *The Murderer and His Victim*. Springfield, Illinois, Charles C Thomas, Publisher, 1961.

National Commission on the Causes and Prevention of Violence: Final Report. New York, Praeger Publishers, Inc., 1970.

Normandeau, A.: Patterns in robbery. Criminologica 1: 2—13, 1968.

Pittman, D. J., and Handy, W. J.: Patterns in criminal aggravated assault. *In* Cohen, B. (ed.): *Crime in America*. Itasca, Illinois, F. E. Peacock Publishers, Inc., 1970.

Pokorny, A. D.: Human violence: a comparison of homicide, aggravated assault, suicide, and attempted homicide. *In* Cohen, B. (ed.): *Crime in America*. Itasca, Illinois, F. E. Peacock Publishers, Inc., 1970.

President's Commission on Law Enforcement and Administration of Justice: *Challenge of Crime in a Free Society*. Washington, D.C., U. S. Government Printing Office, 1967.

Reckless, W. C.: *The Crime Problem*. 5th ed. New York, Appleton-Century-Crofts, 1973.

Spencer, C.: *A Typology of Violent Offenders*. Administrative Abstract No. 23, California Department of Corrections, September, 1966.

Wolfgang, M. E.: *Patterns in Criminal Homicide*. Philadelphia, University of Pennsylvania Press, 1958.

Wolfgang, M. E.: Criminal homicide and the subculture of violence. *In* Wolfgang, M. E. (ed.): *Studies in Homicide*. New York, Harper & Row, Publishers, 1967a.

Wolfgang, M. E.: Victim precipitated criminal homicide. *In* Wolfgang, M. E. (ed.): *Studies in Homicide*. New York, Harper & Row, Publishers, 1967b.

Wolfgang, M. E., and Ferracuti, F.: *The Subculture of Violence*. London, Tavistock Publications Ltd., 1969.

4 SEXUAL OFFENSES

The category of sex offenses encompasses a broad spectrum of behavior, ranging from violent acts that represent a threat to community safety, e.g., rape, to acts that are mildly reprehensible, e.g., exhibitionism, to acts that are engaged in by a large number of adults in the community, e.g., fornication. Ellis and Abarbanel (1967) provide a comprehensive list of the categories of sexual behavior which are commonly penalized and prohibited. These are: (1) forcible sexual assault (without coitus); (2) forcible rape; (3) statutory rape (coitus with a female under the "legal age of consent" — usually 16 or 18, regardless of consent); (4) incest; (5) noncoital sex relations with a minor; (6) exhibitory sexual behavior; (7) obscenity (defined as making indecent or offensive proposals to a member of the opposite sex, using improper language in public, and disseminating "obscene" materials); (8) homosexual behavior; (9) transvestism; (10) voyeurism; (11) murder in a sexual context or sexual circumstances; (12) bestiality; (13) sodomy; (14) adultery; (15) fornication; (16) prostitution; (17) pimping or pandering; and (18) managing a house of prostitution.

Gebhard, Gagnon, Pomeroy, and Christenson (1965) conducted a massive study of 1500 incarcerated sex offenders, under the auspices of the Institute for Sexual Research founded by Alfred Kinsey. Their project represents the largest and most comprehensive study of sex offenders ever conducted, and we shall make frequent reference to their findings in an attempt to sketch an accurate picture of sexual criminals. The authors interpret their vast array of data to show two broad classes of sex offenses. The first category includes offenses in which the behavior involved is "normal" and motivated by desires that most people, including clinicians, would consider typical for the average person. However, while these offenses may be considered normal, they are deemed inappropriate and punishable for various reasons. Such offenses would include sexual intercourse with a willing, unrelated female who has passed puberty and occasional opportunistic peeping. These offenses do not seriously threaten the community, and the individuals who engage in them are generally either psychologically undamaged or minimally damaged. Consequently, our social sanctions should be tempered accordingly and society should expend a minimum amount of time and money on such cases. The second class of offenses comprises behavior which is uncommon and motivated by desires which most laymen and clinicians would consider definitely unacceptable and/or pathological. Such offenses would include those involving force or serious duress, those involving children who have not reached puberty, and most acts of incest, exhibitionism, and compulsive peeping. These offenses tend to disrupt social organization, if only by the furor they cause; the possibility of individual psychological damage is greater; and the offense may constitute a public nuisance. It is on these offenses that society should focus attention and be prepared to spend money for detention, treatment, and research.

PUBLIC VIEWS OF THE SEX OFFENDER

Public misconceptions concerning the sexual offender are numerous, and Coleman (1972) has summarized the more common of these:

1. Sexual offenders are typically homicidal sex fiends.
2. Sexual offenders progress to more serious types of sex crimes.
3. Sexual offenders are "oversexed."
4. Sexual offenders suffer from glandular imbalance.
5. Sexual offenders are usually repeaters.

To the extent that the views of many people are shaped by beliefs such as these, it is not difficult to understand why the sexual offender can come to be regarded as a depraved beast who will attack with violent intent. A compilation of some basic factual information about sex offenders (Abrahamsen, 1960; Karpman,

1962) helps to place these common myths in proper and reasonable perspective:

---

1. The majority of convicted offenders are found to be rather harmless, "minor" deviates rather than dangerous "sex fiends."

2. Only a relatively small number (about 20 per cent) use force or duress upon their victims.

3. When they are not psychologically treated, convicted offenders are found to be frequent repeaters of both sexual and nonsexual offenses, even though their rates of recidivism may be lower than those of nonsex offenders.

4. Very few offenders can be designated as true "sexual psychopaths," since most of them, when intensively examined with modern psychological and psychiatric techniques of investigation, are found to be severely neurotic, borderline psychotic, psychotic, or to have organic brain impairment.

5. Aside from those convicted of statutory rape and incestuous relations, most offenders tend to be sexually inhibited and constricted rather than overimpulsive and oversexed. The great majority of them are distinctly immature emotionally.

6. In comparison to the general population, subnormal intelligence is found in a greater percentage of criminal offenders and bright normal or superior intelligence in a smaller percentage. Subnormal intelligence is more frequently found in offenders convicted of statutory rape, incestuous relations, and bestiality, and less frequently found in offenders convicted of forcible rape, exhibitory acts, and disseminating "obscene" material.

7. The majority of offenders are quite young, being in their teens and early twenties. From 50 to 60 per cent of the convicted offenders are unmarried. Most of the offenders come from relatively poor educational and socioeconomic backgrounds.

The typical sex offender as an individual differs strikingly from the stereotypes portrayed in fiction and the mass media. Overreaction to these distorted images has created much of the misguided public policy with respect to nonviolent sexual behavior. Thus, an individual may be a sex offender, e.g., a statutory rapist, and exhibit conventional (genital) sexual behavior; or he may show considerable deviation in sexual behavior, e.g., compulsive masochism, and never commit a statutory sex offense, *unless that particular category of behavior has been specifically prohibited in that particular jurisdiction.*

VARIETIES OF SEXUAL OFFENSES AND SEXUAL OFFENDERS

During 1975 there were 163,270 arrests for sex crimes in the United States, according to *Uniform Crime Reports (1976)*. These arrests break down into the following categories:

Forcible rape	26,670
Prostitution and commercialized vice	68,200
All other sex offenses	68,400

The last category includes *statutory rape*, defined as sexual intercourse by a male with a female who is under the specified legal age, regardless of consent. The total number of *reported* cases of forcible rape (as distinguished from arrests) for this same period was 56,090 — an increase of 880 offenses over 1974.

Rape

A number of studies (Amir, 1971; Atlanta Regional Commission [undated]; provide a clear picture of the nature of the offense of rape. This section will present the major patterns that this research has uncovered.

Race

All major studies show that rape is predominantly an intraracial crime: it is committed by black men against black women and by white men against white women (Georgia Commission on the Status of Women [undated]). Furthermore, rape has been found to occur more often between blacks than between whites. For example, in Atlanta in 1972, the race of the perpetrator and victim, where identifiable, was: black–black, 62 percent; white–white, 13 per cent; black–white, 24 per cent; and white–black, 1 per cent. In Philadelphia, blacks had, on the basis of population, four times their expected number of victims, and the proportion of black offenders was four times greater than their proportion in the general population (Amir, 1971). The Georgia Commission study indicates that statistics regarding the race of the victim and offender should be regarded with caution since they are based only on reported rapes, which constitute but a fraction of all rapes. The commission further suggests that existing statistics may be misleading because of the possibility that poor women — who are often black — are more likely to report a rape than middle or upper class women — who are more often white. A recent study cited by the Georgia Commission concluded that:

> *White middle class women are likely to take their troubles straight to a family doctor or psychiatrist; their lower income sisters have no better recourse than the precinct house, making them overrepresented in police studies and supporting the bias that rape is a lower class black phenomenon. (p. 3)*

Furthermore in this connection, a victimization study conducted by the Atlanta Regional Commission reports that while 43 per cent of the black rape victims reported the rape, only 22 per cent of the white victims made an official report.

Age

The research indicates that most rapists are young. Amir (1971) found that 81.9 per cent of the offenders were between the ages of 15 and 29, with the age ranges of 15 to 19 (40.3 per cent) and 20 to 24 (25.6 per cent) predominating among both blacks and whites. Chappel and Singer (1973) found that 71.1 per cent of the rapists in their study were between the ages of 15 and 24.

The age pattern for victims is somewhat different in that it spans a much broader range. For example, in Philadelphia the age range for most victims was 10 to 29 (68.8 per cent), with the age groups 15 to 19 (24.9 per cent) and 10 to 14 (19.9 per cent) predominating (Amir, 1971). According to the Georgia Commission report, the average age for victims was 19 to 20 years old. Thus, while offenders and victims tend to concentrate within the same age ranges, victims tend to concentrate at the lower end of the range (10 to 19), while offenders tend to concentrate within the central age categories (15–29).

Occupational Status

Amir (1971) found that in Philadelphia 90 per cent of the offenders of both races occupied the lower end of the occupational scale, i.e., skilled labor down to retired and the unemployed. This is consistent with the data from the Georgia Commission report.

On the other hand, Amir indicates that victims come from mixed occupational backgrounds, and that certain women run a greater risk of victimization because of their occupation (e.g., nurses, waitresses). Amir concludes that sexual victimization is not occupationally bound.

Temporal Patterns

All the studies examined refute the common belief that rape is "a hot season offense." However, there is evidence that rape is associated with certain days of the week and hours of the day. In both Atlanta and Philadelphia, rape occurred more often on the weekends and between the hours of 8 P.M. and 2 A.M.

Special Patterns

Studies on rape reveal that the victim and offender often live in the same area. In Philadelphia, in 82 per cent of the cases the victim and offender lived in the same neighborhood or vicinity, while in 68 per cent of the cases a "neighborhood triangle" occurred, that is, offenders lived in the vicinity of the victim and the place where the offense took place.

The Role of Alcohol

Amir's research dispelled the myth that rape is associated with drinking. He found that in two thirds of the cases alcohol was absent from the rape situation. In the remaining one third of the cases, involving alcohol, it was present in both victim and offender in 63 per cent of these incidents, in victim only in 28 per cent, and in the offender only in 9 per cent. The presence of alcohol was found to be strongly related to violent rapes, particularly those involving black offenders and victims, and also with the sexual humiliation of the victim, particularly forcing the victim to perform fellatio.

Previous Record

Amir (1971) found that a relatively high proportion of offenders had previous records. Victims also were frequently found to have records, although the proportion was not as high as that of offenders. Of the 1292 offenders in his sample, Amir found that 49 per cent had previous arrest records while 51 per cent were first offenders. With regard to specific offenses:

> 1. Of 637 offenders with previous records, 42 percent had a record of at least one or more offenses against property only, 20 percent against person only, and 23 percent against public order only. Two percent had arrest records of use or possession of drugs, four percent of sexual offenses other than rape, and nine percent of forcible rape.

2. Negro offenders had higher arrest records than white offenders for offenses against the person (21 percent and 16 percent respectively), and for rape (10 percent and six percent, respectively). White offenders had higher arrest figures for offenses against property (47 percent and 41 percent, respectively) and for public disorder (26 percent and 23 percent, respectively). (p. 115)*

Of the 648 victims in his study, Amir found that 29 per cent had an arrest record. With regard to specific offenses, 9.7 per cent of the offenses were against property, 10.5 per cent were against the person, 22 per cent against public order.

Modus Operandi

Amir (1971) has used this term to refer to the nature of the offense, i.e., the way in which it is carried out, the behavior of the partners in the rape situation, the condition of the victim prior to, during, and after the assault. On the basis of an analysis of victim accounts, he has identified the following sequence of phases as characteristic of this offense:*

I. The initial interaction and the meeting ground. *This phase includes the place of initial meeting between the offender(s) and his (their) victims. The scene of the crime may be that of the initial meeting place. If the crime is to be committed elsewhere, a "moving of the crime scene" will occur. The offender or offenders may have set their minds on committing this act, thus planning it, or the act may be an explosive one, a situation-induced event. The manipulation of the victim by various degrees of coercion and force begins in the initial meeting.*

II. At the scene. *At the scene of rape, the victim may continue to resist the offender who, as a response, will try to render her submissive by more violent means. Alternatively, the victim may continue giving the offender encouraging cues, or she may already be frightened and subdued.*

III. The crime. *The offender rapes the victim. He may inflict on her more physical abuse and/or subject her to sexual humiliation in the form of perverted sexual acts.*

IV. After the crime. *The victim may be left at the scene or she is kept for some time, raped, and abused again, or she may be taken to another place and left there (a further moving of the crime scene). Later, the victim either immediately reports the event herself, or confronts someone else who summons the police.* (p..137)

Phase I: Initial Contact and Planning of the Offense. Many people believe that rape is mainly a deadend street or dark alley event. Data from both the Philadelphia study and the Atlanta study failed to confirm this view. In Philadelphia, only 48 per cent of the rapes were initiated on the street, with the victim walking on the street (41.8 per cent), waiting for transportation (2.4 per cent), and standing in front of a bar (7.8 per cent). In an additional one third of the rapes, the point of contact was at the victim's home or the place where she was temporarily staying. In the remaining cases, the point of contact was: the offender's home (6.7 per cent), at a party or picnic (2.6 per cent), and in a bar (7.8 per cent). Thus, in the majority of cases, the street and the participant's place of permanent or temporary residence are the places where the initial contact for rape is made.

One of the predominant misconceptions about rape is that it is an explosive event; the Philadelphia study dispelled this myth. Amir (1971) found that 71 per cent of the rapes in Philadelphia were planned — the place was arranged, elaborate enticement was employed, or the victim was deliberately sought and a plan was made to coerce her into sexual relations in the place of the initial meeting or elsewhere. An additional 11 per cent of the rapes were partially planned — vague plans were made hastily, after the offender had encountered the victim and the situation seemed right for the offense. Only 16 per cent of the rapes were designated by Amir as explosive — the offender had no previous idea of committing the crime but opportunities (place of meeting, victim's behavior, etc.) created the impulse, or the offender's judgment was impaired, usually by the consumption of alcohol before the event.

Phase II: At the Scene. During this phase, the offender attempts to secure the submission of the victim through "reasoning or through physical coercion." In addition, if the scene of the crime is not that of the initial meeting, the offender will try to take the victim to the place where he intends to rape her, intimidating her along the way and at the crime scene.

Amir (1971) found that a majority of rapes took place indoors at a participant's residence (56 per cent). An additional 12 per cent of the rapes occurred indoors at other than the participant's residence (vacant houses, housing projects, etc.). Eighteen per cent of the rapes took place in open spaces — school yard, alley, field, vacant railroad lots, parks, or public restrooms. Finally, 15 per cent of the rapes were found to have taken place in autos.

Looking at the phenomenon of "moving of the crime scene," i.e., when the offender moved the victim from the initial point of contact to the place where the rape took place, Amir found that when the meeting place was the temporary or permanent residence of one of the participants, the rape occurred in the same place in 88 per cent of the cases; however, when the meeting place was outside, the rape occurred in the participant's temporary or permanent residence in 33 per cent of the cases. The moving of the crime scene was found to occur mainly with outdoor meetings; Amir (p. 147) noted that among those who met their assailants on the outside, more were raped indoors [i.e., the crime scene was moved] than were raped outdoors after meeting their offenders indoors.

Phase III: The Crime. Rape is a crime not because of the sexual act per se but because the victim is forced to submit to the act against her will. Rapists differ in the amount and kind of physical force that they employ against the victim. In some instances the rapist may employ only verbal overtures, while in others he may beat the victim to death. Victim resistance and the offender's psychological makeup and motives all interact to determine the degree of force employed by the offender. Data relating to the former two factors are not available from studies of police reports; however, we will discuss these factors when we look at the offenders.

Nonphysical Force. Based on an analysis of police interrogations, Amir (1971) developed the following categories of nonphysical force:

> 1. Tempting. *The victim is offered money or a ride; the offender tries to arouse interest by verbal or non-verbal means. This method is used especially against young victims.*
> 2. Coercion. *The victim is threatened with bodily harm, or other kinds of verbal violence are employed by the offender.*
> 3. Intimidation. *Physical gestures and verbal threats are used.*
> 4. Intimidation with a weapon or object. *Threats are reinforced with a weapon or other physical object (a stick, stone, etc.).* (p. 152)*

Data from this study show that the more aggressive forms of duress (the two forms of intimidation) were employed in nearly two thirds of the cases. Verbal coercion was employed in nearly 25 per cent of the cases and temptation was used in approximately 12 per cent.

Physical Aggression. Amir (1971) identified four categories of physical force: roughness — holding, pushing; nonbrutal beating — slapping; brutal beating — slugging, kicking, beating by

---

From Amir, M.: *Patterns in Forcible Rape.* Chicago, The University of Chicago Press, 1971, ©1971 by The University of Chicago Press.

fists repeatedly, etc.; and choking, gagging, etc. Some form of physical force was found to have been employed in 85 per cent of the rape cases in Philadelphia:

> *In almost one-third of the cases (29 percent) the force used was in the form of roughness. In one-quarter of the cases, the victim was beaten non-brutally during the rape situation. In one-fifth of the cases (20.5 percent) the victim was brutally beaten by the offender, and in 12 percent of the cases the victim was choked by her assailant.* (p. 155)*

The most excessive degrees of violence were employed in group rape, with single rape showing the least violence in the rape situation. When the data on pair rapes and group rapes were combined, a significant association was discerned between multiplicity of offenders and violence in the rape situation. This means that the smaller the number of offenders, the less likely that violence will occur.

The most excessive degrees of violence during the rape situation are more likely to occur outdoors than at the victim's or offender's home or temporary place of residence. In outdoor rapes, brutal beating was the lot of the victim before the rape in 51 per cent of the cases, and in 40 per cent she received brutal, severe beating during and after the rape. These results compare to 30 per cent and 36 per cent, respectively, when the rape took place indoors in either the victim's or offender's place.

Sexual Humiliation. Although most people associate rape with sexual intercourse, it also may involve other forms of sexual behavior (humiliation) usually considered to be deviant. Sexual humiliation occurred in 27 per cent of the rapes in the Philadelphia study. An examination of the cases in which it occurred revealed that:*

> . . . *in over one-third of the cases (35 percent) fellatio was enforced on the victim; in 6 percent cunnilingus was used; and in another 6 percent both fellatio and cunnilingus were used; and in another 6 percent pederasty was displayed; in 4 percent the offender used a prophylactic. [This category was included because Amir believed that by using a prophylactic the offender attempts to transform a forced erotic encounter into a regular "affair" or love relationship; or he views his relationship as a danger to himself (fear of VD), with no insight into the true meaning of the whole situation]; and in 43 percent the offender forced the victim to [engage in] more than one [act of] sexual intercourse [this category was included because repeated intercourse entails*

---

*From Amir, M.: *Patterns in Forcible Rape.* Chicago, The University of Chicago Press, 1971, © 1971 by The University of Chicago Press.

*longer captivity of the victim by the offender, and more physical
abuse — besides that of a further sexual shock]* .... (Amir, 1971,
p. 160)

In addition, Amir found that sexual humiliation was significantly associated with a multiplicity of offenders. It was found to
occur in 34 per cent of the group rape events and in 27 per cent of
the pair rape events, while it was displayed in only 23 per cent of
the single rape events. Alcohol was also found to be associated
with sexual humiliation. In 44 per cent of the rape events in which
sexual humiliation occurred, alcohol was present; whereas sexual
humiliation was absent in 70 per cent of the cases in which alcohol
diminished the victim's capacity to resist the rape, and in these
instances her behavior was found to be mainly submissive.

Phase IV: After the Crime. In most instances, the rape is
quickly executed and the offender disappears; but in a small
number of cases, and particularly in those involving group rape,
felony rape, rape committed in the offender's home, or rape committed by someone close to the victim, the victim is kept by the
offender at the scene after the forced intercourse is completed.
Amir (1971) noted that captivity occurred in 9 per cent of the
rapes in Philadelphia. The time span of captivity (after the last
intercourse) ranged from a half hour to four hours or more. The
offenders' confessions revealed that the usual reasons for keeping
the victim captive were either to "cool the victim off' or to hold
her for further sexual abuse in the case of gang rape. In four cases,
the offender was drunk and fell asleep, but the victim was too
frightened to move until he left (p. 175).

Multiple Rape

The rape of a woman by two or more males is a much more
frequent occurrence than is generally recognized. Forty-three per
cent of the victims in Philadelphia (Amir, 1971) and 25 per cent
of the victims in New York (Chappel and Singer, 1973) were
sexually assaulted by more than one offender. Multiple rape can
be further subdivided into (1) pair rape, in which two offenders
rape one victim, and (2) group rape, in which three or more offenders rape one victim. In Philadelphia, 16 per cent of the rapes
were pair rapes and 27 per cent were group rapes.

The Dynamics of Group Rape. In order to understand group
rape* it is necessary to examine not only the motives of the indi-

---

*The term "group rape" as used in this discussion includes both pair rape
and group rape.

viduals involved but also the dynamics of the group process. While the males involved may be predisposed to engage in deviant acts, including forced sexual activity, individually many would not sexually assault a woman. However, groups have the ability to arouse and reinforce certain attitudes and emotions held by group members. In this regard, groups can produce distorted sexual attitudes and conceptions of women. Groups can also eliminate those attitudes and conceptions that conflict with those of the majority and, particularly, with those of the group leader. The group then destroys or neutralizes inhibitions against deviant actions and provides justifications for these activities. Accordingly, group-generated rationalizations and pressures interact to produce behavior that is atypical of some group members. In short, groups bolster the courage of their members and threaten those who do not participate with expulsion or ridicule (an individual who fails to participate is labeled "a chicken").

In addition, individual group members may propose activities simply to generate conversation, in jest, or as a means of impressing their peers. Nevertheless, within the group setting, activities can escalate from discussion to execution without any of the members actually desiring to participate in the activity in question. This results from the fact that in some cases each member believes that the others actually want to carry on the activity, and consequently none of the members indicate their unwillingness to participate for fear of being ostracized.

Also, in some instances, groups get so involved in the discussion and planning of a hypothetical activity that a decision is made to execute it without any thought of its potential consequences. It is not until after the act has been executed that group members become aware of its seriousness and the actual or potential consequences to themselves or others. But obviously there are also many instances in which a group plans and executes a rape with full knowledge of its potential consequences.

Patterns of Group Rape. The following scenarios provided by MacDonald (1971) illustrate typical patterns of group rape:

> *[A group of youths] call at a girl's home. One member of the group claims to know a brother or cousin of the girl. Once inside the home, they take advantage of the absence of the parents and other family members to rape the girl. Sometimes the girl goes to the home of a friend. There she finds a group of boys who tell her that her girlfriend is out but is expected back shortly. She is encouraged to come in and wait for her friend. One or more of the boys who are high on marijuana or alcohol starts making suggestive remarks. The girl becomes uncomfortable and starts to leave, but is taken to a bedroom and raped.*

Young girls who go to a drinking party in a home after school soon find, as they probably anticipated, that petting is a feature of the party. One girl will be taken around the house by one of the boys. A petting session in a bedroom ends up in a group rape while the party continues in the livingroom.

The young woman at a drinking party who consumes too much alcohol and remains long after the other girls have left may find that the men take advantage of the situation . . . .

Another pattern of group rape involves women who have been drinking in a tavern. The victim may be seized by several men as she leaves the tavern and driven away in their car. Sometimes two or three women who are together will be offered a ride home. One woman, two if there are three women, will be driven to her home but the last woman in the car will be driven to a suitable location and raped by all the men . . . .

Occasionally a girl will be seized as she is walking home alone in the evening and forced into a car. She is warned not to cry out under threat of physical violence and is driven to a deserted spot where she is raped by three or four of the men in the car . . . .

Girls with reputations for promiscuity are likely victims of group rape . . . . A 20 year old girl who was known to have had sexual relations with many men was abducted by a group of school boys and raped. (pp. 161–163)*

Characteristics of Group Rape. Amir (1971) noted that more whites than blacks participated in pair rapes, whereas more blacks than whites were found to be involved in group rapes. Also the older the offender the less likely he is to participate in group rape. On the other hand, all the offenders aged 10 to 14 were found to have participated in group rape or pair rape, with the highest proportions of pair or group rapes perpetrated by offenders between the ages of 14 and 19. Furthermore, while group and pair rapes were found to be characterized by a greater use of non-brutal beatings, extreme violence and brutality were more characteristic of single rape events. This is true because a single offender must subdue the victim and does not have the help of others. Finally, Amir found that in many instances pair rapes resembled single rapes more than group rapes, and he therefore suggests that it may be better to see pair rapes as a form of criminal "partnership" rather than as a type of group event.

---

*From MacDonald, J. M.: *Rape Offenders and Their Victims,* 1971. Courtesy of Charles C Thomas, Publisher, Springfield, Illinois.

Victim-Precipitated Rape

A popular misconception about rape is that the victims are in some way responsible for their victimization either consciously or by default. In other words, it has been suggested that the victim by her provocative behavior, dress, talk, or other behavior gives the offender the impression that she is available for a sexual encounter. In order to study this question, Amir (1971) developed the following definition of victim-precipitated rape:

> The term *"victim precipitation"* describes those rape situations in which the victim actually, or so it was deemed, agrees to sexual relations but retracted before the actual act or did not react strongly enough when the suggestion was made by the offender(s). The term applies also to cases in risky situations marred with sexuality, especially when she uses what could be interpreted as indecency in language and gestures, or constitutes what could be taken as an invitation to sexual relations. (p. 266)*

Amir found that 19 per cent of the 646 rapes in the Philadelphia study were victim precipitated. A study of 17 cities conducted by the National Commission on the Causes and Prevention of Violence (1970) found that only 4.4 per cent of the rapes were victim precipitated. Amir indicated that there were several significant factors associated with the victim-precipitated rapes in Philadelphia including: the consumption of alcohol in the rape situation, particularly by the victim and at a bar, picnic or party; and the victim being in a "primary relationship" with the offender but not related to him.

Types of Offenders

Based on clinical research, Cohen, Seghorn, and Calmas (1969) and Cohen, Garafalo, Boucher, and Seghorn (1971) have identified four subgroups of rapists. Their typology is based on the role played by sexual and aggressive components in motivating the act of rape.

Rape — Aggressive Aim. Among offenders in this group, the sexual assault is primarily an aggressive, destructive act with sexual feelings minimal or absent.

> The sexual behavior is used to physically harm, to degrade, or to defile the victim in service of this aggressive intent. The acts are experienced by the offender as a result of an "uncontrollable

---

*From Amir, M.: *Patterns in Forcible Rape*. Chicago, The University of Chicago Press, 1971, © 1971 by The University of Chicago Press.

impulse" and almost always follow some precipitating, disagreeable event involving a woman, girl friend, mother, or friend. The victim is brutally assaulted, and those parts of the woman's body which are usually sexually exciting frequently become the foci for the offender's violence. (Cohen et al., 1969; p. 250)

The role played by aggression is well illustrated in the following case:

> *... [Philip] was driving along a city road when he saw a girl whom he did not know. He stopped his car beside her, stepped out and asked where she was going. He didn't hear her answer and asked her again in an angry manner. She turned to walk away and Philip felt that she was trying to make a fool of him. He believed that she had first shown an interest in him and when he exposed his own interest in her, she was rejecting it. He punched her in the stomach, grabbed her under the chin, pulled her into his car, and drove away to a secluded area. After he had parked the car, he told the girl to get into the back seat. When she refused, he climbed into the back, dragged her over the seat beside him. He undressed her and violently penetrated her. He states that he then withdrew without having an orgasm and let her out of the car, threatening to kill her if she made mention of the attack. When he was arrested thereafter, he immediately admitted his guilt.* (Cohen et al., 1971, pp. 315–316)

Rape — Sexual Aim. In this group, the intent of the act is sexual, and aggression is minimal and devoid of any characteristics of brutality. Offenders in this group are constantly in a state of intense sexual excitement and frequently have an orgasm simply in pursuing a victim or upon making some physical contact. Several additional features characterize the offenses perpetrated by this group:

> *The offense almost always takes place out of doors in isolated places such as darkened streets, a park, a wooded area. Most frequently, the offender embraces the woman from behind touching her breasts or genitals, holding on to her with some force but not to any excessive degree. If the victim should struggle and thus require more physical effort in order to be held, the offender will release her and flee .... Thus, most of the offenders are charged with assault with intent to commit rape. At other times, the victim is so frightened that she passively submits and the rape takes place without any additional force. When apprehended, it is discovered that he has carried out such acts many times.* (Cohen et al., 1971, pp. 317–318)

These features are well illustrated by the case of Ted.

> *He would approach a woman from behind and place one hand on her breasts and the other between her legs. If the neighborhood was sufficiently secluded, he would try to force her to the ground. If the surroundings were more public, he would simply caress and fondle her and flee. The patient admits to over a hundred such assaults. There were two exceptions to the behavior described above. In one instance, he threw the woman to the ground in a deserted park and choked her until she lost consciousness. When he became aware of what he had done, he fled leaving her on the ground. On another occasion in the same park, he held a knife to a woman and in her continued struggle a superficial wound was made. He became frightened and again fled.*
> (Cohen et al., 1971, p. 320)

Rape — Sex-Aggression-Diffusion. In this pattern, the offender's behavior is motivated by both sexual and aggressive elements. In fact, it appears that offenders in this group do not have the ability to become sexually excited without some degree of violence being present. This pattern is further characterized by the presence of a strong sadistic component, the degree of which is quite variable, "with the extreme position seen in lust murders where excessive brutality and mutilation occur before, during, and even after the murder" (Cohen et al., 1971, p. 322). However, this extreme behavior is relatively rare, because offenders typically use violence only as a means of arousal and thus there is no need for further violence after intercourse has been completed. The following is typical of the type of offense committed by such individuals:

> *[Frank] spent the evening dancing with the girl and then offered to drive her and her two girl friends home. He drove one girl to her house but when he reached the home of the second girl, he learned that both she and the girl that he had spent the evening with planned to leave together. He sped away, drove outside of town to a small cemetery, parked the car and told the girls that he wanted to have intercourse with them. The two girls jumped from the car but Frank was able to catch each of them and knock them to the ground. One girl fell on her stomach whereupon he leaped astride her, pressing her face into the earth until she lost consciousness. Leaving her lying there for the moment, he turned to the other girl, throttled her until she, too, was in a semi-conscious state. He then carried them back into the car, forced them to undress, lighting up the interior of the car so that he might watch. He then forced each girl to fellate him under*

physical force and verbal threats that they would be killed.
Following this he had intercourse with one of the girls. He sat
for a while with the two girls, took some money from one, and
then drove them home . . . . (Cohen et al., 1971, p. 374)

Rape — Impulsive Type. In this final group, the act of rape is
attributable to neither sexual nor aggressive desires; it represents
simply another manifestation of the predatory nature of such
offenders. Rape for these offenders is an extension of their criminal activity with the only difference being that in this case they
are forcibly imposing their will on a woman, whereas in the case
of other offenses they are simply depriving victims of their property. The transition is not difficult for this group since they view
women solely as sexual objects whose role in life is to provide
sexual pleasure (Gebhard, et al., 1965). Further, rape is frequently
carried out by these offenders in conjunction with some other antisocial act, such as robbery or theft. In these cases, the victim's
unfortunate presence on the scene provides the motivation for the
rape, which is carried out with relatively little sexual or aggressive
feelings. For example, an offender may enter an apartment at night
with the intent of simply depriving the occupant of property.
However, upon entry he finds the female occupant asleep in bed
and at this point he may decide to both rape her and take her
property. Few of these offenders experience guilt with regard to
this behavior since they belong to a subculture that condones both
the deprivation of property and forced sexual relations.

Voyeurism

Voyeurism is a condition in which sexual gratification is
obtained by observing a nude woman or some part of the nude
female body without consent of the female involved. More commonly, the voyeur is called "a peeping Tom," a term which derives
from the name of the tailor in Coventry who peeped at Lady
Godiva when she took a "bare backed" (this does not refer to the
absence of a saddle) ride through the town market place. As
Mathis (1972) suggests, "Tom was condemned for looking but no
one criticized Lady Godiva for tempting Tom beyond his limits
of resistance by her exhibitionism. This type of semi-rational
thinking is still with us and the law arrests Tom and winks at the
Lady Godivas" (p. 41).

In discussing this phenomenon, it is necessary to distinguish
between the sexual pleasure and stimulation that a normal man

derives from viewing an attractive female body and true voyeurism. While both may obtain pleasure from looking at women, for the voyeur the act of looking is the primary method of sexual gratification and not just a pleasant experience or a prelude to intercourse. Thus, voyeurs may be stimulated to orgasm simply by looking at a nude woman; however, more commonly they masturbate while "peeping" or as soon thereafter as possible. In addition, in contrast to the normal male, the voyeur does not merely avail himself of unexpected opportunities to view nude women but actively seeks out such opportunities in spite of the attendant risks. For example, a peeper may wait hours while a woman finishes some minor tasks in hopes of getting a glimpse of her undressing prior to retiring for the night. Further, as a rule, peepers do their looking from the outside, typically through a bathroom or bedroom window with incompletely drawn blinds or curtains rather than invading a residence to gratify their voyeuristic impulses (Gebhard et al., 1965; Mathis, 1972).

With regard to choice of victim, peepers often have specific criteria. Most prefer at least moderately attractive women, preferably engaged in some sort of sexual activity; some, however, have specific body parts or scenes in mind, e.g., breasts, buttocks, fellatio, masturbation, or love-making between lesbians. The peeper is very optimistic about each escapade and perseveres, hoping that something more provocative will be just around the next corner.

According to Gebhard et al. (1965), peepers are not given to serious antisocial behavior but are very prone to minor criminality. Their criminal record generally stems from arrests for habitual peeping and sometimes exhibitionism. However, unlike true exhibitionists, discussed in the next section, the majority of peepers try to avoid detection. Those few voyeurs who do try to attract attention to themselves generally wish to frighten or humiliate the victim or in some instances elicit some reciprocal interest, characteristics usually associated with the exhibitionist. Gebhard et al. further suggest that "peepers who enter homes or other buildings in order to peep and peepers who deliberately attract the female's attention (tapping on windows, leaving notes, etc.) are more likely to become rapists than are the others" (p. 378).

This discussion has centered on the male voyeur because voyeurism among females is extremely rare. Until recently, it was generally assumed in our society that women rarely derive any pleasure from looking at the nude male body. The editor and publisher of *Cosmopolitan* magazine were among the first to raise questions about this widely held belief. Akers (1973) observes that social and cultural inhibitions may prevent women from reporting arousal to sexually provocative stimuli. However, should the trend toward sexual equality continue, it is quite possible that we may encounter more cases of female voyeurism in the not too distant future.

Exhibitionism

Exhibitionism (indecent exposure) is the inappropriate exposure of male genitalia to females for the purpose of sexual gratification. Like voyeurism, exhibitionism is a compulsive condition; i.e., the individual is compelled to exhibit himself in order to relieve unbearable anxiety. According to Mathis (1972), the exhibitionist is driven by an inner force which is simply beyond his control: "Once he has accomplished the act of exhibiting and has received some show of emotion from the female, there is a gratifying sense of relief and relaxation which Rousseau referred to as 'foolish pleasure'" (p. 37). Following completion of the act, the exhibitionist often feels a sense of guilt and shame, combined with a fear of the possibility of apprehension and its attendant publicity that may result in job loss and disgrace. Given the compulsiveness of this offense and the offender's need for public exposure, it is not surprising that Gebhard et al. (1965) found that, compared with other sex offenders, exhibitionists have the greatest number of convictions for sex offenses (72 per cent) and for specific sex offenses, i.e., exhibition offenses for exhibitionists, rape for rapists.

Varieties of Exhibitionists

Coleman (1972) has divided exhibitionists into two categories based on the factors associated with the causes of this behavior.

Exhibitionism Associated with Personal Immaturity. Coleman cites research by Witzig which showed that 60 per cent of the cases of exhibitionism referred by the courts for treatment fell within this category. He attributes exhibitionism in this group to inadequate information, feelings of shyness and inferiority in approaching the opposite sex, and puritanical attitudes toward masturbation. Closely associated with the exhibitionist's personal immaturity appears to be a second factor: doubts and fears about masculinity, combined with a strong need to demonstrate masculinity and potency. To illustrate the operation of this factor,

Coleman (1972) makes reference to a case cited by Apfelberg, Sugar, and Pfeiffer of an exhibitionist who:

> . . . *achieved sexual satisfaction only when he accompanied the exposure of his genitals with a question to the victim as to whether she had ever seen such a large penis. On one occasion, the woman instead of evidencing shock and embarrassment, scornfully assured him that she had. On this occasion, the defendant stated, he received no sexual gratification.* (p. 464)

Finally, exhibitionism rarely occurs in a setting which is conducive to sexual relations. In short, the exhibitionist wishes to elicit some reaction from the victims confirming his masculinity without having to demonstrate that he can perform sexual intercourse adequately.

Interpersonal Stress and Acting Out. Another factor that appears to precipitate exhibitionism is stress. According to Coleman (1972):

> *Often the married exhibitionist appears to be reacting to some conflict or stress situation in his marriage, and his behavior is in the nature of a regression to adolescent masturbatory activity. In some instances, an exhibitionist may state that exhibiting himself during masturbation is more exciting and tension reducing than utilizing pictures of nude women.* (p. 64)

Also included in this group is the exhibitionist who exhibits himself following a period of intense conflict over some problem — often involving authority figures — with which he feels inadequate to cope.

> *For example, a marine who wanted to make a career of the service was having an experience with a superior that made it impossible for him to reenlist. He could not admit to himself that he could be hostile to either the corps or the superior. For the first time in his life time, he exposed himself to a girl on the beach. Arrested, he was merely reprimanded and returned to the scene of conflict. A short time later he displayed his genitals to a girl on a parking lot. This time he was placed on probation with the stipulation that he seek treatment, and his enlistment was allowed to terminate in natural sequence. He never repeated the act, he was happily married and seemed to be acting out in this instance a vulgar expression of contempt.* (Witzig; cited in Coleman, 1972), p. 464)

Association with Other Psychopathology. Exhibitionism may also be associated with a variety of other types of mental disorders. First, youths, both male and female, who are mentally retarded may exhibit themselves because they are not aware of the fact that their behavior is socially unacceptable. Second, some exhibitionists are older men who as a result of brain deterioration related to aging lose touch with reality and become less bound by ethical standards. Finally, exhibitionism is also associated with psychopathic personality disorders and manic or schizophrenic reactions.

The Nature of the Act

The great majority of exposures occur in public and semi-public places — the street, in parks, within buildings and from parked vehicles. The act itself is quite variable, ranging from the exposure of the flaccid penis without sexual satisfaction to exposure of the erect penis, often accompanied by masturbation and intense sexual satisfaction. The nature of the act can differ with the same individual, according to circumstances and the intensity of the sexual urge. However, there is really very little eroticism involved in exhibitionism. The exhibitionist does not expose himself as a prelude to sex or as an invitation to intercourse (Mathis, 1972); rather, the exhibitionist seems more intent on evoking fear or shock. In many cases, the offender is attempting to get his victim to acknowledge the fact of his masculinity by eliciting a reaction of shock, fear, or embarrassment. It is also generally agreed that the exhibitionist does not usually seek further contact with his victim and may in fact even fear it. With regard to choice of victim, the exhibitionist usually chooses a stranger and in some instances may choose multiple victims as in the case with exposures on playgrounds, crowded streets, and in public parks. It has also been noticed that some exhibitionists prefer particular types of victims. Thus, some choose mature females, still others choose adolescents, and some even choose young children (Mathis, 1972). Children constitute between 20 and 50 per cent of the total number of victims of exposure. Mohr, Turner, and Jerry (1964) noted, however, that the proportion of child victims may be higher among cases in which the offender is charged, because exposure to children is regarded more seriously and is more likely to be prosecuted.

Pedophilia

According to Mathis (1972) "pedophilia [child molestation] is a condition in which a child is the preferred sexual object of an adult" (p. 53). The sexual behavior of the pedophiliac includes the exposure of the genitals, manipulation of the child, penetration (partial or complete), and any indecent or immoral practice using the sexual parts or organs of the child so as to bring the offender in contact with the child's body in any directly sexual manner. Brownmiller (1975) summarized a study of child molestors conducted by DeFrancis for the Children's Division of the American Humane Association. DeFrancis used a sample of 250 cases reported to child protection agencies in Brooklyn and the Bronx, over an 18 month period. This core sample represented only one sixth of all cases reported during this period, and it was cautiously estimated that the actual incidence of child molesting was twice that reported. Cases included within this sample were limited to offenders 16 years and older and victims below the age of 16. Furthermore, only cases involving rape, incest, sodomy, and carnal abuse were included in the sample, thus eliminating noncontact cases involving charges of indecent exposure and impairing the morals of a minor. Some of the major findings of this study are as follows:

> The sexually abused child is statistically more prevalent than the physically abused, or battered, child.
>
> The median age of sexually abused children is 11, but infants have not escaped molestation.
>
> Ten girls are molested for every one boy.
>
> Ninety-seven per cent of the offenders are male.
>
> In three quarters of the Brooklyn–Bronx cases, the offender was known to the child or her family. Twenty-seven per cent lived in the child's home (father, stepfather, mother's lover, brother). Another 11 per cent did not live in the home but were related by blood or marriage. A significant number of offenders were local storekeepers, next-door neighbors, landlords, janitors, and youths entrusted to babysit. Only 25 per cent of the offenders were reported to be total strangers.
>
> In more than 40 per cent of the cases, the sexual abuse was not a single, isolated event but occurred over a period of time ranging from weeks to, in one case, seven years.
>
> Force or threat of force was used against 60 per cent of the children. Another 15 per cent were enticed by money or gifts. For the remaining one quarter, "the lure was more subtle and was based on the child's natural loyalty and affection for a relative or near relative."
>
> Two thirds of all sexually abused children had suffered some form of identifiable emotional disturbance and 14 per cent had become severely disturbed. The most common reaction among children was the taking on of deep feelings of guilt (articulated by victims as "the trouble" that they "had caused the family"),

*shame and loss of esteem. "To shatter the ego even further,"
the report noted, "some parents projected blame on the children
and used every opportunity to upbraid or remind the child of
the consequences of bad behavior."*

*The age of reported offenders ranged from 17 to 68, with a
median age of 31. More than 30 per cent were under the age of
24 and almost 60 per cent were under the age of 34.* (Brownmiller, 1975, pp. 278–279)*

Several of the factors discussed merit further attention. First,
data concerning pedophilia reveal that most pedophiliacs fall
within three distinct age groups: adolescent group (puberty), mid
to late 30's (middle-age group), and mid to late 50's (aged
or elderly). According to Mohr, Turner, and Ball (1962), studies
of offenders, especially those who have been institutionalized,
have shown consistently that the middle-age group is the largest.
The adolescent child molestor is frequently passive, immature, and
insecure about his capacity to have normal sexual relations with a
heterosexual partner of his own age group. He is often shy and
uneasy while in the company of adults yet perfectly at ease among
children or young adolescents, particularly those known to him.
Reinhardt (1957) suggests that some pedophiliacs have resorted to
children after failing repeatedly to experience satisfactory sexual
relations with older partners. This, in part, explains the motivating
force behind the attraction to children for the adolescent and
middle-age group. A different set of factors accounts for this behavior in the older offender group. Men in this group usually have
no previous history of pedophilia prior to the onset of old age.
Within this group, pedophilia has been attributed to the loss of
mental and physical powers, including sexual powers, attributable
to the aging process. According to Mathis (1972):

> *[This] may lead him to approach a child in a seductive man-
> ner simply because he unconsciously perceives himself to be the
> same age on an emotional level. He usually becomes friends with
> the child with no thought of overt sexuality and he may be more
> shocked than anyone else when he finds himself so deeply in-
> volved.* (p. 64)

For the majority of pedophiliacs, acts of pedophilia are more or
less incidental occurrences. It is only for a very small group of
offenders that the behavior becomes chronic.

Second, consideration must also be given to the role that children may play in precipitating their own victimization. MacDonald

---

*From *Against Our Will*. Copyright 1975 by Susan Brownmiller. Reprinted by permission of Simon & Schuster, Inc.

(1971) cites a study by Weis of 73 girl victims of adult sex of-fenders that concluded that victims could be divided into two groups: those who took part in initiating and maintaining the relationship (participant victims) and those who did not (accidental victims). Thus, not only are some little girls willing victims, but in some instances they also may actually initiate sexual play with an adult who seems receptive to them. Further, according to Mathis (1972), another characteristic of these little girls is their seductive behavior toward adults. There is evidence that these children are deprived of the care and affection they need; thus, their seductive behavior represents a search for the love, attention, and approval that is missing from their home environment. A man grappling with a predisposition toward pedophilia may find him-self tempted beyond his ability to control his immature impulses. For example, Mathis (1972) relates the case of a 55 year old electrician who had been attracted to young girls all his life and at the time of the act had recently discovered that his wife was ill with an incurable disease. The circumstances of the case are as follows:

> *[The] electrician was called to make some repairs at a sub-urban home. The mother asked if her 6 year old girl would be bothersome if she remained at home while the mother went grocery shopping. The workman assured her that it would present no problem and that he was very fond of little girls.*
>
> *Shortly after the mother left the home, the little girl squatted by the electrician, pulled down her panties and asked if he had something like she had. The mother, who had forgotten her purse, returned just in time to see the man caressing the nude genital region of her daughter.* (p. 62)

This discussion should not be interpreted as a justification for the behavior of the pedophiliac, but it does provide a better under-standing of the dynamics of this problem.

Third, the American Humane Association study suggested that the emotional trauma experienced by children as a result of being victimized can be attributed at least partially to parental reaction. This point is worthy of further attention since, in some cases, youngsters may be harmed more by parental overreaction, inter-rogation by police and lawyers, and medical manipulation (exami-nation) that follow victimization than by the act itself. To begin with, the offense as a rule is limited to petting or fondling, and physical injury to the victim is minimal. However, in many instances, parents, neighbors, and relatives become so excited and hysterical that the child comes to believe that something horrible has happened. The child may be surprised by this reaction, since she may have viewed the act as boring or disgusting or may even have found it amusing or exciting. As Mathis (1972) suggests "the sexual curiosity of a child and her willingness to cooperate should never be underestimated" (p. 61). A pelvic examination of female victims should be avoided unless there is evidence of actual or attempted penetration, since for a young girl a hastily conducted pelvic examination can be quite traumatic. In short, parents can avoid unnecessarily traumatizing children who are victims of pedophilia by handling the incident as an unfortunate contact with a disturbed individual.

Finally, the American Humane Association found that 3 per cent of their cases involved female offenders. This is interesting in light of the fact that female child molestors are rarely if ever detected and reported because this behavior can be masked by the female role which allows overt displays of affection between women and young children. Since little attention is given to the relationships between such female people as babysitters, teachers, neighbors, and aunts and young boys and girls, there is no way of knowing the actual incidence of this phenomenon. However, studies like those of the American Humane Association and clinical data indicate that female pedophilia does exist.

SUMMARY

This chapter was devoted to a discussion of sexual offenses. A number of myths regarding rape were dispelled, and a fourfold typology of rapists was presented, based primarily on the motivational components associated with the act. The distinctive patterns that were identified were (1) rape — aggressive aim; (2) rape — sexual aim; (3) rape — sex-aggression-diffusion; and (4) rape — impulsive type. The compulsive nature of exhibitionism and voyeurism was examined, as well as the distinctive patterns associated with each of these conditions. It was pointed out that these offenders rarely, if ever, assault their victims, since exhibitionists derive their sexual gratification primarily from public exposure of their genitals, and voyeurs derive theirs from simply viewing a nude female body. The chapter concluded with a discussion of pedophilia. It was noted that acts of pedophilia are incidental occurrences for the majority of offenders. Also discussed was the possible role that some children might play in precipitating their own victimization.

REVIEW

Find the answers to the following questions in the text:

1. What are the characteristics of the two broad classes of sex offenses identified by Gebhard and his associates in their study of incarcerated sex offenders?

2. Discuss some of the widely held public beliefs about sex offenders. How accurate are these conceptions of the sex offender?

3. From the data gathered in the Philadelphia, New York, and Atlanta rape studies, develop a profile for the typical forcible rapist and his victim.

4. How much support is there for the contention that rape is a spontaneous (unplanned) crime? What importance does alcohol have as a precipitating agent?

5. What are some of the major patterns of multiple rape? Who is most likely to be involved in multiple rape as a victim? As an offender?

6. Who was "peeping Tom"? Why has his name become a synonym for voyeur?

7. Sketch the characteristics of the two types of exhibitionists identified by Coleman.

8. Cite the distinct age groups associated with pedophilia and describe the characteristics of the members of each.

TERMS TO IDENTIFY AND REMEMBER

pair rape	exhibitionism	multiple rape
forcible rape	indecent exposure	pedophilia
voyeurism	statutory rape	victim-precipitated rape

REFERENCES

Abrahamsen, D.: *The Psychology of Crime.* New York, Columbia University Press, 1960.

Akers, R.: *Deviant Behavior: A Social Learning Approach.* Belmont, California, Wadsworth Publishing Co., 1973.

Amir, M.: Forcible rape. Federal Probation *31:*51–58, 1967.

Amir, M.: *Patterns in Forcible Rape.* Chicago, University of Chicago Press, 1971.

Atlanta Regional Commission: The Master Plan Update for the Atlanta Impact Program. *In* Georgia Commission on the Status of Women: *Rape and the Treatment of Rape Victims in Georgia.* Atlanta, Georgia, undated report.

Brownmiller, S.: *Against Our Will: Men, Women, and Rape.* New York, Simon & Schuster, Inc., 1975.

Chappel, D., and Singer, S.: *Rape in New York City: A Study of Material in the Police Files and Its Meaning.* Albany, State University of New York, 1973.

Cohen, M., Seghorn, T., and Calmas, M.: Sociometric study of the sex offender. Journal of Abnormal Psychology 74: 249–255, 1969.

Cohen, M., Garafalo, M.A., Boucher, R., and Seghorn, T.: The psychology of rapists. Seminars in Psychiatry 3: 307–327, 1972.

Coleman, J. C.: Abnormal Psychology and Modern Life. Glenview, Illinois, Scott, Foresman and Co., 1972.

Ellis, A., and Abarbanel, A.: The Encyclopedia of Sexual Behavior. New York, Hawthorne Books, Inc., 1967.

Federal Bureau of Investigation: Uniform Crime Reports: 1975. Washington, D.C., U.S. Government Printing Office, 1976.

Gebhard, P. H., Gagnon, J. H., Pomeroy, W. B., and Christenson, C. V.: Sex Offenders. New York, Harper & Row, Publishers, 1965.

Georgia Commission on the Status of Women: Rape and the Treatment of Rape Victims in Georgia. Atlanta, Georgia, undated report.

Guttmacher, M. S.: The Mind of the Murderer. New York, Farrar, Straus and Cudahy, 1960.

Karpman, B.: The Sexual Offender and His Offenses. New York, Julian Press, Inc., 1962.

MacDonald, J. M.: Rape Offenders and Their Victims. Springfield, Illinois, Charles C Thomas, Publishers, 1971.

Mathis, J. L.: Clear Thinking About Sexual Deviations. Chicago, Nelson-Hall Co., 1972.

Mohr, J., Turner, E. R., and Ball, R. B.: Exhibitionism and pedophilia. Corrective Psychiatric Journal of Social Therapy 8: 172–186, 1962.

Mohr, J., Turner, E. R., and Jerry, M.: Pedophilia and Exhibitionism. Toronto, University of Toronto Press, 1964.

National Commission on the Causes and Prevention of Violence: Final Report, New York, Praeger Publishers, Inc., 1970.

Reinhardt, J. M.: Sex Perversions and Sex Crimes. Springfield, Illinois, Charles C Thomas, Publisher, 1957.

5 CONVENTIONAL PROPERTY OFFENSES

Property offenses, which include burglary, larceny, auto theft, and fraud, constitute the major portion of our conventional crime problem. For example, in 1974, property crimes made up 90 per cent of the volume of the crime index.* Property offenders vary in the extent to which they depend upon crime for their livelihood; for some offenders crime represents their exclusive means of support, while for others crime is only a means of supplementing their income. Offenders differ in the skills, planning, and techniques they employ in their criminal activity. Moreover, offenders vary in their attachment to norms that view unlawful deprivation of property as criminal behavior. However, despite these differences, most property offenders can be classified into one of three groups: ordinary career criminals, occasional criminals, and professional criminals.

ORDINARY CAREER CRIMINALS

Offenders in this group commit the majority of the property offenses and compose the major part of the prison population in the United States. Clinard and Quinney (1973) have identified several characteristics of this group. First, these offenders typically either augment their income through property offenses or make their entire living through criminal activity that includes primarily

---

*As indicated in Chapter 2, the offenses included in the Crime Index are: murder, forcible rape, robbery, aggravated assault, burglary, larceny-theft, and motor vehicle theft.

the offenses of larceny, burglary and robbery.* Second, crime represents a major part of the life activities of the career offender. These offenders come to develop a conception of themselves as criminals. Furthermore, they tend to progress from petty to more serious offenses, and during this progression, there is a continual acquisition of both skills and rationalizations to justify their criminal behavior. Although these offenders tend to specialize in either a few types of property crimes or one specific kind of crime, they never become as sophisticated and skillful as the professional criminal.

Career Patterns

Clinard and Quinney (1973) indicate that most conventional offenders begin their careers as juvenile delinquents. Data from the *Uniform Crime Reports (1976)* support their contention: in 1975, persons under 18 accounted for approximately one half of the arrests for burglary, larceny, and auto theft and one third of the arrests for robbery.

The early life histories of these offenders tend to show a pattern of truancy, destruction of property, street fighting, and delinquent gang membership. As a rule, the ordinary career criminal begins his career in a gang with juveniles of similar backgrounds. The delinquent activities of these groups do not represent isolated acts but often are part of the way of life of the slum community in which these youngsters reside. Youth in delinquent gangs begin engaging in delinquent behavior at an early age; some are as young as 6 or 7, and most commit their first delinquent act by the age of 13 (Robin, 1967). There is evidence that following the onset of delinquency, these youths progress to more frequent and serious offenses, and many of them readily proceed from juvenile offenses to adult criminal behavior that is even more frequent, serious, and sophisticated (Clinard and Quinney, 1973). For example, Robin (1967) found that 41 per cent of the gang members he studied were adults who had acquired criminal records. His research further indicates that a large proportion of the gang members who were persistent and dangerous offenders as juveniles become even more serious adult offenders. However, it appears that the adult criminal careers of these offenders are shortlived; a

---

*Robbery is included here because, although it is classified as a violent offense, its primary objective is money or property. Also, offenders in this category commit occasional burglaries.

large number discontinue their criminal activity by age 18, with most of the remainder terminating their careers by their mid 20's and early 30's. This is illustrated by the arrest data presented in Table 5–1, which shows that in 1975, 53.9 per cent of the Crime Index property offenses were committed by offenders 18 and under and an additional 35.6 per cent were committed by offenders in the 19 to 34 age group.

TABLE 5–1. PER CENT OF ARRESTS OF PERSONS FOR PROPERTY INDEX OFFENSES* BY AGE FOR 1975†

AGE GROUP	PER CENT OF ARRESTS
10 and under	2.2
11–12	4.9
13–14	12.5
15	9.3
16	10.1
17	9.0
18	7.9
19	5.9
20	4.7
21	3.9
22	3.3
23	2.8
24	2.5
25–29	8.3
30–34	4.2
35–39	2.5
40–44	1.8
45–49	1.4
50–54	1.0
55–59	.7
60–64	.5
65 and over	.6
Not known	.1

*Property index offenses are: burglary, larceny-theft, and motor vehicle theft.
†Data from Federal Bureau of Investigation: *Uniform Crime Reports: 1975*, Washington, D. C., U. S. Government Printing Office, 1976, pp. 188–189.

It is extremely difficult to say exactly why offenders who pursue a career of crime decide to discontinue their criminal activity. It is likely that when many juveniles reach the age of 18 they stop committing offenses because they recognize that they no longer will be sent to training school but instead will be incarcerated in a state prison. Some may discontinue their activity following their first commitment to a state prison. In the case of the former group, the criminal activity may not be lucrative enough to risk a state prison sentence, while in the case of the latter group, it may not justify subsequent commitments to prison. Marriage and family responsibilities also have been suggested as factors contributing to the termination of criminal careers, because for many this results in a change of life style. Whereas in the past the young male may have spent a good deal of his time on the street corner or in the local pool hall with his delinquent and criminal associates, this time is now spent with his wife, family, and married friends. In addition, following marriage, many former gang members decide to obtain legitimate employment, which further removes them from their delinquent and criminal friends. Still others join the armed service and upon return to civilian life recognize the futility of pursuing a criminal career. In short, delinquent and criminal activities become less attractive as a young male matures, gets married, obtains a job, or joins the service. Werthman (1967) has described the process by which gang boys disengage themselves from delinquent and criminal activities:

> Once a gang boy gets beyond the age of 18 . . . the situation changes rather dramatically. Whether he likes it or not, he now has a choice to make about what identity system to enter. He could get married, get a job, and assume the status of a full fledged "adult"; he could decide to postpone his decision in legitimate ways such as joining the Army and going to school at night; or he could decide to remain a few more years as an elder statesman on the streets in which case he will continue to make use of the identity materials available to youth.
>
> The decision he makes at this point in his career will depend on his situation. If he managed to graduate from high school, he may well decide to go on to college; if he was expelled from high school, he may feel either bitter or reluctant about going back to night school to get the high school degree. He knows that he has been administratively reborn in the eyes of the law, and thus the risks he takes by staying in the streets increase considerably since he now may be processed by the courts as an adult. On the other hand, if his status in the gang world was still high, he may not want to trade it right away for a low paying blue collar job; and he knows that he will be rejected by the Army if he has a jail record of any kind.
>
> In short, it is at this point in his career that the "opportunities" available to him will affect his behavior, his attitudes, and the decisions he makes about his life. If there are no legitimate options open to him, options that at best would not make him suffer a sudden decrease in status and at worst would allow him not to face his ultimately dismal status-fate as an adult, then he may well decide to stay in the streets, despite the great consequences involved in taking risks. He may adopt a "hustle," and

> *he may also adopt a full blown ideology with it. Since he now views the conventional world as a place he is expected to enter he tends to develop a "position" on it. Jobs become "slaves"; going to school becomes "serving time"; and in some cases the assumptions about marriage and getting a conventional job are replaced by fantasies about the quick and big "score."*
>
> *. . . After a few years of this existence, these boys are really at the end of their "delinquent" careers. Some get jobs, some go to jail, some get killed, and some simply fade into an older underground of poolrooms and petty thefts. Most cannot avoid ending up with conventional jobs, however, largely because the "illegitimate opportunities" available simply are not that good.* (p. 170)

Those offenders who continue their careers beyond age 30 tend to spend less and less time out on the streets and more and more time in prison, because with each subsequent conviction they draw longer sentences and parole boards become less willing to grant early parole. A more detailed discussion of the major offenses committed by this group will be presented following the section "The Professional Offender."

OCCASIONAL PROPERTY OFFENDERS

In contrast to the conventional property offender, the occasional offender generally has a criminal record that consists of a single or a few property offenses, such as illegal auto joyriding, naive check forgery, shoplifting, employee theft, and vandalism (Clinard, 1974). Crime is a minor part of the life style of this group. The incidental nature of their criminal activity precludes the possibility that it is a major means of support for these offenders. The offenses committed by this group show little sophistication and skill. Further, their criminal activity is usually fortuitous in nature and is generally done alone, with little if any prior criminal contacts. In other words, these offenders are not, as a rule, part of a juvenile or adult group that engages in and provides support for criminal activities (Clinard and Quinney, 1973).

The occasional offender does not conceive of himself as a criminal because, as a rule, he is able to develop rationalizations for his offenses that enable him to view the offenses as noncriminal acts. For example, an alcoholic in a bar who reaches a high point in his drinking may forge a check in order to obtain additional funds to continue drinking. Likewise, a man away from home on a drinking spree with several others may forge a check if midway through the spree he runs out of money and feels pressure to continue the drinking bout (Lemert, 1967). In both these cases, the individual involved can attribute his criminal act to the fact that he was too drunk to appreciate the nature and consequences of his behavior. In this way, he can rationalize his criminal behavior and still view himself as a noncriminal.

While the occasional offender commits a variety of offenses, vandalism and joyriding have been identified as offenses committed almost exclusively by this group (Clinard, 1974). Vandalism involves the malicious destruction of property, with no utilitarian purpose or objective. Murphy (as cited by Clinard, 1974) comments on the kinds of actions that may occur in vandalism:

> Studies of the complaints made by citizens and public officials reveal that hardly any property is safe from this form of aggression. Schools are often the object of attack by vandals. Windows are broken; books, desks, typewriters, supplies, and other equipment [is] stolen or destroyed. Public property of all types appears to offer peculiar allurement to children bent on destruction. Parks, playgrounds, highway signs, and markers are frequently defaced or destroyed. Trees, shrubs, flowers, benches, and other equipment suffer in like manner. Autoists are constantly reporting the slashing or releasing of air from tires, broken windows, stolen accessories. Golf clubs complain that benches, markers, flags, even expensive and difficult to replace putting greens are defaced, broken, or uprooted. Libraries report the theft and destruction of books and other equipment. Railroads complain and demand protection from the destruction of freight car seals, theft of property, willful or deliberate throwing of stones at passenger car windows, tampering with rails and switches. Vacant houses are always a particular delight of children seeking outlets for destructive instincts; windows are broken, plumbing and hardware stolen, destroyed, or rendered unusable. Gasoline operators report pumps and other service equipment stolen, broken, or destroyed. Theatre managers, frequently in the "better" neighborhoods, complain of the slashing of seats, willful damage of toilet facilities, even the burning of rugs, carpets, etc. (p. 307)

Vandalism is generally committed by juveniles who do not view themselves or their behavior as criminal. Clinard (1974) indicates that, as a rule, these juveniles regard their acts as "pranks." He further suggests that since nothing is stolen during these acts, this reinforces the vandal's image of himself as a prankster rather than a delinquent. The fact that the vandal derives no tangible reward from this activity appears to indicate that vandalism serves no utilitarian purposes for these youngsters. However, while it provides no material rewards, it does give these youngsters fun and excitement and a means of protesting their low status in society. In addition, participation in these acts provides these youths with status and acceptance in their peer group (Clinard, 1974). Direct involvement also enables the individual to avoid becoming a marginal member of the group:

> *One of the kids that I ran around with and I were walking around one night when we came to the motor company. He just picked up a rock and threw it. He didn't tell me he was going to do it. Those were $150 windows, something like that. He picked up a nice, big, juicy rock. He came back and said, "Now it's your chance." Of course, the guys that I ran around with, they call you "chicken." One guy dares another — calls him "chicken" — some guys can't take that. I took it as long as I could until I got into it. They said if you want to belong to our club, you got to break a window. We broke about eight windows that night. Usually, it is started by someone calling you "chicken." If you get into a gang, you gotta break a window if you want to get in our club. So, we stopped, found some rocks, and threw them. Happened in a minute and sped off. We thought it was kinda funny.*
> (Wade, 1967, p. 102)

Wade views vandalism as spontaneous behavior that is an outgrowth of interaction among group members. He identifies the five stages that tend to characterize this behavior: (1) waiting for something to turn up; (2) removal of the uncertainty by an exploratory gesture involving a suggestion for action or an initial act of vandalism by one of the group members; (3) mutual conversion of each group member to the proposed activity; (4) joint elaboration of the act, i.e., once begun the destructive behavior escalates from minor to major property damage; (5) aftermath and retrospect — review of the behavior, followed by a combination of feelings including guilt and shame, awareness of the senselessness of the destruction, rebellion, and malicious delight.

Like vandalism, joyriding is a crime of occasional offenders; it is usually committed by teenagers on a sporadic basis. These juveniles generally take cars in which the owners have left keys, cars whose keys they have access to, or those they can start by jumping the ignition with a hot wire. Typically, the cars are "borrowed," driven around town, and abandoned when the gas tank is empty. These youngsters do not, like the career auto thief, select a special type of car, procure a "fence" for the sale of the car or its parts, or strip the car for their own use.

Social reaction to these offenders is often not severe because the offenses they commit are generally not too serious and they usually have no previous records or at most minor ones. As a result, the charges against these offenders are often dismissed, and those who are convicted are typically placed on probation or given a suspended sentence (Clinard and Quinney, 1973).

PROFESSIONAL OFFENDERS

The term "professional criminal" is applied to a small group of criminals who have the most highly developed criminal careers and the highest status and skill level. As compared with other offenders, they are usually able to avoid detection and therefore rarely spend time in prison. In the past, professional offenders usually limited their activities to nonviolent forms of crime, including pick-pocketing ("cannon"), shoplifting ("the boost"), sneak thieving from stores, banks, and offices ("the heel"), stealing from jewelry stores by substituting inferior jewelry for valuable pieces ("penny weighting"), stealing from hotel rooms ("hotel prowling"), confidence games ("the con"), miscellaneous rackets, such as passing illegal checks, money orders, and other papers ("hanging paper"), and extorting money from others engaged in or about to be engaged in illegal acts ("the shake") (Clinard and Quinney, 1973). However, more recently, several authors (Conklin, 1972; Clinard and Quinney, 1973; Gibbons, 1973; Inciardi, 1975; McCaghy, 1976) have expanded the category of professional offender to include the subgroup identified as the professional "heavy" criminals, who engage in armed robbery, burglary, and auto theft. The professional heavy employs coercion, force, and the threat of violence to deprive the victim of his property, in contrast to the traditional professional thief who acquires the victim's property through fraud, dexterity, distraction, the use of various ingenious devices (trousers with hidden pockets and linings), and other techniques. Although these heavies use weapons to reduce resistance and ensure their getaway, they expect that their skill and smooth operation will enable them to avoid the use of violence. In short, the professional heavy does all he can to avoid killing or injuring his victim in order to avoid a long prison sentence if he is apprehended (which is unlikely).

Recruitment and Training

The use of recruitment and training is one of the factors that distinguish professional from ordinary criminals. The professional offender is accorded high status by other offenders, and a person cannot generally acquire this recognition unless he has had the necessary training, which is only granted to a few selected (recruited) individuals (Clinard and Quinney, 1973).

Professional offenders are drawn from the ranks of the legitimately employed as well as from the underworld. Inciardi (1975) states that professional offenders often recruit waiters and waitresses, cab drivers, bellboys, hotel clerks, and others whose jobs bring them into frequent contact with the offenders. Professionals also tend to be drawn from legitimate occupations that parallel their subsequent criminal pursuits. Thus, "the etcher becomes the counterfeiter; the skilled worker or foreman of a lock company becomes a safecracker; the worker in a stock broker's office gets into 'hot' bonds" (Reckless, 1973, pp. 258–259). Professionals recruited in this manner typically have not been juvenile delinquents and thus do not have records that show a gradual progression from petty delinquencies to more serious crimes. ·On the other hand, there is evidence that some skilled thieves have graduated from petty to professional crime; these offenders generally were reared in slum or working class areas where exposure to the underworld was great (Inciardi, 1975).

Contact with and recruitment of individuals for training as professional offenders may occur in many locations, including places where professional offenders are working, jails and prisons, hangouts such as bars and pool rooms, and hotels and rooming houses. Once selected, an individual receives informal training that involves the learning of skills, techniques, attitudes, and values. Rather than receiving formal verbal instructions, new recruits learn while engaging in criminal activity. During this process, the new recruit assimilates the moral standards of the group, such as the need for "honor among thieves," not cutting in on another's assigned role, and never informing on other offenders, and becomes acquainted with and accepted by other professionals. In addition, during the apprenticeship, the offender learns techniques for stealing and disposing of goods. This is well illustrated by the apprenticeship served by Harry King (1972) in learning to be a "box man" (safecracker):

> I worked for Dick for three years as an apprentice. My job was to steal the dynamite and cook it up; . . . I would also lay on the joints [places they were going to burglarize] that he picked out. It was my job to watch the joint for three or four nights and see when the door shaker [night watchman or policeman] would come by; what time they closed up; what time they opened up in the morning; and just generally watched what they did.

> *I did all the work. He was the brains. It was quite lucrative for me as I got an equal share of the loot. He was very fair and trustworthy as far as dividing the loot. . . . I worked for him for three years before he let me shoot a box. Shooting a box is really touchy because the grease that you use is cooked out of dynamite and it is not the same consistency as nitroglycerine that you buy. Sometime it may be real strong and the next time weak and there's no way to tell until you try it out . . . .*
>
> *I eventually learned how to open boxes by talking to him. Then we would get what we called a cold caper where we really didn't need a point man, because the safe would be out of sight or something like that. He wanted me to learn so he would take me with him in there. I eventually learned all the different types of safes. Some of them you could take a gut shot and open it easy and others you couldn't. You could blow the door all to hell and it still wouldn't take on a gut shot so you have to use a jam shot. He taught me about all the different safes and how they operated. Mostly I learned in conversation.* (pp. 9–11)

Not all professional offenders go through an apprenticeship in order to acquire the skills necessary to effectively commit crime. In some instances, professionals teach themselves, as was the case with two California bank robbers:

> *So we decided to go into crime, and, in order to decide which branch we wanted to go into, since we were both inexperienced criminals at the time, we decided to do as much research as we could and find out which made the most money the fastest and that percentage wise was the safest. I think that you will find that every public library in a city has statistics on the number of crimes committed the previous year, how much money each crime was, and you could figure out, from the amounts stolen, the number of crooks caught, and the number of convictions, what you wanted to know. We spent four days at the public library and we researched, and we came up with armed robbery as the most likely for us.* (Jackson, 1969; cited in Clinard and Quinney, 1973, p. 253)

For other crimes, such as fraudulent check writing, little training is necessary because the skills required are elementary.

The "Fix"

In those rare instances in which the professional is apprehended, he expects to "fix" the case and thus avoid incarceration.

Cases are fixed in a number of different ways: In some instances, the victim is told that his stolen property will be returned if he refuses to push for prosecution or testifies in a manner that would not help to convict the thief. Police may serve as agents of the criminal and convince the victim that a trial is not to his advantage. The victim is told that a trial would cause him a great deal of inconvenience and expense, after which he would still not recover his stolen property. In other cases, police may be bribed not to file a complaint or, if a complaint is filed, to perjure themselves or provide evidence that contradicts that of the victim or witnesses. If the police refuse to cooperate, the prosecutor will be approached and may be induced not to file charges or, if prosecution is inevitable, to present a case that is so weak that the thief will not be convicted. As a last resort, a judge may be bribed to decide the case in favor of the offender or to impose a minor penalty (Sutherland and Cressy, 1974).

Harry King (1972), the "box man" quoted previously, describes how cases are fixed:

> Every town has a criminal attorney who is the fix. The jailor will tell you who the fix in town was or the bull that pinched you because he'd get a commission from the attorney you know, for it. Everybody wants to tell you. Especially a box man. He's usually got money so they all wanna get a cut in on the action. Then they get 10 percent of what the attorney gets as his fee, so you have no trouble findin' out.
>
> The attorney will come to see you and talk to you. He asks you where you are from and usually tries to check to see if you are gonna run or not. After he talks to you a little bit, why you usually know somebody that he knows, another box man around the country or something, and he'll get you out on bail, get the bail cut down, and get you out on it, or take you right that night on bail. Then you go down to see him the next day and ask him what the score is and he'll tell you it will cost you so much to get this cut down to a petty larceny beef and that's all there is to it. It's just that simple. If the town's not hot. (p. 98)

He also provides an illustration of a case that was fixed:

> To give you an illustration of the fix. Recently Danny was released from Montana on parole. He came to Seattle. A short time later he was arrested for possession of narcotics. He had a real sharp lawyer who could do business with the D.A. He went up, got the D.A. straightened around. After getting the case squared around, they went to court. The judge was told that in as much as Danny was going to be violated and taken back to the

*joint, they thought they would save time and money and drop
the charge. The judge did this. Then the attorney for Danny
flew over to Montana. He told the parole board that Danny was
being held and tried for possession of narcotics in Seattle and he
thought they should continue Danny's parole. The parole board
went along with the idea, not knowing that Danny had the
charges dropped here. So, consequently, Danny remains on
parole to this day, no charges against him or anything.* (p. 103)

While there are no official statistics on the incidence and
prevalence of case fixing, there is certainly enough evidence to
indicate that it is not a rare occurrence. In addition to numerous
reports in the mass media, a study conducted by the American
Bar Association indicates that there is widespread case fixing
within the criminal courts that involves bribing judges, inducing
perjured testimony, and "taking care of jurors" (Inciardi, 1975).
In addition, although there are no statistics on the average costs of
a fix, King (1972) indicates that it costs between $4000 and
$5000 to fix the average case.

TYPES OF PROPERTY OFFENSES

Now that we have briefly examined the three basic types of
conventional offenders, attention will be given to the most common offenses committed by these criminal types.

Burglary

Burglary is committed by the ordinary, occasional, and professional offender. Scarr (1973) has identified nine phases of the
burglary cycle (Fig. 5-1), in which the offender:

1. *Has needs that may be satisfied through successful burglary.* Most offenders commit burglary in order to satisfy the need
for money. Addicts and alcoholics commit burglary to obtain
money to support their habit, and some offenders burglarize in
order to maintain a fast and expensive life style. This latter group
may simply supplement their income through burglary or they
may decide to make burglary their primary means of support upon
recognizing that they can make more money in this way than by
working at a regular job.

Burglaries are also committed to satisfy a variety of social
motives. These motives are reflected in the activities of juvenile
gang members, who engage in delinquent acts in part to satisfy

needs for peer group approval, social status, and recognition. Finally, some people commit burglaries for idiosyncratic or eccentric reasons. Included in this group are those for whom burglary: (1) provides an exciting adventure or an opportunity to match wits with the law, (2) provides an opportunity to rebel against the dull routine of a 9 to 5 job, or (3) represents an expression of frustration or a manifestation of neurotic or even psychopathic personality characteristics.

This discussion is not meant to imply that burglary is motivated exclusively by one of the aforementioned needs, since most often it is committed to satisfy more than one. For example, a youth may commit a burglary not only to satisfy a need for group approval and recognition but also to obtain money to buy flashy clothes.

2. *Has or acquires burglary skills.* The number and types of skills employed by those who commit burglaries vary tremendously from throwing a rock through a window to using lock picking tools to defeat a dead bolt lock. A burglar's skill is also measured by the types of goods he steals: The unskilled or amateur burglar generally takes money because he doesn't need to contact a fence to dispose of it and because he can use it immediately to buy items to meet his needs; while the professional, with a greater ability to distinguish between valuable and worthless items and a wider number of contacts with receivers of stolen property, is more likely to have as his objective expensive furs, jewelry, coins, and the like. Indeed, a burglar's level of sophistication is gauged by what is best described as "larceny sense," which includes talents such as "spotting a score" and successfully "taking it off."

3. *Perceives an opportunity to burglarize.* Potential burglars are exposed to a vast number of opportunities to commit burglary in a variety of ways. Youths residing in slum areas frequently observe and are aware of burglaries in their own neighborhoods. Moreover, the victim, often through carelessness or ignorance, provides the potential burglar with clues regarding methods of relatively easy access to his premises. For example, doors are often left unlocked, windows are often left open or unlocked, and doors often have locks that are easily opened with a plastic strip (credit card) or other simple tool. Furthermore, victims alert the burglar to their absence by clues that include several days' accumulation of newspapers, a lone light shining in a living room at three o'clock in the morning, and notices in society columns of forthcoming vacations. Burglars also learn of potential targets from casual comments made by the victim or his associates (friends, servants, beauticians, bartenders) regarding

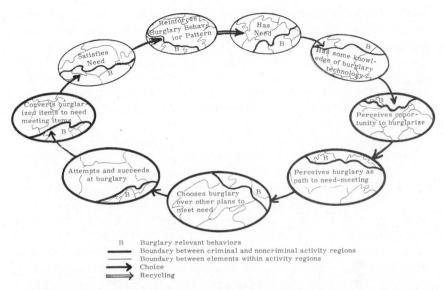

B   Burglary relevant behaviors
     Boundary between criminal and noncriminal activity regions
     Boundary between elements within activity regions
     Choice
     Recycling

Figure 5–1. A specific behavior cycle—burglary. (From Scarr, H. A.: *Patterns of Burglary.* Washington, D. C., U. S. Department of Justice, U. S. Government Printing Office, 1973. Reproduced by permission of the U. S. Department of Justice.)

his general wealth or specific valuables, such as a coin collection, and occasions when the victim will be away from home.

4. *Perceives burglary as a path to need meeting.* Statistics from the Uniform Crime Reports and victimization studies indicate that burglary is considered an acceptable means of satisfying needs by many members of our society. In 1974, an estimated 3,020,700 burglaries were committed in the United States (Federal Bureau of Investigation, 1975b). Offenders who commit burglary justify their behavior in a variety of ways. Some offenders allege that burglary is less harmful than the offenses committed by the respected members of the community. For others burglary represents a means of actively expressing their right to share in the wealth and abundance of our society. Finally, for some who are not career criminals, burglary is viewed as a means of occasionally alleviating financial problems brought on by unusual circumstances; these are categorized as occasional or circumstantial offenders.

5. *Chooses burglary over other paths to meet needs.* Many persons choose burglary over other offenses, as well as over legitimate means of satisfying needs, because it offers the greatest probability of success with the least amount of risk. This is related to the fact that burglary is, for the most part, a passive crime in

that the burglar makes every effort to avoid any contact with the victim. Thus, burglars who break into unoccupied structures minimize the risk of later identification and also increase their chances of being away from the crime scene, and quite possibly of having fenced the stolen goods, before the burglary is discovered. In addition, the burglar knows that even if he is apprehended the penalties for this offense are less severe than those imposed for robbery.

When a person decides to commit burglary he has a variety of options with regard to method and target. Some burglars choose to work during the day, while others prefer to do their stealing at night — like the cat burglar who enters the premises while the victim is there, although he generally tries to avoid direct confrontation. Still others specialize in burglarizing hotels, resorts, or apartments.

6. *Attempts and succeeds at burglary.* In order for the burglary cycle to continue beyond this point, the burglar must successfully complete the offense. The literature on burglary indicates that burglars who are successful continue to commit this crime until they are apprehended. On the other hand, some individuals attempt burglary but are unsuccessful, primarily because they lack basic skills, and these individuals may be deterred from any further attempts. However, in some instances, even the highly skilled burglar will abandon his plan to burglarize a site owing to unforeseen obstacles or signs of danger, such as noise (which is the burglar's main concern). However, once a burglar successfully enters his target he will usually complete the intended theft unless he perceives that someone else is on the premises.

7. *Converts burglarized items to need meeting items.* Following the theft of anything but cash, the burglar must find a means of disposing of the stolen property. Burglars dispose of stolen property in a variety of ways, which range from selling property to friends, neighbors, and strangers on the street to contacting the professional fence, who buys large quantities of goods to supplement his legally acquired merchandise or whose business is based entirely on a stock of stolen goods.

A reliable fence is the key to the success of a good burglary operation because the fence provides the burglar with an outlet for stolen property and a source of credit with which to finance his operations. In addition, the professional thief often avoids apprehension because he is able to dispose of the goods to a fence quickly and thus avoid being caught with hot items in his possession, which is often the downfall of the novice. The price that the burglar will receive from a fence varies tremendously.

A drug addict desperate for a fix will be more likely to sell stolen property at prices far below street value, whereas the more highly skilled burglar, who is not driven by drug induced cravings, is skilled in the art of bargaining, and has associations with more than one fence, is likely to be well compensated for his criminal activity.

8. *Satisfies needs.* Given that all the aforementioned elements of the cycle have been successfully completed, at this point the needs that originally motivated the burglar will be fulfilled. The drug addict can purchase drugs, the compulsive spender can go forth on a spending spree, and the insecure delinquent will feel accepted and approved of by the gang.

For some offenders the cycle ends here and they never commit another offense, but for others the cycle continues. In the case of the circumstantial offender, the cycle terminates at this point because the circumstances that motivated the burglary are not likely to occur again. In the case of the drug addict, the cycle is likely to be repeated as often as he requires funds to purchase drugs. The professional burglar is likely to acquire enough money from a given burglary to last him for several months, and thus he need engage in only a few burglaries a year.

9. *Reinforces burglar's behavior pattern.* Success motivates burglars to continue to commit burglaries until they are apprehended. While for some, arrest and incarceration will terminate their careers, for others these will merely interrupt their careers temporarily. In fact, for younger offenders, incarceration often is a reinforcement of rather than a deterrent to criminal behavior. Many young offenders perceive prison as a test of their ability to endure deprivation, and, in fact, "doing time like a man" raises an individual's status among his peers. In addition, while in prison, the youthful offender is likely to receive a broad-based education in theft from veteran offenders that includes tips on more sophisticated burglary techniques, which many of these offenders enthusiastically employ upon release. On the other hand, it appears that older offenders, whether incarcerated for the first time or having already served several sentences, tend to be more likely to conclude that a life of crime is too costly and to make the decision to go straight when their prison term is completed.

The Professional Burglar

According to Shover (1972) the professional burglar, known among other thieves as "the good burglar": (1) is technically competent; (2) has a reputation for personal integrity; (3) tends to specialize in burglary; and (4) has been at least relatively successful at crime. He further indicates that a man becomes a good burglar through stealing with and learning from other good burglars. However, professional burglars give this opportunity only to individuals who are known and give evidence of good character. An individual can acquire this reputation in three principal ways: First, juveniles who reside in high crime areas may come to the attention of older thieves who then establish an apprentice/little brother relationship, resulting in instruction and experience in burglary. Second, an older man with little or no record of criminal activity may spend much of his leisure time in bars and lounges frequented by thieves or may have maintained relationships with boyhood friends who are involved in criminal activities. This type of individual may become interested in pursuing a career in crime as a result of disruptions in his life style, usually brought about by family breakups. An individual is not given an opportunity to participate in criminal activities unless he has demonstrated that he is tough or close-mouthed, as the following excerpt illustrates:

> *I just come out of the air force and me and the old lady weren't getting along. I was spending a lot of time in this one place where all the thieves hung out. (You know, there are a lot of thieves in J. _____). Well, I had gotten into two or three fights in there and I had got a reputation as someone who wasn't afraid to fight and wasn't afraid of the police.* (Shover, 1972, p. 543)*

Finally, some men obtain a solid reputation while in prison. This represents the major route to sophisticated thievery for men reared in rural areas, since they usually lack criminal contacts. The man who develops a reputation as a person with a solid character while in the "joint" can use this as currency upon release to acquire contacts, instruction, and experience.

An unattached burglar or a burglary crew will recruit a novice for a job for a variety of reasons. In some instances, the unattached burglar who normally works alone may plan a job that requires more than one person, while the crew may require an additional person for a particular job. In other cases, a novice may be employed by a burglar who has just gotten out of prison or whose partner has been apprehended. In still other cases, a person may ask to be taken on a job because he needs to obtain some money fast:

> *[A] person may lose a job, get caught in amateur stealing or may need additional money. If he has developed a friendly re-*

---

*Reprinted by special permission of the Journal of Criminal Law, Criminology, and Police Science, Copyright ©1972 by Northwestern University School of Law, Vol. 63, No. 4, 1972.

*lationship with professional thieves, he may request or they may
suggest that he be given a minor part in some act of theft. He
would, if accepted, be given verbal instructions in regard to the
theory of the racket and the specific part he is to play.* (Sutherland; as cited in Shover, 1972, p. 544)*

Following the establishment of a relationship of trust with "a
good burglar," the new recruit's contacts expand to include fences
and tipsters who can assist him in his work. Tipsters ("spotters,"
"fingermen" or "set up men") provide the burglar with information regarding premises or individuals that represent good targets
for burglary. Burglars are apprehensive about using information
provided by tipsters because it may be grossly exaggerated. On the
other hand, they cannot totally disregard this information because
of the possibility that they will thereby neglect to take advantage
of a large, poorly protected score. Moreover, by operating with
information provided by tipsters a burglar can be more certain
that he will be adequately rewarded for his labors. For example,
tipsters can provide a burglar with information on a cache of
money hidden by someone who has been cheating on his income
taxes. Tipsters come from all walks of life; they may be night-
watchmen, window cleaners, prostitutes, attorneys, catering
service employees, jewelers, gamblers, detectives, used car dealers,
beauticians, and tavern owners and bartenders. While in many
instances a burglar receives unsolicited information, in some cases
he actually searches people out in order to obtain information
regarding a specific individual or premises. In these instances, he
pays cash for the information:

*[T]his particular place was here in town. I knew a girl that
knew a girl that worked there. So, I approached this girl and
said "Hey, I would like some information about this place. Why
don't you ask her and see what she says, course I'll pay for
it?" ... [S]o this girl came back and said, "Yeah, the fifteenth
and the 31st there's money there because they cash the company
payroll checks ...." Then I sent back for some specific information, what kind of safe it was and how the alarm was tied in ....
We got the place and then I gave this other girl $500 and I never
heard any more about it.* (Shover, 1972, p. 547)*

The professional recognizes that if he continues his criminal
activity for an extended period of time he will at some point be
arrested, and in order to prevent this arrest from resulting in a
lengthy prison sentence he establishes contact with attorneys who
are skilled at minimizing the penalties imposed by the criminal

*Reprinted by special permission of the Journal of Criminal Law, Crimi-
nology, and Police Science, Copyright ©1972 by Northwestern University
School of Law, Vol. 63, No. 4, 1972.

justice system. Burglars typically establish contact with two types of attorneys: one is skilled at fixing cases through the use of cash payments and political favors, while the other relies on his legal knowledge and courtroom skill to free his clients.

The Conventional Burglar

Based on an examination of police records and interviews with 97 burglars, Reppetto (1974) has developed a series of burglar profiles. Although there is some overlap among his categories, he suggests that they are sufficiently distinct to permit the development of brief typological profiles. While Reppetto does not make a distinction between the professional and the conventional burglar, an examination of the characteristics of his sample (skill level, size of score, target) reveals that less than 7 per cent of his sample may be defined as professionals, which would not materially affect the accuracy of his profiles with regard to the conventional offender. Also, while he focused on the residential burglaries committed by offenders in his sample, a large percentage of the members of this group (62%) had also been involved in nonresidential burglaries, particularly of stores and offices. The profiles that he developed of these offenders are:

> *The Juvenile Offender. The typical juvenile offender in this study had been arrested a couple of times and placed on probation. Because he lacked both education and experience, he was ill-qualified for legitimate work and demonstrated little skill even in his criminal endeavors. He was more inclined than the older offenders to work with his friends or in gangs, and since he traveled on foot to make his hits, he was more likely to work in or around his own neighborhood, and to rely more on spur-of-the-moment opportunities than on careful selection of targets. ("I'm just walking down the street and a couple of friends say, 'Hey, do you want to break into a house with us?' I say, 'OK, if its a good hit.'"). He was quite likely to be deterred by evidence of a burglar alarm, police patrols, or unfamiliar neighborhoods, which made him feel conspicuous. His lack of skill led him to prefer easy targets over difficult but affluent ones, and consequently, his average score was low. His disposal of the goods was haphazard rather than systematic, in keeping with his apparent attitude that burglary was more of a game than a way of life.*
>
> *The 18–25 Year Old Offender. The extensive overlap between this group and the drug-using group makes the isolation of a distinct age-profile difficult, but a few age-related characteristics may still be noted. The typical burglar in this age range had several previous convictions, but continued to break and enter because he found it easy, not very risky, and relatively lightly*

punished. *("I gave up mugging because it might end in murder."*
"I like breaking and entering because you don't have to contend
with people.") He was more mobile than the younger burglar and
had moved outside his own neighborhood for at least half his hits
(over 50 percent — predominantly drug users — did five or more
hits a week) and his average score was higher than the juvenile's.
He also took a wider variety of goods because he had more highly
developed channels for disposing of them, and his fences *(of*
whom he had several) were often "so-called respectable citizens."

The Older Offender — Age 25 and Upwards. The typical
older offender had been breaking and entering for many years,
and had been in and out of jail several times on many different
charges. Like many in the middle age group, he chose breaking
and entering as preferable to, and more profitable than, other
types of crime. *"I purse-snatched when I was 15. I grew out of*
that into something bigger." "I changed as I learned more . . .
from low class neighborhoods to highrise apartments . . . it's
another step.") That the neighborhood should be affluent was his
first consideration and therefore he spent much of his time working in single-family suburban houses. *("When gains don't*
out-balance the other, you don't take the chance.") He was more
inclined to plan carefully, to get to know the neighborhood
thoroughly before attempting a hit there, and to employ relatively
effective entry methods. *("Any lock made by man can be broken*
by man.") His average score was higher than that of the other
groups and he disposed of the goods immediately through several
trusted fences. On the whole, (unless he were a drug addict) he
made fewer, more profitable hits, thus reducing the chances of
being caught. He was less likely than the younger burglar to be
deterred by burglar alarms, which he felt he could *"handle,"*
but more likely to be deterred by the presence of an occupant or
a dog. Although occasionally he worked at regular employment,
he usually had difficulty holding a job, and might have given up
trying. *("I don't like to work. I haven't had to work for five*
years." "You can make a week's pay in one night.")

Whites. Basically, the methods and skill levels of nonwhite
and white burglars were similar, although some relatively minor
behavioral differences did emerge from the study. The white
burglar was more likely to be married than the black burglar, to
have a semiskilled job, and to have earned a little more money a
week. He was more inclined to prefer single-family houses, regardless of the race of the resident, but he was unlikely to work in a
predominantly nonwhite residential area for fear of violence.
("If you get caught in a black or Puerto-Rican neighborhood you
might get killed.") The white burglar was also less likely to go
into housing projects, more likely to travel further from his
home, and more likely to be cautious in hitting the same neighborhood again.

The white burglar gave a higher estimate of the amount of

money he needed a week than the black burglar, but since his average score was likely to be a little greater, the frequency of operation was virtually the same for both groups. While approximately the same number in each group were drug users, the white burglar was marginally more likely to be a heroin user.

Blacks. The black burglar generally preferred to hit residences owned by white people, largely because he assumed that they would be more affluent. ("If it was a black guy, I'd know that there wasn't too much money. If it was a white guy, I'd know there was.") However, because he was somewhat less mobile than the white burglar, he was frequently forced to work in relatively less affluent black neighborhoods near his own residence. Many also felt conspicuous and out of place in the suburbs and conceived these areas — along with luxury apartments — to be almost prohibitively well-secured, however attractive as targets. (In response to a slide, "Cops over there all the time. Looks like a white neighborhood. You'd have a police escort every corner you turned.") Blacks, in general, were more likely than whites to be deterred by police patrols, particularly younger blacks.

The black burglar was also more likely to get to his target on foot and to travel less than one hour to make a hit. His average score was marginally lower than the white burglar's, and he was more inclined to take the goods home or to a friend's home than to dispose of them immediately.

The adult black gave a lower estimate of the amount of money he needed a week — between $100 and $250, rather than the $250 or more that the white burglar required. If he was a drug user, he was more inclined to use amphetamines than the white burglar.

The Drug User. The typical drug user in the interviewee sample was under 25, with a drug habit (usually heroin, sometimes amphetamines) of several years' standing. He differed from the nondrug user chiefly in that he needed more money and, consequently, made more hits. His habit could cost him $1,500 a week, and rarely cost him less than $150. Since his job, if he still had one, normally earned him between $100 and $200 a week, he had decided to concentrate on breaking and entering because it was the easiest way to get the additional money he needed, and did not involve violence. However, his scores were only a little higher than the nondrug user, and therefore he made many more hits per week — averaging 5–6, compared with 1–2 for the nondrug user. ("On amphetamines you're full of pep, does something to your nervous system. We'd just keep going on and on .... On one of those benders I might do 150 or 200 burglaries. Before that, I'd only done about 10 a year.").

Although the drug user, in principle, preferred single-family suburban houses where the scores were higher, he was more likely than the nondrug user to work around or in his own neighbor-

hood, particularly as his habit increased. ("When I started doing it, it was always there (single-family suburban houses). Then I said to heck with going all the way out there. I wanted the junk, right; I'd look for the quickest way to make more money . . . .")
Because of the urgency with which he needed his money, his view of deterrents was somewhat different from the nondrug user. He did comparatively little planning, and could be more easily deterred by complex security devices. ("If the door was a hassle, I'd go elsewhere.") Although he preferred no one to be home, he was more inclined to be reckless and risk confrontations. ("When I'm strung out . . . I don't care who's at home. I need money.")
    The Nondrug User. Clearly this category includes an analytically intractable cross-section of types, connected only by their common differences with the drug using category. In brief, the nondrug user needed less money, made fewer hits and did more planning. He was more concerned with avoiding personal confrontation and was consequently more likely to be deterred by a full time occupant, by police and security patrols, or even by dogs or neighbors checking on the residence. He was, in contrast, less likely to be deterred by the mechanical obstacles (locks, etc.) which would defeat the patience of the addict. One might also characterize the nondrug user's choice of a career in burglary as more 'disinterested' than the drug user's choice, since (1) the nondrug user was not so obviously incapacitated for legitimate employment and (2) his financial needs were not so extreme as to virtually prohibit living within a legitimate wage. (Reppetto, 1974, pp. 23–26)*

Receiving Stolen Goods

The fence, or criminal receiver, knowingly buys, sells, or otherwise traffics in stolen merchandise (Chamber of Commerce, 1974). Fences differ with regard to the scope, method, and specialization of their operations. It appears that there is a hierarchy among fences. On the one extreme, there are those fences who deal directly with the thief and openly sell to the buyer. Included within this group are local merchants who buy stolen property to supplement their inventory or sell stolen property as an adjunct to their businesses and people who sell small quantities of stolen property from their homes or apartments. Ianni (1974) reports on the operations of a man whom he calls Thomas Irwin, who operates a combination dry cleaning and tailor shop in Harlem. In addition to providing these legitimate services, Irwin also buys and sells stolen property. Thus, his customers know that if they are looking for whiskey, clothing, and the like they can buy it from him at

---

*Reprinted with permission from *Residential Crime* by Thomas A. Reppetto, Copyright 1974. Ballinger Publishing Co.

drastically reduced prices. At another level is a fence who specializes in particular types of merchandise. The following description provided by an assistant district attorney testifying before the Senate Select Sub-committee on Small Business illustrates this type of operation:

> 'Mack,' as we will refer to this fence, is a gnome-like man in his 60's who maintained three electrical outlet stores.... An analysis of 'Mack's' books and records revealed that in 1970, 'Mack' purchased stolen electrical construction materials valued at approximately one million dollars — an amount which must be multiplied in terms of the loss to the construction industry in labor costs, delay, and replacement of the stolen property.
>
> 'Mack's' operation is typical because, as a fence, he would only deal in a speciality, that is, electrical construction materials.... In addition, 'Mack' was also typical in that he acted as a catalyst in causing certain materials to be stolen at certain times. When he was overstocked in certain materials, he would so advise thieves.... But when one of his clients needed particular materials, 'Mack' would put out a 'contract' for the theft of particular items, and take great pains to see that his customers, who paid cash, would receive the property at the time requested. (Testimony given before the Senate Select Sub-committee on Small Business; cited in Chamber of Commerce, 1974, p. 46)

Finally, at the top of the hierarchy is the "master fence," who as a rule does not come into physical possession of or inspect the goods he sells. Master fences typically operate as arrangers for the distribution of merchandise. Thus, they can consummate most of their transactions over the telephone. One witness before a Senate sub-committee investigating fencing provides a perspective on the extent of their operations:

> Witness: ... Well, off hand, I know about four big fences that can come up with a hundred thousand in cash, no sweat. [Rule of thumb: for a fence to earn $100,000 he would have to handle from $750,000 to $1,000,000 in stolen merchandise.] (Testimony given before the Senate Select Sub-committee on Small Business; cited in Chamber of Commerce, 1974, p. 45)

Fences serve as an outlet for any type of stolen merchandise for which there is a demand. They handle securities, steel, credit cards, forged or stolen documents, cigarettes, office equipment, meat, airline tickets, shoes, clothing, liquor, jewelry, and appliances of all kinds.

Some fences also assist in the education of the young burglar by teaching him how to distinguish between valuable and worthless jewelry, paintings, furs, and the like (Shover, 1972). They also educate the burglar in other ways: ·

> *[Johnny] used to tell us a whole lot of things that we didn't know about. He told us how to steal furs and what to do with them afterwards, how to steal silver, and how to go downtown to the places where few negroes went and steal stuff. Johnny told us how to dress. He'd tell us about looking like a delivery boy when you went to Park Avenue to steal something or looking like a working boy when you went down to the garment center to steal things. He knew a lot about stealing and all kinds of crime.* (Shover, 1972, p. 545)*

In addition, fences can sometimes put a burglar in touch with a businessman who is having financial problems and wishes to solve them by a contract burglary. Fences may also provide burglars with tips on places that would be good targets for burglary. In this way, the fence is able to control his inventory and ensure a supply of the kinds of merchandise that are in demand:

> *It was then that Jake had his idea. At the gambling houses he knew all sorts of people. Show people, gamblers, criminals and even guys on the legit bought hot stuff from him. Jake would go to a gambling place and if he saw someone there he was sure would be good for a nice haul, he would call up my room and tell me where the guy lived. I hurry over there and break in. If the guy left the gambling house, Jake would call me at the place I was prowling and I would get out fast. Most of these people were 'sports' and they usually kept quite a lot of cash around their apartments. To them, diamonds were their ace in the hole. The whole thing seemed foolproof. I stole from these people and Jake sold their stuff to others like them.* (Shover, 1972, p. 546)*

Motor Vehicle Theft

Motor vehicle theft accounted for 9 per cent of the Crime Index offenses for 1975, with a total of 1,000,500 vehicles reported stolen (Federal Bureau of Investigation, 1976). In a two month nationwide 1974 study of motor vehicle thefts, the FBI found that 85 per cent of the vehicles reported stolen were passenger cars, while 6 per cent were trucks and buses (Federal Bureau of Investigation, 1975a). Half the vehicles reported stolen were from the 1968 model year or older, 20 per cent were 1969 to 1971 models,

---

*Reprinted by special permission of the Journal of Criminal Law, Criminology, and Police Science, Copyright © 1972 by Northwestern University School of Law, Vol. 63, No. 4.

and 30 per cent were 1972 or newer model vehicles. With regard to the site of the theft, 24 per cent of the vehicles were stolen from private residences or apartments (garages, driveways, off street parking areas), 35 per cent from public streets in residential areas, 13 per cent from public streets in business or commercial areas, 17 per cent from free parking areas (including shopping centers), and the remaining 11 per cent from paid parking areas, car lots, and other areas.

In most instances, law enforcement agencies cannot determine the purpose of a vehicle theft merely by the recovery of the vehicle. However, for the two month 1974 survey period, law enforcement agencies in 44 metropolitan areas in the United States examined stolen late model passenger cars for the purpose of ascertaining the objectives of the theft. They reported that 38 per cent of the recovered automobiles had been stripped, 35 per cent were used for transportation or "joyriding," 3 per cent were used in another crime, and no objective was discernible from an examination of the remaining 24 per cent of the cars. Obviously, a certain proportion of the latter group were stolen specifically for resale, but it is impossible to determine when a car is stolen for this specific purpose unless the thief or theft ring is identified or the car comes to the attention of the police. However, in a parallel study conducted within selected cities, police examined 10,014 cars and determined that 131 had been stolen for resale. This is, no doubt, only the tip of the iceberg since there are numerous car theft rings involved in the resale of automobiles operating around the country.

Motor Vehicle Theft Rings

These theft rings specialize in the theft and resale of all types of motor vehicles. Professional auto theft rings are composed of specialists from the various fields of the automobile industry. The FBI has provided a description of the basic pattern followed by these gangs in the theft and resale of automobiles (Federal Bureau of Investigation, 1975).

Theft Methods. Many professional theft rings have such large operations that they hire amateur thieves to steal cars for them, for which they pay $25 to $50. A rank amateur has little difficulty in locating cars with keys in the ignition because so many auto owners are careless. If the car thief cannot locate a car with the keys in the ignition on the street, he can walk into almost any parking lot, get into a car, and simply drive away. Another method employed by amateur thieves is to steal unlocked cars parked on hills or inclines. This method was used exclusively by amateur thieves supplying cars to a southern car ring several years ago. These thieves would get into the car, place the transmission in neutral, and quickly coast the car off the hill, at which point they would hot-wire the car and drive it away.

Some professionals prefer to employ their own men and methods to acquire cars. For example:

> Members of one east coast ring posed as prospective buyers, approached car dealers, [and] requested to "test drive" new cars. Their actual objective was to acquire the ignition key serial number so that they might later have a key made and steal the car at their convenience. (Federal Bureau of Investigation, 1975, p. 7)

Some rings are extremely selective with regard to the types of cars they steal. For example, one ring would search the area for the model car they needed and obtain the automobile license plate number. They would then contact the state motor vehicle bureau and obtain the name of the vehicle's owner. By calling the owner, they could obtain the name of the dealer from whom the car was purchased. A ring member would then contact the dealer and pose as the owner, indicating that he had lost his key and requesting the key identification number so that he could have a new one made. Then, it was just a matter of awaiting an opportune moment to carry out the theft.

Finally, some thieves are brazen enough to employ the direct, or drive off, method in stealing cars:

> Posing as a customer, the thief approaches either a car dealership or a private citizen who has placed a "for sale" ad in the newspaper. Requesting either to test drive the car or to show it to his wife, the thief drives away and never returns. At times the thief might make a small down payment or issue a worthless down payment check. A similar technique is used when thieves "rent" cars from rental agencies. (Federal Bureau of Investigation, 1975, p. 7)

Preparation for Resale. Following the theft phase of the operation is the alteration phase, which is divided into four segments: document forgery; vehicle identification number (VIN) changes; license plate replacements; and body work. One or all of these may be used to prepare an automobile for resale.

Document forgery essentially involves obtaining a new title for the automobile. In some instances, this is accomplished by going to what is called a "nontitle state," in which little or no proof of ownership is required in order to register a car or obtain license plates for a car. Thus, all the thief has to do is walk into a motor vehicle bureau in one of these states and he can register and obtain a license for a car that he has neither legal title to nor even possession of at the time. Other auto theft rings obtain titles by purchasing late-model wrecked cars from salvage yards. They steal a car that is identical to the wrecked one and alter the vehicle identification number and color of the stolen car to match those on the title of the wrecked one.

In most instances, the next step in the process is the alteration of the vehicle identification number. A variety of methods are employed for this. For example, one accomplished number changer working with an eastern auto ring stamped new numbers directly over the old ones, always stamping the new numbers deeper than the old. He then ground off the old numbers and used acid to make the remaining new numbers look like the old ones. Other car rings simply steal a number plate from a car on the street; most car owners would never miss it. Still other rings acquire blank number plates, which they can number easily with a stamping machine.

A third phase of this process involves the acquisition of license plates for the stolen cars. Some rings take license plates from other cars and use them on the stolen vehicles. Another common method involves the use of a registration obtained from a nontitle state to legitimately obtain a license plate from another state. Some car theft rings cut two license plates in half, switch the halves and then solder them together to obtain two plates with different numbers.

Some theft rings will even do some body work on the cars they have stolen. This usually involves such things as changing the color of the car and repairing minor body damage.

Resale of "Hot" Cars. The sale of these stolen vehicles generally presents no problems because from the same unsuspecting public from whom the cars were stolen come the unsuspecting buyer-victims. In addition, many people are more willing to buy things "no questions asked" if the price is right, and in this respect, the auto theft ring is quite obliging because it is willing to sell late model cars for as little as one half their actual value or, in some cases, even less.

> *An auto theft ring with a large overseas operation in the Scandinavian countries sold stolen late model American cars for as little as one fifth of their actual value and almost destroyed the legitimate car market in these countries before moving on.*
> (Federal Bureau of Investigation, 1975, p. 9)

Car theft gangs also dispose of hot cars at auctions and through newspaper advertisements. Some car thieves approach car dealers and indicate that they must sell a car quickly because they have to leave on a trip. A few rings even establish "legitimate" dealerships in order to market their stolen vehicles:

> Usually accompanying these dealerships are "dummy" companies from which the dealer purportedly buys the stolen car. When an investigation occurs, the "legitimate" dealer brings forth a bill of sale and states that he "believed" he was making a legal purchase. He will deny any knowledge of the dummy company and its illegal activities. Finally, as was suggested earlier, some car theft rings even ship their stolen vehicles overseas to be sold. (Federal Bureau of Investigation, 1975, p. 9)

Figure 5–2 shows (at least in theory) the organizational and procedural structure of an East Coast car theft ring with both domestic and foreign outlets for disposal of the stolen vehicles. The following is a brief description of the ring's operation:

> Typically, in this ring's operation, the car was stolen by amateur thieves and subsequently sold to a middleman, a person in the lower command of the auto theft ring. The car was delivered to a location where false documents and altered numbers were attached. It would be documented as being owned by a "dummy" company, which in turn would "sell" the car to the

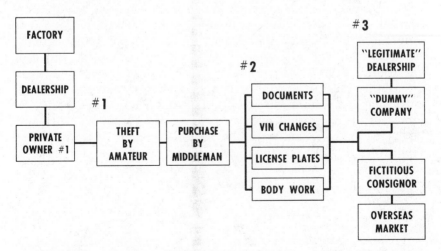

Figure 5–2. Organization and procedural structure of an auto theft ring. From Federal Bureau of Investigation: Auto theft rings. FBI Law Enforcement Bulletin, August, 1971. Reproduced by permission of the U. S. Department of Justice.

ring's "legitimate" car dealership. The car would then be sold to an innocent victim by the dealership.

On the other hand, the same car might be titled to a ring member under an alias. The ring member would pose as the domestic consignor and have the car shipped to the ring's foreign market, where it would usually be sold for much less than its actual value. (Federal Bureau of Investigation, 1975, pp. 9, 28)

Shoplifting

Shoplifting is growing faster than any other Crime Index property offense. Between 1970 and 1975, shoplifting increased by 73 per cent, which surpassed the rates of increase for all types of burglary, other larcenies, and motor vehicle thefts (Federal Bureau of Investigation, 1976). Furthermore, the National Council on Crime and Delinquency reports that this offense rose 221 per cent between 1960 and 1973. The United States Commerce Commission estimates that the number of shoplifting incidents may be as high as 140 million per year, involving losses of two to five billion dollars' worth of goods (Mydans, 1975). Finally, the magnitude of this problem is underscored by results from a recent study in which a team of professional shop watchers observed 500 persons selected at random who walked into a midtown Manhattan store: the team found that one of every ten shoppers walked out with merchandise that was not paid for (Hellman, 1970).

In contrast to other conventional offenders, shoplifters come from all social strata and range in age from as young as 5 to more than 80. For example, a four member gang of children aged 5 to 7 operated in the toy department of Foley's in Houston under the leadership of a 5 year old. When apprehended, the gang was found with a sack containing a hundred dollars' worth of toys. Other cases of shoplifters arrested by store detectives include an 81 year old woman with a $40,000 bank account and a $50,400 home, an office worker with an income of $13,000 a year, a middle aged matron, and a public school teacher (Wright, 1972). Shoplifters can be divided into three categories: professional shoplifters, or "heels"; ordinary offenders, or "boosters"; and amateurs, or "snitches" (Cameron, 1964).

The Professional Shoplifter

Professionals work alone or in teams and often have specific orders to fill. A shoplifting team generally consists of two to three members, including a "stall" who diverts the attention of sales clerks and store detectives, a "clout" who actually takes the goods, and maybe a "cover" who takes the goods from the clout or conceals the clout's exit. Typically, a team will enter the store and the stall will initiate a diversionary action, such as a simulated faint or heart attack or a small fire, which gives the clout the time needed to conceal the preselected items or to transfer them to the cover. At this point, the troupe can make a leisurely exit since there is little chance that the merchandise will be missed immediately. Cameron (1964) notes that the entire operation takes only a few minutes, giving a troupe the opportunity to "clout" several stores in one day. In the course of a day, a professional working either alone or in a team may steal a size 42 long, blue, pinstriped suit for one customer and a silver tea service in a particular pattern for another (Hellman, 1970).

Professionals employ a variety of techniques to conceal stolen merchandise. Specially designed "booster" skirts, pants, bloomers, and coats with pockets or hooks are used by many professionals to hide merchandise. A woman wearing a booster skirt can quickly acquire the contours of an advanced pregnancy, and a detective who has not observed the rapidity with which the pregnancy "symptoms" have developed may well be reluctant to arrest the shoplifter (Cameron, 1964). The recent popularity of the maxi coat has been a blessing to the professional shoplifter because it affords more space for females to secrete merchandise. Both men and women often use specially designed coats with slits in the bottom of the pockets and special linings to conceal merchandise. The female professional, particularly if she is stout, can, with a little practice, become quite adept at a technique called "crotch walking," which involves working the merchandise between the thighs (the ampleness of a stout figure hides the bulge quite well) and then walking out with no apparent change in the normal step. Women employing this technique have been caught taking many sorts of goods out of stores, including small television sets (Hellman, 1970). Undoubtedly, these techniques were learned from other professionals as well as through trial and error. There is reported to be a school in California for professionals that teaches these skills for a tuition of between $1500 and $2000. Graduates of this school are reputed to be able to steal up to five women's suits at one time while talking to a sales clerk and to make up a thousand dollars a week (Wright, 1972).

The Ordinary Shoplifter

These offenders, known as "boosters," are similar to professionals in that they have easily identifiable criminal backgrounds and steal mainly saleable merchandise. Included within this category are alcoholics and drug addicts who shoplift in order to support their habits. Cameron (1964) indicates that the frantic addict with no money to buy drugs who attempts to grab merchandise and run is well known to department store detectives. Such individuals are frequently spotted by store security personnel because they lack the skill of the professional and are often in too much of a hurry to accomplish their objectives. Also included in the booster category are all other ordinary criminals who engage in shoplifting along with other conventional offenses. For example, Cameron (1964) found that several of the boosters whom she studied had been arrested for burglary, auto larceny, robbery, assault with a deadly weapon, and carrying concealed weapons and that several were subsequently arrested for murder.

The Amateur Shoplifter

The majority of shoplifters are amateurs ("snitches"), a group that includes such diverse types as housewives, office workers, subteens, and foreign visitors (Hellman, 1970). Retail reports indicate that the typical shoplifter is a white female aged 20 to 25 who has one child and is married to a man who earns more than $10,000 a year (Wright, 1972).

Snitches do not think of themselves as thieves nor do they have any criminal associations. They shoplift for a variety of reasons, which include irritation over poor service, a need to feed their families, a desire to square a grudge with the store, and a wish to acquire luxuries that they cannot afford. The wealthy pilfer just for kicks or because they feel they have spent too much at a store and expect a bonus. In addition to the aforementioned reasons, teenagers shoplift as a form of rebellion, as part of initiation ceremonies for high school clubs, as a means of keeping their wardrobes as up-to-date as those of their peers, in order to embarrass their parents so that they will pay attention to them, and for peer group acceptance (Davidson, 1968).

Hellman (1970) has identified an elite group of shoplifters sometimes called "shadow professionals," whose greater skill distinguishes them from other amateurs. This subgroup of pilferers steal for themselves or intimate friends but do not steal as a means of livelihood. They have an acquired taste for shoplifting that is constantly bolstered by successful undetected forays:

> The very model of a first class shadow professional is a 26 year old assistant to a New York foundation executive. Joanne is clean featured and clear skinned, with striking grey eyes and a bouncy walk. She enjoys talking about her shoplifting: "My job

routine use to be very dispirited, very dull," she explains. "I would come in on the subway in the morning, trudge out to the sandwich shop at 12:30, trudge back at 1:30 and work until 5, get on the subway, go home to my guy in Brooklyn. What a bore. Well, the routine is still the same — except now I bring a sandwich in wax paper which I gobble down in a minute, then I spend my lunch hour going around lifting stuff we need. The first thing I took was a bottle of soy sauce I needed for a Polynesian chicken dish I was going to make for company. It was just the spirit of the day — I was looking at it, turning around like a housewife — I dropped it into my handbag. So simple."

"I really mean it when I say it turned into something that makes me look forward to my lunch hour. On the subway in the morning I think, 'What can I lift today?' 'Where will I go?' I plan dinner; usually I can pick up most of what we need. We are saving for a trip to Europe, and it seems silly to spend good money for food when we could be sticking it into our savings account. It's funny — all the girls have little cupboards at the office, and mine is always filled with things like lettuce heads and lamb chops. There isn't much that won't go into a purse: a split of champagne; a nice gold plated flashlight I found in a gift shop on Madison Avenue; Arygle socks for when it gets cold; a copy of Hemingway's short stories in hardcover. It all goes in the bag — plunk — plunk — plunk. I've gotten so that I honestly feel I have 360-degree sensory perception. I can be facing a shelf and know whether somebody is behind me watching. If I get bad signals, I put them back."

"There is an esthetic to this: I always end my trips by dropping in the bag either a can of Beluga caviar or a bottle of Macadamia nuts. It's like my signature at the end of working hard on a painting that comes out well."

"When I'm on the subway at nights now, I don't like to sit there like a gloom bunny waiting for the stops to go by. I take out the stuff, piece by piece, look it over, gloat a little. Then I am home. I perform the same routine for my guy — an unveiling of the new line."

"So now I have a craft. It's more rewarding in some ways than my job. It gives me something to look forward to — on the train in the morning, at lunch, on the way home. You could say it makes my day." (Hellman, 1970, p. 39)*

Con Games and Swindles

Bloch and Geis (1970) claim that the "confidence game stands at the top rung in the prestige hierarchy of professional crime"

---

*©1970 by The New York Times Company. Reprinted by permission.

(p. 172). The status of this activity derives from the fact that the victim voluntarily delivers his money or property to the swindler because of the confidence the victim has in him. The basic distinction between a true confidence game and a swindle is in the nature of the victim's involvement. The confidence game is based on the victim's greediness and dishonesty. The element common to all confidence operations is showing the victim a means to make money or gain some other benefit fraudulently and then taking advantage of his dishonesty. Thus, a true confidence game really leaves no innocent victims. Swindlers, on the other hand, prey on the victim's innocence, ignorance, or gullibility (Gasser, 1970). However, at best this is a tenuous distinction, particularly in the case of elderly victims. Prior to his assignment to the New York City Police Department's Pickpocket and Confidence Squad, Lt. Campbell had been convinced that only the greedy were victimized by confidence schemes. However, after three years of working in this area, his views have changed:

> "For old people, especially the ones with nothing but a bank account and Social Security, that amount they have in the bank is like an index of how long they are going to live. A hope of another $3,000 means another year of life." (Kaufman, 1973, p. 49)*

Typically, confidence men (and swindlers) are smooth, skillful, convincing talkers who live by their wits and their ability to manipulate people (Roebuck and Johnson, 1970). The following case related by a con man illustrates the artistry employed in these operations:

> He [said] that he once had a woman ready to enter into a dishonest scheme which involved cheating an exclusive store out of an expensive fur coat. It meant, however, that the woman would have to go to the bank and withdraw money. She decided not to do this because she was afraid of what her husband might say when he learned of it. The con man felt that he had lost the score, but kept talking to the woman while trying to think of a way to induce her to take her money out of the bank. While talking to her he remembered that he had first met her standing in front of a fur store admiring a coat. He took her to the store so that she might see the coat again. She wanted it so much she went to the bank, withdrew the money, and gave it to the con man. He pointed out that this was what he meant by putting the right "touches" into the game — sometimes the difference between making the score or losing it. (Gasser, 1970, p. 265)

---

*©1973 by The New York Times Company. Reprinted by permission.

Schur (1957) points out that "con" games of any type follow a pattern. The first step is the selection of a "mark" or victim. The con man then establishes rapport with the intended victim, and when he feels the mark has sufficient "confidence" in him, he "shares" with the victim a scheme by which they can make some fast money. Too late, the mark realizes that he has been the betrayed victim — the "moms" or "lamb" — rather than the clever participant in a swindle. The number of confidence operators involved in a swindle, the time and money devoted to setting up the victim and taking his money ("trimming"), and the amount taken from the victim determine whether a given confidence operation or trick falls into the category of the "big con" (also known as the "long con") or the "short con" (Roebuck and Johnson, 1970).

The Big Con

These "games" involve numerous accomplices, props, and, in some instances, sums of money ranging from a few thousand to hundreds of thousands of dollars. These operations generally include a series of preplanned steps in which several operators (each with a specific role) work at persuading the victim to invest all the money he possesses or can secure in a transaction they have devised. In a typical operation, a victim is selected by the "roper" or "steer" who introduces the victim to the scheme. For instance, the victim may be told that the inside man is a disgruntled employee of a gambling club who wishes to quit but before doing so wants to "take" the place for a sizable sum of money. The victim is told that if he wishes to participate he can keep all or part of the winnings. In many cases, the victim is allowed to win a small sum of money to demonstrate that the scheme works. The victim is then sent home to secure a sizable amount of money. Upon his return, he is deftly deprived of this sum through a series of maneuvers that on the surface appear to be the result of errors or a misunderstanding. The victims of a big con are "shaken off" or "cooled off" in order to prevent them from making a report to police. Victims who are "shaken off" are often reminded that if they make a complaint to the police they may go to jail as well because of their role in the illegal act. In addition, the victim is reminded that even if he doesn't go to jail he risks exposure, ridicule, and contempt from his friends and the police if he reports his loss (Gasser, 1970). In other instances, the victim is "shaken off" through the use of a "cackle bag" — a plastic bag filled with chicken blood that is broken in the course of a fierce fight between the roper and the inside man in which it appears that the roper has been shot by the inside man. The mark, upon being told that he may be an accessory to a homicide, is usually more concerned with being able to leave the area quickly and rarely asks any further questions about his lost money (Bloch and Geis, 1970). In contrast, in the "cooling off" process, the con man concentrates on consoling the victim rather than making him realize he's been just another "easy mark." Thus, the victim is comforted and an attempt is made to induce the victim to accept the inevitable and retain his self respect (Gasser, 1970).

Cavan (1962) provides us with an illustration of a confidence scheme that operated for several years:

> The criminals in this case were six men with long criminal records of larceny, fraud, burglary, and cheating at cards, punctuated with short terms in prison. They made use of other people such as messengers and secretaries who were not actively involved in any criminal act. The victim was a Mr. Cunningham, an honest and respected businessman in an Eastern city. Several of the criminals first met Cunningham in the 1920's when they were engaged in selling worthless stock. He invested over one hundred thousand dollars and lost it all. In 1951, the swindlers of the 1920's again made contact with Cunningham, telling him that a mythical Dr. Parker had made a fortune on an invention and died, leaving a will bequeathing his fortune to the three investors who had lost heavily in the failure of the company in the 1920's. Cunningham accepted this story and then for six years was induced to make one cash contribution after another for expenses in settling the estate, to buy off other contenders for the fortune, to buy off people supposedly infringing on the patent, to pay a widow of a co-heir who had died, and so forth. Finally, he was told that the money for the will, supposedly 28 million, was being brought from California by armored car to avoid payment of taxes (illegal operation). Unfortunately, the car was intercepted and more payments from Cunningham were needed. By this time he had paid the swindlers $439,121. He was finally induced by his banker to reveal where all the cash withdrawals had gone and the banker reported the affair to the police. . . . [T]he swindlers were tried on charges of using the mail to defraud and received sentences of two to five years. During the time they were bilking Cunningham they also defrauded seven other people of more than $300,000. (p. 114)

Short Con Games

These schemes involve fewer participants and props, less planning, and less finesse and originality than big cons. In addition, the score in short con games is usually limited to the amount of money the victim has in his possession or can obtain by making a withdrawal from a nearby bank, and unlike big con games, these operations are conducted in a relatively short period of time. Thus, the con man must "hook the sucker" and get rid of him fast. Short con men usually move from area to area, hitting a location suddenly and then moving to the next one quickly in order to avoid contact with victims and the police (Roebuck and Johnson, 1970).

Short con schemes take a variety of forms, with con men improvising variations and new forms to fit changing times and circumstances. The following are representative of some of the more common games employed by these offenders.

High Dice. This operation requires two confederates. In the past, the schemes were typically staged at railroad stations, while today they are initiated at shopping centers or on the street. Operator one will select a well-dressed man or woman who appears to have resources. While establishing rapport with the mark, operator two comes on the scene, looking and acting like a bewildered yokel. Operator one goes to him in the guise of offering aid and returns to the victim with the story that the farm boy has come to the city with substantial savings and is concerned that he will be cheated of his funds unless he can find some honest person to help him handle his money.

Operator one confides to the victim that it would be easy to relieve this yokel of his money. The yokel, he explains, is too dumb to call the police. The "plot" thickens as the yokel expresses a fear of banks but is willing to part with his money if the victim will withdraw some of his own money and place it with his. Under this condition, the yokel will allow the victim to deposit both lots of money in any safe place he chooses. The victim goes to the bank, withdraws his money, and is persuaded by the seemingly naive yokel to place both lots of money in a large brown envelope. While the yokel diverts the victim with animated conversation, operator one cleverly makes a switch, placing the envelope with the two rolls of money in his breast pocket and handing the victim a similar envelope containing folded paper. The yokel, satisfied that his money is safe, obtains the victim's address and promises to come to his house within an hour. Each operator departs in separate directions while the victim hurries home to count his "easy" money (Roebuck and Johnson, 1970). This scheme is illustrated by the following case:

> A 64-year-old Columbus man was approached on the street by a stranger who said he was looking for "Reverend Jackson." He said he was carrying $42,000 in cash and wanted the minister's advice about how to keep it safe. Then a second stranger came

along, and joined in the conversation and suggested that the money should be put in a bank, but the man said that he had beem warned before he left Alabama not to trust banks in the North. He said he had been told that it might be difficult to get the money out again when he wanted it. The Columbus man, who didn't know that he was being foxed by a couple of experts, became indignant about this accusation against Northern business and insisted that it was not true. The other two suggested that he draw some of his own money out of the bank to prove that it could be done. He withdrew $1,000 from his account and put it in a handkerchief which he was told to hold. Later, when he opened the handkerchief he found that it contained only small pieces of toilet paper. His $1,000 had disappeared and so had the strangers. (Waldron, 1969, p. 42)

Pigeon Drop (Pocketbook Drop). This is an ancient con game, reportedly introduced into this country by Chinese immigrants, which is based on the victim's own greed. The plot has three acts. In the first act, the "catchman" approaches the victim with a tale designed to win his sympathy and trust. In the second act, the "hit" partner enters the scene with the news that he has found some money, usually bookie receipts. In order to partake of this "windfall," the victim is asked to produce his own "earnest money," and in a "switch," the money the victim is asked to put up in "good faith" comes into the possession of the players. In the third act, the "blow off," the victim is given some final bogus instructions that allow the confederates to leave his presence before he realizes he has been victimized (Roebuck and Johnson, 1970). Lt. Campbell of the New York City Pickpocket and Confidence Squad indicated that there are some confidence operators who run stables of confidence teams, some of which earn as much as $100,000 a year with this scheme (Kaufman, 1973).

The following cases illustrate two of the many variations of this scheme that have been employed over the years:

Mrs. A. is a 72 year old widow who has lived carefully on a modest income. . . . [One] particular day she had walked only a block or so after leaving the bank and she was approached by another woman who asked for directions. While they were talking a third woman came along and blurted out excitedly, "Look, I just found this envelope on the street. It's full of money; there must be $75,000 here. What shall I do with it?"

The three discuss the matter. The finder said that she did not want to take it to the police because she was afraid they would ask too many questions. The woman who had asked for directions said she knew an attorney in the city who handled some *business for her. She returned shortly with the word that he suggested that they should wait two weeks, and if they still did not know the owner at the end of that time, it would be alright to keep it. The finder generously agreed to split it three ways, providing the other two would show good faith in some way. Mrs. A. showed them her bank book listing a $1,500 balance. She was urged by the others to withdraw the money from the bank and put the cash in a good-faith kitty. She did, and they put it in an envelope along with the other money. The other two women agreed to let Mrs. A. hold the envelope until a time agreed upon to meet and split the $75,000 windfall.*

The three then separated. Mrs. A. took the envelope home with her, but in a few days she began to wonder if she had done the right thing. Just to reassure herself that the money was safe, she steamed open the envelope and was shocked to find only some worthless scraps of paper inside. She had lost all her hard earned savings. (Waldron, 1969, p. 42)

[T]he victim left the doctor's office and was walking along the street to a bus stop when she was approached by a woman of about 25 who inquired about the location of "the Cuban Foundation." Another woman appeared on the scene and she, too, asked about the Foundation.

The first woman volunteered that she had $30,000 in cash to turn over to the organization. The second woman suggested that since this organization apparently did not exist the three women could divide the $30,000.

There was one catch. There always is. The widow would have to put up $5,000 "good faith" money. The two "benefactors" drove the woman to a nearby savings and loan firm where she withdrew the money even though the personnel at the savings company tried to talk her out of it.

She walked out of the bank and handed the $5,000 to one of the women who in turn gave her an envelope supposed to contain her share of the windfall. An instant after the two women drove away, the widow found that she had been duped. The envelope was stuffed with file cards. (Karsko, 1970, p. 8a)

The Bank Examiner Swindle. In this scheme the con artist poses as a bank official or examiner who is investigating the bank or one of its employees. The victim is called and asked to assist the investigation by withdrawing some funds from the bank and temporarily turning them over to the bank examiner. The con man obtains the mark's money and disappears. The following illustrates how this con game operates:

One con artist posed as a bank official to bilk a 70 year old woman out of $2,800 savings. He phoned her at home, warning

*her that she should take her money out of the bank, and he of-
fered to hold it for her so it would be safe. He sent a taxi to pick
her up. She complied, turned the money over to him, and that is
the last she has seen of either him or the cash. In a variation of
this same scheme, a man who claimed to be a bank official said
he wanted a depositor's help in trapping a dishonest employee.
The depositor was to go to a certain teller and draw out $1,500,
then leave and walk down the block. She would be approached
by a detective, to whom she should give the money, and he would
take it back to the bank and redeposit it for her. Of course, he
kept the money and disappeared.* (Waldron, 1969, p. 44)

Spanish Prisoner Game. This con game would warm a
novelist's heart. The mark is approached with an impressive looking "smuggled" letter from a prisoner (ordinarily a Latin
American). The prisoner's letter promises the mark a sizeable
portion of his estate and his daughter's hand in marriage if the
mark will effect his daughter's escape from this terrible country
by sending a large sum of money to a certain courier. (A picture of
a beautiful girl is attached to the letter.) Thus, avarice, sex, ro-
mance, and intrigue all combine to make a Walter Mitty fantasy
a realistic con game (Roebuck and Johnson, 1970).

The Greasy Pig or the Shell Game. One of the oldest of con
games is the old shell game of state fair fame. Three nutshells are
used, and a pea shaped object is shifted from one cover to another
by a nimble fingered operator. On most occasions, the pea is
held under the operator's fingernails instead of under the shell.
The victim is allowed to win just enough to whet his appetite, and
this is used to fuel his interest in gaining some fast money
(Roebuck and Johnson, 1970).

Other Con Games and Swindles. Con men also practice two
related games known as the "badger game" and the "Murphy
game." In the former, a prostitute brings the mark to her room
and during their activities a confederate breaks in upon them,
posing as a shocked and outraged husband. The mark pays off
the "aggrieved husband" and slinks away, both embarrassed and
poorer. A spin-off of this game is the Murphy game, in which a
con man poses as a pimp and accepts money from a mark to
secure a prostitute and then simply disappears (Roebuck and
Johnson, 1970). Finally, Lt. Campbell of the New York City
Pickpocket and Confidence Squad relates a swindle involving the
sale of phony merchandise:

*This confidence game begins when "a lamb" is called on the
phone and told by the caller that "Joe the garbage man or Sam
the mailman suggested I call."*

The caller then says he represents a large department store that is faced with the problem of clearing out its floor models of color television consoles to make room for new shipments.

There aren't enough of these sets to justify a sale, he continues, so he is offering them in lots of five to recommended individuals at a cost of $200 each but the transaction has to be in cash and the buyer must pick up the sets himself. If the perspective victim bites, a meeting is arranged at the parking lot of a shopping center department store. The confidence man waits by the delivery bays for the station wagon that the buyer has described to him.

The con man approaches the car, takes the envelope with the money, and beckons the buyer to back up to the bay. Then he returns to the delivery area and disappears, leaving the shorn lamb to wait for his non-existent bargain. (Kaufman, 1973, p. 49)*

SUMMARY

This chapter focused on the characteristics of conventional property offenses and offenders. Three distinct types of property offenders were identified: ordinary criminals, occasional criminals, and professional criminals. Differences among these types with regard to training, skill level, specialization, and commitment to criminality were discussed.

The second portion of this chapter briefly examined certain types of property offenses. Burglary was discussed, with specific reference being made to nine behavior phases associated with this offense. In addition, characteristics of both the professional burglar and the conventional burglar were examined. Attention was also drawn to the vital role played by the fence, or criminal receiver, in all property offenses, and sketches of the major types of these offenders were presented.

The section on auto theft presented the statistics relating to the prevalence, site, and objectives of this offense, and the modus operandi of professional auto theft rings was also discussed. Next, the crime of shoplifting was examined. Three types of shoplifters, the professional, ordinary, and amateur, were identified and their characteristics discussed. This chapter concluded with a section on con games and swindles. Attention was given to the differences between big con games and short con games, and such short con games as high dice, the pigeon drop, the bank examiner swindle, and the greasy pig were described.

REVIEW

Find the answers to the following questions in the text:

1. Identify and briefly describe the characteristics of the three types of conventional property offenders.

2. List the nine phases of the burglary cycle.

3. Briefly sketch the characteristics of the professional burglar.

4. List the types of conventional burglars.

5. What is the role played by the fence in property offenses?

6. What are the procedures followed by the professional auto theft ring in the theft and resale of automobiles?

7. Do most shoplifters have the same characteristics as other conventional property offenders?

8. What are the major types of shoplifters? Cite some factors that differentiate these types.

9. What are the differences between the big con and the short con games?

10. Identify and briefly describe four short con games.

TERMS TO IDENTIFY AND REMEMBER

professional offender	fence	high dice
ordinary career criminal	boosters	pigeon drop
occasional criminal	heels	bank examiner swindle
the fix	snitches	greasy pig
burglary cycle	big con	shadow professional
tipsters	short con	

REFERENCES

Bloch, H. A. & Geis, G. A.: *Man, Crime and Society.* New York, Random House, Inc., 1970.

Cameron, M. O.: *The Booster and the Snitch: Department Store Shoplifting.* Glencoe, Ill., The Free Press, 1964.

Cavan, R. S.: *Criminology.* New York, Thomas Y. Crowell Co., 1962.

Chamber of Commerce of the United States: *A Handbook on White Collar Crime: Everyone's Problem, Everyone's Loss.* Washington, D.C., 1974.

Clinard, M. B.: *Sociology of Deviant Behavior,* 4th ed. New York, Holt, Rinehart and Winston, Inc., 1974.

Clinard, M., & Quinney, R.: *Criminal Behavior Systems: A Typology,* 3rd ed. New York, Holt, Rinehart and Winston, Inc. 1973.

Conklin, J. E.: *Robbery and the Criminal Justice System.* Philadelphia, J. B. Lippincott Co., 1972.

Davidson, B.: They steal just for the hell of it. The Saturday Evening Post May 18, 1968.

Federal Bureau of Investigation: Auto theft rings. F.B.I. Law Enforcement Bulletin, August, 1975.

Federal Bureau of Investigation: *Uniform Crime Reports: 1975.* Washington, D.C., U. S. Government Printing Office, 1976.

Gasser, R. L.: The confidence game. *In* Cohen, B. J. (ed.): *Crime in America: Perspectives on Criminal and Delinquent Behavior.* Itasca, Illinois, F. E. Peacock Publishers, Inc., 1970.

Gibbons, D. G.: *Society, Crime and Criminal Careers: An Introduction to Criminology.* Englewood Cliffs, New Jersey, Prentice-Hall, Inc., 1973.

Hellman, P.: One in ten shoppers is a shoplifter. The New York Times Magazine March 15, 1970.

Ianni, F.: *Black Mafia: Ethnic Succession in Organized Crime.* New York, Simon & Schuster, Inc., 1974.

Inciardi, J. A.: *Careers in Crime.* Chicago, Rand McNally & Co., 1975.

Karsko, B.: Sure sign of spring: con artists bamboozle $5,000. The Columbus Dispatch March 11, 1970, p. 8a.

Kaufman, M. T.: Elderly warned of con games as complaints rise. The New York Times March 28, 1973, Section 2, p. 49.

King, H.: *Box-Man: A Professional Thief's Journey.* New York, Harper & Row, Publishers, 1972.

Lemert, E. M.: An isolation and closure theory of naive check forgery. *In* Clinard, M., and Quinney, R. (ed.): *Criminal Behavior Systems: A Typology.* New York, Holt, Rinehart and Winston, Inc., 1967.

McCaghy, C. H.: *Deviant Behavior: Crime, Conflict and Interest Groups.* New York, MacMillan, Inc., 1976.

Mydans, S.: Shoplifting: a fast-growing crime. The Tampa Tribune December 12, 1975.

Reckless, W. C.: *The Crime Problem,* 5th ed. New York, Appleton-Century Crofts, 1973.

Reppetto, T. A.: *Residential Crime.* Cambridge, Massachusetts, Ballinger Publishing Co., 1974.

Robin, G. D.: Gang delinquency in Philadelphia. Klein, M. W. (ed.): *Juvenile Gangs in Context: Theory, Research and Action.* Englewood Cliffs, New Jersey, Prentice-Hall, Inc., 1967.

Roebuck, J. B., & Johnson, R. C.: The "short-con" man. *In* Cohen, B. J. (ed.): *Crime in America: Perspectives on Criminal and Delinquent Behavior.* Itasca, Illinois, F. E. Peacock Publishers, Inc., 1970.

Scarr, H. A.: *Patterns of Burglary.* Washington, D. C., U. S. Department of Justice, U. S. Government Printing Office, 1973.

Schur, E. M.: Sociological analysis of confidence swindling. Journal of Criminal Law, Criminology and Police Science *48*:196–309, 1957.

Shover, N.: Structures and careers in burglary. Journal of Criminal Law, Criminology and Police Science *63*:540–548, 1972.

Sutherland, E. H., & Cressey, D. R.: *Criminology.* Philadelphia, J. B. Lippincott Co., 1974.

Wade, A. L.: Social process in the act of juvenile vandalism. *In* Clinard, M., and Quinney, R. (ed.): *Criminal Behavior Systems: A Typology.* New York, Holt, Rinehart and Winston, Inc., 1967.

Waldron, B.: Swindling made easy (with help of the victims). The Columbus Dispatch Magazine June 1, 1969.

Werthman, C.: The function of social definitions in the development of delinquent careers. *In* President's Commission on Law Enforcement and the Administration of Justice: *Task Force on Juvenile Delinquency.* Washington, D. C., U. S. Government Printing Office, 1967.

Wright, R. A.: Nation's retail merchants mobilize security systems to combat fast growing shoplifting trend. The New York Times May 21, 1972, p. 51n.

6 ORGANIZED CRIME: HISTORY AND STRUCTURE

The Wickersham Commission in 1931 and the President's Commission on Law Enforcement and the Administration of Justice in 1967 identified organized crime as a serious national problem.* Public attention has been drawn to organized crime by televised Senate hearings and by such books and films as *The Valachi Papers*, *My Life in the Mafia*, *The Godfather* (Parts I and II), *The Brothers*, and *Capone*. Despite the interest shown in this problem by both the popular and the professional media, there is still some skepticism on the part of the law enforcement community and the public regarding the existence of organized crime and its extent and influence. There is even greater confusion over the nature of criminal syndicates and their relationships. Even when the existence of organized crime is acknowledged, the tendency has been to give it second billing, with the primary emphasis being accorded to street crime — i.e., burglary, robbery, larceny — and this has led to the assumption that street crime and organized crime are not related. One need only examine the involvement of organized crime in narcotics traffic to see that this assumption is unfounded. A single heroin addict requires between $20 and $100 a day to maintain his habit. This money is obtained through robberies, burglaries, shoplifting, and other offenses, with

*Much of the material in this chapter and in Chapter 7 was drawn from lectures by and discussions with Ralph Salerno, formerly a Supervisor of Detectives with the Central Investigation Bureau of the New York City Police Department and currently a nationally recognized consultant on organized crime.

164

addicts receiving from fences only about 20 to 30 per cent of the value of the property stolen. Thus, the addict who depends on theft to secure drugs must steal more than $35,000 worth of property each year in order to maintain his habit.

DEFINING ORGANIZED CRIME

There are a number of reasons for the confusion regarding the nature of organized crime. First, it is not a crime in a traditional sense; nobody has ever been arrested, prosecuted, or convicted for an offense called "organized crime." Furthermore, cases involving certain types of crimes, such as gambling or narcotics, are not *ipso facto* organized crime cases. In determining whether a case involves organized crime figures, other factors in addition to the violation of a specific section of the criminal law are taken into account. Another similar misconception that clouds our understanding of syndicated crime is the belief that it is the people involved that determines whether or not a case is an organized crime case. Some people are under the impression that if the participants in a crime have Italian surnames, then the case is by definition an organized crime case. This reasoning would exclude Meyer Lansky, who is considered by some to be the single most important figure in the history of organized crime; Bumpy Johnson, a black man who dominated the rackets in Harlem from the 1940's to the mid-1960's; Murray Humphreys, Dutch Schultz, Bugsy Siegel, certain Cubans in Miami, and many others within the ranks of organized crime. While it is true that the Italians have dominated organized crime for some time, they at no time have exclusively controlled it.

Some people focus on the term "organized" and lump together all offenses involving criminals operating in groups in the category of organized crime. Using this definition, groups of offenders who band together to commit a specific crime (e.g., rob a bank) and teams of criminals who operate as a group for varying periods of time (e.g., auto theft rings, pickpocket mobs) would all be considered as organized crime groups. However, the fact that a group of criminals organizes to commit an offense or a series of offenses does not constitute a sufficient condition to warrant identification of such groups as organized crime syndicates. It is not the specific activities, the people involved, or the fact that a crime is committed by a group of offenders that defines organized crime.

Perhaps the extent of the confusion over the nature of organized crime is best illustrated by the fact that it took 40 experts meeting at Oyster Bay, Long Island, in May, 1965, for the purpose of examining this phenomenon an entire day to agree upon a definition. They defined organized crime as:

> ... the product of a self-perpetuating criminal conspiracy to wring exorbitant profits from our society by means — fair and foul, legal and illegal. Despite personnel changes the conspiratorial entity continues. It is a malignant parasite which fattens on human weakness. It survives on fear and corruption. By one or another means, it obtains a high degree of immunity from the law. It is a totalitarian organization, a way of life that imposes rigid discipline on underlings who do the dirty work while the top men of the organization are insulated from the criminal act and the consequent danger of prosecution. (Salerno and Tompkins, 1969, p. 303)*

Several features of this definition are worthy of further elaboration. One of the factors that distinguishes organized crime from other types of criminal activities is that it is "self-perpetuating." This means that if any of the leaders die or are sent to prison, the organization continues to operate — in much the same way as a corporation like General Motors would continue to function if its president were to die or become incapacitated. For example, Vito Genovese, reputed "king of organized crime," was imprisoned in 1959 and died there in 1969. While he was in prison, his New York operations were reported to have been run by Jerry Catena, who was the underboss, Tommy Eboli, who was the acting boss, and Mike Miranda, who was the counselor, with Catena assuming command upon Genovese's death. Moreover, this same "family" has been in existence since before Prohibition. No other type of criminal organization (gang) has continued to operate under such circumstances for as long a period of time, because once the ringleaders are imprisoned a criminal group usually disintegrates. Thus, most traditional law enforcement methods are ineffective against organized crime.

A second important aspect of organized crime is that it is a "continuing criminal conspiracy." This refers to the fact that syndicate members have agreed to follow certain procedures in operating their enterprises. Following Prohibition, all major syndicate leaders agreed to stop fighting each other because they realized that it was "bad for business." While violent feuds have not been

---

*From *The Crime Confederation* by Ralph Salerno and John S. Tompkins. Copyright © 1969 by Ralph Salerno and John S. Tompkins. Reprinted by permission of Doubleday & Co., Inc.

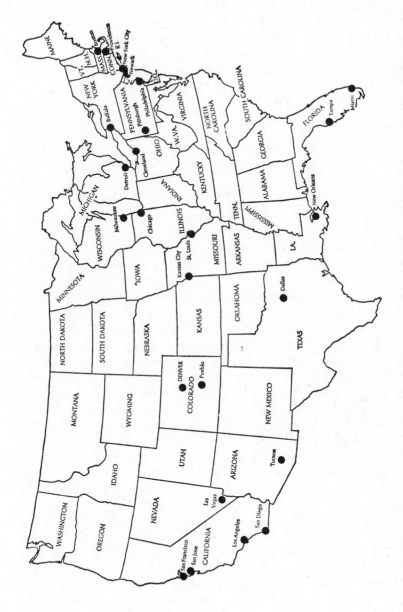

Figure 6–1. Location of Major Syndicate Operations in the United States. From *The Crime Confederation* by Ralph Salerno and John S. Tompkins. Copyright © 1969 by Ralph Salerno and John S. Tompkins. Reproduced by permission of Doubleday & Co., Inc.

entirely eliminated, fighting within and among syndicates has been minimized and most disputes have been settled through negotiation.

The scope of this criminal conspiracy is also significant. Figure 6–1 shows the location of major syndicate operations in the United States. In addition, the syndicate is reported to have spheres of influence in Toronto and Montreal, Canada, and in the Bahamas and other Caribbean islands. Belguim, Luxembourg, and Switzerland must also be included, because it is through these countries that the syndicate funnels stolen securities and launders money from its illegal operations. Its narcotics operations span Italy, Turkey, France, Mexico, South America, and Southeast Asia. This conspiracy, in short, is global in character. It is not some group of petty thieves, but a worldwide operation with an annual income conservatively estimated at $7 to $10 billion, which probably is twice or three times that amount. According to McCulloch (1970), if U. S. Steel, American Telephone and Telegraph, General Motors, Standard Oil of New Jersey, General Electric, Ford Motor Company, IBM, Chrysler, and RCA were all joined together into one conglomerate, their total profits would still be less than that currently accrued by organized crime.

Finally, attention must be given to the role played by fear and corruption in syndicate operations. Corruption is essential to the successful functioning of both legal and illegal syndicate enterprises. Corruption enables organized crime to provide illicit goods and services relatively free from the risks incurred by conventional offenders who violate the law. Corruption is used in legal endeavors to gain contracts, to operate businesses in violation of licensing laws and other regulations, and to cover up the use of inferior materials in construction projects and in products supplied to both government and industry. The syndicate reaches into government at all levels, from the patrolman on the street to federal judges and legislators. The service provided by each of these functionaries depends on his position and influence, while the compensation he receives is based on his position and the importance that the syndicate attaches to the service performed. For example, a sergeant on the vice squad who can provide advance notice of raids on gambling operations will be paid more than a patrol sergeant and certainly more than a beat patroman. Figure 6–2 presents a typology of organized crime payoffs, developed by Pace and Styles (1975), which shows the types of government officials that are likely to be approached by the syndicate, the services these officials typically provide, and the form of compensation they

Participants	How Obligations Are Incurred	How the Debts Are Paid
Elected Officials (Federal)	Support in political campaigns. Trips, vacations on company expense accounts, cash through foundations, and cash bribes through lobbyists, etc.	Political appointments Contracts Personal favors Paroles, pardons
Appointed Staff	Campaign workers Liaison with revenue sources Cash payoffs	Hired as staff worker Retains contact with revenue sources Conducts business for elected official
The Elected Official	**State** Campaign contributions Trips on private accounts Cash through lobbyists Tips on investments, i.e., public franchises and licensees **Local** Campaign contributions Promise to self interest groups—gamblers, etc. Money to citizens' committees during pre-election campaign Cash payoffs through lobbyists	Contracts Allocations of franchises Granting licenses such as liquor Contracts for local service—garbage, ambulance, towing, etc. Abstain from enforcing certain type of laws
The Judge	**All Levels** Campaign contributions Cash payoffs	Favorable decisions Probation, parole and select court assignment
The Lawyer	Client contacts and referrals Campaign workers Liaison with business and criminal clientele Cash payoffs (fees)	Appointments to positions to keep contacts with proper clients Consultants on contracts, crime commissions, etc.
The Police	**All Levels** Political patronage Campaign contributions to elected offices Budget manipulation Cash payoffs	Select enforcement methods Preferential treatment in the degree of enforcement Lack of enforcement

Figure 6–2. A Typology of Organized Crime Payoffs. From Pace, D. F., and Styles, J. C. *Organized Crime: Concepts and Control.* Englewood Cliffs, New Jersey: Prentice-Hall, 1975, p. 31. Reproduced by permission of the authors and publisher.

generally receive. The only major group missing from this list is correctional personnel — prison guards and officials, parole commissioners, probation and parole officers — who provide such services as giving favorable presentence investigations, special privileges to the imprisoned, and early parole and overlooking parole and probation violations. The following provide some specific examples of corruption at various levels:

> [In 1970 Will Wilson, Assistant Attorney General of the State of Ohio, reported that the] Chief of the Intelligence Bureau of the Columbus, Ohio, Police Department received $40,000 over a three year period and patrolmen on-the-beat received approximately $250 per month to protect a numbers operation in Columbus with an annual gross of multi-millions of dollars. The daily intake of one operator, Frank Baldasarro, was estimated to exceed $15,000. (McClellan, 1970, p. 88)

> In 1967, a national magazine suggested that Senator Edward V. Long, a zealous Missouri investigator of wiretapping abuses, was using his committee to help teamster boss James Hoffa establish that he had been improperly convicted on wiretap evidence. The Senator was accused of taking $48,000 from a St. Louis lawyer who represented Hoffa. The Senate Ethics Committee looked into the affair, cleared Long and mentioned that he and the lawyer, who represented many racketeers and gamblers had been friends for 25 years. (Salerno and Tompkins, 1969, p. 253)*

> A former senatorial campaign manager for President Truman admitted that he got the United States Board of Parole to free Paul ("The Waiter") Ricca, Lewis ("Little New York") Campagna, Charles ("Cherry Nose") Gioe, and Phil D'Andrea after [they had served] one-third of their ten year sentences for extortion. (Salerno and Tompkins, 1969, p. 248)*

> William Phillips, then recently assigned as a plainclothes man in the division covering lower Manhattan testified [before the Knapp Commission] that on the basis of his own experiences and conversations with fellow plainclothes men that the average monthly share [of the gambling payoffs] per man ranged from $400 to $500 in midtown Manhattan divisions to $800 on the upper west side, $1,100 in lower Manhattan and $1,500 in Harlem. He stated that [the reported share per man] in two Queens divisions was $600, that in the three Bronx divisions it was $600, $800, and $900 and that in one Brooklyn division it

---

*From *The Crime Confederation* by Ralph Salerno and John S. Tompkins. Copyright © 1969 by Ralph Salerno and John S. Tompkins. Reprinted by permission of Doubleday & Co., Inc.

> *was $800. These figures corroborated quite precisely those received by the [Knapp] Commission from many sources [who were] willing to talk privately but did not want to take the risk of public testimony, and further corroboration has come from similar sources since the Commission's hearings.* (Knapp Commission, 1972, p. 75)

> *The FBI disclosed that among those "owned" by [Raymond] Patriarca [syndicate boss of New England] were top officials in state government, a high ranking court administrator, two licensing officials, a police chief, and numerous state legislators. It also revealed that the going rate for corrupting high state officials in New England was $100,000.* (Dorman, 1972, p. 136)

> *In Elizabeth [New Jersey], Union County District Court Judge Ralph De Vita was convicted in 1970 of obstructing justice by offering a $10,000 payoff to a prosecutor to dismiss a case against two underworld figures charged with bookmaking and attempted bribery of a policeman. Prosecutor Michael R. Imbriani testified that De Vita told him the indictment against the defendants "has got to be killed" and that, if it were, "there are 10 big ones in it for you." De Vita resigned his judgeship and was disbarred after conviction.* (Dorman, 1972, p. 70)

In addition to money, fear, and in some cases violence, are employed by the syndicate to ensure the success of its operations. Threats of bodily harm and destruction of property are used to eliminate competition, to ensure the payment of overdue loans, to persuade a witness not to give damaging testimoney, to assure cooperation, and to persuade businessmen of the need for "protection." More specifically, threats, as well as the actual commission, of such offenses as arson, assault, coercion, mayhem, sabotage, and even murder may be used to take control of a city's garbage collection business, to take over independent bookmakers, and to dominate the restaurant supply industry in a particular area.

HISTORY AND DEVELOPMENT OF SYNDICATED CRIME IN THE UNITED STATES

The history of organized crime in the United States can for the most part be traced in the process of "ethnic succession" whereby each new immigrant group used organized crime as a means to acquire wealth and power before gaining a foothold in legitimate business (Ianni, 1973). In other words, as Daniel Bell (1963) suggests, each immigrant group handed to the next a "queer ladder of social mobility" which had organized crime as the first few rungs.

The roots of organized crime extend far back in our history to the street gangs of hoodlums present in New York as early as the late 1700's, and later in Chicago and San Francisco. These early gangs, spawned in the slums of these cities, typically consisted of a group of juveniles under the leadership of men a few years older than their followers. Quite rapidly, these gangs learned that there was money in muscle. After a gang gained control of an area, the local houses of prostitution and gambling, opium dens, and legitimate businesses were required to pay a fee for "protection." Gang members also hired themselves out as mercenaries, either as a group or individually, to persons or "causes" (Tyler, 1962). During the 1850's, coalitions developed between these gangs and the political machines, particularly in New York and Chicago. Through coercion and violence these gangs could ensure that a certain politician would win an election. They could also virtually guarantee that a ward leader would win nomination for himself or his chosen candidates by simply filling an assembly hall with "shouters and fighters" who were quite able to influence those around them to vote in a particular manner.

The Irish were the first immigrant group to become involved in organized crime on a large scale. In fact, the Irish were such a predominant element in the underworld between 1820 and 1890, that many students of this problem concluded that crime was hereditary among the Irish (Tyler, 1962). Typical of their involvement were McDonald's gambling syndicate in Chicago and John Morrissey's syndicate in New York.

McDonald arrived in Chicago in 1854, and by 1872 he had become a force to be reckoned with in city politics. As the owner and operator of a plush gambling establishment known as "The Store," he played host to politicians, gamblers, city officials, wealthy members of society seeking excitement, and more disreputable elements of the Chicago underworld who came to rub elbows with high society. With the help of those same elements, McDonald extended his control over most of the profitable gambling operations within the city. With the large profits from his various illicit enterprises, McDonald reached out to shape the political fortunes of ward leaders, city officials, and legislators. Those he favored with his attentions received substantial campaign contributions and support, but McDonald's influence did not stop there. He had acquired control of *The Chicago Globe*, a leading metropolitan newspaper, whose editorial columnists were put to work in support of McDonald's handpicked candidates. McDonald amply deserved the title he bore until his death in 1907 — "The Boss of Chicago."

The career of John Morrissey offers a New York parallel to the career of Mike McDonald. Morrissey became the leader of a gang known as the Downtowns while he was still in his teens. By 1855, he had acquired a partnership in a lucrative gambling establishment. Twenty years later he was a wealthy and influential figure in the Irish community — a Godfather-like patron to his fellow Irishmen and a powerful client for Tammany Hall, the political machine of the New York Democratic Party. He ran successfully for political office in the United States Congress and won two terms as a Senator. Albini (1971) points out:

> As a political figure Morrissey could offer both police and political immunity to the gambling establishment under his protection. Before his election to Congress this protection came from services he performed to Tammany Hall. With his election, he himself became a powerful force in the dispensing of protection. . . . In return for this protection before every election those gamblers who were protected made contributions to Morrissey, who retained some of the money for his own personal use and distributed the rest to help meet the needs of the political machine. (p. 188)

The wealth acquired by Irish gangsters like McDonald and Morrissey enabled the Irish to make inroads into the political structure of our major cities. As they eventually gained control of the political machinery of the large cities, the Irish won wealth, power, and respectability by expanding their legitimate business interests and came to dominate such diverse fields as construction, trucking, public utilities, and the waterfront.

Following the Irish, the Jews dominated organized crime, with Arnold Rothstein, Lepke Buchalter, and Gurrah Shapiro controlling gambling and labor racketeering for a decade (Ianni, 1973). Arnold Rothstein, known as "The Brain," was the most prominent of this group. During the 1920's, he was New York's foremost racketeer and he put together the largest gambling empire in the nation. In addition, Rothstein, who worshipped money, was involved in loan sharking, bootlegging, phony securities, gambling, drugs, fencing stolen liberty bonds, and anything else that might result is a payoff (Katz, 1975). In fact, he is credited with providing the initial game plan for sports betting, rum running, and narcotics smuggling (Messick, 1971). The Jews did not dominate organized crime for long; they moved quickly up the ladder into the world of legitimate business and were gradually replaced by the Italians, who did not truly dominate organized crime until the 1930's (Ianni, 1973).

The early involvement of the Italians in criminal activity was not organized. During the 1900's, Black Hand gang activities, which typically involved extortion through the use of threats of death, bodily harm, and kidnapping, were the predominant type of criminal activity in the Italian-Sicilian communities. However, Prohibition provided a new source of illegal profits for the Italian gangsters. They were in an ideal position to take advantage of this source of profits since they had traditionally produced their own wine and the conversion of a home winery to a still was a relatively simple matter. In a short time, central organizations developed that collected alcohol from hundreds of home stills in the same manner that dairies collected milk from independent farmers. While the older immigrants were reluctant to leave the security of the Italian community, thereby hindering their involvement in the distribution process, their sons, who had been socialized into the non-Italian world of gangsters, were more willing to make outside contacks with the distributors. Furthermore, many Italians like Frank Costello assumed lower-echelon positions in Jewish and Irish bootleg gangs, and some, like Al Capone, even became distributors (Ianni, 1972).

The enormous profits in bootlegging did not result from the home stills, which, at most, could turn out a few gallons of alcohol a day. Instead, the real income came from giant illegal breweries, which could serve whole cities or even states. Big money could also be made by bringing liquor in from the French islands off the coast of Canada, across the border, and from beyond the 3-mile ocean limit. Katz (1975) notes that an importer could make $250,000 in profits on one shipload of liquor. But an operation of this kind required organization:

> An organization consisting of a small army of men had to be recruited and supervised to smuggle in a load that size. First the ship had to be bought or chartered, then a competent ship's captain and crew had to be hired. When the ship arrived for secret rendezvous off the coast, speed boats had to meet it and unload the precious cargo while keeping an eye out for hijackers and the Coast Guard. The speed boats then had to make a run for some little inlet. . . . The trip by land was even more treacherous than the one by sea. Split second timing between the speed boats and the men on shore had to be developed so the load of liquor would be exposed as short a time as possible. The booze was loaded in international trucks while the local police were paid to look the other way. Once loaded, the trucks rumbled on the narrow deserted highways into the city. The run resembled an army convoy during war time. Two cars loaded with men armed with shotguns and machine guns preceded the convoy. Everyone was

*on edge watching for hijackers or police. Another armed car
protected the rear.* (Katz, 1975, pp. 53–54)

These types of operations required big money, and they also
required the establishment of appropriate connections with government agents. More importantly, the struggle for the control of
alcohol resulted in tight interstate and international alliances. Thus,
the major figures of organized crime began to carry out their
strategies and operations on a national scale, and this led to the
aggregation of various ethnic gangs into a coast-to-coast network
(Tyler, 1962). The first of these alliances "consisted of seven east
coast syndicates including such underworld notables as Waxy
Gordon, Charles 'Lucky' Luciano, Lewis 'Lepke' Buchalter,
Gurrah Shapiro, Frank Costello, Dandy Phil Kastel, Longy
Zwillman, Benjamin 'Bugsy' Siegel, Owney Madden, and William
'Big Bill' Dwyer (Albini, 1971, p. 201).

The current structure and organization of the Italian criminal
syndicate (often referred to as the Cosa Nostra) emerged from a
bloody struggle in 1930–1931, called the "Castellamarese Wars,"
which started between Italian and Sicilian gangs in New York
and eventually spread throughout the country. This was essentially
a conflict between the old "Moustache Petes" who had controlled
the gangs in the Italian communities since before the turn of the
century and a group of younger immigrants and second-generation
Italian-Americans who have been in control of them ever since.
The war was started by Giuseppe Masseria, who was the single
most powerful figure in Italian crime at that time, in order to
consolidate his power base. Allied with Masseria were mobsters of
future note, including Lucky Luciano, Vito Genovese, Willie
Moretti, Joe Adonis, and Frank Costello. Opposed to Masseria
were such prominent Castellamarese powers as Joe Bonnano and
Joseph Profaci in Brooklyn, Buffalo's Stefano Magaddino, and
Joseph Aiello in Chicago (Maas, 1968). The most frequent victims
of this war were the old "Moustache Petes," particularly the
Castellamarese; in one 48-hour period, 30 to 40 of the old Sicilian
leaders were reportedly killed. However, despite these victories,
Masseria was soon losing the war to Maranzano, and peace feelers
were sent by Masseria to Maranzano. Realizing that the war was
already lost, several of Masseria's lieutenants secretly surrendered
to Maranzano, and in exchange for their promise to have Masseria
killed, Maranzano agreed to halt the war. On April 20, 1931, the
Castellamarese Wars came to an end when three of these lieutenants
killed Masseria while lunching with him in a Coney Island restaurant (Ianni, 1972).

Maranzano declared peace and called a meeting of from 400 to 500 gangsters at which he outlined the structure for each of the families in the New York metropolitan area. He decreed that everyone would become part of a "family" that would consist of a boss and an underboss who together would be responsible for a group of regular members designated as soldiers. Further, he named himself dictator — or as he put it, *capo di tutti capi*, meaning "boss of all bosses." Maranzano failed to recognize, however, that one of the reasons why the younger men had fought the war was because they wanted to run their own gangs without having to answer to a "Mr. Big." Fearing (correctly) that Maranzano was setting them up for assassination, Vito Genovese and Lucky Luciano arranged to have Maranzano killed. Following Maranzano's assassination, some 40 Italian-Sicilian gang leaders, practically all of them old timers, were slain within a 72-hour period (Salerno and Tompkins, 1969).

With Maranzano eliminated, Luciano met with the gang leaders of the New York metropolitan area and formed a council of six bosses. In the same year (1931), leaders from all of the Italian syndicates in the United States met and decided to form a national crime cartel. In 1934 the non-Italian groups, including such gangs as the Bugs and Meyer Mob, and the Cleveland syndicate headed by Moe Dalitz, became part of the cartel at a meeting held at the Waldorf Astoria in New York. In light of the involvement of these other groups, there may be some question regarding the applicability of the label "Cosa Nostra," to this collective syndicate. The term "Cosa Nostra" applies only to the inner core of organized crime, which is composed of persons of Sicilian-Italian parentage who are members of the Italian syndicate. Moreover, even the term "Cosa Nostra," which was popularized by the testimony of Joseph Valachi before the McClellan Committee, is not a correct label for the Italian criminal syndicate as a whole because it is only used in the New York metropolitan area. In New England the Italian syndicate is referred to as "the Office," in Chicago it is called "the Outfit," and in Buffalo it is known as "the Arm" (Messick, 1971).

Salerno and Tompkins (1969) indicate that law enforcement personnel have felt that the most appropriate term for this national criminal cartel is "Confederation." While the Confederation is dominated by the Italian syndicate, it also includes Jews, Armenians, Poles, Germans, blacks, Puerto Ricans, and Cubans. Thus, while Meyer Lansky is not a member of the Italian syndicate, he is an important associate of the Confederation and is the equal of any family boss and superior to some in both power and influence.

Meyer Lansky is one of the singular figures in the Confederation. Before World War II he was engaged in illegal gambling activities in Florida and elsewhere. He had the foresight to see what could happen to gambling in Las Vegas. He could see the boom coming. Seeking expansion, he established gambling operations in Cuba. When Cuba's helpful dictatorship fell, to be replaced by Castro, Lansky was invited to leave. He got to a member of Parliament in Jamaica but the whole effort failed. He then set up shop in the Bahamas. All along, Mr. Lansky has always been smart enough to cut in the men with the Italian-sounding names. He became the bridge to the export of bigtime gambling in England. He is a wizard in the transmission of cash. He has always had the confidence to corrupt, to make the approaches, to take the chances, to start the wheels rolling. When Lansky dies, it will be the end of a pioneer and an era. He is no candidate for the Hall of Fame but organized crime will find him impossible to replace. In a sense, he is more important than any single Cosa Nostra boss. (Salerno and Tompkins, 1969, p. 88)*

STRUCTURE OF THE ITALIAN CRIMINAL SYNDICATE

The testimony of Jospeh Valachi before the McClellan Committee, as well as information gathered from informants and from wiretaps, has provided us with a clear picture of the structure of the Italian criminal syndicate. The core of the syndicate today comprises approximately 24 families operating as criminal cartels in large cities across the country. Included within this group are five families in New York City and one each in Buffalo, Boston, Newark, Chicago, Detroit, San Francisco, Los Angeles, San Jose, New Orleans, and Tampa.

The syndicate is governed by a "commission" that over the years has consisted of 9 to 12 bosses of the most powerful local syndicates. The commission is by no means a representative body; those with the largest families, the longest tenure, and the most money command the greatest respect. Until a few years ago, the balance of power on the commission rested with the leaders of New York City's five families: Vito Genovese, Carlo Gambino, Joseph Profaci, Thomas Lucchese, and Joseph Bonnano. (Salerno and Tompkins, 1969).

---

*From *The Crime Confederation* by Ralph Salerno and John S. Tompkins. Copyright © 1969 by Ralph Salerno and John S. Tompkins. Reprinted by permission of Doubleday & Co., Inc.

The commission serves as a combination supreme court, legislature, board of directors, and arbitration board, but its principal functions are judicial. Syndicate members look to the commission as the ultimate authority in organizational and jurisdictional disputes. Furthermore, while the commission does not actually choose new bosses, syndicate members are required to obtain the advice and consent of the commission prior to installing a new boss.

Each family is headed by a boss whose authority is absolute and unquestioned within his group, his geographical area, and any extended territory under his influence that does not conflict with that of other recognized syndicates. As shown in Figure 6–3, each boss has an underboss (*sottocapo*); or vice president, in charge of relaying instructions and collecting information. On the same level as the underboss is the buffer. His functions are much like those of an administrative assistant and therefore his title does not appear on the organization chart. In addition to being an aide, the buffer may serve the boss on occasion as a driver, messenger, counselor, and bodyguard. The buffer insulates the boss by serving as a go-between through whom money, commands, information, and complaints can flow back and forth from the men to the boss. In this way, the boss cannot be directly tied to any of the family's illegal activities.

Consigliere (counslor) is another position within the command structure. The person serving in this capacity is generally an elder statesman who is partially or fully retired. His major function is to provide advice to the boss or any other member of the family. However, he occupies a staff position, and therefore the advice he offers does not carry with it the mandate of an order or command. Next in rank below the underboss is a position variously described as "lieutenant" (*capodecina*), "captain" (*caporegima*), or simply "head" (*capo*). The person occupying this position functions in the same way as a platoon or squad leader in the army or a manager within a business organization, i.e., as chief of an operating unit. Each lieutenant generally has one or two associates who work closely with him and operate as messengers and buffers between him and the other members of his group. The number of lieutenants within a family, as well as the number of men under a given lieutenant, varies with the size and activities of each family.

The lowest level members of a family are called "soldiers" (*soldati*) or "button men." Soldiers may operate in illicit enterprise for their bosses on a commission basis, or they may "own their own business" and pay a percentage to the boss for the right to operate. Partnerships between two or more soldiers and between

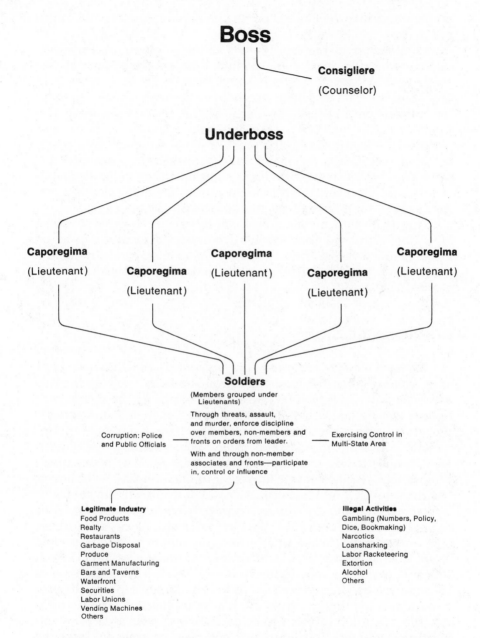

Figure 6–3. An Organized Crime Family. President's Commission on Law Enforcement and Administration of Justice. *Task Force Report: Organized Crime.* Washington, D. C.: U. S. Government Printing Office, 1967, p. 9. Reproduced by permission of the U. S. Department of Justice.

soldiers and men higher up on the command structure are quite common.

Membership in the family ends at the soldier level. However, soldiers generally have many people working under their supervision who are not members but are "eligibles,"* employees, and functionaries. In fact, these are the people who actually operate the various enterprises. They answer the telephones, drive the trucks, sell the narcotics, take the bets, make collections, and work in the legitimate businesses. For example, in a black neighborhood in Chicago the major lottery business was operated by black workers, with the bankers for this operation being Japanese-Americans. However, this entire operation, including the bankers, was licensed for a fee by a member of the Chicago family.

The number of members in a family ranges from about 20 to 800. It is estimated that the total number of members in all of these families ranges from 5000 to 7500 members (President's Commission on Law Enforcement and the Administration of Justice, 1967).

ETHNIC SUCCESSION

We have already suggested that organized crime has been used as a stepping stone for immigrant groups on their way up the ladder of social mobility. The question is which group, if any, will replace the Italian-Americans — as the Italian-Americans replaced the Jews, who themselves replaced the Irish before them. Observers of the organized crime scene indicate that blacks, Puerto Ricans, and, to a lesser extent, Cubans are moving in this direction. Blacks are aggressively moving into higher positions of power in urban politics, and both blacks and Puerto Ricans are gradually displacing Italians in some organized crime operations. For example, in New York City, the Puerto Ricans, blacks and Cubans are now replacing Italian-Americans in the numbers racket. In some areas, such as East Harlem and Brooklyn, this succession has been peaceful, with the Italian-Americans in effect leasing the rackets to these groups on a concession basis. The family supplies the protection and the money while the blacks or Puerto Ricans actually run the operation. However, in other areas, such as Central and West Harlem, this transition has not been so peaceful, and the Italian syndicate members are in reality being driven out. Recent

---

*Eligibles are persons who have met all of the requirements for membership in a family, but have not been admitted because there are no vacancies.

estimates indicate that upwards of one fourth of the operation and control of the numbers racket in New York City has thus far changed hands (Ianni, 1973).

The enterprises operated by these newer groups cannot be characterized as "big" operations, in comparison to those of the Italian-American families with their many levels of authority and countless employees and associates, many of whom are not aware of the activities of the others involved. At the present time, black and Puerto Rican enterprises are still relatively small, specialized operations that have not as yet developed into large empires (syndicates) or even into interconnected baronies. Nevertheless, a recent study conducted by Ianni (1974) of the activities of these groups indicated that there are a number of connections among criminal networks engaged in the same types of businesses (e.g., narcotics). Evidence from this study suggests that "the present pattern of loosely structured, largely unrelated networks has not reached its highest stage of development and that what seems to be necessary for these networks to become elaborated into large combines, like those now present among Italians, is (1) greater control over sectors of organized crime outside of as well as inside the ghetto, (2) some organizing principle that will serve as kinship did among the Italians to bring the disparate networks together into larger criminally monopolistic organizations and (3) better access to political power and the ability to corrupt it" (Ianni, 1974, pp. 316–317). Ianni suggests that drug trafficking is an area that blacks and Puerto Ricans could possibly monoplize and thereby use as a base for expansion both within and outside the ghetto. Within the ghetto, drug producers and wholesalers can expect that neighbors will provide them with protection from the police for their operations. The movement toward tougher drug laws and stiffer penalties will increase the risks associated with drug trafficking and thereby reduce competiton from outside the ghetto. Moreover, while blacks and Hispanics may find whites reluctant to deal with black loan sharks or fences, drug addicts are colorblind when it comes to securing drugs to meet their needs. In addition, the enormous profits associated with drug trafficking will provide blacks and Hispanics with the money to corrupt police and other government officials, without whose protection no syndicate operation can long endure. Ianni feels that if blacks, either in partnership or in competition with Hispanic groups, can take control of local drug trafficking, this will provide the basis for a national or even international operation. Furthermore, they can take their profits and, like the Italians, reinvest them in other illicit enterprises.

According to Ianni, the organizing principle for coalescing black and Hispanic crime networks into syndicates is currently visible within their respective networks. The Hispanics, and particularly the Cubans, may well adopt the existing "family" model of organization employed by the Italians. On the basis of his research, Ianni maintains that the bond of kinship seems stronger in Hispanic criminal networks than in black networks. Also there is evidence that Hispanics are working collaboratively with Italian families to a much greater extent than blacks. For example, in September, 1972, "Cubans operated the gambling concessions at the San Gennaro Festival, New York's annual Italian street fair. Until 1972, the gambling tables and wheels had always been operated by Italians. Obviously some arrangement must have been made for the Italians to allow the Cubans to operate, even under franchise, in the heart of "Little Italy" (Ianni, 1974, p. 322).

However, while there is a cultural basis for a family-type organization among the Hispanics, this is not true among the blacks. Ianni believes that "black militancy" is the "organizing principle" that will serve to strengthen the structure of black organized crime and, more importantly, unite the various groups under one code of behavior. The Jews, Irish, and Italians who became involved with organized crime were striving to become "Americans." However, blacks are entering organized crime during a period when being black, being a "brother" or a "sister," gives rise to a family-type structure based upon militancy. Blacks involved in organized crime may also feel a common bond as a result of being victims of an oppressive system that rejects their attempts at political and social mobility.

Before black criminal networks can become syndicates and extend their activities outside the ghetto, they must have better access to and be able to corrupt the political power structure. Ianni questions whether blacks will be able to develop the kinds of social relationships with white politicians that provide the setting in which deals are made, bribes are offered or solicited, and protection developed. It is quite possible that those Italians who remain involved in organized criminal activities will come to serve as power brokers for black and Hispanic syndicates, thus providing them with the protection they need to expand their activities outside the ghetto.

The movement of the blacks and the Hispanics into a dominant position in organized crime is predicated upon the disengagement of the Italians from their organized crime–related activities. There is some evidence that the Italians are moving in this direction. For example, Ianni (1975) indicates that in the families associated with the Italian criminal syndicate he studied progressively fewer members of each generation have become involved in syndicate-related activities. While both sons of the syndicate's founder remained in the business, and most of their sons did likewise, only one third of the fourth generation men are involved in the family business. The rest of the fourth generation sons became physicians, lawyers, college teachers, or ran their own businesses, and most of the daughters married business or professional men who were usually, but not always, of Italian descent. Most of them would like to forget how their grandfathers made the money that put them through college and supported their "upper class" lifestyle. Ianni feels it is likely that fifth generation males will divorce themselves from their family's illegitimate activities and become involved exclusively in legitimate businesses. The likelihood of this is increased by the fact that those who are currently involved in family criminal enterprises are becoming more and more dissatisfied with the present state of these operations. This is evident in the following discussion of a family's loan sharking operation:

> At a family baptism, Charlie Lupollo's* son Patsy remarked, "I wouldn't put money even at 15 percent now — half the guys who borrow are on dope and no matter what you do they aren't going to pay you back because they end up on Riker's Island [county jail] or getting shot by the cops. I told Joey (his cousin, who is a stockbroker) that I like his stock market thing much better even if it ain't sure, you don't have all those creeps and bums to work with." (Ianni, 1975, p. 92)

What Ianni has observed with respect to the Italian extended family that he studied is the same process of ethnic succession that the Jews followed in previous decades. That is, some of the Italians associated with organized crime families are disengaging themselves from their illicit enterprises and fewer of the sons of syndicate members are taking positions in the crime familes. However, there are indications that bosses of the Italian syndicates are bringing over young males from Sicily to operate syndicate enterprises. If these young immigrants follow the same pattern of involvement in syndicate activities that Ianni observed, the Italian syndicates will remain operative for at least several generations to come.

---

*Lupollo is a pseudonym that Ianni gave to the New York City Italian crime family that he studied.

The question is: What position will the new black and Hispanic syndicates occupy relative to their Italian counterparts. At this time the blacks and Hispanics are pushing the Italians out of the ghettos and are taking over control of the narcotics, gambling, and loan sharking activities in those areas. However, it is likely that for some time to come the blacks and Hispanics will still use the Italian layoff banks. The Italian syndicates will continue their bookmaking, gambling and loan sharking activities in middle and upper class areas and in those lower class areas not dominated by black or Hispanic syndicates. They will also remain active in narcotics importation, particularly heroin brought in through the Turkish-French connection, because of their close ties with the Corsican syndicates. Finally, the Italian syndicates will continue to expand their penetration of legitimate businesses, using techniques adapted from their illicit operations to gain control of and to manage these enterprises.

SUMMARY

The history and organizational structure of organized crime are briefly described in this chapter. The definition of organized crime presented emphasizes that organized crime is a continuing and self-perpetuating criminal conspiracy that relies heavily upon the use of fear and corruption to carry on its activities. The roots of organized crime reach far back into our national history; at various times, nearly every national or ethnic group has been represented in the ranks of organized crime. While the Italian-Sicilian syndicates have dominated the scene, there are indications that black and Hispanic groups are moving into organized crime in growing numbers (illustrating the principle of "ethnic succession") as the latest generation of Italians finds safer and more attractive opportunities in the legitimate business sector.

REVIEW

Find the answers to the following questions in the text:

1. Discuss some of the reasons for the common misconceptions regarding the nature of organized crime.

2. What is meant by the assertion that organized crime is a "continuing and self-perpetuating criminal conspiracy"?

3. Why are intimidation and corruption crucial to the operation of organized crime?

4. Which immigrant group was the first to become involved in organized crime on a large scale? How did this happen?

5. Describe the development of Italian-Sicilian syndicates during Prohibition. Why did bootlegging provide such a major impetus to the process of syndication?

6. What were the Castellamarese Wars? Who were the principal victors and who were the principal victims in that conflict? What was the major result of these wars?

7. Outline the structure of a typical Italian-Sicilian organized crime family. Identify the duties and responsibilities of the various persons in the hierarchy.

8. What is meant by the "commission"? How does it relate to the independence and autonomy of family operations?

9. Discuss the concept of "ethnic succession." What groups at present are moving into organized crime on a growing scale?

10. What accounts for the apparent disengagement of Italians from organized crime—related activities? How do prospects appear for the future of the Italians in organized crime?

TERMS TO IDENTIFY AND REMEMBER:

family	buffer	*capo*
ethnic succession	button men	*consigliere*
Confederation	syndicate	*caporegima*
sottocapo	Cosa Nostra	*soldati*
capodecina		

REFERENCES

Albini, J. L.: *The American Mafia: Genesis of a Legend*. New York, Appleton-Century-Crofts, 1971.

Bell, D.: The myth of the Cosa Nostra. New Leader 46:12–15, 1963.

Dorman, M.: *Payoff: The Role of Organized Crime in American Politics*. New York, David McKay, Co., Inc., 1972.

Ianni, F. A. J.: *A Family Business: Kinship and Social Control of Organized Crime*. New York, Russell Sage Foundation, 1972.

Ianni, F. A. J.: *Ethnic Succession in Organized Crime: Summary Report*. Washington, D. C., U. S. Government Printing Office, 1973.

Ianni, F. A. J.: *Black Mafia: Ethnic Succession in Organized Crime*. New York, Simon & Schuster, Inc., 1974.

Ianni, F. A. J.: The Godfather is going out of business. *Psychology Today* 9:87–92, 1975.

Katz, L.: *Uncle Frank: The Biography of Frank Costello*. New York, Pocket Books, 1975.

Knapp Commission: *Report on Police Corruption*. New York, George Braziller, Inc., 1972.

Maas, P.: *The Valachi Papers*. New York, Bantam Books, 1968.

McClellan, J.: Testimony before the Committee on the Judiciary of the House of Representatives on the Control of Organized Crime in the United States. 91st Congress, 2nd Session, May 20, 1970.

McCulloch, W.: Testimony before the Committee on the Judiciary of the House of Representatives on the Control of Organized Crime in the United States. 91st Congress, 2nd Session, May 20, 1970.

Messick, H.: *Lansky.* New York, Berkeley Medallion Books, 1971.

Pace, D. F., and Styles, J. C. *Organized Crime: Concepts and Control.* Englewood Cliffs, New Jersey, Prentice-Hall, Inc., 1975.

President's Commission on Law Enforcement and Administration of Justice: *Task Force Report: Organized Crime.* Washington, D. C., U. S. Government Printing Office, 1967.

Puzo, M.: *The Godfather.* Greenwich, Connecticut, Fawcett Publications, 1969.

Salerno, R., and Tompkins, J. S.: *The Crime Confederation: Cosa Nostra and Allied Operations in Organized Crime.* Garden City, New York, Doubleday & Co., Inc., 1969.

Tyler, G.: *Organized Crime: A Book of Readings.* Ann Arbor, University of Michigan Press, 1962.

7 ORGANIZED CRIME: CRIMINAL AND LEGITIMATE ENTERPRISES

Organized criminal syndicates are involved in illegal activities that provide maximum profit and minimal risk of law enforcement intervention. Salerno (1976) has suggested that an appropriate symbol for organized crime syndicates would be a scale similar to that used to depict Justice, with one side labeled "Risk" and the other side labeled "Profit." The possible risks associated with syndicate activity are arrest, trial, and incarceration, but with rare exceptions, the scale is generally tilted heavily toward the profit side.

As we have already noted, organized crime is involved in a variety of legitimate businesses. In this chapter, we shall examine both the criminal and the legitimate enterprises conducted by organized criminal syndicates.

CRIMINAL ENTERPRISES

Among the illegal activities carried on by organized criminal syndicates are gambling, loan sharking, narcotics trafficking, cigarette smuggling, counterfeiting, frauds involving the use of arson, sale and distribution of illegal alcohol, prostitution, protection rackets, and fencing stolen property. Since it is beyond the scope of this book to examine all these activities in detail, we shall focus on those enterprises that provide the major source of income for the syndicates.

187

Gambling

Gambling is the major source of income for organized crime. A survey conducted for the President's Commission on Law Enforcement and the Administration of Justice, using extremely conservative ratios in order to avoid the astronomical estimates made by previous surveys, indicated that illegal gambling brings in $20 billion a year gross, with a net income to organized crime of $7 billion (Salerno and Tompkins, 1969). The syndicate is involved in a variety of illegal gambling activities that include illegal casino gambling, use of illegal gambling devices (e.g., slot machines, sports pool cards, numbers [policy]), and bookmaking, with the latter two providing the major source of gambling income.

The Numbers Game

"The numbers," "policy," and "Bolita" (used in the southern part of the United States) are all terms used to describe a daily illegal lottery in which a player selects a one, two, or three digit number, with three digit numbers predominating. The winning numbers are derived each day from some public source, such as payoffs at the race track or the U. S. Treasury balance. The numbers has always been popular in ghetto areas because it permits small bets — 50¢ and $1.00 — provides hope for a new life at the end of the rainbow.

> A hit can change a guy's whole life around," says a veteran Harlemite, who has seen it happen many times. "The guy who wins sometimes sets himself up in business in a grocery store or bar. I know cases where fellows made so much from a good hit that they set themselves up as numbers runners. Others paid off their bills, their mortgages. And some have sent their kids to college with the money they made on numbers." (Cook, 1971, p. 27)

The numbers game is very simple. A player bets that a certain combination of three figures will turn up, for example, the last three digits in the amount bet for the day at a given race track. If the total amount bet at the track for a given day is $3,716,602, then the winning number for that day is 602. While the player gets paid off at the rate of usually 500, 550, or 600 to 1, he has only one chance in a thousand to win. Furthermore, he is generally obligated to pay 10 per cent commission to the runner who took his lucky bet. Thus, it is clear that the odds favor the numbers operator, who has at least 400 extra points working for him.

As shown in Figure 7–1, a typical numbers operation is a three-tiered pyramid. The numbers men, or "runners," are at the bottom of the pyramid. They deal with the bettors and may be housewives, barmaids, butchers, grocers, pizza parlor owners — virtually anyone. A numbers runner may operate from a stationary place of business or within a specified area. Because numbers

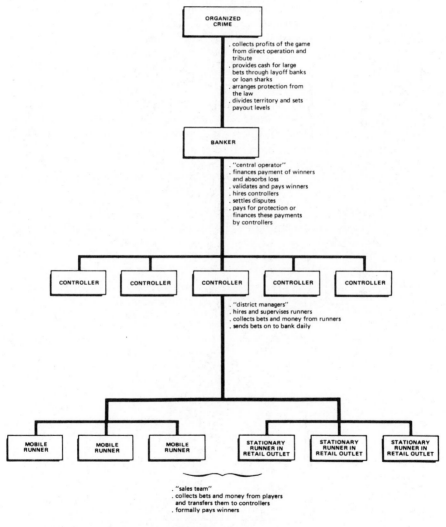

Figure 7–1. Fund for the City of New York: *Legal Gambling in New York: A Discussion of Numbers and Sports Betting.* New York, 1972.

runners operate out in the open, they are the agents of the game who are most likely to be arrested. For taking this risk, they are paid a commission of 25 per cent of their receipts. Some may also receive the additional fringe benefits of bail and legal counsel in case of arrest. After deducting this 25 per cent, the runner delivers the remaining 75 per cent and the betting slips to a "controller," who may handle from five to fifty runners. The controller makes a record of the numbers covered and which runner brought in the bets. A controller generally receives 10 per cent of the original bet. In a typical operation, neither the runner nor the controller takes any risks of loss. A "bank pick-up man" collects the remaining 65 per cent of the money and a list of the numbers bet and delivers it to a "policy bank."

A policy bank may receive bets from as many as a dozen or two dozen controllers. From the 65 per cent of the bet money he receives, the banker must pay off the winners, pay for police protection, and pay office costs (salaries for pick-up men and adders [bookkeepers] and in some instances rental for office space). Table 7–1 shows a breakdown of the estimated operating costs and profits of numbers banks. Banks giving odds of 500 to 1 make a profit of approximately 5.5 per cent and banks that give odds of 600 to 1 make a profit of approximately 14 per cent. The bank's volume is dependent upon the number of runners it employs (25 to 2500) as well as the size of the community in which it operates. Singer and Candela (1973) estimate that the total daily

TABLE 7–1. ESTIMATED COSTS AND PROFIT (AS A PERCENTAGE OF SALES) OF NUMBERS OPERATIONS*

	PAYOFF	
	500 to 1	**600 to 1**
Sales costs, runners	25.0%	25.0%
Sales costs, controllers	5.0	5.0
Payback to winners, net	48.5	57.5
Protection	5.0	5.0
Office costs	2.0	2.0
Total costs	85.5	94.5
Profit	14.5	5.5

*Data from Fund for the City of New York: *Legal Gambling in New York: A Discussion of Numbers and Sports Betting*. New York, 1972, pp. 30–31.

bets for banks in New York City range from $10,000 to $100,000. The following are profiles of different size numbers operations:

> One of the largest banks in Philadelphia was raided by IRS intelligence agents on February 27, 1967. The bank employed over two hundred writers and runners, did a daily business of $50,000 and a yearly volume of $12.5 million. . . .

> On December 17, 1969, Philadelphia police raided the head-quarters of a West Philadelphia bank [the Robinson bank]. Carl Robinson and two office workers were arrested. Records seized indicated that the bank's average daily volume of business was between $5,000 and $10,000, or between $1.25 and $2.5 million per year. The bank employed 78 writers and received an average of 25,000 bets per day. . . .

> The Grosso operation in Pittsburgh was found to handle an annual volume of $12 million. At the Maloney trial Grosso, who had voluntarily submitted to a polygraph and passed it, testified to the following: (a) He handled a daily volume of between $40 thousand and $60 thousand with 3,000 to 5,000 numbers writers; (b) Maloney, Assistant Superintendent of Police, was paid $1,000 per month plus money for holidays and vacations; (c) $15,000 per year was paid by Grosso to bag men for political officials in Pitts-burgh; (d) Bribes were paid to police and other officials totaling $25,000 annually. . . .

> Erie [County, Pennsylvania] police raided a $1,000 a day numbers operation of Salvatore Calafato which was believed to be laying off large bets with organized crime syndicates in Pittsburgh and Youngstown. (Pennsylvania Crime Commission, 1970, pp. 28–32)

The numbers banker uses a layoff bank in order to minimize his losses from heavy bets on particular numbers. The layoff bank operates as a "super bank" for numbers bankers. By taking some of the money gambled on a heavily bet number and betting it with a layoff bank, the numbers banker can minimize his losses if the number hits, since the layoff bank would then be responsible for making the payoff. The layoff business requires a large amount of money, and therefore only the wealthiest syndicate leaders can provide this service. For example, in Philadelphia the layoff bank for a majority of bankers is operated by the lieutenants of Cosa Nostra boss Angelo Bruno (Pennsylvania Crime Commission, 1970).

The direct involvement of syndicates in the numbers business follows several patterns: (1) independent banks operated by non-syndicate members may pay a percentage of their receipts (usually 1 per cent) to the local syndicate boss; (2) banks may be operated by a soldier or lieutenant of a syndicate for the boss or as an independent franchise for a percentage of the operations; (3) the syndicate may operate the layoff banks, which in some areas may represent its sole source of income from the numbers; (4) the syndicate may provide loans to independent bankers when their cash reserves are not sufficient to pay off winners (Cressey, 1969; Fund for the City of New York, 1972). In addition, local syndicates provide independent bankers with protection by means of their capital and wide range of contacts with politicians and high level police officials. Organized crime also provides other forms of needed protection. If a banker wants to earn a steady living from the game, he must avoid the disruption of his operations caused by territorial wars. In addition, it is to the advantage of the banker to maintain low payoff odds and to avoid having these odds forced up by competition. The syndicate has the power to enforce and determine the payoff levels and divisions of territory (Fund for the City of New York, 1972). For example, in the New York City area, police intelligence information confirmed the existence of "a standing committee which met regularly to control the industry and many facets of it beyond the payoff ratio, including the regulation of non-raiding of employees and the adjudication of territorial disputes" (Salerno and Tompkins, 1969, p. 356).

Bookmaking

The bookmaker, or "bookie," is in the business of taking bets on horse races, football games, baseball games, and other contests. With regard to betting on team sports, the bookmaker handles bets that cannot be made comfortably between friends. Thus, he performs the role of broker between those who wish to bet on opposing teams, for which he charges a commission on the total amount wagered. His objective is to equalize the amount wagered on each team so that the losses of one set of bettors will pay for the winnings (less his commission) of the other. In order to equalize the bets on each side, the bookmaker employs a point spread in the case of football and basketball and odds in the case of baseball.

The point spread operates as a handicap to the stronger team. For example, if the Dolphins are favored by 7 points to beat the Buccaneers, then Dolphin backers will win only if their team wins by more than 7 points. However, should the Dolphins win by exactly 7 points, then the betting is tied and all wagers are returned. (This is often avoided by giving point spreads in half points, e.g., 7-1/2.) Furthermore, in order to encourage backing for a team that is being inadequately bet, a bookmaker will change the point spread as betting develops before a game. Bookmakers can also protect themselves from losses by simply refusing to take bets on a given team if the point spread fails to equalize bets on a given game. Moreover, the bookmaker can compensate for the imbalance of his bets by laying off with another bookmaker. Bookmakers who balance their books keep 4.5 per cent of the total football and basketball "handle," or "take," as their commission because a bettor must put up $11 to win $10. For example, if a bookmaker has one $10 bet on each team, he will take in $22 and pay out $21. On this transaction, then, his commission is $1, which is 4.5 per cent of a $22 handle.

The percentage that a bookmaker receives on baseball bets is more complicated to compute, as the following illustrates:

> *Suppose that odds on a game between Baltimore and Cleveland is 7-1/2 to 5. The bookmaker will list the game as 7–8 Baltimore favorite. This means that the bettor on Baltimore must risk $8 to win $5. A Cleveland backer must bet $5 to win $7. With one wager on each side, the bookmaker takes in $13. If Baltimore wins, he pays $13; if Cleveland wins, $12. Assuming that the odds are accurate and Baltimore wins three of five games, the bookmaker takes in $65 (5 × $13) and pays out $63. His commission over the five games is $2 or 3.1 per cent.* (Fund for the City of New York, 1972, pp. 40–41)

A bookmaker's commission may vary with the odds he gives, which depends upon the size of the bet and whether he is taking layoff action from other bookmakers. However, on the whole he makes less on baseball bets than he does on football and basketball.

Horse racing provides the bookmaker with a much larger commission than sports betting. Bookmakers pay track odds and thus in effect receive the same 17 per cent taken by the track if their bets are in the same proportion as those made at the track. Also, bookmakers normally have maximum payoffs that in some instances are less than those paid at the track. However, despite the fact that they make more on horse race bets, many large-scale bookies seem to prefer sports bets for several reasons, including the fact that they often don't get enough betting on horse races to balance their books, track odds are often uncertain, and they must keep informed about which tracks are reasonably protected against fixes (Singer and Candela, 1973).

Bookmaking operations have very simple organizational structures. Typically, at the bottom of such an operation is the "street bookie," who is also known as the "handbook," "street agent," "commission man," or "runner." His function is to take the bets from the public. He does this in person, over the telephone, or both. Some street agents operate out of fixed locations, such as record shops, grocery stores, bars, and corner newsstands. Usually they work for either a salary or a percentage of customer losses (LEAA Technical Assistance Division, 1972).

The bookmaker occupies the next level in the organizational structure of bet-taking enterprises. Persons occupying this position usually have title to a neighborhood, which they divide up among their street agents. Each street agent funnels his bets to the book-makers's "office," which is usually staffed by a "tabber" who keeps track of the bets and is responsible for deciding when to change lines or spreads and when to lay off bets. The bookmaker is either a low level member of a criminal syndicate or an independent entrepreneur. As a member of a criminal syndicate, a bookmaker will operate his business in exchange for a percentage of the profits or for a straight salary. Some syndicate members and independent entrepreneurs operate their enterprises on a franchise basis, paying the local syndicate a percentage of profits and in some cases laying off all bets with the syndicate bank. Table 7–2 provides an illustration of the weekly income and expenses of a bookmaking operation with 22 runners. If this office

TABLE 7–2. ONE WEEK STATEMENT OF THE INCOME AND EXPENSES OF A BOOKMAKING OPERATION*

Income			
Horse racing	$ 35,000		
Football	141,000		
Gross income	$176,000		
Less payments to betters		$163,500	
Net income before expenses			$12,500
Operating Expenses			
Payroll, including			
Manager's salary	1,500		
Rent and telephone	200		
Arrest expenses	1,000		
Runner commissions @ $300 each	6,600		
Total expenses			9,300
Balance before protection costs			3,200

*Data from Fund for the City of New York: *Legal Gambling in New York: A Discussion of Numbers and Sports Betting*. New York, 1972, pp. 42–43.

had a weekly handle of $176,000, approximately one fifth ($35,000) of it coming from horse racing and the remaining four fifths ($141,000) from football, it could expect a profit of less than 2 per cent.

The layoff man occupies the next level of the betting hierarchy. He is likely to be a lieutenant or underboss in the "family" hierarchy. A bookmaker who wants to minimize his risks will place a bet with the layoff man that is equal to the amount of his overload — the amount needed to pay off winners minus the amount bet on losses (Cressey, 1969). For example, if a bookmaker has 60 $2 bets on Fancy Dancer and 50 $2 bets on Prince George in the fifth race at Aqueduct, the books would be out of balance. In order to balance his books he would have to bet $20 with a layoff man on Fancy Dancer.

There are several additional levels in the bet-taking operation occupied by layoff men, each of whom serves a larger geographical area. The "big layoff man" accepts bets from all layoff men in a large metropolitan area. He operates in much the same way as a city or county clearinghouse. On the next level is the layoff man who takes bets from all layoff men in a state or region. On the highest level are layoff men who take bets from state or regional layoff bankers, functioning as a national clearinghouse. One national layoff man is reputed to operate out of Chicago, with others living in Las Vegas and other cities. One such national layoff man who operates out of Las Vegas is reported to take in about $20 million a year, with an annual profit of about 4 per cent of the gross, or $800,000 (Cressey, 1969).

The sports pool card business represents another popular gambling activity that is connected with organized crime. A typical pool, such as a football pool, works as follows: Each week during the season, football cards similar to the one shown in Figure 7–2 are distributed by individuals who deal with the public, such as newsstand dealers, barbers, and bartenders. Some bookies, particularly the smaller ones, may also handle pool cards. Each card typically lists all the major football games, both college and professional, for the week, with the point handicap for each game. Each bettor chooses between 3 and 16 winners and indicates the amount he desires to bet. His payoff is at stated odds such as 4 to 1 for three winners out of three picks or 250 to 1 for ten winners out of ten picks (nine out of ten gets 15 to 1) (Fund for the City of New York, 1972; Singer and Candela, 1973). Not very much is known about pool betting organizations. It is believed that operators are organized and do business with the sanction of organized crime.

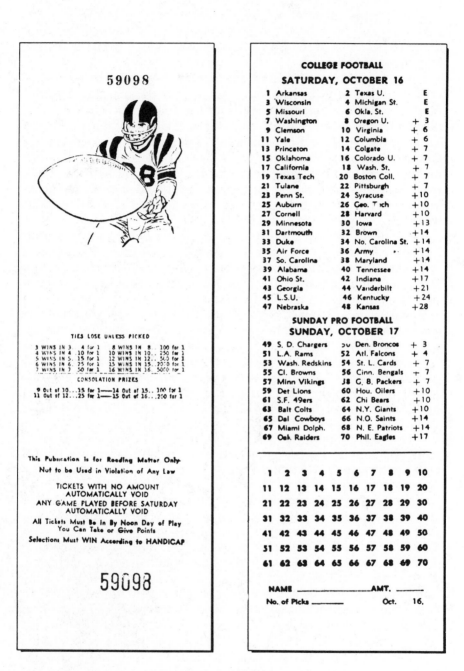

59098

TIES LOSE UNLESS PICKED

3 WINS IN 3.	4 for 1	8 WINS IN 8.	100 for 1
4 WINS IN 4	10 for 1	10 WINS IN 10..	250 for 1
5 WINS IN 5.	15 for 1	12 WINS IN 12..	500 for 1
6 WINS IN 6.	25 for 1	15 WINS IN 15.	2000 for 1
7 WINS IN 7	50 for 1	16 WINS IN 16.	5000 for 1

CONSOLATION PRIZES

9 Out of 10...15 for 1——14 Out of 15.. 100 for 1
11 Out of 12...25 for 1——15 Out of 16...200 for 1

This Publication is for Reading Matter Only
Not to be Used in Violation of Any Law

TICKETS WITH NO AMOUNT
AUTOMATICALLY VOID
ANY GAME PLAYED BEFORE SATURDAY
AUTOMATICALLY VOID
All Tickets Must Be In By Noon Day of Play
You Can Take or Give Points
Selections Must WIN According to HANDICAP

59098

COLLEGE FOOTBALL

SATURDAY, OCTOBER 16

1	Arkansas	2	Texas U.		E
3	Wisconsin	4	Michigan St.		E
5	Missouri	6	Okla. St.		E
7	Washington	8	Oregon U.	+	3
9	Clemson	10	Virginia	+	6
11	Yale	12	Columbia	+	6
13	Princeton	14	Colgate	+	7
15	Oklahoma	16	Colorado U.	+	7
17	California	18	Wash. St.	+	7
19	Texas Tech	20	Boston Coll.	+	7
21	Tulane	22	Pittsburgh	+	7
23	Penn St.	24	Syracuse	+10	
25	Auburn	26	Geo. Tech	+10	
27	Cornell	28	Harvard	+10	
29	Minnesota	30	Iowa	+13	
31	Dartmouth	32	Brown	+14	
33	Duke	34	No. Carolina St.	+14	
35	Air Force	36	Army	+14	
37	So. Carolina	38	Maryland	+14	
39	Alabama	40	Tennessee	+14	
41	Ohio St.	42	Indiana	+17	
43	Georgia	44	Vanderbilt	+21	
45	L.S.U.	46	Kentucky	+24	
47	Nebraska	48	Kansas	+28	

SUNDAY PRO FOOTBALL

SUNDAY, OCTOBER 17

49	S. D. Chargers	50	Den. Broncos	+	3
51	L.A. Rams	52	Atl. Falcons	+	4
53	Wash. Redskins	54	St. L. Cards	+	7
55	Cl. Browns	56	Cinn. Bengals	+	7
57	Minn Vikings	58	G. B. Packers	+	7
59	Det Lions	60	Hou. Oilers	+10	
61	S.F. 49ers	62	Chi Bears	+10	
63	Balt Colts	64	N.Y. Giants	+10	
65	Dal Cowboys	66	N.O. Saints	+14	
67	Miami Dolph.	68	N. E. Patriots	+14	
69	Oak. Raiders	70	Phil. Eagles	+17	

1	2	3	4	5	6	7	8	9	10
11	12	13	14	15	16	17	18	19	20
21	22	23	24	25	26	27	28	29	30
31	32	33	34	35	36	37	38	39	40
41	42	43	44	45	46	47	48	49	50
51	52	53	54	55	56	57	58	59	60
61	62	63	64	65	66	67	68	69	70

NAME .... AMT. ....

No. of Picks ....   Oct.   16,

Figure 7–2. A Football Pool Card

The Relationship Between Gambling and Other Crimes

Gambling is a popular activity that is widely considered to be, at most, a technical infraction of the law. This attitude is supported by general ignorance of the key role that gambling plays in other syndicate activities. Gambling justifies and pays the overhead for a sizable organization that can and does engage in other illegal activities. It provides profits that are used to finance such syndicate enterprises as the importation of narcotics, loan sharking, and the infiltration of legitimate businesses. Gambling profits are also used to pay for protection for other illegal activities and to corrupt police, judges, and others in the criminal justice system who must be subverted in order for a gambling organization to operate. Inevitably, gambling breeds violence; debtors are assaulted as part of the enforcement process and competition is eliminated by the use and threat of force.

Several methods have been proposed for attacking organized crime's gambling empire. One scheme calls for the state to establish gambling operations that compete directly with those currently conducted by organized crime. Plans have been devised for legal sports betting, pool cards, and horse betting operations, as well as for state-operated numbers businesses, that could compete effectively with those operated at present by organized crime (Fund for the City of New York, 1972; Singer and Candela, 1973). Legal gambling operations are only one aspect of a broad-based attack on illegal gambling that might also include a campaign to induce bettors to stop betting with illegal numbers operators and bookmakers and criminal prosecution and imprisonment for large scale operators.

Loan Sharking

The usury business, better known as "loan sharking," represents the second major source of revenue for organized crime. The profit that accrues to organized crime from this business is estimated to be in the multi-million dollar range (Mitchell, 1970). Based on his research, Seidl (1968) indicates that criminal loan sharking involves three major elements:

> The lending of cash at very high interest rates by individuals reputed to be connected with underworld operations.
>
> A borrower-lender agreement which rests on the borrower's willingness to place his and his family's physical well-being as collateral against the loan.
>
> A belief by the borrower that the lender has connections with ruthless criminal organizations. (p. 30)

Gambling and previous loan sharking activity provide the primary continuing source of new loan sharking funds. In addition, loan sharks can borrow from legitimate lending agencies, relatives, friends, or underworld sources and then lend these funds to their customers. Loans from legitimate lending institutions such as banks and finance companies made directly to loan shark borrowers represent a third source of funds. These loans are generally provided through collusion between one or two members of these lending institutions and loan sharks for sizable kickbacks or other considerations, for example, reduction of gambling debts (Seidl, 1968).

Funds are provided by criminal syndicates to loan sharks under two different sets of conditions. In some cases, funds are supplied "with strings attached." Under these circumstances, the loan shark must operate under a strict set of guidelines with regard to loan policies, profit rates, default rates, and collection procedures. The loan shark thus has limited discretion in lending funds and must keep his bosses informed regarding the details of his transactions. According to Seidl (1968), Detroit is an example of an area in which most loan sharking activities are carried on "with strings attached." In this city, the loan shark industry is centralized and under the supervision of the local criminal syndicate. The syndicate allocates territories to loan shark organizations, standardizes interest rates, and restricts competition between different loan shark organizations. Six to ten loan shark organizations are reported to operate in Detroit under the supervision of the local criminal syndicate. Each of these organizations has a leadership structure and numbers between 10 and 15 individual loan sharks who are responsible for different territorial markets. The leaders in these organizations lend money directly to large borrowers, and their subordinates are responsible for smaller loans. If a borrower requires more money than a particular loan shark has available or can loan without approval, the loan shark must obtain the consent of a superior or take the borrower to a superior in order to complete the transaction.

In other areas, funds are supplied to loan sharks "with no strings attached." In these instances the local syndicate exercises no direct control over the use of the funds. For example, a syndicate boss may give each of his lieutenants $100,000, with the stipulation that each man is to repay him $150,000 within a year.

Loans provided to loan shark borrowers from legitimate lending institutions follow a different pattern. First, the loan shark and his customer agree upon the size of the loan and the fee the loan shark is to receive for securing the money from the lending institution. The borrower then signs a note for the loan payable to the loan shark for the total amount of the transaction, i.e., principal plus service charge. This note is then given to a specific loan official who discounts it and gives the proceeds of the loan to the borrower. The borrower pays the loan shark his fee off the top and is then responsible for paying the total amount plus normal interest to the lending institution. Of course, the loan shark is still responsible for the borrower meeting his repayment schedule. In general, only certain loan officials or individual executives of the lending institutions are involved in these transactions, with the companies themselves generally not knowingly being a party to them. Evidence that these transactions take place is provided by the New York Commission of Investigation, which found that prior to its failure the Crown Savings Bank had granted loans of $4,141,900 to four principal out-of-territory loan brokers and loan sharks. The commission's investigation also revealed that "a loan officer in a branch bank in New York City had okayed $800,000 worth of loans for one loan shark who had obtained close to one and a half million dollars in bank loans for his customers" (Seidl, 1968, p. 38).

Interest charges for loans are a function of a variety of factors. Loan shark organizations that loan funds to other loan shark organizations generally charge 3 to 5 per cent a week. Small loan sharks, who typically make individual loans ranging from $50 to $1000, generally charge 20 per cent per week. (Figured on a yearly basis this represents an effective rate of 960 per cent). The small loan shark works in areas such as industrial plants, docks, construction sites, and blue collar and lower middle class residential areas. People in these areas borrow because they need money to tide them over to pay day, to pay gambling debts, to meet family emergencies, and to pay bills. Large loan sharks generally charge their customers a much lower rate than small loan sharks. Seidl (1968) found that the standard rate for large loans was 5 per cent per week in all the metropolitan areas he visited. The large loan shark can provide loans ranging from a few hundred dollars to $50,000 and up.

There appear to be three major reasons why people patronize these large loan sharks. First, small businessmen use them to obtain working capital to meet their creditors and payrolls. Garment manufacturers, building contractors, and other businessmen are often placed in a position in which they need money to meet their payrolls and to buy materials in order to finish jobs for which they will receive payment upon completion. Secondly, some speculators, promoters, and producers who require capital to finance a new project or venture will seek it from loan sharks.

Real estate and stock speculators borrow in order to obtain venture capital to finance various projects; the following is an example of such speculative borrowing:

> The matter began when three "quick money" promoters bought a community center in a racially changing white neighborhood for $90,000 and planned to sell it to a Negro civic organization for $165,000. The promoters could raise all but $13,500 and for this amount they went to a notorious loan shark in Jersey City, Harold Konigsberg. . . . Konigsberg agreed to lend the $13,500 for 30 days, and he demanded to be repaid $25,000 — almost a 100 per cent per month interest (almost 1200 per cent if figured on an annual basis). For a time the promoters were able to meet their payments but at the end of 30 days they were unable to complete the terms. Konigsberg then granted them a 30 day extension — for an additional $5,000 interest.
>
> In order to help them meet Konigsberg's terms, Jimmy Roberts [the man who had originally taken them to Konigsberg] negotiated an additional loan from a south Philadelphia loan shark, Armand Colianni, who, through Roberts, lent them $5,500 and demanded $11,000 in return. Konigsberg continued his threats to the trio, so one of them, Joseph Zavod, went directly to Colianni for help. Finally, Cosa Nostra boss Angelo Bruno found out about the affair, and demanded a meeting with Konigsberg and his boss, Cosa Nostra Caporegima Joseph Zicarelli in Jersey City. At an arbitration meeting Bruno ruled that the promoters had a remaining debt of $15,000 to be paid to Bruno's under boss Ignazio Denaro. Bruno arranged for Konigsberg to receive $4,000 while Colianni and Denaro were to get $11,000. Still unable to meet these adjusted terms, Zavod went to the FBI and a prosecution ensued. (Pennsylvania Crime Commission, 1970, p. 41)

The third group of loan shark customers comprises individuals who need funds for personal expenses of a kind to which conventional money lending agencies are not likely to be sympathetic: replacing embezzled funds, maintaining a mistress, or paying large nightclub bills. It seems almost superfluous to note that most people who seek funds from either large or small loan sharks do so not voluntarily but because they have been refused credit by legitimate lending institutions that view them as bad risks for a loan.

The Borrower-Lender Agreement

Locating a loan shark from whom to borrow funds is not too difficult. People already acquainted with the underworld generally know a loan shark or at least someone who can "steer" them to one. Those not familiar with the underworld must look for a "steer" or "shill" who can introduce them to a loan shark. Steers may receive a finder's fee for providing a loan shark with customers. Normally, people who work in service occupations, such as bartenders, cab drivers, hat check girls, elevator operators, barbers, and doormen, serve as steers. Bookmakers can also direct a person to a loan shark.

As a rule, a loan shark will not lend money to a total stranger. Most require that a person have a voucher or guarantor — a person known to and trusted by the loan shark. Generally the guarantor only guarantees the principal in a transaction, although in some instances he may also have to guarantee both principal and interest. Guarantors are not always required to repay loans when a borrower leaves the area or makes himself unavailable in some other manner, but in those cases in which they are required to repay the loans, they are often reminded of this obligation in a violent manner. Some people are not aware that by introducing a borrower to a loan shark they automatically guarantee repayment of their friend's loan.

Several factors affect the amount of money that a loan shark will lend to a borrower. These include the loan shark's personality, his evaluation of the borrower's repayment capabilities (on large loans credit checks are often run), and limitations placed upon the loan shark by his superiors. Many loan sharks will lend a borrower only what they believe he can afford to repay. This assessment is based upon the borrower's income or his expected profits as a result of the loan. However, some loan sharks will lend a borrower just a little more than he can afford to repay so that he becomes "hooked." It is often to the advantage of the loan shark to get a borrower hooked, because in a very short period of time, owing to the high interest rate, the borrower will have paid back the loan shark's original investment, and all subsequent payments will then be pure profit. For example, if a loan shark lends a man $500 at 20 per cent interest per week, his original investment will be returned to him within five weeks. Furthermore, the size of the customer's weekly payment to the loan shark often forces him to borrow additional money on pay day to augment his already depleted income. In this way, some borrowers are placed in such a position that their interest payments are so high that they can never repay the principal. After a while, a person in this situation no longer thinks about repaying the principal but instead simply considers the interest payment he owes the loan shark as a regular bill, much like rent, that must be paid.

Loan sharks employ two types of repayment plans. Under one plan, the borrower pays interest every week until he can save up enough to pay the principal back in full. This plan often works to the disadvantage of the borrower since it is usually quite difficult for him to save enough to pay the principal back in full. In these cases, the borrower becomes a permanent customer of the loan shark, often increasing his weekly interest payments as situations arise in which he needs additional funds. Under the second plan, the customer is allowed to make weekly payments that include both principal and interest. It is generally easier for a person to finally repay the loan under this type of plan.

When people borrow from a loan shark they are generally aware of the nature of both their relationship with him and the collateral they have pledged for the loan. In most cases, the borrower is not required to sign a note, a loan contract, or any other paper indicating that he has borrowed the money; usually a handshake confirms the bargain. Borrowers recognize that the collateral for the loan is their own physical safety and the well-being of their families. In some cases, the nature of this collateral is made explicit. For example, after one loan shark gave three brothers $50,000 in cash, he matter-of-factly said that "the final security on the loan will be the brother's eyeballs" (Salerno and Tompkins, 1969, p. 238).

The Collection Process

Seidl (1968) states that a loan shark organization's reputation for ruthlessness and violence is the key element in inducing a person to repay a loan. This reputation is largely a function of the borrower's perception of the organizational structure and operational methods of the loan shark industry and of the individual loan shark from whom he has borrowed. Customers who are aware of the sinister reputation of the industry present fewer collection problems.

While customers may be threatened frequently, the actual employment of violence is minimal, for if violence were used extensively it would prove counterproductive for the loan shark organization. Lavish employment of violent collection methods would no doubt bring the activities of the industry to public attention, resulting in pressure for increased law enforcement activity. Moreover, a person who has been severely injured is usually in no position to repay a loan.

According to Seidl, the collection process follows six steps. The first is the weekly payment meeting at which the loan shark collects his weekly installment. In some cases, borrowers make their weekly payment without having contact with the loan shark by dropping their payment at a specified location. Most borrowers are acquainted only with the first step in the collection process, but if a borrower misses a weekly payment, he then becomes aware of the second step. Loan sharks are quick to make contact with delinquent borrowers in order to remind them of their obligation. Usually at this stage the reminders are pleasant; however, the borrower is penalized for his tardiness. The penalty in these cases is normally a fine that is added to the already late payment, or in some cases, a loan shark will fine a borrower by increasing the amount of his loan.

The third step is likely to be the first time the loan shark uses aggressive action to induce repayment from delinquent borrowers. This action takes the form of harassment, which may involve continuously telephoning the borrower at home in the early morning hours, constant telephone interruptions at his place of work, and public embarrassment.

> *A large loan shark in New York would harass his delinquent customers unmercifully after they had missed one, or at the most, two payments. He would do anything to infuriate the borrower, so he would pay just to get the loan shark off his back. The loan shark would spit in the delinquent borrower's face in public, call him vile names in front of his wife, or ring his doorbell or phone in the early hours of the morning.* (Seidl, 1968, p. 56)

In the fourth stage, implicit threats are employed to induce repayment. At this point, the loan shark often visits a delinquent borrower's home or place of employment accompanied by his associates, whose appearances readily reveal their function. In addition, members of the borrower's family may receive phone calls in which the caller simply leaves his name and a message that the borrower must keep a specific appointment if business troubles are to be averted.

During the next stage, explicit threats are employed to persuade the borrower to meet his obligations. Generally the borrower is threatened with violence against himself, his family or other relatives, or his property.

> *Typical threats include showing the borrower two sticks of dynamite and telling him his house will be blown up without regard to his wife and children; or warning the victim that his daughter may have an accident on the way home from school.* (Seidl, 1968, p. 57)

Also during this stage, some loan shark organizations will use demonstrations of violence to threaten a delinquent borrower.

One effective method is a bombing or a fire preceded by a warning and followed by additional explicit threats. In addition, some loan shark organizations still take their victims for "a ride" in a big Cadillac or its equivalent to further persuade them to repay the loan. The borrower is usually taken to the waterfront or some other deserted area where he is verbally threatened.

Loan shark organizations employ actual violence, the sixth step, when they feel that the borrower is not making an effort to meet his obligations. The violence inflicted upon delinquent borrowers can be very harsh and painful. In most instances, the loan shark's enforcers use their fists and feet to beat delinquent borrowers; however, weapons such as brass knuckles, iron pipes, baseball bats, bicycle chains, sledge hammers, and razor blades have also been employed. As we have already pointed out, throughout any period in which the borrower has failed to meet his scheduled payments, his indebtedness is increased, because the loan shark assesses a fine each time the borrower misses a regular payment.

When the loan shark realizes that the borrower cannot make any further payments, he generally follows one of three courses of action. First, in a rare case, the loan shark may have the borrower murdered. Secondly, the loan shark may "stop the clock," meaning that he will stop charging the borrower interest on the loan. In some cases, the clock is stopped for an indefinite period of time — until the borrower "gets back on his feet" — however, most often it is stopped for a limited period of time, such as a year (Cressey, 1969). A third course of action followed by loan sharks is to cancel the loan in exchange for a part interest in or full ownership of the borrower's business. This is how Joe Valachi acquired an interest in a restaurant and a dress factory (Maas, 1969). Finally, in some cases, a loan shark will cancel a loan if the borrower performs some service for the criminal organization, such as setting up a burglary or highjacking, adding a racketeer to his payroll, shipping stolen goods, or stealing securities. For example, a truck driver in debt to a loan shark would receive 10 per cent of whatever he helps to steal, which would then be marked off his loan shark bill, and these thefts would be arranged in such a way that the driver would be protected from arrest.

Conclusion

The major reason for the involvement of organized crime in loan sharking is its high rate of return. Sherrid (1975) illustrates just how lucrative a business this is:

Suppose you were a member of organized crime and were given $100 by your boss. You were told to lend the $100 out at the going rate of 20 per cent for every seven days. At the end of the week you were told to again lend out the $100 plus the interest at the same 20 per cent rate. You were to continue this process of lending out the principal and all the earned interest each week. All the money was to be working at all times. How much money would you have at the end of the year? . . . [T]he answer [is] a little over $1,310,000! (p. 59)

A further reason why organized crime finds this business so attractive is that it is easy to operate and has relatively low overhead. All the loan shark needs is money and borrowers. A loan shark does not need an office or any employees. He meets his customers in restaurants, bars, and other pre-arranged locations. He can call upon his syndicate backers or enforcers to assist him in making collections. Since the loan shark carries on his business inconspicuously, he generally does not have to pay protection costs.

Various methods are available for dealing with the loan shark industry. To begin with, it is important to re-emphasize the fact that the loan shark industry is currently the only available source of funds for people who require high risk loans. Perhaps the most effective curb would be to create an alternative lending system designed to provide such loans. There are several ways in which this could be accomplished. First, the government might provide this service by charging interest rates that are high enough to cover the losses from borrowers who default. A second alternative is the licensing of private firms that would be able to charge higher than normal interest rates for high risk loans. Finally, a system of judicial restraint could be established, patterned after that currently in operation in England. Under this system:

No statutory maximum interest rate exists for any loan. Courts can declare any transaction usurious and decree a reasonable arrangement for the parties concerned. English statute reads that interest in excess of 48 per cent per year will be presumed to be excessive unless proved otherwise. Thus, freedom of contract subject to good faith and fair dealing is the English approach to interest regulation. (Seidl, 1968, pp. 185–186)

Narcotics Trafficking

Although the Italian syndicates have been trafficking in narcotics since the end of Prohibition, they have not held a complete monopoly in this trade. They have limited their involvement to the importation and initial distribution of drugs — primarily heroin and some cocaine. The risks associated with low level drug dealing are considerable; hence, one does not find syndicate members selling drugs to junkies on the street.

Heroin

Heroin traffic in the United States was dominated in the beginning by Jewish gangsters like Legs Diamond, Dutch Schultz, and Meyer Lansky, who were the controlling force in organized crime in the 1920's. During this period, Italian syndicates were content with the substantial profits they were reaping from their illegal liquor operations. When the end of Prohibition came into sight and the legalization of alcohol consumption appeared imminent, it was obvious to Lucky Luciano and others that the Italian syndicates would require a new source of income. Heroin seemed an attractive alternative to booze and beer because its relatively recent prohibition provided a market that could easily be exploited and expanded. Consequently, in the 1930's, the Italian syndicates moved into the heroin market.

Luciano was convicted and imprisoned in 1936. Ten years later, he was released from prison and deported to Italy — ostensibly in exchange for services he had rendered to the Army and Navy during World War II. Upon his arrival in Sicily, he began to rebuild the heroin distribution apparatus that had fallen apart during the war. Initially, he obtained heroin by diverting it from one of Italy's most respectable pharmaceutical companies, Schiaparelli. But when the U. S. Federal Bureau of Narcotics disclosed in 1950 that a minimum of 700 kilos of heroin had found its way into Luciano's possession from that company over a four-year period, Italy tightened its pharmaceutical regulations. This move had no effect on Luciano's operations, however, since by then he had built up a network of clandestine laboratories in Italy and had made contact with the Lebanese for the purpose of obtaining *morphine base*, the white powdery substance that constitutes the key stage in heroin manufacture. Luciano had recognized, however, that if his operations were to continue at their current level, he would have to expand his own clandestine laboratories, seek new ones, or locate another source of supply. He had discovered that while Sicilian Mafiosi were extremely capable smugglers, they seemed to lack the ability to effectively manage clandestine labs. Almost from the start his illegal heroin operations had been plagued by a series of arrests that were attributable largely to Mafia incompetence in moving materials in and out of the laboratories. If this situation were to continue, he might face the prospect of being arrested himself. In an effort to protect himself, Luciano shifted his laboratory operations to Marseille, France.

There is good reason to believe that Meyer Lansky's 1949–1950 European trip was instrumental in establishing contacts between the Italian and the Corsican syndicates. While in France, Lansky, a close associate of Luciano, is reputed to have met with high ranking Corsican syndicate leaders on the French Riviera and in Paris. These discussions reportedly resulted in a tentative agreement concerning the international heroin traffic, and the fact is that just after Lansky returned to the U. S., heroin laboratories began appearing in Marseille — the first step in Marseille's as the eventual emergence as the heroin capital of the world (McCoy, 1972).

The Turkish-French Connection. Until 1972, the bulk of the heroin brought into the U. S. came from Turkey. Estimates of the exact percentage of Turkey's contribution to the U. S. supply of heroin have ranged from 50 per cent (Domestic Council on Drug Abuse Task Force, 1975) to 80 per cent (Newsday, 1974).

The opium poppy, from which heroin is derived, has been cultivated by Turkish farmers on the Anatolian plateau since the 11th century A.D. These farmers have developed uses for nearly every part of the poppy: the oil for cooking, the leaves for salads, the pods for livestock feed, and the stalks for cottage ceilings. The only part of the poppy not used by the villagers is the gum, from which opium is made. Although all of the gum produced by the farmers is supposed to be sold to the Turkish government, which in 1972 paid $7.47 for each pound of gum, the farmer can receive a higher price by selling the gum to drug smugglers. The Turkish government attempts to control diversion of opium to the illegal drug market through the use of inspectors, but their efforts are rendered largely ineffectual by inadequate resources and personnel and the remoteness of many of the rural areas where the crop is grown.

"Collectors" (also known as "commission-men") are the first link in the illegal heroin distribution chain. They collect the gum from the farmers, pay for it, and transport it to depots where it is stored. Collectors are usually persons well known to the villagers: wealthy farmers, merchants, village officials, or even traveling salesmen.

Next, the opium gum is converted to morphine base. Collectors frequently send their own "chemists" to the villages to handle this process. In addition, big collectors generally maintain their own conversion laboratories, which operate on a semipermanent basis in the opium growing provinces. Opium gum is converted to morphine base at this point in order to reduce the volume and weight. Ten kilograms of raw opium is converted to one kilogram of morphine base; hence, smuggling the base powder is far easier than smuggling the bulky gum.

"Patrons" — a term that in Turkey denotes persons who specialize in the financing and planning of large-scale smuggling operations — are the next step in the heroin distribution system. They maintain contacts with the Corsicans, who convert morphine base to heroin and who ship it to their syndicate contacts in the United States.

Morphine base, a powder, is an ideal material for smuggling. It is not harmed by water and it can be shaped into any form or fitted into any type of container: a car radiator or gas tank, a false-bottom suitcase, a spare tire, a hollowed-out axle, or a ship's ballast. This base is moved out of Turkey along many sea, land, and air routes, hidden in cars, buses, planes, ships, and vehicles known as "TIR trucks."* Smuggling drugs out of Turkey is not too difficult because it is impossible to search all the vehicles leaving the country and also because many police officers are open to bribery. Some smugglers prefer to ship morphine base by sea since there are no international boundaries or customs posts on the high seas. The smugglers further protect their cargo by transferring it from the large ship to small fishing and pleasure boats before arrival at the port of Marseille because these small boats receive less attention from French customs officials than a ship arriving from Turkey. A common procedure followed on these large ships is to pack the morphine base in water-tight bags attached to a 300-foot rope weighted at both ends. The rope is thrown overboard with a marker bouy, in a predesignated area thus allowing the ship to sail into Marseille clean. Then small boats are dispatched before dawn to pick up the morphine (Newsday, 1974).

Most of the morphine base from Turkey is processed in clandestine laboratories operated by the Corsican syndicate in Marseille. The Corsican syndicate lacks the formal organization of the Italian syndicate in the U. S., being instead a loose organization of clans whose members can drift from one group to another. In addition

---

*By international treaty, trucks bearing the TIR sign (an abbreviation for *Transports Internationaux Routiers*) are sealed by customs in the country of origin and are usually not searched at border crossings unless a tip has been received that the truck is carrying contraband. The purpose of this is to facilitate transportation of perishable items. It also facilitates the movement of morphine base (Newsday, 1974).

to being specialists in heroin manufacture, the Corsicans are experts in sophisticated international smuggling, art theft, and counterfeiting. They are also involved in such traditional activities as prostitution, armed robbery, and car theft. Corsican gangsters have not restricted their operations to Marseille; some have migrated to Indochina, North Africa, the Middle East, Latin America, Canada, and the South Pacific. Regardless of the enormous distances between them, Corsican racketeers have managed to keep in contact and to work together smoothly and efficiently in complex international smuggling operations, thus stymying law enforcement efforts for a quarter of a century. One of the major reasons why the Italian syndicate has been able to circumvent every effort U. S. officials have made at reducing the flow of heroin into the United States since the end of World War II is the cooperation between Corsican smugglers and syndicate drug distributors.

When a shipment of morphine base arrives in Marseille it is delivered to a receiving point. The man receiving the shipment is generally not the buyer. In fact, the importer or buyer will as a rule never see the shipment. However, the importer will have made arrangements for a "chemist" to convert the base into heroin. The base is taken to a laboratory by a courier who also does not know who the importer is. Thus, if the police intercept the courier or raid a laboratory, the people they arrest cannot tell them who the importer is, where the base came from, or where the heroin was to go.

Most morphine base is converted to heroin in crude temporary kitchen labs by "chemists" who have learned the process through "in-service training." Upon receiving the shipment, a chemist will work virtually around the clock for a period ranging from one to seven days, depending on the size of the shipment, in order to get the converted merchandise out of his possession and into the hands of the buyer as quickly as possible. A chemist is well compensated for the risks he takes in working in an illicit laboratory. Typically a chemist works on only three or four shipments a year, but since he receives $500 for each kilogram he converts, four shipments of 50 kilograms each net him $100,000, which places him among the highest paid of those who profit from heroin (Newsday, 1974).

After the morphine is converted to heroin, it is brought by courier to one of the various points of departure. Small amounts — 5 or 10 kilos — are generally flown to North or South America from any of the western capitals (Madrid, Amsterdam, Lisbon, Paris, London, or Rome) that has a direct airway to North or South America. Larger shipments are transported by ship but rarely directly from Marseille.

No ingenuity is spared in devising techniques for smuggling heroin into the United States. The drug enters the country strapped to the thighs of "mules," or couriers; sealed into tins that supposedly contain fish; in the heels and soles of traveler's shoes; in ski poles; in picture frames; in the luggage of diplomats; in false-bottom wine bottles; in oriental dolls. Ships offer the smuggler an unlimited number of hiding places. Heroin routed through South America and the Caribbean is flown into the U. S. in small planes, which unload their cargoes at one of the more than one hundred remote air fields in Florida, Georgia, South Carolina, and Alabama.

Other Sources of Heroin. When Turkey announced plans in 1967 to reduce and eventually abolish opium production, both the Corsican and the Italian syndicates recognized the need to find an alternative source of opium. A number of other countries, including Mexico, the nations of Southeast Asia, India, and Afghanistan, could serve as this new source of supply. Mexico had been producing small amounts of low-grade, brownish-colored heroin for several years, although she had never been able to produce the fine white powder demanded by American addicts. While India and Afghanistan had been involved in lively local opium production, they did not have any connections with the international criminal syndicates. On the other hand, Southeast Asia had been growing more than 70 per cent of the world's illicit opium, and the Chinese laboratories in Hong Kong, which refined much of this opium, were producing some of the world's best heroin. For a decade, Corsican-based syndicates in Viet Nam and Laos had been regularly supplying the international markets, including Marseille and Hong Kong, with opium and morphine base. The so-called "golden triangle," the tri-border area where Burma, Laos, and Thailand meet, had been producing opium since the 1800's when Meo and Yeo tribesmen fled China to escape the brutal Chinese pacification campaign. These tribesmen brought with them a knowledge of poppy cultivation. According to McCoy (1972), in the 1960's "a combination of factors — American military intervention, corrupt national governments, and international criminal syndicates — pushed Southeast Asia's opium commerce beyond self-sufficiency to export capability" (p. 245). As things turned out, however, Southeast Asia, which had the potential to become the major source of U. S. heroin supply when Turkey banned opium production, failed to provide heroin in sufficient quantities to fill the void. Instead, the United States Drug Enforcement Administration estimates that up to 80 per cent of the heroin coming into the U. S. today is Mexican grown.

Opium is cultivated illegally in Mexico in the far reaches of the Sierra Madre Mountains, which are located in the western part of the country. Because a farmer may lose his land if he plants opium on it, he usually goes at least a mile from his house and plants the opium crop on government land. These impoverished farmers plant opium for exactly the same reason as their counterparts in Asia and Turkey: for them, opium represents a cash crop, which, when planted two or three times a year on 2-1/2 acres of land, yields them a relatively large income of $4000. After the crop is harvested, it is picked up by middlemen who frequently do not even see the peasants. They just pick up the opium gum and leave the money in a hiding place. It is then taken to makeshift labs to be converted into heroin. The equipment and the processing techniques employed by the Mexicans are crude; consequently, the heroin they produce is clay-colored and only 68 per cent pure, in contrast to the snow-white, 98 per cent pure heroin processed in France and Southeast Asia. In come cases, the Mexicans reduce ("step on") the purity levels of the heroin they export to the U. S. to levels below 20 per cent. This eliminates dealers who would cut it further and enables the Mexicans to retain more of the profits for themselves (Salmons, Marro, and Schmidt, 1976).

The Mexican connection differs from the French and Southeast Asian connections in several respects. Mexican drug traffickers do not appear to have any tie-ins with Italian criminal syndicates. Their organizations, however, are structured in the same way as Italian criminal families. The Mexican drug traffic is controlled by several clans (families) bound together by blood ties of trust and loyalty. These clans operate the business all the way from providing opium poppy seeds to the Sierra Madre farmers to distributing the heroin from the *barrios* of cities like Chicago.

The Future of Turkish Opium Production. Until 1972, as we have noted, the Turkish-French connection was a major source of American heroin, accounting for an estimated 50 to 80 per cent of the heroin consumed in this country. Between 1968 and 1971, under considerable pressure from the U. S., Turkey reduced the number of provinces in which poppy cultivation was allowed from 21 to 4, and in 1972, opium production was entirely prohibited. This ban remained in effect for two years. In July, 1974, the Turkish government authorized an autumn poppy planting in 7 provinces. Despite an official promise to strictly enforce the laws against illicit diversion, John T. Cusack (1974), Director of the International Operations Division of the Drug Enforcement Administration points out:

> It is simply impossible to control the production of opium by
> a hundred thousand farmers on half acre plots in Turkey. This

> *production is simply too vulnerable to criminal elements in Turkey and abroad, and there is no system that can prevent substantial diversion. The cost of attempting to develop and implement such a system would be economically prohibitive.* (p. 7)

The Drug Enforcement Administration (Cusack, 1976) reported that in 1975 the Turkish-French connection provided a very small amount of heroin for the illicit U. S. market and that all of this supply was believed to come from stocks diverted from pre-1972 opium production. There are indications, however, that Turkish opium is once again finding its way into the illicit world market. In June, 1976, Egyptian authorities recovered 270 pounds of opium — enough to make a million dollars worth of heroin — from a Turkish freighter. This was reported to be the largest seizure in that area in five years.

It is too soon at this point to determine whether Turkey will resume her position as the major source of supply for heroin in the U. S., but given that Turkish-French heroin is of high quality and preferred by addicts over low-grade Mexican heroin, there can be little doubt that this is a distinct possibility in the event that sizable quantities of opium are diverted to the illicit market.

The Heroin Distribution System in the U. S. Heroin is distributed in this country by a system that operates on several levels. We shall describe the system as it functions in the New York City metropolitan area since this particular operation encompasses all stages in the system. Other parts of the country may have a more circumscribed system, with their highest level of operation at one of the lower stages.

At the top of the system are the "importers" who usually purchase 20 to 100 or more kilograms of "pure" (approximately 80 per cent pure) heroin. While importers control the movement of heroin into the United States, they normally do not personally see the heroin they import. Importers must have substantial amounts of capital since they must pay for the merchandise before it can be resold. Generally, they receive shipments of between 10 and 100 kilograms, which cost between $50,000 and $500,000. Their sales transactions range between two and eight a month, with each transaction involving 2 to 4 kilograms of heroin at a price of between $15,000 and $60,000. Importers doing this level of business make profits of between $5 and $10 million a year (Moore, 1970; Singer and Newitt, 1970).

Kilo connections form the next level of the distribution system. A kilo dealer usually makes two to eight purchases per month of 1 to 10 kilograms of heroin (80 to 95 per cent pure) at a price of between $15 and $20,000 per kilogram. The profit at this level is often made by diluting the heroin with milk sugar, quinine, and other dilutants so that 2 kilograms can be sold for every kilogram bought. These dealers sell 1/2 to 4 kilograms of heroin (40 to 45 per cent pure) two to four times per week at a price of $20,000 per kilogram.

While in the past, the Italian criminal syndicate controlled the upper two levels of the heroin distribution system, today there are independent blacks, Cubans, and Mexicans operating at these

TABLE 7–3.   THE HEROIN DISTRIBUTION SYSTEM*

Level of Distribution	Purchase Price per Kilogram	Selling Price	Per Cent of Heroin When Sold	Value of 1 Kilogram of 80% Pure Heroin at Different Levels	Cut	Per Cent Return on Investment
Importer	$ 5,000	$15,000 per kilogram	80–85	$ 15,000	None	200
Kilo connection	$15,000	$20,000 per kilogram	40–45	$ 40,000	1:1	167
Connection (ounce man)	$20,000	$700 per ounce	20–22	$ 98,000	1:1	147
Weight dealers	$24,700	$600† per ounce	10–11	$182,400	1:1-1/8	84
Street dealers	$22,800	$650 per ounce	6–8	$293,400	1:1-1/2	61
Pusher addict (jugglers)	$22,900	$875 per ounce	6–8	$395,500	None	35
Addict	$30,000	–	6–8	$395,500	–	–

*Data from Singer, M., and Newitt, H. J.: *Policy Concerning Drug Abuse in New York State: The Basic Study*. Croton-on-Hudson; New York, Hudson Institute, 1970, pp. 50–51; and Moore, M.: *Policy Concerning Drug Abuse in New York State: Economics of Heroin Distribution*. Croton-on-Hudson, New York, Hudson Institute, 1970, pp. 69–70.

†"Short ounces" appear at different levels of the marketing system. However, they are most likely to appear at this level because this is the last stage before the heroin hits the street. Therefore, about three short ounces were added to account for some extra profit at this level. Thus, the weight dealer has 38 short ounces to sell instead of the normal 35.3 ounces per kilogram.

levels. People who conduct these operations take great care to deal only with people they know and never buy from or sell to addicts whom they regard as unreliable. They further insulate themselves by not personally handling drugs; other members of their organization are employed to deliver the drugs and collect payment. They have enough money to protect themselves against conviction and punishment in the event that they are arrested. For example, it is not unusual for dealers operating on this level or their couriers to carry large sums of money ($20,000 to $100,000) to be used to bribe police should they be intercepted during one of their transactions. They also pay for police protection and for intelligence information on the operations of narcotics units.

People who operate on the next level of the distribution system are generally called "connections" or in some cases "ounce men." They buy between 1/2 and 4 kilograms of heroin (40 to 45 per cent pure) three to six times per month at a price of approximately $20,000 per kilogram. They dilute the heroin to 20 to 22 per cent pure and sell it in quantities of 2 to 15 ounces (in ten to 20 transactions per week) at a price of approximately $700 per ounce ($24,000 per kilogram). While some ounce men have organized crime connections, the majority do not. Connections play a vital role in the heroin distribution system, since they serve as a link between the small number of people at the top who import and distribute drugs to the system and the large number of heroin users and dealers below them who make up the bulk of the system. Connections are estimated to make profits of approximately a few hundred thousand dollars per year. Furthermore, while only a few of the connections use heroin, the majority of the people below them in the system are heroin users. In fact, it is estimated that about half the heroin flowing through the system is consumed by people who are part of the distribution system. In other words, "probably approximately one-half of the heroin consumed is paid for at wholesale prices by the work involved in heroin distribution" (Singer and Newitt, 1970, p. 49).

From the connection to the retail purchaser, heroin follows a variety of different paths which have up to four levels. Singer and Newitt (1970) provide a description of one common pattern of distribution:

> Connections commonly sell to weight dealers who buy lots of several ounces or a fraction of a kilo, and who sell to Street Dealers who buy units which are called "pieces" or "spoons" (which are less than an ounce) or as much as an ounce. The Street Dealers typically put the heroin in bags (and recently capsules) and sell what are called half-loads or bundles which are sets of

15 or 25 bags. Street Dealers sell to jugglers who sell at retail, often one or two bags at a time. Typically the juggler buys 15 bags and sells ten, or buys 25 bags and sells 15, in each case using the rest himself. Sometimes users from other areas such as suburbs, buy a few bags at retail, bring them home, divide them in samller or more dilute doses and sell them to others. (p. 49)

The Heroin Factory. At several points in the distribution system heroin is diluted. This process is handled by heroin factories or mills. The heroin factory can be two people diluting a small amount of heroin in a tenement to be used on the premises — (a "shooting gallery"). It can also be an operation involving a dozen people seated at a table, each performing a specific function as the bits of heroin are passed down the table. Usually dealers who operate factories have a regular crew of dependable people, including their lieutenants, who cut, package, bind, and distribute the drugs. Most mill operators will recruit young women when they find themselves short of help, and some operators prefer to staff their factories entirely with female workers. Factory workers can expect to earn between $200 and $250 a week. All factory operators worry about pilferage, since it is easy for a mill worker to overcut the heroin and get out with a quarter of an ounce of relatively pure heroin for which an addict will pay quite handsomely. For this reason, mill hands are carefully watched, and some dealers require their workers to work in the nude or wear special pajamas in which it is difficult to conceal heroin (Newsday, 1974).

Cocaine

When Turkish heroin became scarce in the 1970's, many addicts switched to cocaine, which increased the demand for this drug many-fold. Cocaine is supplied to the U. S. by distribution rings under the direction of Latin businessmen and professionals who have become so politically and economically powerful that they can operate in their respective areas virtually immune from arrest and prosecution (Gage, 1975b). Cocaine traffic within the U. S. is also dominated by rings of Latins. In many ways, these groups are similar to the Italian criminal families. The members are often bound together through close family relationships. Disputes in these groups are generally settled by discussion, and while violence is used to maintain discipline, it is not employed as frequently as in Italian groups. Moreover these groups have maintained much closer ties to main criminal organizations back home than Italian groups did with their Sicilian counterparts. While some Italian syndicate members have become involved in cocaine traffic, the majority have not. Federal authorities attribute this to the fact that these groups do not have well established relationships with suppliers in South America (Gage, 1975a).

Cusack (1976) reports that the coca leaf, from which cocaine is derived, grows wild in the Andean regions of Peru and Bolvia and, to a much lesser degree, in Colombia and Ecuador. The coca plant is cultivated by poor farmers, mostly Indians, for the same reason that the poppy is cultivated in Turkey, Southeast Asia, and Mexico — because it provides them with a cash crop. Thus, it is not surprising that when the Peruvian government gives newly cleared land to farmers, they almost always plant coca. The government appears to wink at this practice because it allows these farmers to support themselves without any training or financial support (Gage, 1975a). After the farmer harvests the crop, he sells the coca leaves to small laboratory operators for $600 a half ton. These laboratories operate in the growing area because of the large quantity of leaves that are required to produce cocaine — over 300 pounds for 1 kilo. The chemist, using about $600 worth of chemicals, extracts 2 kilograms (4.4 pounds of coca paste) from this half ton of leaves. He sells this paste to a middleman processer for $3000 a kilogram. The middleman, often using Indian women, who generally are not searched when they walk across the borders, ships the paste to northern Chile, Argentina, or southern Colombia, where it is processed into refined cocaine in clandestine laboratories. A variety of routes and techniques are used to ship this refined cocaine to the United States.

The methods employed to smuggle cocaine into the United States are similar to those used for heroin. "Mules" (couriers) are typically used to carry small quantities of cocaine. One of the more ingenious methods is to soak the mule's clothing in a solution containing cocaine; upon arrival in the United States, the clothing is put in a solution that releases the drug (Gage, 1975a). In addition to using their own countrymen as mules, Latin American drug traffickers also recruit Americans with no prior criminal involvement. These recruits are enticed by the "easy money" they believe they can earn — $100 to $6000 per single trip. Unfortunately, most of these recruits are not aware of the severe penalties and conditions of incarceration to which they will be subjected if arrested. For example, American men imprisoned in Mexico are given the most degrading jobs which include scrubbing toilets and scraping up excrement. American women in Mexican prisons appear to be subjected to even worse treatment (Time, 1974).

Large quantities of cocaine are shipped via Mexico or Puerto Rico to Miami, Tampa, Los Angeles, New York, and Canada by ship, private air craft, or automobile or hidden in commercial shipments. In 1976, 183 pounds of cocaine valued in the neighborhood of $42 million dollars were brought into Tampa harbor by a Liberian freighter.

While the price spiral (i.e., the increase in price at each level of distribution) for cocaine is not as dramatic as it is for heroin, it is quite substantial. The following illustrates the profits to be made in this business:

> To smuggle a manageable quantity of nine kilograms into the U. S., for example, may cost $36,000: $1,000 for each of the two couriers, $2,000 for a pick up man at destination, $5,000 for airport officials and police, $1,000 for air fares, and $27,000 for raw materials and processing. The operator will charge customers $15,000 to $18,000 per kilo, netting him more than $100,000 for the job. The smuggler's cocaine arrives in the U. S. nearly 100 per cent pure, but it doesn't stay that way long. Wholesalers and their pushers may cut it as often as three times, using everything from milk sugar to corn starch and powdered milk. By the time the mixture finds its way to the final customer, its price tag may top $30,000 per kilo . . . . (Crittenden, 1974, p. 17)

Narcotics Control Methods

A comprehensive discussion of narcotics control methods would require a great deal more space than we can devote to the topic in this chapter. However, we would like to provide some perspective on this important issue by citing several of the recommendations on control that were made by the Domestic Council on Drug Abuse Task Force (1975):

Durg Priorities

> The Task Force recommends that when resource constraints force a choice, priority in both supply and demand reduction should be directed toward those drugs which inherently pose a greater risk — heroin, amphetamines (particularly when used intravenously) and mixed barbiturates.

Supply Reduction

> The Task Force recommends that a continuous process of identifying the most vulnerable segments of the illicit distribution system be launched, and that resources be continually reallocated to focus on the most vulnerable portion of the system.

> Enforcement (1)   The Task Force recommends that federal law enforcement efforts focus on major trafficking organizations and particularly on the leaders of those organizations.

(2) *The Task Force recommends that greater attention be given to the development of conspiracy cases, which often are the only way to apprehend high-level traffickers.*

(3) *The Task Force endorses the President's proposal for mandatory minimum sentences for persons trafficking in hard drugs, and suggests that consideration be given to expanding the proposal to include traffickers of barbiturates and amphetamines.*

(4) *The Task Force recommends mandatory consecutive sentencing rather than concurrent sentencing for persons who are arrested and convicted for narcotics trafficking while on bail for another trafficking offense.*

(5) *The Task Force recommends revoking parole in the event that a parolee is rearrested on narcotics trafficking charges.*

(6) *The Task Force recommends that the Internal Revenue Service reemphasize its program of prosecuting drug traffickers for violation of income tax laws under strict guidelines and procedures.*

(7) *The Task Force recommends continuation and expansion of LEAA [Law Enforcement Assistance Agency] and DEA [Drug Enforcement Administration] activities aimed at strengthening state and local law enforcement agencies.*

International (1) *The Task Force recommends that a high priority be given to the development of international cooperation in preventing illicit production of drugs and that special attention be given to Mexico as a major source country for U. S. markets.*

(2) *The Task Force recommends that the U. S. government intensify diplomatic efforts to heighten other governments' concern over violation of international treaty obligations, and continue participation in institutions that promote international awareness of drug abuse.*

(3) *The Task Force recommends that additional emphasis be placed on the collection, analysis and utilization of overseas operational intelligence, and recommends that U. S. agents stationed overseas concentrate their activities on international trafficking chan-*

nels believed to be headed for the United States.

(4) *The Task Force recommends that continued attention be given to crop substitution as a means of reducing the supply of raw materials used in making drugs, and believe that this should be one of the major focuses of the [United Nations Fund for Drug Abuse Control].*

(5) *The Task Force recommends creating a DEA/Justice/State Committee on international narcotics control to coordinate efforts to seek U. S. jurisdiction over foreign drug traffickers through extradition or expulsion.*

(6) *The Task Force recommends that the opium policy task force accelerate its evaluation of* Papaver bracteatum *as a substitute for morphine-base* Papaver somniferum *in the production of codeine.*

Science & Technology

The Task Force recommends a specific set of priorities for the research efforts; highest among these are projects aimed at providing better equipment for use in border interdiction, improving intelligence information systems, and better support and communication equipment for enforcement officers. (pp. 98–100)

PENETRATION OF LEGITIMATE BUSINESS BY ORGANIZED CRIME

Few people are aware of the extent to which organized crime has penetrated legitimate businesses. Some idea of the scope of this involvement can be gleaned from the following excerpt from a speech given by Senator John McClellan before the Senate:

Legitimate business is another area in which organized crime has begun most recently and widely to extend its influence. In most cities, it now dominates the fields of juke box and vending machine distribution. Laundry services, liquor and beer distribution, and nightclubs, food wholesaling, record manufacturing, the garment industry, and a host of other legitimate lines of endeavor have been invaded and taken over. The Special Senate Committee To Investigate Organized Crime in Interstate Commerce, under the leadership of Senator Estes Kefauver noted in 1952 that the following industries had been invaded: advertising, amusement, appliances, automobile, baking, ballrooms, bowling alleys, banking, basketball, boxing, cigarette distribution, coal, communications, construction, drug stores, electrical equipment, florists, food, football, garment, gas, hotels, import-export, insurance, juke box, laundry, liquor, loan, news services, newspapers, oil, paper products, radio, real estate, and transportation. (Chamber of Commerce of the United States, 1969, pp. 9–10)

Criminal syndicates have become involved in legitimate business for several reasons, the primary one being to make money, since a legal enterprise simply provides another source of revenue. A legitimate business serves several other purposes: (1) By being on the payroll of a legitimate business, a syndicate member can point to a legitimate source of income that reflects his observable expenditures. He is more than happy to pay taxes on this income since it provides an opportunity for him to evade the substantial taxes he would have to pay for his illegal enterprises. (2) Involvement in a legal business provides a syndicate member with a respectable occupation that can be used to mask his participation in illegal activities. Furthermore, it provides both him and his family with a semblance of respectability and social standing. (3) It furnishes a second source of income that can be used to offset losses from illegitimate enterprises resulting from vigorous law enforcement efforts. (4) A syndicate member can pad his business' payroll to show payment of seemingly legitimate wages to criminal associates who are actually involved in his illegal enterprises.

Syndicates acquire business interests in a variety of ways. In some cases, syndicate members acquire businesses by investing profits obtained from gambling and other illegal activities. Syndicate profits were used to build many of the casinos in Las Vegas, beginning with the Flamingo in 1945 (Messick, 1971). The syndicate is reported to have skimmed millions of dollars from casino profits and smuggled them out of Nevada without paying taxes on them (Salerno and Tompkins, 1969). As we have already indicated, syndicates acquire interests in businesses as payment for gambling debts or in exchange for cancelling usurious loans.

Syndicate members may receive their percentage of the profits from these businesses through various channels. Profits may be paid directly to the syndicate member, or a brother-in-law, uncle, cousin, or friend may be added to the company payroll. In other cases, he may be paid by requiring the company's owner to buy some or all of his supplies at exorbitant prices from companies owned by other syndicate members. Some of these supplies so purchased may never be delivered, and the funds are thereby diverted entirely to the company's "silent partner."

Extortion is another method by which organized crime penetrates legitimate business. In a limited number of cases the syndicate member will walk into a business and announce, "I am your partner." A variation of this is the protection racket. A businessman will be visited by a syndicate member and "asked" to pay for protective services or insurance. For example, a beauty shop owner may be approached and asked to pay $30.00 a week for protection against having her premises stink-bombed or having bees or mice released among her patrons. Another method is to send some thugs into a business like a nightclub and have them beat up a few people, break some furniture, smash the bar, and then storm out. The following day a syndicate member will visit the club and solicit protection money. In some cases the club owners will even come to the syndicate and request protection. Vincent Teresa, a former syndicate member, claims that he was able to extort $1000 a month from 20 nightclubs in the Boston metropolitan area using this technique (Teresa and Renner, 1973). A more refined method of extortion employed by some syndicates entails selling merchants products they do not need, brands they do not wish to stock, or merchandise they stock at above market prices. For example, in 1958, Joseph DiVarco, a reputed northside Chicago syndicate boss, was involved in a business that sold glass-washing machines to Chicago bars and taverns. His salesmen experienced no difficulty placing these machines in northside bars, employing a simple but persuasive sales pitch in which the merchant was informed that Joey Caesar (a name by which DiVarco was better known) wanted him to purchase one of these machines (Cressey, 1969).

Another favorite syndicate business technique is the counterfeiting of nationally famous products. In one such operation, a syndicate-controlled company produced auto parts and stamped them with the name of a well-known company. These parts were packaged in company cartons and shipped for sale in South America. This operation came to light only when a customer complained to the legitimate company about a defective part. Another syndicate-controlled company flooded the record distribution and juke box industry with cheap reproductions of popular records with counterfeit labels affixed to them. There are now indications that the syndicate has infiltrated the prescription drug industry and is involved in the illegal manufacture of prescription drugs (Chamber of Commerce of the United States, 1969).

In the next two sections, we will present more detailed discussions of two additional methods employed by organized crime to infiltrate legitimate businesses.

Bankruptcy Fraud

Organized crime perpetrates bankruptcy fraud — also called "planned bankruptcy," "bustout," and "scam" — because of the rather substantial profits and minimal risks associated with these schemes. The U. S. Chamber of Commerce indicates that there are approximately 200 syndicate related bankruptcy frauds perpetrated each year, each involving up to 250 or more creditors and merchandise or material valued at upwards of $200,000. All scam operations have as a common denominator the abuse of credit (Chamber of Commerce of the United States, 1969). While bankruptcy fraud can take a variety of forms, syndicates generally employ one of the following four types:

The Three-Step Scam

> *A new company is formed, headed by someone (front man) with no prior adverse record. "Nut money" of $30,000 or so is deposited in a bank to establish visible evidence of the firm's creditworthiness. A classy company name is conjured up and a public accountant often prepares a balance and income statement — with a note attached indicating that the financial reports have not been verified by him. If requested, references are supplied — often names of cooperative racketeer controlled firms. Modest initial orders are placed with suppliers. Creditors are paid in full for initial shipments. Gradually, orders are increased and payments decline as the percentage of what is due. The final step is the placement of large orders. When the goods are all in, they are sold at bargain rates or concealed elsewhere [in some cases the goods are sold to a fence]. Nut money is withdrawn and the scam operators vanish or explain away the resulting bankruptcy by blaming it on a theft (so true), a fire that destroyed the warehouse, an urge to gamble that consumed all of the profits, etc.*
> (Chamber of Commerce of the United States, 1969, p. 27)

Because the three-step scam requires several months to complete, the less time-consuming one-step scam is more frequently employed. According to De Franco (1973), this scam involves the following elements:

The One-Step Scam

1. *A successful business with a good credit rating is purchased [or acquired as payment for a gambling debt or usurious loan].*
2. *No notice of the change in management is provided to Dunn*

and Bradstreet or other credit agencies, thus trading on the previous owner's good credit reputation.

3. *Manufacturers are approached in person or at trade shows to arrange for the purchase of merchandise.*

    a. *Since the orders placed are usually of a large quantity, suppliers who did not sell to the company previously are politely informed by the scam operator that if he does not sell to him, some other company would be glad to do so. This is known as "the sketch."*

4. *Large orders are then placed, including orders for many items not previously purchased by the company.*

5. *After the orders have been received, the merchandise is sold as with the three-step scam; the money is milked from the business; and the company is forced into bankruptcy, just as the scam operator had planned.* (p. 6)

The Same Name Scam

The following is a variation of the one-step scam:

> *The scam group company is given a name almost identical to that of a well known and highly creditworthy corporation. If the latter is Gidget, Inc., the scam's operation is dubbed Gidget Sales, Inc., whose address may even be on the same street as that of the reputable firm. Capitalizing on the favorable credit rating of the well known firm, racketeers proceed to order goods from misled suppliers, except in this case the bustout can proceed faster because there is a preestablished credit rating and financial statements are often unnecessary.* (Chamber of Commerce of the United States, 1969, p. 28)

While scams may never be completely eliminated, the key to minimizing losses from these schemes is alertness on the part of the business community.

Manipulation and Theft of Stocks and Bonds

Theft and manipulation of stocks and bonds is a relatively new enterprise for organized crime. The following statement in the President's Crime Commission report illustrates how new this involvement is:

> *The greatest gambling enterprise in the United States has not been significantly touched by organized crime. That is the Stock Market. (There has been criminal activity in the Stock Market, but not on the part of what we usually call "organized crime.")*

The reason is that the market works too well. Furthermore, federal control over the Stock Market, designed mainly to keep it honest and informative, aimed at maximizing the competitiveness of the market and the information for the customer, makes tampering difficult. (President's Commission on Law Enforcement and Administration of Justice, 1967, p. 124)

While it is difficult to trace the movement of organized crime into this area on a large scale, Murphy (1971) states that the volume of thefts from Wall Street brokerage firms has risen markedly since 1966. Between 1967 and 1970, the value of securities reported lost to the New York City Police Department rose from $8-1/2 million to $38-1/2 million. The National Crime Information Center reported that the combined figure for losses of private and government securities for 1970 was $226 million (McClellan, 1971). Organized crime is reputed to play a major part in the theft and conversion of these stolen securities. While the Italian syndicates dominate these activities, a number of other syndicate groups and combinations of criminals in a loosely organized confederation are also involved. Organized crime figures became interested in securities after they had developed a sufficient background in business to understand the low risks and high rewards of marketing stolen securities (Mitchell, 1971). There are four main sources from which organized crime acquires stolen securities: (1) brokerage houses (including stock exchanges); (2) banks; (3) the mails; (4) individuals — which includes thefts from private homes, corporate offices, and the like (Manuel, 1971).

Many of the thefts from brokerage houses are inside jobs. Owing to the unprecedented volume of business on Wall Street in the late 1960's and early 1970's, brokerage houses were forced to increase the size of their staffs. The tight labor market for qualified clerks led many firms to hire personnel without checking references and without making background investigations (Grutzner, 1973). This high volume of business also resulted in an almost casual handling of securities (Gross, 1971). An employee with a will or a need to steal found few obstacles.

Employees who steal securities from brokerage houses can be grouped into three categories (Gross, 1971). First, some heretofore honest employees steal because they see this as an easy means of making money. The second group of employees pilfer securities because of pressure exerted — threats of bodily harm to the employee or his family — by bookmakers and loan sharks as a result of gambling debts or loans. The employee receives a percentage of the value of the securities stolen, which is applied against his outstanding debt or loan. A third group of employees are placed in brokerage houses for the specific purpose of stealing securities. Syndicate members working through employment agencies have placed "budding criminals" with falsified references in brokerage houses in New York and other cities. The position obtained by the planted employee is of no consequence, since any position offers direct access to securities, the opportunity to recruit another employee, or the possibility of obtaining information on a shipment that can be used to intercept it at some point in the course of its trip. Employees planted in brokerage firms by organized crime not only steal securities but also are involved in other related thefts.

The mechanics of securities theft are really quite elementary. In many cases, an employee of a brokerage house or bank that handles large quantities of securities — corporate stocks, bonds, and various kinds of government notes and bonds — will simply take some certificates with him when he goes home in the evening. In a recent case, an employee successfully removed $2-1/2 million worth of securities from a brokerage firm by carrying them out in his attaché case (Gross, 1971). In some instances, a small fire is planned to cover the theft. A far more sophisticated method known as the "switch" is also used:

> An employee in stock house (A) steals a hundred shares of IBM. The stolen stock is given to an employee in stock house (B) who steals a hundred shares of IBM, replacing them with the stolen stock from house (A).
>
> When stock house (A) does their audit they discover the loss, put stops on those shares that are quietly sitting in stock house (B). When (B) does its inventory, all books balance. Thus, the underworld is free to peddle (B's) stock on which there is no stop order. (Gross, 1971, p. 74)

While many thefts of securities occur in brokerage firms, the most common means of obtaining stolen securities is burglaries of public carriers, mail receptacles, private homes, and businesses and occasionally thefts from safe deposit boxes and bank vaults (Gross, 1971). Thefts from bank vaults are often carried out by employees using the same methods and having the same motivations as those working in brokerage houses.

Thefts of air freight, registered mail pouches, and REA value boxes, particularly from airports, represent a lucrative source of securities as well as other merchandise for the syndicate. Until 1970, airports were an easy target because the rapid expansion of the air transportation industry and its growing capability to carry mail were not matched by the development of adequate security systems within the industry (Cotter, 1971). Even today, airports are not as well protected as they should be.

The thief who actually takes the securities generally receives only between 2 and 10 per cent of their face value. Lacking the contacts or the expertise to make direct use of these stolen securities, the thief is forced to pass them along for a fraction of their face value to a bookmaker, fence, or small loan shark who has the knowledge and contacts to dispose of them. Gross (1971) mentions a thief who was reputed to have stolen $2.2 million worth of securities, which he sold for a new Mustang. Securities are passed upward through the ranks of organized crime until they eventually reach the hands of someone who has the expertise, the capital, and the personnel to effect a profitable disposition (Murphy, 1971). Each person who handles the securities gets a slice of the profits; however, the bulk of the gain is made by those who handle the final disposition.

Control Measures

In the late 1960's when the thefts of securities skyrocketed, the securities industry began to take steps to tighten up security procedures. Many brokerage firms developed security systems that involved the use of armed guards, the requirement of identification badges for employees working in sensitive areas, and the use of closed circuit TV systems and other advanced techniques. Brokerage houses also began to do more thorough background investigations on new employees. Another important development was the creation of a securities validation system. Under this system a computer data bank containing information on lost and stolen securities provides brokers and banks with a quick means of determining if securities presented to them for sale, transfer, or as collateral are stolen.

On a long-term basis, the industry is moving toward the elimination of the stock certificate. It has been suggested that the industry adopt some kind of book-entry computer system. Under the proposed system, computers would be utilized to maintain records of stock ownership. Thus, when a customer bought stock, instead of receiving certificates as he does at present, he would receive only a memorandum indicating how many shares of the stock he then owns (Zarb, 1971). The first system of this kind was implemented by the Federal Reserve Banks in 1968 and covered treasury securities owned by member banks and held in custody at their Federal Reserve Bank. Eventually, this procedure was extended to securities owned by customers of banks. It is anticipated that in the near future most treasury securities will be converted to book-entry form and that ultimately there will be very few pieces of paper in existence evidencing a government debt obligation (Debs, 1971).

The substantial thefts at airports prompted them to tighten their security systems. At John F. Kennedy International Airport in New York City, where thefts have probably been the most serious, personal security has been tightened by an improved system of screening prospective employees likely to have access to cargo and through the use of identification badges for more than 14,000 employees with access to cargo terminals and ramp areas. More security officers and guards have been hired by the airlines, and a reward program has been established for information concerning cargo thefts. Dual lens cameras, closed circuit TV, alarm systems, and other mechanical devices have been installed. The Post Office Department has instituted a program at Kennedy and several other airports for the containerization and convoy of registered mail, known as the Con-Con system (Landry, 1971). The Chamber of Commerce of the United States (1974) has provided businessmen with a list of danger signals that should alert them to possible transactions involving stolen securities.

LABOR RACKETEERING

Organized crime became involved with labor unions in the 1930's when they were attempting to organize workers in major industries. Confederation men took advantage of this situation and hired out to both labor and management. They worked as strongmen for companies anxious to avoid unionization and hired out to unions to intimidate factory guards and beat up nonstrikers (Salerno and Tompkins, 1969).

Labor racketeering occurs in several guises. One common technique involves the establishment of self-chartered dummy unions and paper locals for the purpose of shaking down employers and exploiting workers. A fictitious local will be established and employers will be induced to send dues deducted from worker's salaries to the local's office, with the workers receiving nothing in return for their union dues. For example, Benny "the Bug" Ross is reported to have set up a phony union with a name almost the same as that of Local 124 Bakery and Confectionary Workers International, an AFL-CIO affiliate. Having set this union up, he then induced employers to send the dues deducted from their worker's salaries to his office, which was located in the same building as the legitimate union (Grutzner, 1968).

Labor racketeers also make use of the control they have over certain unions to solicit money from both businessmen and workers. At Kennedy Airport the syndicate obtained control of the unions and trucker trade association and used them to get cuts of businessmen's profits, worker's wages, and shipper's freight charges (McClellan, 1970). In one specific case, a union secretary-treasurer told a large trucking firm that $5000 would assure the company trouble-free access to Kennedy Airport.

Syndicate members may also use the control they exert over labor unions to further their outside business interests. A syndicate member is reported to have once demanded that supermarket chains purchase kosher products from his company in exchange for minimal labor relations difficulties (Chamber of Commerce of the United States, 1969).

Another common practice by labor racketeers is to pressure companies to pad their payrolls with names or to hire workers whose only job is to handle horse race and policy bets and collect loan shark payments. In May, 1969, a wildcat strike was called because a waterfront employer refused to comply with a union local's suggestion that the company hire someone it neither desired nor needed.

Another common ploy used by syndicate labor leaders is to require that the company hire them as labor consultants in exchange for maintaining labor peace:

> After experiencing the nightmare of a labor situation, a company employed a well-known racketeer as a labor consultant. There was no more trouble from the union. The company paid $15,000 yearly to the consultant, who was at the same time receiving $22,500 in severance pay from a union of which he had been secretary-treasurer. When a union official, he was indicted for unlawfully receiving money from employers. (Chamber of Commerce of the United States, 1969, p. 36)

Syndicate members with strong associations in organized labor use their positions to extort money from contractors for allowing them to operate their projects without union labor. In these deals, the syndicate members serve as middlemen. They make contact with the builders and indicate that for a price their construction project can use nonunion labor. They collect the fee from the contractors and pay off union delegates. Everyone benefits from this except the workers, who are paid below union scale. By paying below union scale, the contractor has a decided advantage in underbidding his competitors. These agreements can save contractors in some areas more than $1000 on the price of each apartment unit.

The "sweetheart" contract represents still another method by which workers are deprived of benefits through collusion between labor and management. These contracts are arrange to benefit management, thus defeating the whole purpose of collective bargaining. In return for a favorable contract — one that brings no or only minimal benefits to employees — an employer pays a fee to racketeers or permits pilfering, gambling, and loan sharking on his premises. In some cases, sweetheart contracts are negotiated through the vehicle of a paper or dummy local, and employees do not realize that they are members of a union until the contract is signed and dues payments begin (Chamber of Commerce of the United States, 1969).

One of the major objectives of syndicate penetration of labor unions has been to gain access to union pension and welfare funds, which amount to approximately $100 billion and are growing at a multi-billion dollar annual rate. Once in control of these funds, the syndicate uses them (1) for investment in the stock market either in a "high flyer" (a speculative stock whose backers are of questionable integrity) or in a security whose price can be manipulated upward through heavy purchases by syndicate members; (2) to establish a welfare program for union members that fellow racketeers are hired to administer at exorbitant salaries; and (3) to loan out to anyone who will provide a requisite kickback (Chamber of Commerce of the United States, 1969).

In addition to the aforementioned practices, syndicate members have been involved in assisting businessmen to eliminate their competitors through strikes, picketing, sabotage, and discriminatory wage scales. Their support has allowed businessmen to evade the payment of required contributions to union welfare and pension funds. One of their most reprehensible practices has been requiring workers to pay kickbacks in order to get and hold jobs (Grutzner, 1968).

SUMMARY

In this chapter we have surveyed both the criminal and legitimate enterprises in which organized crime is involved. Gambling, with an estimated annual take in the billions, is the principal revenue source for organized crime. The organizational structure and operations of the numbers racket and bookmaking were examined in some detail. Attention was also devoted to loansharking, a low risk, high return enterprise that ranks second only to gambling as a lucrative field for syndicate criminals. Our major emphasis in this chapter was upon the illegal importation and distribution of narcotics, principally heroin and cocaine, because drug abuse is one of our gravest social problems and a contributing factor to the constantly rising urban crime rate. The chapter concluded with a discussion of the penetration of legitimate business and labor union racketeering by organized crime.

REVIEW

Find the answers to the following questions in the text:

1. Describe the organizational structure and operations of the numbers racket. Identify the functions of the runner, controller, and bank pick-up man.

2. Describe the organizational structure and operations of bookmaking.

3. Of what importance is gambling to other organized crime activities?

4. Why has loan sharking been referred to as the safest and most remunerative racket of the underworld?

5. Who are the principal clients of loan sharks? How can the activities of loan sharks be curbed?

6. What role did Lucky Luciano play in setting up the Turkish-French connection?

7. Trace a "bag" of heroin from the opium poppy fields of Turkey to the arm of the addict purchaser in the United States.

8. What are some of the sources of heroin supply other than Turkey?

9. Who are the principals dominating the cocaine traffic?

10. Discuss the recommendations of the Domestic Council on Drug Abuse Task Force for the control of narcotics importation and distribution in this country. How would you assess the feasibility of the various proposals?

11. What are some of the ways in which organized crime can acquire control of legitimate business enterprises?

12. What is involved in scam operations? Sketch the steps that occur in a one-step and a three-step scam.

13. What are the features of securities theft that make this activity particularly attractive to organized crime?

14. What is a "sweetheart" contract?

15. Why did organized crime become involved with labor unions? What use is made of legitimate union financial resources by organized crime?

TERMS TO IDENTIFY AND REMEMBER:

Bolita	golden triangle	big layoff man
runner	one-step scam	"stop the clock"
bank pick-up man	sweetheart contract	morphine base
policy bank	controller	ounce man
loan sharking	layoff bank	three-step scam
TIR trucks	bookmaker	

REFERENCES

Chamber of Commerce of the United States: *Deskbook on Organized Crime*. Washington, D. C., 1969.

Chamber of Commerce of the United States: *White-Collar Crime: Everyone's Problem, Everyone's Loss*. Washington, D. C., 1974.

Cook, F. J.: Pari-mutuel handle: The black Mafia moves into the numbers racket. The New York Times Magazine April 4, 1971, pp. 26–29, 107–112.

Cotter, W. J.: Organized Crime: Stolen Securities. Hearings Before the Permanent Subcommittee on Investigations of the Committee on Government Operations. 92nd Congress, 1st Session, 1971, Part I, pp. 8–35.

Cressey, D. R.: *Theft of a Nation: The Structure and Operations of Organized Crime in America*. New York, Harper & Row, Inc., 1969.

Crittenden, A.: Cocaine: The champagne of drugs. The New York Times Magazine September 1, 1974, pp. 14–17.

Cusack, J. T.: Turkey lifts poppy ban. Durg Enforcement Fall, 1974, pp. 3–17.

Cusack, J. T.: A review of the international drug traffic. Drug Enforcement Spring, 1976, pp. 34–37.

Debs, R. A.: Organized Crime: Stolen Securities. Hearings Before the Permanent Subcommittee on Investigations of the Committee on Government Operations. 92nd Congress, 1st Session, 1971, Part I, pp. 8–35.

De Franco, E. J.: *Anatomy of a Scam: A Case Study of a Planned Bankruptcy by Organized Crime*. U. S. Department of Justice, Washington, D. C., U. S. Government Printing Office, 1973.

Domestic Council on Drug Abuse Task Force: *White Paper on Drug Abuse*. Washington, D. C., U. S. Government Printing Office, 1975.

Fund for the City of New York: *Legal Gambling: A Discussion of Numbers and Sports Betting*. New York, 1972.

Gage, N.: Latins now leader of hard-drug trade. The New York Times April 21, 1975a, pp. 1, 26.

Gage, N.: Drug smuggling logistics bizarre and often fatal. The New York Times April 22, 1975b, pp. 1, 24.

Gross, M.: Organized Crime: Stolen Securities. Hearings Before the Permanent Subcommittee on Investigations of the Committee on Government Operations. 92nd Congress, 1st Session, 1971, Part I, pp. 8–35.

Grutzner, C.: Union racket cases crowding courts. The New York Times August 11, 1968, pp. 1, 74.

Grutzner, C.: Organized crime and the businessman. *In* Conklin, J. E. (ed.): *The Crime Establishment: Organized Crime and American Society*. Englewood Cliffs, New Jersey, Prentice-Hall, Inc., 1973.

Landry, J. E.: Organized Crime: Stolen Securities. Hearings Before the Permanent Subcommittee on Investigations of the Committee on Government Operations. 92nd Congress, 1st Session, 1971, Part I, pp. 8–35.

LEAA (Law Enforcement Assistance Agency) Technical Assistance Division: *Police Guide on Organized Crime*. Washington, D. C., U. S. Government Printing Office, 1972.

Maas, P.: *The Valachi Papers*. New York, Bantam Books, 1969.

Manuel, P. R.: Organized Crime: Stolen Securities. Hearings Before the Permanent Subcommittee on Investigations of the Committee on Government Operations. 92nd Congress, 1st Session, 1971, Part I, pp. 8–35.

McClellan, J. L.: Testimony Before the Committee on the Judiciary of the House of Representatives on the Control of Organized Crime in the United States. 91st Congress, 1st Session, May 20, 1970.

McClellan, J. L.: Organized Crime: Stolen Securities. Hearings Before the Permanent Subcommittee on Investigations of the Committee on Government Operations. 92nd Congress, 1st Session, 1971, Part I, pp. 8–35.

McCoy, A. W.: *The Politics of Heroin in Southeast Asia*. New York, Harper Colophon Books, 1972.

Messick, H.: *Lansky*. New York, Berkely Medallion Books, 1971.

Mitchell, J. M.: Organized Crime: Stolen Securities. Hearings Before the Permanent Subcommittee on Investigations of the Committee on Government Operations. 92nd Congress, 1st Session, 1971, Part I, pp. 8–35.

Moore, M.: *Policy Concerning Drug Abuse in New York State: Economics of Heroin Distribution*. Croton-on-Hudson, New York; Hudson Institute, 1970.

Murphy, P.: Organized Crime: Stolen Securities. Hearings Before the Permanent Subcommittee on Investigations of the Committee on Government Operations. 92nd Congress, 1st Session, 1971, Part I, pp. 8–35.

Newsday: *The Heroin Triad*. New York, Signet Books, 1974.

Pennsylvania Crime Commission. *Report on Organized Crime*. Harrisburg, Office of the Attorney General, 1970.

President's Commission on Law Enforcement and Administration of Justice: *Task Force Report: Organized Crime*. Washington, D. C., U. S. Government Printing Office, 1967.

Salerno, R.: Lectures delivered before the Seminar on Vice Control and Drug Abuse, Florida Institute for Law Enforcement. St. Petersburg Beach, Florida, February 2–6, 1976.

Salerno, R., and Tompkins, J. S.: *The Crime Confederation: Cosa Nostra and Allied Operations in Organized Crime*. Garden City, New York, Doubleday & Co., Inc., 1969.

Salmons, S., Marro, A., and Schmidt, W. The Mexican connection. Newsweek March 15, 1976, pp. 28–30.

Seidl, J. M.: *Upon the Hip — A Study of the Criminal Loanshark Industry*. Unpublished Ph.D. dissertation, Harvard University, 1968.

Sherrid, S. D.: The mathematics of loansharking. Police Chief *42*:59, 1975.

Singer, M., and Candela, B.: *Increased Legal Gambling in New York: A Policy Analysis*. Croton-on-Hudson, New York, Hudson Institute, 1973.

Singer, M., and Newitt, H. J.: *Policy Concerning Drug Abuse in New York State: The Basic Study*. Croton-on-Hudson, New York, Hudson Institute, 1970.

Teresa, V., and Renner, T.: *My Life in the Mafia*. Greenwich, Connecticut, Fawcett Books, 1973.

Time Magazine. Latin America: A tragic trail's end for the Yankee mules. August 12, 1974, p. 36.

Zarb, F. G.: Organized Crime: Stolen Securities. Hearings Before the Permanent Subcommittee on Investigations of the Committee on Government Operations. 92nd Congress, 1st Session, 1971, Part I, pp. 8–35.

8 WHITE-COLLAR/ ECONOMIC CRIMES

Criminologist Edwin H. Sutherland introduced the concept of *white-collar crime* in his presidential address to the American Sociological Association in 1939. Defining white collar crime as "crime committed by a person of respectability and high social status in the course of his occupation" (1949, p. 9), Sutherland employed this concept to direct attention to crimes of the "upper world," as distinguished from those conventional crimes committed by the lower classes. He suggested that white-collar crime can be found in all occupations and provided the following illustrations for some of the most common illegal practices within business and the medical profession:

> *White-collar criminality in business is expressed most frequently in the form of misrepresentation in financial statements of corporations, manipulation in the stock exchange, commercial bribery, bribery of public officials directly or indirectly in order to secure favorable contracts and legislation, misrepresentation in advertising and salesmanship, embezzlement and misapplication of funds, short weights and measures and misgrading of commodities, tax frauds, misapplication of funds in receiverships and bankruptcy. These are what Al Capone called "the legitimate rackets." These and many others are found in abundance in the business world.*
>
> *In the medical profession, which is here used as an example because it is probably less criminalistic than some other professions, are found the illegal sale of alcohol and narcotics, abortion, illegal services to underworld criminals, fraudulent reports in testimony in accident cases, extreme cases of unnecessary treatment, fake specialists, restriction of competition, and fee splitting.*
> (Sutherland, 1949, as quoted by Geis, 1968, p. 42)

233

Sutherland's definition of white-collar crime is far too restrictive because it fails to recognize that many such crimes bear no relation to the offenders' occupations. These crimes include making fraudulent claims for unemployment insurance, filing false personal and nonbusiness income tax returns, and making numerous credit purchases with neither the intention nor the capability of ever paying for them. Sutherland's definition also fails to include those businesses in which crime is the central activity of the operation; e.g., pyramid clubs, fraudulent land sale corporations, bogus home improvement companies, and phony accident rings.

Edelhertz (1970) has developed an expanded definition of white-collar crime that encompasses the many areas excluded by Sutherland's definition. He defines white-collar crime as "an illegal act or series of illegal acts committed by nonphysical means and by concealment or guile, to obtain money or property, to avoid the payment or loss of money or property, or to obtain business or personal advantage" (p. 3). He discerns the following elements in any white-collar crime:

- *Intent to commit a wrongful act or to achieve a purpose inconsistent with law or public policy.*
- *Disguise of purpose or intent.*
- *Reliance by perpetrator on ignorance or carelessness of victim.*
- *Acquiescence by victim in what he believes to be the true nature and content of the transaction.*
- *Concealment of the crime by —*
  (1) preventing the victim from realizing that he has been victimized, or
  (2) relying on the fact that only a small percentage of victims will react to what has happened, and making provisions for restitution to or other handling of the disgruntled victim, or
  (3) creation of a deceptive paper, organizational, or transactional facade to disguise the true nature of what has occurred. (p. 12)

While Sutherland's definition places its major emphasis on the people who commit the crimes, Edelhertz's approach concentrates on the *modi operandi* and the objectives of the crimes. In addition to providing us with an expanded definition of this concept, Edelhertz (1970) has also developed a four-fold classification system of white-collar crime, which is presented below, along with examples of some of the criminal activities that fall within each of these categories.

A. **Personal Crimes:** *Crimes by persons operating on an individual ad hoc basis. Some examples are:*

1. *Purchases on credit with no intention to pay, or purchases by mail in the name of another.*
2. *Individual income tax violations.*
3. *Credit card frauds.*
4. *Bankruptcy frauds.*
5. *Title II home improvement loan frauds.*
6. *Frauds with respect to social security, unemployment insurance, or welfare.*
7. *Unorganized or occasional frauds on insurance companies (theft, casualty, health, etc.).*
8. *Violations of Federal Reserve regulations by pledging stock for further purchases, flouting margin requirements.*
9. *Unorganized "lonely hearts" appeal by mail.*

B. **Abuses of Trust:** *Crimes in the course of their occupations by those operating inside business, government, or other establishments, in violation of their duty of loyalty or fidelity to employer or client. Examples include:*

1. *Commercial bribery and kickbacks, i.e., by and to buyers, insurance adjusters, contracting officers, quality inspectors, government inspectors and auditors, etc.*
2. *Bank violations by bank officers, employees, and directors.*
3. *Embezzlement or self-dealing by business or union officers and employees.*
4. *Securities fraud by insiders trading to their advantage by the use of special knowledge, or causing their firms to take positions in the market to benefit themselves.*
5. *Employee petty larceny and expense frauds.*
6. *Frauds by computer, causing unauthorized payouts.*
7. *"Sweetheart contracts" entered into by union officers.*
8. *Embezzlement or self-dealing by attorneys, trustees, and fiduciaries.*
9. *Fraud against the Government:*
   (a) *Padding of payrolls.*
   (b) *Conflicts of interest.*
   (c) *False travel, expense, or per diem claims.*

C. **Business Crimes:** *Crimes incidental to, and in furtherance of, business operations, but not the central purpose of the business. Some examples:*

1. *Tax violations.*
2. *Antitrust violations.*
3. *Commercial bribery of another's employee, officer or fiduciary (including union officers).*
4. *Food and drug violations.*
5. *False weights and measures by retailers.*

6. *Violations of Truth-in-Lending Act by misrepresentation of credit terms and prices.*
7. *Submission or publication of false financial statements to obtain credit.*
8. *Use of fictitious or over-valued collateral.*
9. *Check-kiting to obtain operating capital on short term financing.*
10. *Securities Act violations, i.e., sale of nonregistered securities, to obtain operating capital, false proxy statements, manipulation of market to support corporate credit or access to capital markets, etc.*
11. *Collusion between physicians and pharmacists to cause the writing of unnecessary prescriptions.*
12. *Dispensing by pharmacists in violation of law, excluding narcotics traffic.*
13. *Immigration fraud in support of employment agency operations to provide domestics.*
14. *Housing code violations by landlords.*
15. *Deceptive advertising.*
16. *Fraud against the Government:*
    (a) *False claims.*
    (b) *False statements:*
        (1) *To induce contracts.*
        (2) *AID frauds.*
        (3) *Housing frauds.*
        (4) *SBA frauds, such as SBIC bootstrapping, selfdealing, crossdealing, etc., or obtaining direct loans by use of false financial statements.*
    (c) *Moving contracts in urban renewal.*
17. *Labor violations (Davis-Bacon Act).*
18. *Commercial espionage.*

D. Con Games: *White collar crime as a business or as a central activity of the business. The following are illustrative:*
1. *Medical or health frauds.*
2. *Advance fee swindles.*
3. *Phony contests.*
4. *Bankruptcy fraud, including schemes devised as salvage operation after insolvency of otherwise legitimate businesses.*
5. *Securities fraud and commodities fraud.*
6. *Chain referral schemes.*
7. *Home improvement schemes.*
8. *Debt consolidation schemes.*
9. *Mortgage milking.*
10. *Merchandise swindles:*
    (a) *Gun and coin swindles.*
    (b) *General merchandise.*
    (c) *Buying on pyramid clubs.*

11. *Land frauds.*
12. *Directory advertising schemes.*
13. *Charity and religious frauds.*
14. *Personal improvement schemes:*
    (a) Diploma mills.
    (b) Correspondence schools.
    (c) Modeling schools.
15. *Fraudulent application for, use, and/or sale of credit cards, airline tickets, etc.*
16. *Insurance frauds:*
    (a) Phony accident rings.
    (b) Looting of companies by purchase of over-valued assets, phony management contracts, self-dealing with agents, inter-company transfers, etc.
    (c) Frauds by agents writing false policies to obtain advance commissions.
    (d) Issuance of annuities or paid-up life insurance, with no consideration, so that they can be used as collateral for loans.
    (e) Sales by misrepresentations to military personnel or those otherwise uninsurable.
17. *Vanity and song publishing schemes.*
18. *Ponzi schemes.*
19. *False security frauds, i.e., Billy Sol Estes or De Angelis type schemes.*
20. *Purchase of banks, or control thereof, with deliberate intention to loot them.*
21. *Fraudulent establishing and operation of banks or savings and loan associations.*
22. *Fraud against the Government:*
    (a) Organized income tax refund swindles, sometimes operated by income tax "counselors."
    (b) AID frauds, i.e., where totally worthless goods are shipped.
    (c) FHA frauds:
        (1) Obtaining guarantees of mortgages on multiple family housing far in excess of value or property with forseeable inevitable foreclosure.
23. *Executive placement and employment agency frauds.*
24. *Coupon redemption frauds.*
25. *Money order swindles.* (pp. 73–75)

More recently, Finn and Hoffman (1976) have suggested that we label this type of criminal activity *"economic crime"* rather than "white-collar crime," because the term "economic crime" more accurately reflects the objective of these types of offenses — economic gain — and does not imply that only the wealthy or those in executive positions perpetrate such crimes. We agree with these authors and anticipate that this new label will eventually replace "white-collar crime" as the designation for this type of criminal behavior.

In the following section, we shall discuss Edelhertz's four general categories of economic crime. While an exhaustive coverage of the entire range of economic crimes is beyond our capabilities in the present context, we have sought to provide sufficient detail in selected instances to exemplify the main characteristics of each of Edelhertz's categories.

CATEGORIES OF ECONOMIC CRIME

Personal Crimes

Fraud, according to Black's Law Dictionary (1968), is a "generic term, embracing all multifarious means which human ingenuity can devise, and which are resorted to by one individual to get advantage over another by false suggestions or by suppression of truth, and includes all surprise, trick, cunning, dissembling, and any unfair way by which another is cheated" (p. 788). Edelhertz's list of fraudulent activities, ranging from home improvement loan schemes to illegal stock market manipulations, provides only a sample of the "multifarious means" that human beings have managed to devise in seeking personal advantage, but the feature common to all is that they are practiced as a form of individual criminal entrepreneurship.

Credit Card Fraud

One of the newest areas of criminal endeavor within this category of personal crimes is the use of credit cards to defraud. Credit cards were first issued by petroleum companies back in the 1930's to preferred customers who were recommended by local dealers. Monthly billing and the ease of credit payment attracted customers to these companies, and it is this customer attraction that continues to justify the risk and expense of issuing credit cards on the part of individual companies. In 1950, a New Yorker named Frank MacNamara devised a plan for credit card use in restaurants, motels, and places of entertainment that eventually became established as the famous Diners Club. Following the success of this venture, other multipurpose credit card systems were designed, among them American Express, Master Charge, and BankAmericard. Major retail stores and airlines entered the competition with their own credit plans. The Chamber of Commerce of the United States (1974) estimates that there are approximately 300 million credit cards in circulation, with annual fraud-related losses amounting to $100 million.

In obtaining credit cards to defraud, the simplest way is usually the easiest and safest: 60 per cent of cards used fraudulently were either lost or stolen. Twenty per cent of fraud-related losses represent cards that were issued to, but never received by, legitimate applicants, and the remaining 20 per cent are cards obtained by fraudulent application. Counterfeiting of credit cards is extremely rare, but there is growing concern that it will develop into a major problem as the more traditional methods of credit card fraud become less and less successful (Chamber of Commerce, 1974).

Theft of credit cards is generally a secondary crime, because most thieves were after either money or easily fenced items. Leading the list of high-theft areas for credit cards are motels and hotels. Thefts by pickpockets and thefts from glove compartments of automobiles rank second and third, respectively. Credit cards can be lost or stolen in bars and restaurants by the absent-minded customer who forgets his card; by the crooked waiter or waitress who hides the credit card under a plate or napkin in the hope that the customer will not notice; or by the waiter or waitress who switches the card with one that has outlived its usefulness, gambling that the customer will fail to recognize the substitution. Cards stolen from hotels or motels have a life of from 1 to 10 days; those stolen from mailboxes before reaching the legitimate applicant have a life of 28 days.

Fraudulent credit card applications can be made in various ways. One method is to obtain the name and address of a legitimate card-holder from a used charge-slip carbon, then write to the company requesting a change of address and another card for a wife or husband. Another method requires the connivance of an employee of the card-issuing company whose position allows him to issue cards to accomplices. A much more elaborate scheme involves the creation of fictitious identities. One enterprising criminal named John Spillane managed to obtain more than 1000 credit cards and $660,000 in loans by establishing at least 300 phony identities for himself. The scheme worked like this:

> In July 1970, Spillane set up several fraudulent businesses by incorporating, securing post office boxes and ordering telephones. Somehow, he managed to get five New Jersey banks to give the "businesses" loans, and because he was prompt with interest payments, the loans were increased.

> *To pay the interest, Spillane needed more income, so he begun creating the fraudulent personal identities to get credit cards. Once he had the credit cards — mostly BankAmericard and Master Charge — he could get cash advances of between $500 and $1,500 from banks.*
>
> *To set up the phony identities, Spillane needed two things: jobs for his aliases and good credit ratings for them. The jobs were easy. He set up several more phony businesses that consisted of just a telephone. Lieutenants would receive calls from credit card companies, pretend to be personnel department workers and give verifications of employment for the aliases.* (Tampa Tribune, January 29, 1976, p. 18)

Schemes and Methods Used To Defraud. Most credit card frauds are variations on two basic transactions: the use of the stolen or fraudulent card to "purchase" goods for resale, or the illegal use of the card to receive a cash advance. The criminal may simply use a stolen or spurious card as long as he thinks he can to amass a pile of merchandise which can be sold or fenced. Or he may collude with the owner or employee of a store to make a fraudulent purchase and split the proceeds. An employee may engage in a practice known as "double-slipping"; i.e., he makes out two charge slips, one for the correct amount and the other to be filled out later. The customer pays in cash, which is pocketed by the employee; he then fills out a charge slip for a stolen or fraudulent card. Other employee frauds are perpetrated by writing in falsely high amounts on charge slips.

As a convenience to their card holders, credit card companies guarantee payment on checks cashed in one of their outlets. A fraudulent credit card may be used by the criminal to cash books of checks underwritten by the credit company guarantee. If there is a limit as to amount, then the check may be written for just under that amount (Farr, 1975).

Coping With Credit Card Frauds. Some recommendations which might help to reduce credit card frauds include the implementation of security measures provided to merchants by law enforcement agencies and the credit card companies. Over and above any other action which might be taken to prevent or deter credit card abuses, the individual credit card companies should redouble their efforts to employ all the security precautions and devices that are economically feasible to protect against credit card frauds. A free exchange of information concerning criminal use of credit cards between the credit card industry and the various law enforcement agencies is necessary, but at present the flow of information between law enforcement agencies and the credit card industry is often impeded by local laws or departmental regulations. This information is necessary not only in the investigation of criminal suspects but also in the screening of prospective employees by credit card companies. Increased and better enforcement of existing credit card laws by all agencies involved, cooperation between the credit card companies and law enforcement officials, and education of the public are all essential for coping with credit card frauds.

Abuses of Trust

Employee Theft

Inventory shrinkage — an accounting euphemism for losses due to employee pilferage — has been estimated at three times the total losses from robbery, burglary, and larceny-theft in any given year (Newsweek, 1974). The pilferer may be a loner who steals from petty cash, or he may be part of an extensive and well-organized operation that systematically loots the firm of thousands of dollars worth of goods or merchandise. Whatever his *modus operandi*, he contributes to the bankruptcy of nearly 1000 businesses each year (Barmash, 1973).

Who are the pilferers? According to Lipman (1973):

> *Some are punks and some are executives, but the average company thief is a married man, has two or three children, lives in a fairly good community, plays bridge with his neighbors, goes to church regularly, is well thought of by his boss. He is highly trusted and a good worker, one of the best in the plant. That's why he can steal so much over such long periods and why it's so hard to discover his identity.* (p. 160)

It would be difficult to describe a more typically middle-class, respectable individual.

Actual techniques of employee theft are many and varied and depend upon the job or position held by the individual and his access to merchandise. Among the more common techniques listed by McCaghy (1976) are:

> *1. Cashiers who ring up a lower price on single item purchases and pocket the difference, or who ring up lower prices for "needy" friends going through the checkout.*
> *2. Clerks who do not tag some sale merchandise, sell it at the original price, and pocket the difference.*

> 3. *Receiving clerks who have duplicate keys to storage facilities and who return to the store after hours.*
> 4. *Truck drivers who make fictitious purchases of fuel and repairs, and who split the gains with truck stops.*
> 5. *Employees who simply hide items in garbage pails, incinerators, or under trash heaps until they can be retrieved later.*
> (p. 179)

In employee theft, as in many other areas of criminal entrepreneurship, ingenuity in devising new methods of pilferage tends to remain comfortably ahead of methods for the detection and apprehension of the pilferer.

Embezzlement. The real stars among employee thieves, in McCaghy's (1976) view, are *embezzlers* — persons who fraudulently appropriate money entrusted to them by their employers. The methods used by the embezzler depend upon the nature of the transactions over which he has control in the performance of his duties. In the banking business, the employee may have control of the recording of amounts and may manipulate several accounts so that the loss cannot be detected except by a complete audit. The criminal usually has a thorough understanding of the financial operations of the organization that employs him. In some instances, such as when the criminal is the firm's accountant or bookkeeper, he may be the only person in the organization with a comprehensive knowledge of the workings of the company's finances. His criminal operations may take place over a period of months or even years.

The crime of embezzlement involves no violence and is usually committed at the expense of a large organization that is perceived as wealthy and impersonal; hence, no great odium attaches to the embezzler. Indeed, he may be described as a "mastermind" by newspaper reporters, and his criminal feats may be recounted with barely concealed admiration.

Why do people become embezzlers? The obvious reasons that suggest themselves are indebtedness, a desire to live beyond one's means, and drinking or gambling problems. Cressey (1973) concluded that:

> *Trusted persons become trust violators when they conceive of themselves as having a financial problem which is non-shareable, are aware that this problem can be secretly resolved by violation of the position of financial trust, and are able to apply to thier own conduct in that situation verbalizations which enable them to adjust their conceptions of themselves as trusted persons with their conceptions of themselves as users of the entrusted funds.*
> (p. 30)

This description, of course, excludes individuals who have sought positions of trust with the specific intention of committing embezzlement.

Embezzlement often goes unprosecuted. Employers tend to view the matter from a strictly economic perspective: as long as the money is repaid, they are indifferent as to whether it is replaced by the embezzler, his family, or the insurance company. Most employers accept restitution, and this reduces embezzlement to almost a private transaction. Prosecutors are reluctant to take cases to court, they dismiss many of the cases they initiate, acquittals are frequent, and judges are quick to suspend sentence or grant probation to convicted offenders if restitution has been made or arranged.

By taking certain preventive measures, employers can minimize the risks of embezzlement. Rotating employees without warning when they are in key positions, providing an employee's loan fund, and using complex accounting procedures help to reduce the conditions that foster embezzlement. Other measures include the use of internal checks and audits, closer stock inventory, intricate registers and other recording devices, book control, and electric eyes and recording locks and the systematization of receipts and payments. The policing of employees by specially trained personnel unknown to the regular members of the company's work force is a preventive method used within government agencies, but one that is generally not tolerated in the private sector. When this system is used in private business it is only for limited periods of time and for special investigations.

Computer Abuse. The advent of high-speed electronic data processing (EDP) has added a new dimension to economic, or white-collar, crime. While computers are a valuable resource to business, industry, and government, they provide matchless opportunities for criminal exploitation. EDP-related crimes are wide-ranging. According to the Chamber of Commerce of the United States (1974):

> This is so because computer data bases frequently contain ... information encompassing the full scope of business operations. As a result, computer abuse can take the form of embezzlement, misappropriation of computer time, theft of programs, and illegal acquisition of such proprietary information as marketing plans and forecasts, product design, secret manufacturing processes, and confidential technical data. (p. 20)

Whatever the actual cost of computer abuse — and it has been estimated at between $1 billion and $3 billion per year — it seems likely that it will increase. It is expected that 170,000 computers will be in use by 1980, with direct employment in the computer field reaching more than 2½ million people — more than 3 per cent of the total work force.

EDP-related crimes offer scope for a much higher level of sophistication and technical skill than are required by the more common forms of theft. The typical computer criminal is a bright, energetic, highly motivated young male, 18 to 30 years old (Parker and Nycum, 1974). He is often the master of a body of technical information that borders on the esoteric; in fact, he may find it nearly impossible to explain the details of his crime to someone lacking knowledge of computer operations (Farr, 1975).

Limiting access to the computer to carefully screened personnel is considered a key factor in reducing vulnerability to computer abuse. Other security measures include dividing operational responsibilities among a number of people in order to avoid excessive reliance on one or a few persons; maintaining logs to keep track of what the computer has been programmed to do; conducting periodic investigations of company personnel to determine whether anyone is in debt, living beyond his means, and so forth; and hiring computer security specialists trained in detecting the telltale signs of computer abuse. However, perhaps the most significant safeguard against computer abuse that is available to business and industry is a heightened awareness among top management executives of the abuses to which computer operations are susceptible. Fraud of any kind is not likely to flourish under conditions in which close scrutiny is part of the regular routine.

Business Crimes

In the previous section, we discussed economic crimes that are perpetrated by individuals in violation of trust within business or industry. In this section, we shall be concerned with economic crimes that are incidental to and in furtherance of business operations, but not the central purpose of those operations. These "crimes in the suites" represent behavior that is consistent with the goals of profit-seeking in a competitive society. As McCaghy (1976) points out, they are committed by persons within a corporation "who make and implement decisions concerning planning, manufacturing, distribution, pricing, and advertising" (p. 204). They may be top-ranked executives or middle-management personnel, but they "act for and in the name of the corporation" in dealing with other employees and the public. In their pursuit of corporate objectives, McCaghy notes, they may cause the organization to engage in such illegal actions as:

> 1. *undermining the effectiveness of collective bargaining efforts by unions;*
> 2. *conspiring with competitors to keep prices on a level with theirs, or not to cut prices on certain products;*
> 3. *drastically cutting prices in only one product area for the purpose of eliminating competition;*
> 4. *misrepresenting products in advertising or in sales practices.* (p. 204)

Antitrust Legislation

Practices or arrangements that disparage honesty in commercial transactions are detrimental to our free enterprise system of capitalism. In order to be successful, competition must be fair as well as free. As Kintner (1971) puts it:

> *Honest competitors must be protected from predators and shielded from the temptation to adopt the tactics of tricksters in the battle for business survival. And consumers must be protected against commercial chicanery, because fairness requires that they receive an honest product honestly represented, and because consumers are citizens and will ultimately determine the degree of control that government will exercise over business.* (p. 14)

Beginning with the passage of the Sherman Antitrust Act in 1890, the government has sought to bring under legal sanction a broad spectrum of inimical trade practices, ranging from monopolization to price-fixing. These business crimes are known in the aggregate as *antitrust violations.*

Senator John Sherman of Ohio introduced the antitrust bill that bears his name. The Sherman Antitrust Act outlawed "every contract, combination in the form of trust or otherwise, or conspiracy, in restraint of trade or commerce among the several states, or with foreign nations" (Areeda, 1967, p. 785). The act provided criminal penalties of up to $50,000 in fines or imprisonment not exceeding one year for illegal monopolization.*

---

*All monopolies are not illegal. As Kintner (1964) explains: "If the monopoly is achieved through sheer efficiency, if it is granted by the government or it is thrust upon the monopolist in some manner, the status of monopoly is . . . not condemned" (p. 102).

Inadequacies in the Sherman Antitrust Act led to the passage by Congress in 1914 of the Clayton Antitrust Act, which explicitly defined such practices as price discrimination, exclusive dealings, tie-in arrangements, mergers, and interlocking directorates as violations of the law. The greatest effect of the Clayton Act on restraint of trade and monopolistic practices was the provision it made for the prosecution of illegal operations *in their incipiency*. The Clayton Act refers to practices which "tend to" create a monopoly or "may" substantially lessen competition, while the Sherman Act deals with the final result of such practices.

In 1936, the Robinson-Patman Amendment to the Clayton Act was passed. This amendment was designed to provide additional protection to small businesses by curbing and prohibiting all devices by which large purchasers can gain discriminatory preference over small purchasers through their greater purchasing power (Handler, 1967).

Along with the Clayton Antitrust Act, the Congress passed a bill in 1914 that established the Federal Trade Commission, which at that time was intended to be an independent commission to assist the Department of Justice in antitrust violations. Over the years, however, the FTC has enlarged its power and authority over unfair trade practices. Section Five of the Federal Trade Commission Act states that "unfair methods of competition in commerce, and unfair or deceptive acts or practices in commerce, are hereby declared unlawful" (Areeda, 1967, p. 785). Armed with this extremely broad mandate, the FTC has investigated and prosecuted a lengthy series of precedent-setting cases.

Violations and Violators. The three principal types of antitrust violations are boycott, price collusion, and agreement to refrain from competition. In addition to these, there are many practices that, if not actually illegal, are at the very least unethical.

Boycott, or restraint of trade, has been defined as "a conspiracy or confederation to prevent the carrying on of business, or to injure the business of anyone by preventing potential customers from doing business with him or employing the representatives of said business, by threats, intimidation, coercion, etc." (Black's Law Dictionary, 1968, p. 234). For example, Store A advertises and sells a name brand recliner chair for a certain price. Store B obtains the style number and advertises the same item at a considerably lower price. Store A, which has been doing a substantial business with the name brand recliner firm for quite some time, informs the brand company that unless they discontinue shipments to Store B, all the Store A accounts will be terminated.

Name brand company agrees, resulting in an antitrust violation.

Another method of boycott involves several local stores jointly threatening to discontinue all accounts with a supplier for selling to a new store that drops its prices below competition levels. When this is done on a large scale, such as boycotting national brands of gasoline, the result is a monopoly on goods or services and excessively high prices.

Price collusion, or price-fixing, can take many forms and can occur at almost any level of retail transaction. A fairly common method by which price-fixing is accomplished occurs in the setting of prices for new merchandise. A retail store may set a price on an item that is as much as 150 per cent higher than the wholesale price at which the item was purchased. Even when advertised at an alleged "lower sale price," the item may cost the customer nearly twice as much as the store paid for it.

In another form of price collusion, the customer winds up paying for the advertising costs. This method is called "loading." Since each department in a retail store may spend only a certain amount of their total budget for advertising, a system is used in which the store buyer has the supplier bill him for, say $110 rather than the $100 he actually paid. This $10 is returned to the buyer for use in advertising. Because the price the customer pays will include this additional amount, the customer ends up footing the bill for the advertising costs. Although store regulations usually prohibit such activities, they are not only overlooked but also expected in many cases.

The third major violation of antitrust statutes comes under the heading "agreement to refrain from competition." On a large scale, this would include monoplies, mergers, and cartels. By vertical integration, a large corporation virtually swallows up competing dealers. Another merger method occurs through *diversification*, by which an already complex corporate structure creates new business under its control in new areas. An example might be a franchise operation that primarily retails fast food preparations. After diversification, it might also produce brand-name supplies, youngsters' T-shirts, decals, and similar items that advertise the products.

The Incredible Electrical Conspiracy. In what turned out to be the largest criminal proceeding in the history of antitrust violations, 29 of the country's leading manufacturers of heavy electrical equipment, including Westinghouse and General Electric, and their top executives were indicted on a number of charges. Forty-five defendants were convicted of conspiring to fix prices, rig bids, and divide markets on electrical equipment valued at

$1,750,000,000 annually. Fines totaling $1,787,000 were levied against the corporations, with General Electric and Westinghouse paying the largest amounts. Jail terms of 30 days were meted out to seven of the defendants, four of whom were vice presidents, two division managers, and one sales manager (Smith, 1961).

The *modus operandi* of these upper world business leaders would have been a credit to the Mafia. They invented fictitious names, used public pay phones when discussing illicit business, were careful to mail material in plain manila envelopes, and were extremely cautious about what went into wastepaper baskets at the close of a meeting.

The penalties imposed by the court were viewed by the defendants themselves and many of their business colleagues as excessive, but the fines must be seen in perspective. As Geis (1968) put it: "The original fines were . . . negligible: for General Electric, a half-million dollar loss was no more unsettling than a $3 parking fine would be to a man with an income of $175,000 a year" (p. 142). As for serving a 30 day jail sentence for helping to perpetrate a multi-billion dollar fraud, it is something less than the traditional city court sanction of "ten dollars or ten days." Said an anonymous Pullman porter, "Steal ten dollars and you go to jail; steal the railroad and you go to the Senate."

Con Games

In Chapter 5, we discussed a number of more or less "traditional" bunco games, including Spanish Prisoner, Greasy Pig, and Pigeon Drop. These con games trade on the greediness of the potential "mark"; they show the victim a way to make money or gain some other benefit fraudulently, then take advantage of his dishonesty.

The con games we shall discuss in the following sections depend on the faith and trust of innocent victims who have no reason to question the intent of the seller and have no "larceny in their hearts." The perpetrators of this kind of swindle prey on the innocence, ignorance, or gullibility of the victim, who is often elderly or poor.

Home Improvement Frauds

Complaints about home improvements or repairs are close to the top of the list of complaints received by consumer protection agencies in the United States (Nader, 1974). Among the deceptions most frequently complained of are claims of bargain prices when no real bargain is actually offered, false claims concerning products and guarantees, and promises of prizes or refunds for referring friends to the contractor. Other practices complained of include misrepresenting the interest charges accruing in "low monthly installments," obtaining signatures on blank contracts before the transaction is actually completed, adding unauthorized charges to contracts that have already been signed, and even executing second mortgages without the full knowledge of the home owner.

Many home improvements are once-in-a-lifetime projects, and often the home owner has had no previous experience with contractors; hence, when he looks for someone to do a job, anyone calling himself a contractor can compete on an equal basis. In addition, few people have any point of reference for determining what is a reasonable price for home improvements. When the average person shops for a car or TV set, he is able to inspect the finished product before he makes a choice; he can shop around and compare the prices of the various retailers. In contrast, home improvement projects involve work that is yet to be done. It is difficult to make price comparisons since the quality of workmanship and materials used can vary greatly. The typical home owner is therefore vulnerable to (1) overcharging, if the contractor does the work at all; (2) unsatisfactory results when the contractor has quoted a low price in order to secure the commission and then has used the cheapest materials and slapdash work methods; or (3) outright loss, e.g., in instances in which extremely low bids were submitted because the contractor had no intention of performing the work.

Home improvement frauds fall into recognizable patterns. There is the "bonus boy" salesman who moves from city to city, representing himself as an all-purpose contractor who will undertake any job around the house. His objective is to get the home owner to order the most work at the highest prices, then to find a local workman to do the job at the lowest prices; he pockets the difference and moves on. The hapless home owner is caught in a bind. The local workman usually identifies himself as an employee of the company that the salesman works for so that any customer dissatisfaction with his work can be bucked back to the company — if its offices can ever be found. The local workman does not put his own reputation on the line, and he too is interested in making as much as possible from the job. Since the customer has paid or signed an installment contract that was then sold to a finance company, he cannot express his dissatisfaction by withholding payment (Springer, 1970).

The elevated price scheme is worked by a salesman who offers to do a job for a low price that is escalated to a much higher price by the time the job is completed. The home owner will usually be threatened or otherwise intimidated into paying the escalated amount (Nader, 1974).

In the "bait and switch" scheme, a salesman pushes a home improvement product at an attractively low price. Once the customer has expressed interest in buying the product, the salesman will try to talk him into buying a more expensive product. He will tell the customer that the inexpensive product really does not meet his needs, or he may try to make the customer feel guilty by implying that he must not really care about his family or property if he insists on buying that product. If that approach does not work, the salesman may tell the customer that the inexpensive product line has been discontinued or that it is no longer available in that part of the country (Nichols, 1974).

In the "reco" dodge, a salesman sells the customer a product or service and promises to pay a commission to the home owner for every new customer he is able to refer for the same item or service. He is told that the commissions will probably exceed the cost of the product or service, and hence he will get the item or service free. A variation on this scheme is the "model home" pitch. The customer is told that his home has been selected to serve as a model for the display of the product being pushed (aluminum siding, storm windows, etc.) in his community. Thus, every time someone in the neighborhood buys the product, the customer will receive a commission on the sale.

The "hit-and-run" operator works out of a pickup truck and can cover a large amount of territory in an average working day. His typical pitch is that he has just completed a job (painting a house, sealing a driveway) in the neighborhood and has enough materials left over to perform another job. Since he is already in the neighborhood, he can do the same job on the customer's home for an unbelievably low price. By the time the job has been done and has already begun to fall apart or turn shabby, the hit-and-run operator has vanished into thin air.

Perhaps the most spectacularly successful hit-and-run operators at large in the United States is a tribe of gypsies known to law enforcement officials as the "Terrible Williamsons" (Kobler, 1957). Of Scottish origin, they began operating on this side of the Atlantic around 1885, after generations as bunco artists abroad. By 1914, this prolific tribe was a fixture of the American underworld. Since then, neither frequent arrests nor the vigilance of Better Business Bureaus, the Federal Trade Commission, or state and local police has noticeably curtailed their activities. Kobler (1957) has described their *modi operandi*:

> In the course of a year, traveling two or three families together in trucks, trailers and glossy late model cars, they may invade every state and parts of Canada.
>
> Combining pleasure with business, they follow the sun to Florida and Texas in the winter. In their ceaseless roamings they stay at deluxe motels and trailer camps.
>
> The name Williamson predominates among the clan but many of the kinsmen bear other common Celtic names such as McDonald, Stewart, Greggs, or Johnston.
>
> Accomplished actors and masters of deceit, members of this clan are experts in the hit and run type of home repair fraud.
>
> The male members of the clan prowl residential neighborhoods in pick up trucks loaded with asphalt, paints, and spraying equipment. Flashing business cards, ten year certificates of guarantee and cans of nationally known paint, they offer a fast cut rate job. The jobs are usually the painting of a house or the resurfacing of a driveway. They stretch a few dollars worth of paint or asphalt with so much crankcase oil that with the first rain it washes off, leaving the house or grounds in a hideous mess.
>
> Another swindle operated by the Williamsons is the installation of lightning rods. Impersonating electrical engineers, complete with phony university diplomas, endorsements from insurance companies, and factory guarantees of free maintenance, they try to frighten their prey by showing them photographs of houses gutted by lightning. They promise that their customers will automatically get a 50% reduction in their fire insurance premiums. The rigging that they sell at a high price and install on your house consists of rope or wood painted to look like metal and offers no protection against lightning.
>
> The Williamsons have endured mainly because, though their profits are enormous, their operations generally involve mere misdemeanors such as operating without a license or misrepresentation. Moreover, victims often hesitate to stand up in court and admit that they have been swindled. Nor are authorities themselves always aggressive. In many towns with overcrowded jails and jammed court calenders they are content to chase the clan away and let some other community worry about them. (pp. 117–121)

Land Fraud

The Bible records one of the earliest victims of land frauds: Esau, who was swindled out of his inherited real estate by Jacob.

In our own colonial past, Manhattan Island changed hands for a reputed $24.00, but it was the Dutch who got swindled in the deal: the Indians who sold them Manhattan Island had no title to the land, they were merely squatters! Hancock and Chafetz (1968) have noted that, as early as 1870, land promoters in the west were luring immigrants with promises of rich farm land, and during the gold rush days, speculation in land was even more common.

Fraudulent promoters have lately enjoyed particular advantages, such as modern communications facilities, computerized banking, and jet air travel. In addition, there is a maze of overlapping jurisdictions among government agencies, and this situation is exacerbated by numbers of antiquated laws, which are almost impossible to enforce. These conditions favor the fraudulent realtor or land hustler.

Land frauds typically invove either misrepresentation of land values or assets, or duplicity in the manipulation of financing. Land hustlers generally operate as one of the following types of dealers:

> 1. *Acreage peddlers* who sell "investment" parcels of land
> 2. *Land merchandisers* — companies that sell large numbers of lots with few improvements
> 3. *Vacation* or *second home developers* who specialize in "sight unseen" sales
> 4. *Community builders* — creators of whole communities, which are sometimes offered for sale before they have even been laid out on the drafting board

Operations of this kind flourish in sun belt states such as California, Florida, Arizona, and New Mexico, which are characterized by large transient and growing retirement populations. In many of these transactions, the buyer is separated from his purchase by a considerable distance, the sales contracts are designed to appeal to avarice, and advertising is often grossly misleading.

The following are some of the "tools of the trade" used by fraudulent sellers:

The Money-Back Guarantee. This is a strong selling tactic, especially when dealing with "sight unseen" property. The developer stipulates in his contract that if the buyer inspects the property within a specified period of time *and* finds that it was misrepresented in any way, he is entitled to receive his money back. However, even if misrepresentation can be proved, costs of recovering the initial payment will often be prohibitive. Ironically enough, a good many purchasers are high pressured into buying *additional* land when they arrive to reclaim their down payment.

The Hidden Waiver of "Cooling off" Rights. According to the fedral truth-in-land-sales law, if a buyer is not provided a property report within 48 hours prior to the signing of a contract, he automatically receives a 48 hour "cooling off" period during which he may change his mind for any reason, notify the seller, and demand the return of his money. This legal safeguard proved detrimental to many salesmen, who were accustomed to taking a prospect to view a piece of property, pressuring him for an immediate sale, and obtaining a signed contract on the spot. To circumvent this stipulation, they requested and received from Congress the right to insert a waiver in the contract, according to which the buyer, by signing, relinquishes his cooling off rights. This waiver is almost invariable part of the "fine print" in the contract.

Concealment of Recision Rights. The federal truth-in-land-sales law provides that if a person, through financing, buys a piece of land, that may be used in the future as a place of primary residence, he may cancel the transaction within 72 hours for any reason. This is called the right of recision. Developers of second-home and investment properties are not obligated to inform the buyer of his recision rights unless they know that the purchase is intended to be used as a primary residence. To counteract this provision, many sellers employ an elaborate form called the "Buyer's Understanding and Declaration," in which several main portions of the contract are restated. However, in the midst of the fine print is a statement declaring that the property will not be used as a primary residence — and by signing the form, the buyer surrenders his rights of recision.

Other Techniques. Some of the other gimmicks or techniques used by the fraudulent land seller include:

> The annual price boost, which is intended to show the prospective customer that "prices are constantly rising," and therefore now is the time to buy
>
> Free "vacation trips," in which the "winner" of company-sponsored drawings or contests is blitzed by a tour and highpowered sales pitch
>
> "Research reports" and "advisory opinions" extolling the merits of the property that purport to be written by unbiased, independent experts but which actually are composed by the developer and his sales staff

Dinner parties in which the captive audience is treated to a powerpacked sales pitch from salesmen scattered throughout the room at individual tables

Lot exchange privileges, "buy-back" offers, the free lot ploy, gifts of dishes or appliances, add-ons "to help lower payments" — the list is interminable. The ancient admonition *caveat emptor* (let the buyer beware) might have been devised specifically for the prospective land purchaser.

THE IMPACT OF ECONOMIC CRIME

White collar/economic crimes are among the most underreported and undetected of all offenses, and this makes it difficult to assess the impact of these crimes on our society. Moreover, changes in our economic structure, particularly with respect to marketing, distribution, and investment, have resulted in increases in economic crime at a rate that exceeds the rate of population growth. One type of change that has occurred in our marketing system involves a shift in the relationship between proprietors and customers. A generation ago, most people purchased goods from stores that were managed and serviced by their individual owners — people who, for the most part, lived in the communities in which their stores were located or who had close ties with these areas. They were well known to their customers and recognized that they would confront them *after* a purchase as well as before. Competition among propietors were based primarily on reliability and service. While their products might be pre-sold by advertising, they were aware that they would bear the brunt of customer dissatisfaction. Today most consumer products — drugs, food, cosmetics, appliances — are sold by large chain stores whose personnel are as mobile as the customers they serve. Current transactions at the retail level are relatively impersonal — a circumstance that increases the possibility of consumer fraud.

The greater complexity of our society has also made us more vulnerable to economic crime because it has increased our dependency on the courts in order to obtain reimbursement for any losses we have suffered. Private attorneys are expensive, investigators are overloaded, and court calendars are backlogged for months. Under these circumstances, victims are compelled to weigh the time, effort, and money that must be expended to obtain legal redress, and these factors increase the unwillingness of victims to report these offenses. In a considerable number of economic crimes, victims are not in a position to take action against their "assailants" either because they are ignorant of the fact that they have been victimized or because they are not in a position to take legal action against those who have defrauded them. Reference here is made to instances in which victimization results from such practices as false advertising, adulteration of food, and failure to adequately test drugs. Violations of this kind are supposed to be prevented by federal, state, and local regulatory agencies, but these agencies are generally understaffed and often are not given sufficient authority to curb these violations. Obviously this further contributes to the low visibility of these offenses.

Although it is impossible to obtain reliable estimates of the extent of white-collar crime, it is possible to provide a rough estimate of its impact on our society. Several different types of harm result from white-collar crime. It may and frequently does result in serious monetary losses, in some cases to single individuals or businesses, and in others to the business community as a whole, the consumer public, or the entire nation. Some examples are given below of the kinds of financial losses that are caused by these offenses:

> The exact financial loss to the government caused by tax fraud is difficult to determine but undoubtedly is enormous. Estimates of the amount of reportable income that goes unreported each year range from $25 to $40 billion. Some of this is inadvertent but undoubtedly a sizeable amount is deliberate, criminal evasion.
>
> The financial loss to the public caused by a single conspiracy in restraint of trade may be untold millions in extra costs paid ultimately by the buying public.
>
> It is estimated that the cost to the public annually of securities frauds, which are impossible to quantify with any certainty, is probably in the $500 million to $1 billion range.
>
> A conservative estimate is that nearly $500 million is spent annually on worthless or extravagantly misrepresented drugs and therapuetic devices.
>
> Fraudulent and deceptive practices in the home repair and improvement field are said to result in a $500 million to $1 billion loss annually.
>
> In the automobile repair field alone, fraudulent practices have been estimated to cost $100 million annually. (President's Commission on Law Enforcement and the Administration of Justice, 1967, pp. 103–104)

> *The yearly cost of embezzlement and pilferage reportedly exceeds by several billion dollars the losses sustained throughout the nation through burglary and robbery.*
>
> *Fraud was a major contributing factor in the forced closing of about 100 banks during a 20-year period.*
>
> *An insurance company reported that at least 30 percent of all business failures each year are a result of employee dishonesty.*
>
> *The annual bill for all purchases by a state is said to have dropped an estimated 40 percent following exposure and prosecution of businessmen and government officials for bribery and kickbacks.*
>
> *Dishonesty by corporate executives and employees has increased the retail cost of some merchandise by up to 15 percent and, in the case of one company, caused shareholders to suffer a paper loss of $300 million within just a few days.*
>
> *Restitution in the amount of $696,000 was obtained by a state for its residents who were victims of a single consumer fraud scheme which operated nationwide.* (Chamber of Commerce of the United States, 1974, pp. 4–5)

At the present time there is no total dollar figure available for the annual losses associated with these offenses; however, the Chamber of Commerce of the United States has estimated the monetary losses associated with a select group of these offenses. It calculates that not less than $40 billion annually is lost as a result of bankruptcy fraud; bribery, kickbacks, and payoffs; consumer-related crimes; consumer fraud, illegal competition, and deceptive practices; credit card and check fraud; embezzlement and pilferage; insurance fraud; receiving stolen property; and securities thefts and fraud (see Table 8–1). It is interesting to note by way of comparison that the President's Commission on Law Enforcement and the Administration of Justice (1967) has estimated the combined annual losses from burglary, robbery, and larceny at $474 million.

White-collar crime may also cause physical harm or involve the risk of such harm. Death and serious injury may result from misconduct by physicians, from drugs marketed before they have been sufficiently tested, and from tainted food products sold in violation of local health laws or the Pure Food and Drug Act. Insufficient quality control in the manufacture of automobiles, as well as inept repairs by auto mechanics, can also cause serious injury or death. Housing code violations can create fire or other serious health hazards. While the vast majority of white-collar offenses do not involve risk of personal injury, the potential number of victims from the small proportion that do may be quite high.

White-collar offenses also do serious harm to our social and

TABLE 8-1. THE ANNUAL COST OF SOME WHITE-COLLAR
CRIMES*

	(BILLIONS OF DOLLARS)†	
Bankruptcy Fraud		$ 0.08
Bribery, Kickbacks, and Payoffs		3.00
Computer-Related Crime		0.10
Consumer Fraud, Illegal Competition,		
Deceptive Practices‡		21.00
Consumer victims	$ 5.5	
Business victims	$ 3.5	
Government revenue loss:	$12.0	
Credit Card and Check Fraud		1.10
Credit Card	$ 0.1	
Check	$ 1.0	
Embezzlement and Pilferage		7.00
Embezzlement		
(cash, goods, services)	$ 3.0	
Pilferage	$ 4.0	
Insurance Fraud		2.00
Insurer victims	$ 1.5	
Policyholder victims	$ 0.5	
Receiving Stolen Property		3.50
Securities Thefts and Frauds		4.00
	TOTAL (billions)	$41.78§

*Chamber of Commerce of the United States: *White Collar Crime: Everyone's Problem, Everyone's Loss.* Washington, D.C., 1974, p. 6. Reproduced by permission of the Chamber of Commerce of the United States.

†The dollar amounts pertain only to that aspect of each listed crime which is directed at, or committed by or within, business, industry, and the professions. These estimates do not include the cost involved in combating white-collar crime.

‡Estimates related to price-fixing and industrial espionage are not included. Among the schemes or practices that victimize ethically run businesses are the following: advance fee, counterfeit products, illegal hiring of aliens, sweetheart contracts, etc. The figure for Government revenue loss refers to business-related tax fraud, which has been reported as relatively prevalent among the self-employed (especially in the medical, legal, and accounting professions).

§This total is more than the $40 billion referred to in the text because the listed crime categories are not necessarily mutually exclusive. For example, a portion of the embezzlement figure is also part of the estimate for computer-related crime.

economic institutions — although it is extremely hard to assess the extent of this damage. In this regard, the Chamber of Commerce of the United States (1974) indicates that "a major long-term impact of white collar crime is loss of public confidence in business, industry, and the professions and debasement of competition" (p. 7). Edelhertz (1970) provides some specific illustrations of how these offenses affect our system of competition:

> *Every stock market fraud lessens competition in the securities market. Every commercial bribe or kickback debases the*

level of business competition, often forcing other suppliers to join in the practice if they are to survive. The business which accumulates capital to finance expansion by tax evasion places at a disadvantage the competitor who pays his taxes and is compelled to turn to lenders (for operating and expansion capital). The pharmaceutical company which markets a new drug based on fraudulent test results undercuts its competitors who are marketing a properly tested drug, and may cause them to adopt similar methods. Competitors who join in a conspiracy to freeze out their competition, or to fix prices, may gravely influence the course of our economy in addition to harming their competitors and customers. (p. 9)

In addition to debasing competition, an indifference to ethical practices can retard economic growth. For example, many companies refuse to conduct business in a particular state in which payoffs to government officials are expected (Chamber of Commerce of the United States, 1974). In some cases in which abuses become flagrant, public pressure will result in legislation or regulations that adversely affect the innocent as well as the guilty. The Chamber of Commerce reports that as a result of numerous verified abuses, the District Attorney in one county has in effect banned door-to-door salesmen. This policy is supported by local businessmen who are afraid that the unethical practices of many of these salesmen will undermine the public trust in local business and reduce the patronage of local businesses. Unfortunately, such a policy makes it nearly impossible for ethical companies employing honest door-to-door salesmen to operate in this county.

On a much broader basis, white-collar offenses affect the whole moral climate of our country. When corporate executives and government officials, who are usually in positions of leadership in their communities, commit offenses and receive light penalties for them, this tends to undermine our criminal justice system and provide conventional offenders with the opportunity to rationalize their own misconduct. Those involved in Watergate committed a number of offenses, including burglary. No doubt this provided many burglars with a rationale for their offenses and led them to question the penalties imposed upon them by the criminal justice system.

DETECTION OF ECONOMIC CRIMES

White-collar offenses are detected in much the same way as conventional offenses. The primary sources of detection are (1) complaints by victims, (2) informants, and (3) affirmative investigations by enforcement agencies.

Complaints by Victims

Victims of conventional crimes generally are immediately aware that they have been victimized. A person who has been assaulted, robbed, or burglarized has suffered injury and/or loss of property in some readily observable manner. The victim then has the option of reporting or not reporting the crime to the police. However, some victims of white-collar offenses may never learn that they have been victimized or may become aware of their victimization when it is too late to obtain redress or to give assistance to law enforcement agencies. For instance, people who make small contributions to bogus religious and charity organizations are unlikely to recognize that they have been defrauded because they do not give much thought to the possibility of loss under these circumstances and because the practical consequences of the deception are nil except for the remote chance that the contribution will be disallowed on an income tax return. Edelhertz (1970) illustrates what little thought people give to making contributions to charities:

> In 1955 following charity investigations in New York, a Philadelphia newspaper sent collectors into the street, whose collection cans bore the legends "Society For Twinkle-Toed Children," and "Fund For Unregenerate Nazis." Collections were good. One clergyman asked the collector for Twinkle-Toed Children what the collection was for. When she told him he put a quarter in her collection can and said "I'm always glad to contribute to a good cause." (p. 23)

Magazine subscription frauds provide a further example of an offense in which the victim is unlikely to recognize that he has been defrauded. Salesmen selling subscriptions usually gain the victim's sympathy by claiming that they are working their way through college or medical school or are attempting to obtain funds for some high school project. They will offer the buyer subscriptions to magazines at supposedly discount prices; however, these prices may well be higher than regular subscription rates, although most victims will never know this. Usually victims become aware they have been defrauded only when they fail to receive the magazines to which they have subscribed.

Some white-collar offenses depend upon predictable delays in victims' recognition that they have been swindled. Arid desert land in Nevada and Arizona, Florida land that is under water, and land that is inaccessible, e.g., on mountains, has been sold sight unseen to far too many unsuspecting buyers. Work-at-home schemes, chain referral schemes, fraudulent self-improvement schemes, advance fee schemes, and credit card frauds also depend upon delay in victim realization.

There are some frauds that by their nature make it nearly impossible for victims to learn that they have been defrauded. A check kite — a worthless check used to raise money to obtain credit — is an example:

> An otherwise legitimate business man who cannot obtain a loan but needs [$50,000] operating capital to tide him over his business season . . . may put millions of dollars of checks in circulation between several bank accounts and, if his season goes as planned, he settles up. The banks have, in fact, made a $50,000 loan without interest to one who might be an ineligible credit risk for this amount, and they may have been exposed to loss without knowing it. In most cases, these check kites work out, and, although a mail fraud has been committed, law enforcement authorities will never have the violation brought to their attention. (Edelhertz, 1970, p. 24)

Along the same lines, many frauds that are committed against government are based upon the perpetrator's playing the odds that the victims will never discover the frauds, and if they do will be willing to accept a financial settlement (Edelhertz, 1970). A good example of this is when taxpayers take false deductions for entertainment expenses on the premise that these will not be disallowed unless the tax return is closely audited, in which case the only penalty imposed will be a 6 per cent interest charge on the extra tax that should have been paid.

Once an individual makes a determination that he has been the victim of a white-collar crime, he must decide whether he should report the crime. If he decides to report the offense he must then ascertain which agency handles that type of complaint. In the case of conventional crime, the victim need only call the police to make a complaint. However, most white-collar crimes are not within the jurisdiction of police agencies but instead are handled by regulatory agencies on the (1) local level (Department of Weights and Measures, Health Department, Housing Department, County Consumer Protection Agency, Better Business Division); (2) state level (Comptroller's Office, Department of Agriculture, Attorney General's Office, Insurance Department);

and (3) federal level (Securities and Exchange Commission, Interstate Commerce Commission, Federal Trade Commission, Food and Drug Administration). The difficulty of determining which agency has jurisdiction is certainly a factor in deterring many victims from making a complaint. A victim may also cease his efforts to complain in cases in which regulatory agencies lack clear procedures for the intake of complaints. Nevertheless, the development of consumer protection agencies and the greater awareness and persistence on the part of the public have done much to increase the number of white-collar offenses that are reported.

Informants

Traditionally, people have provided government agencies with information concerning such white-collar offenses as tax or customs violations for which there is a reward or bounty. Informants have also played a role in cases involving securities violations, frauds against government, and banking violations. Although they represent a valuable resource in the prosecution of con games and consumer frauds, informants have been used minimally to develop cases in these areas (Edelhertz, 1970). The development of local consumer protection agencies with investigative powers will doubtless result in the more extensive use of informants, because after a few months of operation, local investigators will become too well-known to merchants to be effective. Therefore it will prove necessary to rely on informants (volunteers or other city employees) to develop evidence for cases against retail establishments. Volunteers have already been used in investigations against automotive repair garages.

Investigations by Appropriate Regulatory Agencies

In assessing the extent to which regulatory agencies perform affirmative investigations of white-collar crime, one must take into consideration the probability of consumer complaints, as well as the desirability and cost effectiveness of such actions. Using the Edelhertz classification system of white-collar/economic crimes described previously, it is easy to recognize that there is a greater likelihood of complaints by victims in cases of abuses of trust, personal crimes, and con games than in cases of business crimes. Given the far-reaching impact of business crimes on the community, we are fortunate that the most comprehensive pattern of affirmative investigations occurs in this area. The following illustrates some of these affirmative searches:

> The Anti-trust Division of the Department of Justice and the Federal Trade Commission maintain oversight with respect to mergers, trade association activities, and pricing policies of dominant firms in important markets. The Internal Revenue Service and state tax authorities strive to more carefully audit larger returns. The Department of Agriculture and the Food and Drug Administration make qualitative and quantitative examinations of food and drug products. The Securities and Exchange Commission examines new stock issues and monitors over-the-counter exchange trading. (Edelhertz, 1970, pp. 25–26)

Although all of these activities are undertaken with non-prosecutive objectives, such as the collection of taxes, the imposition of civil injunctions, the maintenance of qualitative standards of food and drugs, and prevention of offenses, and as a means of protecting the interests of the investing public, these investigations can result in criminal prosecution. Since these agencies cannot rely upon the business community to provide the information they need to protect the public interest, they must have the capability to conduct affirmative investigations for violations. In terms of the broad-based potential for harm and actual damage caused by business crimes to all segments of our population, it is certainly both desirable and practical to increase the investigative capability of agencies responsible for the prevention and control of violations in this area. In the case of consumer frauds and con games, we must first ascertain which offenses have a substantial impact on the community and are not currently being adequately and fully dealt with and then develop or provide existing agencies with the investigative capability to deal with these violations.

CONTROLLING ECONOMIC CRIME

Unlike conventional crime, which is handled by the police and courts, white-collar/economic offenses are dealt with for the most part, as we suggested, by federal, state, and local administrative agencies. These agencies were established with provisions for the employment of specialized staffs with the expertise necessary to regulate and control business because the police, courts, and legislative bodies were not in a position to adequately perform these functions. For example the public health agencies require people who are experts in disease control, while the Federal Communications Commission requires a staff that is familiar with the economics and engineering aspects of the telephone, telegraph, radio, and television.

Administrative agencies often are empowered to perform executive, legislative and judicial functions (Auerbach, Garrison, Hurst, and Mermin, 1961). Their executive functions include inspecting businesses, granting licenses, and investigating violations. In their legislative capacity, these agencies establish rules that govern the segment of the business community within their jurisdiction, the violation of which can involve criminal penalties. Their judicial role involves conducting hearings and administering punishments or sanctions short of prison terms. These administrative hearings are not trials and therefore formal criminal procedures often are absent, as are many of the protections afforded defendants in criminal proceedings. Nevertheless, the rulings of these commissions can be appealed to conventional courts, thus affording a defendant his due process rights should he wish to appeal the decision of the hearing officer. Following the determination of a violation, agencies may issue warnings or cease and desist orders, obtain court injunctions, seize and destroy property, revoke or suspend licenses, withdraw privileges, (such as second class mailing privileges) and, in some cases, even levy fines. Finally, in some instances, these agencies will proceed against the violator in civil court, and in rare instances, criminal court action will be taken.

While these regulatory agencies are charged with the responsibility for controlling corporate crime, their response to their mandated responsibility has been less than satisfactory. Senator William Proxmire, at the conclusion of congressional hearings on corporate crime, provided a perspective on this situation:

> *"The problems of corporate crime . . . are more serious than most people understand. The federal government's response has been mixed and less than whole-hearted. Congress is not doing enough to investigate the abuses and there is a reluctance on the part of most agencies to go after corporate wrong-doers."* (Brown, 1976, p. 5b)

A report by Ralph Nader and his staff castigated the FTC for waiting two years to use its authority to compel Firestone Tire Company to stop making deceptive safety claims regarding its wide oval tires, which included the claim that these tires could stop "25 per cent quicker." "Not only did Firestone refuse to substantiate the claims upon request, but their truth is also directly contradicted by numerous tests that show the Firestone tire to be among the most unsafe" (Nader, as quoted by Hills, 1971, p. 178).

Nader also summarized the major derelictions by the Federal Trade Commission:

> As the tide of consumer dissatisfaction rose in the 1960's, the FTC droned on, seemingly oblivious to the billions of dollars siphoned from poor and middle-class consumers alike by deceptive practices hiding shoddy and harmful products and fraudulent services. The Commission's vast information-procurement powers were little used. Hearings were rarely conducted, and never were the transcripts printed. Empirical studies of grass-roots business practices, especially in urban slums, were non-existent until 1968. Moreover, the Commission's enforcement policies were ridiculous. It did not have and did not actively seek from Congress powers of temporary injunction or criminal penalty. It almost ignored the enforcement tools it did have. The strongest of these is the cease and desist order, which merely chastises a culprit after it has pocketed millions with impunity. And before the Commission invokes even this mild sanction, it is willing to accept profuse assurances of voluntary compliance. This process creates delay and encourages the offender's attorneys to create further delays. Cases of unadulterated thievery have stretched on and on before being resolved, while the offender reaped profits never to be returned and devised new schemes not covered by the cease and desist orders. (Nader, as quoted by Hills, 1971, p. 179)

The same Nader report not only indicates that the legal tools available to the FTC are inadequate but also shows that the commission is reluctant to put to vigorous use the tools it already possesses:

> For example, with complaints to the Commission running annually at almost 9,000 in deceptive practices alone, only 1 in 35 results in even the informal wrist-slap of securing a promise of voluntary compliance by the business offender — "a Boy Scout's oath not to practice the deception the same way again." Subsequent willful violations merely bring about another assurance from the offender that he will comply. Only 1 out of every 125 initial complaints results in any kind of formal action. (Nader, as quoted by Hills, 1971, p. 179)

Even more startling is the fact that when the FTC does issue cease and desist orders following hearings and appeals, it relies primarily on the offending company to provide evidence of compliance. Thus, instead of independently ascertaining if the company has ceased its illegal actions, the commission requests the company to file a compliance report within 60 days indicating that this activity has ceased and that action has been taken to prevent its recurrence. But the commission has no authority to impose penalties for false reports. A procedure of this kind raises some questions regarding the extent to which this agency can carry out its mandated responsibilities. As the Nader report acidly comments, "Imagine, if you will, a judge writing a convicted bank robber, whom he has freed without sentence: 'Dear Sir, please let me know if you have stopped robbing banks' (Nader, as quoted by Hills, 1971, p. 179).

Roderick M. Hills, Chairman of the Securities and Exchange Commission, in testimony in the congressional inquiry into corporate crime, stated that his agency had brought suits against nine of the nation's largest public corporations — including Gulf Oil, Minnesota Mining and Manufacturing, and the Northrop Corporation — for doling out bribes to foreign and domestic businessmen and politicians. He also indicated that an additional 30 firms were under investigation by the commission's staff.

> Although Hills said the SEC has the manpower to handle the wideranging and complex investigations, (Ralph Nader) and (Senator William Proximire) (at the same congressional inquiry) both expressed skepticism about the ability of the agency's enforcement section, which has only 200 Washington and 200 field employees, to actively pursue the seemingly broad corporate crime patterns. (Brown, 1976, p. 5b)

The Food and Drug Administration was criticized severely in a report that resulted from a two-year study of the agency by Ralph Nader and 20 volunteers, most of whom were law and medical students. In this report:

> Nader accused the FDA of a conspiracy with the food industry not only to defraud customers but also to endanger their health. The report, in addition, charges this understaffed agency with squandering its meager resources in investigations of relatively harmless (and powerless) quacks while virtually ignoring the giant, blue chip corporate offenders. The FDA is also condemned for depending too heavily on reports supplied by industry-employed scientists of the probable dangers of additives, rather than conducting its own study. But there is no assurance that even the results of agency-conducted experiments will significantly influence policies of the Food and Drug Administration. In 1969, the chief pathologist in the FDA's Bureau of Science charged that for years middle-level bureaucratic agency officials have deleted certain conclusions and recommendations from

> scientific reports of laboratory-animal experiments that cast
> doubt on the FDA's policy positions concerning the safety of
> certain food additives and pesticides. A subsequent probe by
> outside investigators found conclusive evidence confirming
> the charges — raising serious questions as to the agency's scientific
> credibility. (Hills, 1971, pp. 180–181)

Sherrill (1973) questions the degree to which the U.S. Department of Agriculture's Pesticides Regulation Division (PRD) is protecting our country from harmful pesticides. PRD has been in operation since 1947 and is reported to have registered by 1970 approximately 60,000 pesticides, of which some 40,000 are still on the agency's books. New pesticides are registered at the rate of about 5000 per year. Sherrill (1973) reports that:

> In all that time, and although hundreds of these poisons
> proved to be mislabeled or dangerous either to wild life or plants
> or human beings, only twice has the PRD used its suspension
> powers to remove an imminent hazard from the market im-
> mediately. A third suspension — ordering Aeroseal Company's
> vaporizing test-strip off the market — was not motivated by
> danger, but simply to protect Shell Oil Company from competi-
> tion. (Aeroseal's product contained exactly the same ingredients
> as Shell's No-Pest strip, which is still being sold.)
> One of the two authentic uses of its suspension power was
> against the herbicide 2-4-5-T after this poison received pages of
> thoroughly documented bad publicity in the New Yorker and
> other magazines, and after the National Cancer Institute found
> that 2-4-5-T produced cancer in laboratory mice. However the
> suspension was only against household use of the poison; its
> primary use has always been as an agriculture weed killer, and
> it's still permitted for that. You will be eating it, willy-nilly. The
> other use of suspension was against products containing mercury,
> an effort which the PRD bungled critically. (p. 245)

Sherrill (1973) further indicates that when the PRD discovers that harmful or dangerously labeled pesticides are being sold, it does not examine the manufacturer's file to determine where else the pesticide is being marketed so that it can be seized everywhere:

> For example: rodent poisoning containing thallium was
> killing children so abundantly that in 1960 the PRD ordered
> manufacturers to lessen the amount of thallium in their formulas,
> to see if that would make the massacre of children a little less
> noticeable. It didn't do the job; in 1962 and 1963, the Public
> Health Service reported 400 cases of thallium poisoning among
> children, and predicted that probably 10 times that many in-

stances went unreported. So on August 1, 1965, the registration for thallium products was cancelled. However, because the PRD made no effort to withdraw these products from the market, or by using company records, send its investigators out to find and seize the product, rat poisons containing thallium were still on the market three years later — and may still be on the market today. The PRD doesn't know. (p. 246)

Thirty-one inspectors and five supervisors comprise the entire PRD enforcement staff. They are responsible for collecting specimens of produce on which pesticides have been employed. These specimens are then tested by one of the five PRD analytic laboratories to determine if the poison contained the chemicals at the strength levels the manufacturer claimed. If the manufacturer claims the poison will kill weeds then it is tested as a weed killer. Thus, all the PRD is initially interested in is whether or not the pesticide contains and will perform what the manufacturer claims. "Testimony given before the Congress indicates that the PRD does not test for safety to human beings until after somebody is killed by the pesticide or until there are enough serious injuries or enough adverse publicity to force them to make the test" (Sherrill, 1973, p. 247). A look at the procedures employed by the PRD to protect the public raises serious questions concerning the extent to which this agency is carrying out its mandated responsibility. It would appear that these procedures are designed more to placate the public than to protect it.

PROSECUTING ECONOMIC CRIMES

John B. Swainson, former governor of Michigan and a judge of that state's supreme court, was convicted in 1975 of three perjury charges. He could have been sentenced to 15 years in prison. Instead, he received a sentence of 60 days.

Ralph L. Cummins, a former official of the U.S. Department of Transportation, could have been sent to prison for 20 years for accepting $40,000 in bribes. Instead, his sentence was two to six years.

The Cummins sentence prompted a polite but unusual courtroom "protest" by nearly a dozen federal prosecutors in the District of Columbia who objected to the lenient treatment given to white-collar criminals. U. S. District Court Judge Howard Corcoran, who had several days earlier sentenced a Maryland investment counselor convicted of bilking clients of $2 million to a one-year jail term, was not moved by the protest. He chose to blame Cummins' crimes on "easy access to whiskey."

Federal court records support the contention that white-collar offenders generally have received more lenient treatment than other offenders. According to a newspaper report (*Tampa Tribune*, August 11, 1976) statistics compiled by the administrative office of the federal courts show that in fiscal year 1975, 1158 persons were sentenced for income tax fraud. The majority were released on probation, and 112 received fines. Of the 367 who were jailed, only 13 received sentences of five years or more; 154 were given sentences of six months or less, followed by probation.

Fewer than 1000 of the more than 3000 persons who were sentenced for all types of fraud went to jail, most of them for one year or less. Only 285 of the 1605 embezzlers received jail terms, and more than half were for one year or less.

Persons convicted of price-fixing and other violations of antitrust laws fared even better. Out of 112 antitrust offenders, only 8 were given jail terms, none of them for more than one year.

By way of contrast, federal judges sentenced 1853 bank robbers and sent all but 185 to prison. Terms of five years or longer were handed out to 1313.

White-collar criminals usually complain that damage to their reputation from conviction is punishment enough for their crimes. For example, former Governor Swainson claimed that he had been "destroyed" by his conviction. But federal prosecutors and officials of the Department of Justice are increasingly receptive to the use of criminal sanctions against economic criminals for the twofold purpose of punishment and deterrence. In the same newspaper article that reported the Swainson conviction (*Tampa Tribune*, August 11, 1976), Assistant Attorney General Richard L. Thornburgh, head of the department's criminal division, stated that "imposition of prison terms, joined with appropriately high fines, should be the rule" (p. 3-F) in white-collar criminal cases. As Thornburgh observed with regard to the economic criminal:

> We must increase the costs to him of committing such crimes by ensuring his detection, quick prosecution, and punishment more severe than the mere loss of his reputation and community standing. . . . It is hard to justify incarcerating the ghetto youth for theft of a car while at the same time putting on probation the corrupt government official or crooked attorney who has abused his position and milked the public for larger sums of money. (p. 3-F)

Thornburgh's statements echo the comments of criminologist Gilbert Geis (1973), who observed that:

Jail terms have a self-evident deterrent impact upon corporate officials who belong to a social group that is exquisitely sensitive to status deprivation and shame. The white collar offender and his business colleagues, more than the narcotic addict or the ghetto mugger, are apt to learn well the lesson intended by a prison term. In addition, there is something to be said for noblesse oblige, *that those who have a larger share of what society offers carry a greater responsibility to obey its laws.* (pp. 337–338)

Criminal Sanctions

The use of criminal sanctions in the prosecution of economic crime poses a number of problems. Finn and Hoffman (1976) point out some of the weaknesses implicit in the use of criminal law to attack the problem of fraud:

- *the difficulty of "penetrating the corporate veil;" i.e., identifying and holding responsible those individuals within corporations actually responsible for the criminal actions;*
- *the stiff legal requirements for using criminal sanctions; i.e., problems of proof — "beyond a reasonable doubt" — and* mens rea *(state of mind of defendant when taking action or issuing statement);*
- *the ease of using "incompetent business judgment" as a defense;*
- *the reluctance of judges to use criminal sanctions in cases involving commercial sales.* (p. 73)

Despite these problems, law enforcement authorities are moving ahead with programs that seek to supplement civil investigations and prosecutions of fraudulent activities with criminal sanctions. With the support of the Law Enforcement Assistance Agency (LEAA), the King County Fraud Division in Seattle, Washington, and the San Diego County Fraud Division in California have carried on projects designed to concentrate energies and resources upon criminal prosecution of economic crimes. Both programs have targeted false advertising, corporate scandals, automotive repair frauds, financial swindles, and land frauds for their investigative efforts. In deciding which cases to file, members of the units assign top priority to those which (1) have a high probability of successful prosecution, (2) involve large economic losses, and (3) may have a high deterrent value. In both programs, a substantial number of cases are received as referrals from other agencies, businesses, and the local bar association. The San Diego project, however, generates more than two-thirds of its caseload from direct citizen complaints.

During the period from July 1972 through December 1974, the Seattle fraud division handled 106 cases involving an economic loss of $3.4 million. Guilty pleas were obtained in 84 cases, a total of $32,352 was collected in fines, and court-ordered restitution amounted to $1,511,008. Thirty-five of the defendants received jail sentences. Encouraging reports were received on the deterrent impact of the fraud division's operations. As stated in the LEAA phamphlet *Exemplary Projects: The Prosecution of Economic Crime* (U. S. Department of Justice, 1976):

> *At the sentencing of a well-publicized prosecution of a market for fraudulent meat-pricing, the defendant claimed that it suffered sales losses of $100,000 the week after the fraud division filed and publicized its charges. In addition, a large food chain telephoned the fraud division to get information on meat pricing to avoid any possible violations.*
>
> *After the prosecution of a charities case involving the sale of circus tickets, other charities called to ask if what they were doing was legal.*
>
> *The reputation of Washington State for being a good location for securities fraud has reportedly vanished.* (p. 9)

Comparable achievements have been recorded by the San Diego fraud division.

At the federal level, stepped-up investigative activity by the FBI involving economic crime resulted in 3427 convictions during fiscal year 1975 — an increase of nearly 15 per cent over the previous year. The investigations uncovered mail fraud, income tax evasion, obstruction of justice, securities fraud, industrial espionage, and land fraud; resulting fines, savings, and recoveries of misused funds totaled $208 million (Tampa Tribune, November 11, 1976). One reason cited for the increase in effective measures against economic crime is the hiring of special agents with expertise in accounting and other financial specialities. According to FBI Director Clarence Kelley, task forces have been created to investigate specific areas of fraud. For example, special squads of FBI agents have investigated fraud in federal housing projects; other task forces have been assembled to investigate fraud against Veterans Administration educational programs. To prepare more agents to take part in investigative efforts against economic crime, the FBI Academy at Quantico, Virginia, has introduced a four-week course in bank automation and computer operations of the type that are frequently misused in fraudulent enterprises.

Alternative Sanctions for White-Collar Offenders

An article entitled "White Collar Justice" (*United States Law Week*, 1976) reported that in 1974, U. S. District Court Judge Charles B. Renfrew of San Francisco conducted an experiment in sentencing of economic criminals: He ordered a group of individuals convicted of price-fixing to deliver a dozen speeches of contrition apiece, rather than serve time in prison. Judge Renfrew then queried judges, prosecutors, defense attorneys, and the defendants themselves in an attempt to assess the deterrent effect of his alternative to incarceration. The following are excerpts from some of the responses he received:

> A Defendant in the Case: *The stigma of conviction had a strong impact on me and it has not died away with the termination of my sentence and probation. The year of probation in which I carried out the sentence with twelve speeches is something that I shall never forget. The consequences of the publicity on me and my family in our social and business relations was beyond anything I had expected. I'm determined never to be exposed to such a risk again through any of my own actions. Perhaps a jail sentence might have been more punitive and shocking; it could not possibly have been more effective as a deterrent for me.* (p. 14)

> A Defense Attorney: *I am certainly in agreement with your decision not to send these defendants to jail. All of them were, I am sure, exemplary citizens for the most part who had spent years paying their "dues" to their communities and to society while building a good reputation. Once these defendants were convicted of a felony, their general reputations were either destroyed or badly damaged. A mere conviction, therefore, is about as severe as any sentence which you can impose upon an individual of that type.* This differentiates the normal antitrust defendant from the normal defendant in non-White-Collar-Crimes. (emphasis added) (p. 14)

One of the judges who replied to Renfrew's query took strong exception to the sentiments expressed above. In his view:

> *Jail for "white-collar" defendants is the only real deterrent. It carries a social obloquy and brands the offender for what he is. It is not appropriate in truly technical offenses, but fraud is another thing and certainly many per se violations of the Sherman Act fall in the same category. We judges tend to forget the suffering of those who are victimized by such offenses.*
> *My experience at the bar was that one jail sentence was worth 100 consent decrees and that fines are meaningless because the*

defendant in the end is always reimbursed by the proceeds of his
wrongdoing or by his company down the line. (p. 14)

Other respondents (including two judges and one antitrust division attorney) expressed the belief that, although Judge Renfrew's unusual sentencing alternative may have worked in this particular case, it is doubtful whether it would prove effective as a *general deterrent* to white-collar offenses. As one judge observed, "I would consider such judgment as a one-time form of judgment and definitely not a *pattern* for future practice" (p. 14).

Spearly and Kaufman (1976) have suggested that "participation in the delivery of human services" may represent another alternative to imprisonment for economic criminals. According to the authors:

> *By placing the corporate crime offender juxtaposed to a variety of individuals requiring human services, their executive intelligence and perceptual skills may have an opportunity to become focused on the social structural dynamics contributing to these human conditions. Rather than wasting the talents such individuals have by isolating them within a prison setting, society may receive some restitution for the diffuse harms caused by their crimes by having these abilities applied to pressing human problems.* (p. 14)

Spearly and Kaufman draw an analogy to the circumstances of "alternative service" proposed for the conscientious objector. Before their proposal receives any serious consideration from the judiciary, however, Spearly and Kaufman will have to spell out in some detail the precise nature of the "delivery of human services" they recommend as an alternative to incarceration.

Conclusions

After having been almost neglected by the criminal justice system in the years since Sutherland coined the term "white-collar crime" in the 1930's, economic crime is receiving long-deferred attention. It is interesting to reflect on some of the possible reasons why economic crimes have become a national issue in recent times. Consumer advocacy has undoubtedly been a powerful stimulus to raising public consciousness regarding economic crime. Complaints about the rudeness, stridency, and partisan zeal of such groups as "Nader's Raiders" can probably be taken as a testimonial to the effectiveness of their activities — and an indication that many of their barbs manage to hit the mark.

Civil rights activism also seems to have played an important role in arousing indignation over gross disparities in the sentences handed out to poor minority persons convicted of conventional property crimes and middle class or affluent whites convicted of white-collar crimes. Indeed, the ideological polarization that led to the emergence of the radical (new, critical) criminology would appear to be one of the direct consequences of long-standing judicial inequities.

The impact of Watergate is rather difficult to assess. Although the "post-Watergate morality" gets tagged with the credit for everything from the defeat of Gerald Ford in the presidential race in 1976 to the firing of Secretary of Agriculture Earl Butz, there is little direct evidence that Watergate political connivery is linked in the public mind with white-collar crime. The Watergate criminals were generally perceived as men who were motivated by personal loyalties to Richard Nixon or by a hunger for political power — not by covetousness or greed. The large sums of money that were mishandled by the conspirators were incidental to the main theme of criminal conspiracy in the original burglary and its subsequent cover-up.

Nevertheless, Watergate drew attention to the minimal sentences generally received by persons convicted of nonconventional property crimes, in contrast with the relatively more severe sentences meted out to conventional offenders. Watergate and its aftermath may have had an indirect effect in creating public pressure for more effective prosecution and more stringent sentencing in economic crimes. In addition, the continuing revelations concerning political finance abuses (e.g., allegations of irregularities and illegal practices in campaign funding) may have prompted a closer scrutiny of the possible collusive types of relationships between politicians and leaders of business and industry. It may well be that henceforth the political/industrial connection will be subject to closer examination. Already there are indications of growing concern over appointments of business and industrial executives to federal regulatory agencies and the proprieties involved when high-level appointees leave the government to assume positions of responsibility and authority in businesses and industries over which they so recently exercised control.

Ecology and environmental protection advocates have made substantial contributions toward increasing public awareness of economic crime. Ever since the offshore oil spill that blackened the beaches of Santa Barbara, organizations like the Sierra Club and Common Cause have brought unrelenting pressure to bear upon the government for the passage of legislation, or the effective enforcement of existing legislation, intended to prevent further despoliation of irreplaceable natural resources. The major focus of their efforts has been the concept of corporate accountability.

In the final reckoning, our current economic difficulties may have had more to do with increased national concern about white-collar crime than all the factors cited above. Traditional American indifference to economic crime and its perpetrators may prove to be one of the luxuries of the "affluent society" of the 1950's and 1960's that is headed for extinction, along with cheap gasoline and the eight-cylinder family automobile. Now that the glare of official scrutiny has been turned upon economic crime, a return to public apathy seems unlikely, even if our national economic fortunes take a turn for the better. For the white-collar criminal, it may prove increasingly difficult to make a dishonest dollar.

SUMMARY

The term *"economic crime"* has been proposed as a more accurate and comprehensive alternative to Sutherland's "white-collar crime" in designating illegal acts committed by individuals or businesses to obtain money or property. Among the types of economic crime considered in this chapter are personal crimes, abuses of trust, business crimes, and con games. Each of these categories was defined and exemplified, and an attempt was made to gauge the economic and social impact of such criminal activities. Methods used in the detection of economic crimes were discussed, together with the issue of control of economic crime by local, state, and federal regulatory agencies. The growing use of criminal as well as civil sanctions in the prosecution of economic crimes was covered in the concluding section of the chapter.

REVIEW

Find the answers to the following questions in the text:

1. How did criminologist Sutherland define the term "white-collar crime" when he introduced the concept back in 1939? On what grounds do contemporary criminologists object to the term?

2. What are the elements of any white-collar crime according to Edelhertz?

3. Name the four categories of economic crime identified by Edelhertz and give at least one example of each.

4. Describe some typical credit card frauds. What are some of the methods that have been suggested for dealing with these offenses?

5. How does Cressey deal with the crime of embezzlement in terms of motivation and opportunity?

6. Define and give illustrations of three major types of antitrust violations.

7. Who are the "Terrible Williamsons" and how did they acquire their reputation?

8. Describe some of the tactics employed by fraudulent land sellers to (1) induce people to purchase property and (2) take unfair advantage of the buyer in contractual arrangements.

9. Discuss some of the various ways in which economic crime produces an adverse impact on American society. Do you consider the estimates of the economic impact of white-collar crime by the U. S. Chamber of Commerce realistic?

10. Cite three principal methods used in the detection of economic crimes.

11. Are the federal regulatory agencies doing an effective job in attempting to control white-collar crime? What are some of the criticisms raised by consumer advocates like Ralph Nader?

12. Discuss the use of criminal and noncriminal sanctions in the prosecution or economic crimes.

TERMS TO IDENTIFY AND REMEMBER

white-collar crime	"reco" dodge	Clayton Antitrust Act
economic crime	"cooling off" rights	Federal Trade Commission
personal crimes	recision	"loading"
abuse of trust	con game	"bait and switch"
business crime	computer abuse	"hit-and-run" operator
"double slipping"	Sherman Antitrust Act	the Terrible Williamsons
acreage peddler		

REFERENCES

Areeda, P.: *Antitrust Analysis*. Boston, Little, Brown and Company, 1967.

Auerbach, C. A., Garrison, L. K., Hurst, W., and Mermin, S.: *The Legal Process: An Introduction to Decision-Making by Judicial, Executive, and Administrative Agencies*. San Francisco, Chandler, 1961.

Barmash, I.: Pilferage abounds in the nation's stores. *The New York Times*, October 28, 1973, p. 9.

Black's Law Dictionary. St. Paul, West Publishing Co., 1968.

Brown, M.: Nader cites extent of corporate crime. *Tampa Tribune*, January 17, 1976, p. 5-B.

Chamber of Commerce of the United States: *White Collar Crime: Everyone's Problem, Everyone's Loss*. Washington, D. C., 1974.

Cressey, D. R.: *Other People's Money: A Study in the Social Psychology of Embezzlement.* Belmont, California, Wadsworth Publishing Co., Inc., 1973.

Edelhertz, H.: *The Nature, Impact, and Prosecution of White Collar Crime.* Washington, D. C., U. S. Government Printing Office, 1970.

Farr, R.: *The Electronic Criminal.* New York, McGraw-Hill Book Co., 1975.

Finn, P., and Hoffman, A. R.: *Exemplary Projects: Prosecution of Economic Crime.* Washington, D. C., U. S. Government Printing Office, 1976.

Geis, G.: White collar crime: the heavy electrical equipment antitrust cases of 1961. *In* Clinard, M. B., and Quinney, R. (eds.): *Criminal Behavior Systems: A Typology.* New York: Holt, Rinehart and Winston, 1967.

Geis, G. (ed.): *White Collar Criminal.* New York, Atherton Press, 1968.

Geis, G.: Deterring corporate crime. *In* Nader, R., (ed.): *The Consumer and Corporate Accountability.* New York, Harcourt Brace Jovanovich, Inc., 1973.

Hancock, R., and Chafetz, H.: *The Compleat Swindler.* New York, The Macmillan Co., 1968.

Handler, M.: *Trade Regulation.* New York, Foundation Press, 1967.

Hills, S.: *Crime, Power, and Morality: The Criminal-Law Process in the United States.* Scranton, Chandler, 1971.

Kintner, E.: *An Antitrust Primer.* New York, The Macmillan Co., 1964.

Kintner, E.: *A Primer on the Law of Deceptive Practices.* New York, The Macmillan Co., 1971.

Kobler, J.: The terrible Williamsons. Readers Digest *70*:117–121, 1957.

Lipman, M.: *How America's Employees Are Stealing Their Companies Blind.* New York, Harper's Magazine Press, 1973.

McCaghy, C. H.: *Deviant Behavior.* New York, The Macmillan Co., 1976.

Nader, R.: Home repair frauds. Ladies Home Journal *61*:86–147, 1974.

Newsweek. To catch a thief. September 23, 1974, p. 79.

Nichols, W.: How to protect yourself from home improvement frauds. Good Housekeeping *178*:155–156, 1974.

Parker, D. B., and Nycum, S.: The new criminal. Datamation, January, 1974, pp. 56–58.

President's Commission on Law Enforcement and Administration of Justice: *Task Force Report: Crime and Its Impact — An Assessment.* Washington, D. C., U. S. Government Printing Office, 1967.

Sherrill, R.: The real villains. *In* Nader, R. (ed.): *The Consumer and Corporate Accountability.* New York, Harcourt Brace Jovanovich, 1973.

Smith, R. A.: The incredible electrical conspiracy. Fortune *63*:132–180, 1961 (April); *63*:161–224, 1961 (May).

Spearly, J. L., and Kaufman, J. J.: Participation in the delivery of human services as an alternative sanction for corporate crime offenders. Paper presented at the annual meeting of the American Society of Criminology. Tucson, Arizona, November, 1976.

Springer, J.: *Consumer Swindlers and How to Avoid Them.* New York, Award Books, 1970.

Sutherland, E. H.: *White Collar Crime.* New York, Holt, Rinehart and Winston, 1949.

Tampa Tribune. Phony credit trick nets man $660,000. January 29, 1976, p. 3-A.

Tampa Tribune. White collar crime . . . light sentences for VIPs stir debate. August 11, 1976, pp. 1-F, 3-F.

Tampa Tribune. White collar crime feels FBI crackdown. November 11, 1976, p. 15-A.

United States Department of Justice. *Exemplary Projects: Prosecution of Economic Crime.* Washington, D. C., U. S. Government Printing Office, 1976.

United States Law Week. White collar justice: A BNA special report on white collar crime. *44*:1–16, 1976.

9 SPECIAL CATEGORY OFFENDERS

Drug addiction has proved refractory to nearly every type of rehabilitation or treatment program thus far attempted, and vigorous enforcement of the narcotics laws has caused no appreciable reduction in the volume of illicit drugs that enter the United States each year through clandestine channels. Statutory redefinitions of alcoholism as a disease, such as Florida's Myers Act, have failed to provide a solution for the perennial problem of public drunkenness, nor have they helped to curb the involvement of alcohol in other kinds of crimes. The psychotic criminal, the mentally retarded offender, and the psychopathic deviate all require special handling by the criminal justice system. The small but steadily growing numbers of female offenders present problems for a criminal justice system that is primarily equipped to deal with male offenders. Juvenile offenders are handled by a system of justice that, until recently, functioned almost entirely outside the adult criminal justice system. However, distinctions between these two systems have become blurred in recent years, and to an increasing extent, juveniles who have committed serious crimes of violence are being turned over to the adult criminal justice system for processing.

We have designated these types of offenders as *special category offenders*. They share the common characteristic of posing special problems for the criminal justice system and process. As in preceding chapters, we shall try to delineate the salient features of these offenders.

DRUG ADDICTION AND CRIMINALITY

In 1975 (based on a compilation of reports from 2726 law enforcement agencies), 291,061 persons were arrested for violations of narcotic drug laws (Federal Bureau of Investigation, 1976). This represents an increase of 1025.7 per cent over the figure for 1960, when 25,534 persons were arrested for the same offenses. Even more staggering is the increase in arrests of young persons: 65,864 of those arrested in 1975 were under 18 years of age, as compared with 1458 arrested for the same offenses in 1960. This is an incredible increase of more than 4000 per cent!

Another perspective on drug abuse was provided recently by a Census Bureau prison survey (*Tampa Tribune*, 1976). The bureau questioned 191,400 inmates in state correctional institutions and found that, on the basis of their sample, nearly two thirds of state prison inmates (61 per cent) had used drugs regularly, and approximately 25 per cent were serving time for crimes they had committed while under the influence of drugs. Marijuana was the most prevalent drug — used by 92 per cent of the 116,500 drug users. But "hard" drugs also received high percentage rankings: heroin, 50 per cent; and cocaine, 45 per cent.

It is instructive to compare these findings with previous estimates of the incidence of narcotics addiction in the United States. They would appear to offer some support for the Bureau of Narcotics and Dangerous Drugs'* estimate of 559,000 addicts in 1971; but on the other hand, they suggest that the estimate of 250,000 addicts by the director of the National Institute of Mental Health errs on the side of conservatism (Goldfarb, 1975).

Patterns of Drug Use

The National Advisory Commission on Criminal Justice Standards and Goals (1973) has distinguished five types of drug users:

---

*The BNDD was the forerunner of the Drug Enforcement Administration, the "superagency" created in 1973 to coordinate law enforcement efforts against drug importation and distribution.

1. Drugs play no special or regular role in the *experimental user's* life. Use is episodic and reflects a desire to see what the drugs are like or to test their effect on other activities ordinarily experienced without drugs.

2. Drugs are associated with *social or recreational* activities in which this type of user would take part whether or not drugs were present.

3. Drugs play a significant role in the *seeker's* life. Time is dedicated to seeking them out or making connections to obtain them.

4. The *self-medicator* uses legally distributed tranquilizers or stimulants. While this type of use may have beneficial characteristics, it also can become a habitual way of responding to boredom, loneliness, frustration, and stress.

5. Drugs begin to dominate the life of the *dysfunctional* drug user. This process of securing and using drugs interferes with essential activities. The narcotics addict is usually in this category.

The National Advisory Commission found ample evidence that many addicts were pursuing criminal life styles prior to their drug use. For example, in a random sample of black males in St. Louis, Missouri, 73 per cent of those who became addicted to heroin had police records before addiction. Although it is clear that many addicts do have problems with the law before they turn to drugs, it is also true that drug addiction can intensify their illegal activities.

Addiction to a "hard" drug such as heroin is the end product of a complex pattern of causation. The addict is typically a member of an ethnic minority, comes from an impoverished background, and is lacking in education and readily marketable job skills. He perceives his chances for a decent job, adequate housing, material security, and modest recognition as virtually nil. He is bored, restless, rootless, alienated, and generally embittered; these characteristics he shares with members of his peer group. To the question of why they got started on drugs, most addicts return the almost stock answer: *to kill time.* Drugs offer the prospect of a break in monotony, the prospect of a "kick."

In the case of heroin, what begins as a search for kicks ends up as an attempt to maintain the status quo. When the heroin addict injects the drug intravenously ("mainlining"), he experiences an almost orgasmic reaction, the "boss feeling"; this is followed by a drowsy state of relaxed euphoria, and finally he starts "coming down." As the effects of the drug wear off (they last up to four hours), he begins to experience minor sensations of discomfort and mild distress. Depending on the length of time he has been addicted and the number of "bags" of heroin he has been using daily, the severity of the *withdrawal symptoms* that follow abstinence from the drug increases with each passing hour. Restlessness, dysphoria, and irritability are among the immediate behavioral manifestations that may appear; excessive sweating, nausea, severe abdominal cramps, back pains, diarrhea, vomiting, fever alternating with chills, and delirium are some of the physiological reactions that usually occur. The flushing, chills, and sweating are accompanied by excessive piloerection, which produces the familiar "cold turkey" appearance of the skin of the addict.

The compulsive search for the narcotic "high" soon becomes the addict's whole life. His habit, or advanced state of addiction, leaves him functionally disabled. He generally cannot hold a job, continue school, or get enough money by legal means to obtain the heroin and support his family (if he has one.)

Periodically, when his habit becomes too expensive to maintain, the addict may submit himself voluntarily to the "wringing out" process, using other analgesic drugs to relieve the withdrawal pangs. He may accomplish this at a hospital, or, if he can obtain the necessary analgesics, at home. Sometimes he becomes the victim of compulsory withdrawal as the consequence of incarceration. In any event, once he has completed the withdrawal process and is "clean," he usually resumes the addiction pattern.

Incarceration provides no guarantee of abstinence from drugs. Narcotics are smuggled into jails and prisons in a variety of ingenious ways or even retailed to inmates by guards themselves. Withdrawal distress may be reinforced by law enforcement officials as a device to help them trap pushers, and informers may be recruited in jail by the police. The police sometimes offer the addict leniency if he agrees to turn in a pusher, or the informer may be allowed to continue his habit.

There are now some programs to get the addict out of jail as soon as possible. An example is the pretrial-release-to-treatment program in Washington, D. C. Persons being held for arraignment voluntarily undergo screening in which a urine sample is taken and each person is interviewed concerning his history of drug use and treatment. The interviewer explains that some identified addicts are released pending trial to participate in a National Treatment Administration treatment program but makes no promises to secure a prisoner's co-operation. The test results and interview are used only to determine conditions of release and are not available as evidence at trial (Goldfarb, 1975).

There are also addict diversion programs in most states in which addicts are removed from the criminal process temporarily to participate in community-based rehabilitation programs. If the addict can meet the specific requirements of the community-based program, charges are dropped. Advocates of large-scale addict diversion argue that most state and federal statutes are too restrictive and inflexible and urge that more addicts be allowed to participate in such programs (Goldfarb, 1975).

Addiction Treatment Approaches

The National Advisory Commission (1973) suggests a multi-modality approach to drug treatment, recommending: crisis intervention and drug emergency centers; facilities and personnel for methadone maintenance programs; facilities and personnel for narcotics antagonist programs; therapeutic community programs staffed entirely or largely by ex-addicts; and closed and open residential treatment facilities as well as halfway houses staffed primarily by residents.

Crisis Intervention and Emergency Treatment Programs. These supply addicts with both emergency medical aid and psychological services such as hotline telephone help and various types of counseling.

Methadone Maintenance. Addicts treated by this method are provided with a daily oral dose of methadone, usually in a closely controlled clinical setting (Nelkin, 1973). The addict receives increasing amounts of methadone until he reaches a dose regarded by the physician as sufficient to provide a cross-tolerance that will block the euphoric effects of heroin. However, since the methadone does not dull depression or anxiety as does heroin, this method of treatment is successful only if the addict is highly motivated to discontinue his use of heroin.

The National Advisory Commission (1973) considers methadone maintenance a more satisfactory mode of treatment than the heroin maintenance system used in Great Britain. As Dorothy Nelkin (1973) points out, "Unlike heroin, methadone is absorbed effectively through the gastrointestinal tract and is effective for a full twenty-four hours. It is, therefore, administered orally only once a day" (p. 38). Also, the addict does not require increasingly larger does of methadone to remain comfortable, and withdrawal symptoms are less intense.

The possibility of complete withdrawal from methadone remains uncertain. One study claims that withdrawal from methadone is harmless, with little danger of severe physical reaction, but many programs have had limited success in withdrawing patients stabilized on methadone.

Methadone maintenance has been criticized because it offers only a technological (medical) solution to a complex social, political, and psychological problem. On a more practical basis, it has also been argued that since methadone does not produce euphoria, addicts will seek other drugs. Another problem is illegal use of methadone: If a stabilized addict is allowed to take home a few days' supply, the drug may fall into the hands of addicts not participating in the program.

Narcotic Antagonist Treatment Programs. These use chemotherapy to block the effects of heroin and other narcotic drugs. The goal is to create a pharmacological state whereby the effect of any narcotic will be nullified, with the ultimate aim of removing the patient from all drug use.

Therapeutic Communities. In these drug-free environments, the drug user is viewed as an underdeveloped, immature personality. Residents are expected to remain in therapeutic communities for extended periods of time, ranging from 18 months to 2 years or more. These have been criticized on the grounds that only a small number of residents are rehabilitated and returned to the community.

Residential Treatment Facilities. The National Advisory Commission recommends that residential programs include closed, open, and halfway house facilities. The closed facility provides a therapeutic environment in which addicts can live free of their drug use, with the help of constraints, including locked doors. The open center makes available the same basic services as the closed center but lacks the physical and other restraints to keep residents in the facility. The halfway house provides lodging and supportive services for residents who are making the transition from a structured institutional setting to the open community. It is also available to those already in the community who temporarily require the additional supports provided by such a center.

Other Programs. The National Advisory Commission supports programs like those mentioned previously in which addict defendants are referred to treatment programs prior to trial. If treatment is successful, criminal charges may be dropped altogether; if the addict relapses or commits a new offense during treatment, prosecution can then be initiated.

It is difficult to identify particular individuals who will become drug abusers and direct prevention programs toward them. However, current knowledge permits certain generalizations about which persons are likely to become involved with drugs. Large target populations can thus be identified for certain types of prevention work.

Conclusion

One of the most persistent popular myths about drug addiction is that it is essentially a problem of physiology. According to this view, once the person who has become enslaved to the habit frees himself of its physical demands, he thereby becomes able to reorient his life toward the achievement of conventional goals. As we have already seen, the torment of withdrawal pangs is a price the addict is willing to pay repeatedly in order to revert to a lower, less expensive dosage. Anyone who subscribes to the belief that addiction is primarily physiological would be well advised to read Jeremy Larner's *The Addict in the Street* (1964). In this anthology, thirteen heroin addicts give first-person accounts of their lives as heroin addicts in frank and graphic language. For these people, addiction is a life style; the daily quest for drugs and the wherewithal to secure them provide pattern and purpose to what would otherwise be a futile, meaningless existence. Says Larner:

> *Without heroin there would be pain and uncertainty, the empty anonymity of people on the bottom. But as nearly every subject in this books explains:* when you are high on heroin, you don't feel a thing; nothing bothers you . . . . *In contrast to the prescribed social model of contentment-building, the addict fills his hours, days and years with the cycle of search and discovery, need and fulfillment, cures and backslidings, despair and nirvana. And paradoxically, through the presence of heroin in his system, this most alienated of men finds himself utterly involved in his life-process. He, at least, is quit of boredom and empty role-playing. He reduces himself to a need and becomes that need.* (p. 19)

To alter this pattern requires nothing less than a reorganization of the addict's personality and life style. While impressive results have been achieved selectively and on a limited scale in therapeutic enclaves such as Synanon and Daytop Village, such programs are not appropriate to handle the estimated half-million drug addicts. In the absence of any effective alternatives, programs that have already been shown to be largely ineffectual will probably continue to be used.

DRINKING AND CRIME

Beverage alcohol is America's drug of choice. Its widespread use and abuse are related to criminality in two ways: (1) *directly*, in the case of public drunkenness or driving while under the influence of alcohol; and (2) *indirectly*, when alcohol consumption is a contributing or precipitating factor in the commission of serious crimes. Approximately one third of the more than nine million arrests made in 1975 were for the following offenses, which directly involved alcohol abuse:

Public drunkenness	1,217,000
Driving while under the influence	947,100
Liquor law violations	340,100
Disorderly conduct	748,400
Vagrancy	40,000

The involvement of alcohol consumption in criminal homicide has been documented by Wolfgang and Strohm (1956), who found a significant relationship between drinking in the victim and/or the offender in more than 60 per cent of the cases they examined. Haskell and Yablonsky (1974) refer to a California study in which 98 per cent of a sample group of incarcerated felons consumed alcoholic beverages and 29 per cent of them indicated that they were intoxicated at the time they committed the offense for which they were imprisoned. Similar findings have been reported for other states.

The "Revolving Door" Syndrome

Public drunkenness is a misdemeanor. Offenders are apprehended and prosecuted under a variety of statutes covering vagrancy, loitering, disorderly conduct and so forth, in addition to those statutes that specifically prohibit public inebriation. Although anyone who has had too much to drink and appears in a public place in an intoxicated state can be arrested as a public drunk, most arrests for public drunkenness involve skid row derelicts with a lengthy history of chronic alcoholism. These men are arrested and rearrested in a dreary cycle that has been called the "revolving door" syndrome (Pittman and Gordon, 1958). Offenders are typically nonviolent and are often in a precarious condition of physical debilitation.

The most outstanding characteristic of the skid row alcoholic is the chronicity of his offense — a feature that helps to account for the fact that public drunkenness arrests account for about 50 per cent of all misdemeanor arrests made in this country in any given year. One study revealed that 6 offenders had amassed a total of 1409 arrests for public drunkenness and had spent a total of 125 years in various penal institutions, doing a "life sentence on the installment plan" (President's Commission on Law Enforcement and Administration of Justice, 1967). On any given night, drunks constitute from one half to two thirds of the jail population (about one million per year are arrested), and it is not unusual for a "drunk court" to parcel out "justice" at an average of one case every two minutes.

Detoxification Centers

In *Robinson v. California* (1962) the United States Supreme Court held that a California statute making it a criminal offense to be addicted to a narcotic drug was unconstitutional since it amounted to cruel and unusual punishment. This decision was based on a view of addiction as an illness rather than a crime. The argument of cruel and unusual punishment was also applied in the lower court cases of *Driver v. Hinnant* (1966) and *Easter v. District of Columbia* (1966). In the latter case, chronic alcoholism was adjudged a defense to a charge of public intoxication.

The United States Supreme Court in *Powell v. Texas* (1968) upheld the conviction of a chronic alcoholic charged with the crime of public intoxication. However, the vote in this case was 5 to 4, and the language of the opinions indicates that a similar test case involving the same constitutional questions might be decided differently by the Court in the future.

At any rate, the trend had been set by these cases and by the findings and recommendations of several commissions, including the President's Commission on Law Enforcement and Administration of Justice (1967). The recognition of alcoholism as a disease rather than a crime was furthered by the passage of the federal Uniform Alcoholism and Intoxication Treatment Act, more commonly known as the Hughes Act. Guided by this national model, several states drafted laws that sought to decriminalize the status of public intoxication in order to remove its control from the criminal justice system. As in the case of Florida's Myers Act (otherwise known as the Comprehensive Alcoholism Prevention, Control, and Treatment Act), these laws treat alcoholism as a disease rather than as a crime and seek to provide treatment for the alcoholic through health and rehabilitative services.

The underlying rationale incorporated in laws of this kind found implementation when the St. Louis, Missouri, Police Department in 1966 opened the nation's first *civil detoxification center*. A federal demonstration grant provided the financing; a standing order from the chief of police codified the new procedure.

An arrested drunk was offered the choice between criminal processing and "voluntary" detoxification (Nimmer, 1971).

If a qualified offender chose detoxification (a person requiring hospitalization for a physical disease or a person charged with a more serious crime did not qualify), he was transported to the detoxification center for a seven-day stay. A summons charging the "patient" with public drunkenness and setting a court date was left with the detox center staff. If the person completed the seven-day program, the summons was torn up on his release. If he left against medical advice, the criminal process that had been temporarily halted was resumed and the patient/offender was then subject to prosecution for drunkenness.

The St. Louis program continues to operate under these guidelines. It offers some drunks emergency medical care of the highest quality, but it reaches only a fraction of those who could benefit from it. In addition, it provides no effective aftercare for the patient/offender after detoxification.

This program has succeeded in conserving court time and jail space — but that is about all it has done. No convincing evidence has been produced to show that the detoxification program has managed to intervene successfully in the degenerative, repetitive life cycles of most of its skid row patients.

DWI Offenses

Public drunkenness is largely a public nuisance; offenders are rarely violent and their prosecution is often a matter of esthetic rather than criminal concern. Drunken driving, on the other hand, is a serious offense. The gravity of this problem is not conveyed by the sheer magnitude of the number of arrests for "driving while under the influence" (DWI) offenses, although these reached a record high in 1975 of 947,100; of greater concern is the fact that more than 50 per cent of the nation's traffic fatalities in a given year (25,000 to 30,000 victims) occurred in accidents in which alcohol consumption was directly or indirectly involved. Although the official designation of "driving while under the influence" makes no distinction between the effects of alcohol and narcotics, it is alcohol consumption that accounts for the overwhelming majority of such arrests.

In an effort to cope with the highway carnage caused by the drunken driver, the United States Department of Transportation, through the National Highway Safety Administration, initiated ASAP, the Alcohol Safety Action Project. ASAP is a series of 21 countermeasures involving law enforcement agencies, courts, schools, and public relations efforts aimed at enlisting support for the various programs. Included in ASAP is DWI Counterattack, an 8-hour course for drinking drivers enrolled by the court. It is designed to teach the participant about the effects of alcohol on the body and to improve attitudes toward drinking while driving.

Conclusion

Like the heroin addict, the skid row alcoholic exhibits a deviant life style in which all the conventional needs, drives, and incentives have been subordinated to the daily quest for booze. To interpret this complex and self-perpetuated cycle of self-destructive behavior as an illness or a disease raises some extremely controversial issues that are outside the scope of this discussion. Few would dispute the contention, however, that on the grounds of humanity alone it is preferable to replace the squalor of the "drunk tank" with the more civilized surroundings of the detoxification center. Moving the "revolving door" from the jail to the detox center is a move in the right direction.

PSYCHOTIC, RETARDED, AND PSYCHOPATHIC OFFENDERS

Insanity and Incompetency

Under our system of criminal jurisprudence, there are two methods by which an offender can be absolved of criminal responsibility for his actions: the first is by being found "not guilty by reason of insanity," and the second, by being declared "incompetent to stand trial." In the first instance, the offender admits to having committed the act, but the defense claims that at the time of the act he did not have the capacity to understand the nature of the act or that it was wrong. The issue of competency to stand trial involves the common law criteria that a defendant must be able to understand the charges against him and to cooperate with his counsel in the preparation of his own defense. The procedures for determining competency vary considerably from jurisdiction to jurisdiction but most require a court decision based on psychiatric testimony. In some states a jury may be impaneled if the defendant so requests, and in three states the court has the discretion to impanel a jury to determine competency (Brakel and Rock, 1971). If a defendent is found to be incompetent to stand trial, he is usually committed to a mental institution until such time as he is certified to be competent by the medical or psychiatric authorities at the institution.

Both these defenses were outgrowths of the overuse of the death penalty in England. The common law development of the insanity plea saw a major shift away from the excessively sanguinary practices of the early 19th century. The defense of *insanity*, which is a *legal* and not a *medical* term, stems from the famous M'Naghten case.

In 1843, Daniel M'Naghten, a native of Scotland and a political fanatic, was found not guilty on grounds of insanity for the murder of a man who was secretary to the Prime Minister, Sir Robert Peel. M'Naghten had mistaken the secretary for Peel, who as Prime Minister was regarded as a highly conservative upholder of the status quo. Though the form of the personality disturbance that M'Naghten exhibited was not designated at the time, contemporary psychiatrists would probably categorize his behavior as paranoid. He seems to have been entangled in an elaborate system of delusions, including the fixed belief that he was pursued by spies and that the Tories and the Prime Minister were after him because he had voted against them in the previous election.

Many segments of Victorian society, and, in fact, Queen Victoria herself, were indignant at M'Naghten's acquittal. As a consequence, the House of Lords requested an authoritative statement of existing law from the judges of England. They answered, in part, as follows:

> To establish a defense on the grounds of insanity, it must be clearly proven that, at the time of committing the act ... the party accused was laboring under such a defect of reason from disease of the mind, as not to know the nature and quality of the act he was doing, or if he did know it ... he did not know he was doing what was wrong. (Glueck, 1962, p. 44)

Since its pronouncement, the M'Naghten rule has been the focal point of legal and psychiatric controversy. Nevertheless, the defense of insanity gave the courts another option for the disposition of serious offenders short of sentencing them to death. This led to a whole new category of individuals in the criminal justice system: the "criminally insane."

Stone (1975) points out that the significance of the

competency issue has generally been obscured by its confusion with the insanity defense:

> *Consider the case of an obviously mentally ill person who commits some criminal act. Such an offender is typically arrested shortly after the crime. Since mental illness is apparent to everyone, two important legal questions arise. First, if this person is tried, will he be able to consult with his lawyers and participate in his defense? Second, was he responsible for the crime with which he is charged? The first is the question of competency to stand trial, the second is the question of insanity. Before a criminal trial can be held to answer the second question, the defendant must be restored to competency. Thus, in the typical case it is the question of competency that arises first, and its resolution often determines the fate of the defendant.* (p. 202)

As Stone goes on to note, far more persons are confined on the basis of incompetence than on the basis of insanity. He reports that in 1972, 8825 men were committed as incompetent.

With the advent of legal insanity and incompetency as defenses against criminal conviction came the development of special asylums for the "criminally insane," which in most cases were just another form of prison, without due process protections. According to the National Institute of Mental Health (1972), these types of institutions are used for the following categories of persons:

> a. persons adjudicated incompetent to enter a plea or stand trial
>
> b. defendants found not guilty by reason of insanity
>
> c. persons adjudicated under special statutes, e.g., "sexually dangerous persons," "defective delinquents," "sexual psychopaths," etc.
>
> d. convicted and sentenced offenders who have become mentally disturbed while serving a prison sentence and have been transferred to a mental health facility
>
> e. other potentially hazardous mentally ill persons requiring special security during the course of their evaluation and treatment.

There are presently 73 such institutions in the United States.

The Mentally Retarded Offender

Opinions concerning the possible relationships between mental retardation and criminality, according to Menolascino (1975), have tended to converge upon the following "simplistic viewpoints":

> 1. *The retarded are "born criminals" — i.e., congenital "moral idiots."*
> 2. *The retarded characteristically commit dangerous crimes of physical assault, especially sexual assault.*
> 3. *Retarded individuals are more prone to commit crimes because they lack the capacity to grasp the social values of their culture — including its social and legal definitions of "right" and "wrong."*
> 4. *The retarded cannot foresee the consequences of their actions and hence cannot be effectively deterred by normal punishments.*
> 5. *The retarded are more highly vulnerable to suggestion and therefore respond indiscriminately to the criminal leadership of brighter persons.*
> 6. *Retarded individuals more frequently are reared in families and neighborhoods in which early and continuing identification with delinquent models is common.* (p. 57)*

Interest in the mentally retarded offender, as Menolascino notes, has "outstripped factual information." For example, the incidence of mental retardation among incarcerated offenders is difficult to establish with any reliability. The judgment that mental retardation is present requires psychometric evaluation, i.e., an intelligence test, yet a survey by Brown and Courtless (1971) of all correctional institutions in the United States showed that, on the basis of 80 per cent return of questionnaires, only about half the inmates had been so tested. Approximately 9.5 per cent of those who had received psychometric evaluation had IQs below 70, and nearly 1500 inmates had IQ scores below 55. Allen (1970), projecting the findings of this survey on to the total prison population, stated: "There are in American prisons today nearly 20,000 adult offenders (10 per cent of the total prison population) who are substantially impaired, some 3,300 of whom are classifiable as moderately to profoundly retarded" (p. 601). The nature of the crimes committed by these offenders is not specified, but Allen indicated that there is a higher incidence of crimes against the person among the retarded than among the nonretarded.

As Allen (1970) has pointed out, our society has pursued three

---

*Reprinted with permission of the National Council on Crime and Delinquency, from *Crime and Delinquency*, January 1975, p. 57.

different courses with regard to mentally retarded offenders: "We have ignored their limitations and special needs, or have sought to tailor traditional criminal law processes to fit them, or have grouped them with the mentally ill . . ." (p. 602). The lowered social-adaptative capabilities of the retardate that make him prone to commit illegal actions leave him particularly vulnerable in his contacts with the criminal justice system. He is unaware of his constitutional rights and is not likely to comprehend the full import of the Miranda warnings when they are given to him by the arresting officer.

Contemporary services for the mentally retarded offender are perhaps the least adequate of those provided for any category of offender. Conventional probation and parole procedures prove unsuccessful for the majority of retarded offenders, but neither the mental health nor the correctional authorities have been able to provide adequate institutional facilities for the care and management of such offenders.

Menolascino (1975) believes that the first obstacle to be overcome in improving programs for the mentally retarded offender is the problem of "defining him by a common measure with stable dimensions." He suggests a classification that utilizes two age-specific categories, each subdivided into behavioral descriptions, as a basis for identifying the treatment needs of these individuals:

1. **Mentally Retarded Adolescents and Young Adults**
   (a) **Behavioral problems:** *Teen-agers and young adults referred for the first time. Usually adolescents with IQs of 40 to 80 who are management problems, are sexually promiscuous, or lack salable or social skills required in our complex society.*
   (b) **Consistently antisocial, uncontrolled, or self-destructive behavior:** *Usually individuals who failed previously to respond to residential services or who have come directly from the community with a long history of social offenses.*
2. **Mentally Retarded Adults**
   (a) **Delinquent-criminal** behavior with some community judgment of unsafe or unacceptable conduct: *Individuals exhibiting a generally low level of successful socio-educational-vocational experiences before admission to an institution or a treatment setting. Actual or potential threat for physical assault toward others documented.*
   (b) **Severe retardation with a history of habitual unacceptable social behavior:** *Individuals admitted to an institution because their families or general society can no longer tolerate their low abilities and poor behavior. Typically, their problem behavior spills over beyond the power of the family, agencies, and community to control, modify, or contain them.* (p. 63)*

*Reprinted with permission of the National Council on Crime and Delinquency, from *Crime and Delinquency*, January 1975, p. 63.

Allen (1970) has made a series of recommendations for improvement of the handling of mentally retarded offenders, beginning with the establishment of an "Exceptional Offenders Court" to permit early identification of retardates who can be diverted from the criminal justice system. Emphasis is placed on the importance of special education and vocational training to help the retardate acquire skills needed to get along outside the institution, together with effective treatment of emotional problems and realistic prerelease planning. Reintegration into the community should be accomplished by the use of halfway houses and a parole system that uses officers specially trained in the management of mentally retarded offenders.

The Antisocial (Psychopathic) Personality

Until relatively recent times, it was assumed that intellectual factors were the overriding determinants of the condition called "mental illness."* This assumption, however, did not explain the actions of those who committed extremely bizarre acts but still seemed completely "normal" in their intellectual functioning. It was the 18th century physician Philippe Pinel who first described the "moral idiot" — a person suffering from *manie sans délire* (madness without delusions). An American physician of the same period, Benjamin Rush, spoke of moral alienation, defective organization of moral faculties, and deranged will. Rush, like Pinel, saw that the condition called "mental illness" may involve other than intellectual faculties. The 19th century criminologist Cesare Lombroso endorsed the concept of the moral imbecile, noting that such individuals were guiltless, impulsive, highly aggressive, boastful, and particularly insensitive to both social criticism and physical pain. These various meanings and interpretations came to repose in the category designated the "psychopathic personality."

The term "psychopath" was used first by the ancient Greeks to indicate those behaviors not possible to identify through

---

*We shall enclose the term "mental illness" in quotation marks throughout this section to remind the reader that many experts, including psychiatrists like Thomas Szasz, seriously question the validity of this concept and medical model of deviant behavior.

medicine. The etymological definition of the term "suffering mind" reveals the cautious approach of our ancestors toward this type of behavior, whose characteristics lacked sufficiently definable properties for medical classification. Historically, psychiatrists have been ambivalent in accepting the term "psychopath" into their nosology. As shown previously, Pinel and others chose to refer to this condition as some form of "moral insanity." Giving specific content to the term has been extremely difficult because of the relativity of such definitions. In American psychiatry, the term "psychopath" serves as anything from a strict categorization to a vague catchall. H. Cleckley (1970) established an effective case for the existence of a distinct psychopathic condition and listed 16 characteristics common to persons with the condition:

1. *Superficial charm and intelligence*
2. *Absence of delusions and other signs of irrational thinking*
3. *Absence of "nervousness" or neurotic manifestations*
4. *Unreliability*
5. *Untruthfulness and insincerity*
6. *Lack of remorse or shame*
7. *Antisocial behavior without apparent compunction*
8. *Poor judgment and failure to learn from experience*
9. *Pathologic egocentricity and incapacity for love*
10. *General poverty in major affective relations*
11. *Specific loss of insight*
12. *Unresponsiveness in general interpersonal relations*
13. *Fantastic and uninviting behavior with drink and sometimes without*
14. *Suicide threats rarely carried out*
15. *Sex life impersonal, trivial and poorly integrated*
16. *Failure to follow any life plan* (pp. 355–356)

While psychiatry continued to try to find a way to identify and treat this kind of condition, the law began to see special problems with this type of offender, one not troubled by various forms of delusions or other gross disturbances in affect or cognition. These offenders, when placed in a mental institution, were able to show rapid progress and were released, only to get into trouble again. The response to this perceived threat to society was the first of the psychopathy laws, passed by Massachusetts in 1911. Known as the Briggs Act, it created a distinct class of habitual criminal offenders, known as "defective delinquents" (Kittrie, 1971).

THE FEMALE OFFENDER

Long before the term "women's lib" entered the national vocabulary, the FBI's *Uniform Crime Reports* had begun to register sharp increases in crime rates for women. In the decade and a half from 1960 to 1975, crime in all categories by male offenders increased 22.8 per cent, as compared with an overall increase of 101.7 per cent for female offenders during the same period. The pattern of accelerated increase is clearer when one looks at particular types of crimes. The number of women arrested for armed robbery increased by 380.5 per cent, as compared with a rise of 214.3 per cent for men; fraud and embezzlement rose 488.5 per cent for women, 91.1 per cent for men; larceny-theft was up 464.6 per cent for women, 117.7 per cent for men; burglary increased 288.8 per cent for women, 132.0 per cent for men. Table 8–1 shows the distribution of FBI index offenses by sex for calendar year 1975.

TABLE 8–1. TOTAL ARRESTS, DISTRIBUTION BY SEX, 1975*			
	NUMBER OF PERSONS ARRESTED		
OFFENSE CHARGED	Total	Male	Female
Criminal homicide:			
Murder and non-negligent manslaughter	11,083	9,376	1,707
Manslaughter by negligence	1,509	1,331	178
Forcible rape	13,844	13,844	—
Robbery	96,900	89,985	6,915
Aggravated assault	263,634	249,615	14,019
Burglary (breaking and entering)	573,555	387,571	185,984
Larceny-theft	76,227	71,021	5,206
Motor vehicle theft			

*Data from Federal Bureau of Investigation: *Uniform Crime Reports: 1975.* Washington, D. C., U. S. Government Printing Office, 1976.

The only exceptions to this general picture of steeper increases in crime rates for women as compared with men occurred in the categories of criminal homicide and aggravated assault. Although both criminal homicide and aggravated assault were on the increase for men and women alike, there were no substantial differences in rates for male and female offenders.

For reasons that feminists tend to ascribe to chauvinism on the part of members of a male-dominated profession, criminologists have been selectively inattentive to the problems of female criminality. Freda Adler (1975) maintains that throughout the centuries men have approached the "mysteries" of feminine behavior as though women belonged to a wholly different species, as though women did not share male needs for security and status, as though their motivations were entirely foreign. Female criminals were looked upon as freaks.

Lombroso (1903) was one of the earliest criminologists to deal with the subject of female criminality. In keeping with his efforts to identify the inherent characteristics of criminals, Lombroso gathered skeletal remains of female offenders, paying particular attention to the measurement of jawbones and craniums. He found that female offenders exhibited markedly fewer anomalies than were noted among male offenders. According to Lombroso, women were more likely to be "occasional" criminals than "born" criminals.

Lombroso credited the occasional-type female criminal with possessing the higher virtues present in "normal" women. He suggested that such women were led into crime by lovers, husbands, or fathers, and often had little or no taste for criminal activity. He was apparently convinced that women have many traits in common with children — that they are revengeful and jealous and suffer from undeveloped intelligence. He presumed that these defects were ordinarily neutralized by piety, maternity, sexual coldness, and a want of passion. A common theme among 19th century writers was that when a woman was found to have criminal tendencies, she was observed to surpass men in her capacity for wickedness. Lombroso characterized her cruelty as more refined and diabolical: killing her enemy would not satisfy her, she must see him suffer.

Thomas (1923), writing about the delinquent girl, suggested that women are not motivated by sexual desire but manipulate the sexual needs of men in order to achieve their goals. He also believed that criminal activity is comparatively infrequent among middle class women because they are socialized to sublimate their natural desires and behave with conventional decorum, treasuring their chastity as a potential marriage investment. Lower class women, on the other hand, are more prone to crime — for reasons of *amorality* rather than immorality.

"Masked Criminality"

One of the earliest in-depth studies of female criminality was conducted by Otto Pollak (1950). His work challenged a number of widespread myths about the nature and extent of female in- volvement in crime. Pollak believed that women had received a great deal of undeserved praise for their significantly lower crime rate, since, in fact, their participation in crime compared with that of men. In his study, he sought the answers to three questions:

> 1. Are those crimes in which women seem to participate exclusively, or to a considerable extent, offenses which are known to be greatly underreported?
> 2. Are women offenders generally less often detected than are men offenders?
> 3. Do women, if apprehended, meet with more leniency than do men? (p. 1)

Pollak's analysis of the available statistics on female criminality led him to answer all three questions in the affirmative.

Shoplifting of a nonprofessional character, illegal abortions, thefts by prostitutes, domestic thefts, and episodes involving dis- turbances of the peace are consistently underreported in official crime tallies. Shoplifting is an offense that seems especially acces- sible to women. It is not at all unusual or suspicious for a woman to spend a good deal of the day out shopping, and feminine cloth- ing styles often make it relatively easy for a female shoplifter to conceal "boosted" merchandise on her person.

Pollak contended that the criminal behavior of women is easily hidden or "masked" by the traditional roles assigned to women by our culture and society. In addition, he believed that women use more deceit than men in the commission of their crimes. Women are taught deceit for physiological reasons: faking orgasm and concealing menstruation, according to Pollak, give women practice in the art of deceit.

With regard to the third question, Pollak found plenty of evidence that women are given favorable, even preferential, treat- ment at every stage of the criminal justice system and process, from arrest to corrections. Some offenses that typically lead to prosecution if the offender is male go unprosecuted if the offender is female; e.g., homosexual contacts between women, exhibi- tionism, and being an accessory to statutory rape. Reckless and Kay (1967) concluded their review of various explanations for low crime rates among women with observations that provide support for Pollak's contentions:

> Perhaps the most important factor in determining reported and acted-upon violational behavior of women is the chivalry factor. Victims or observers of female violators are unwilling to

take action against the offender because she is a woman. Police are much less willing to make on-the-spot arrests of or "book" and hold women for court action than men. Courts are also easy on women, because they are women . . . . Overlooking, letting-go, excusing, unwillingness to report and to hold, being easy on women are part of the differential handling of the adult females in the law enforcement process from original complaint to admission to prison. The differential law enforcement handling seems to be built into our basic attitudes toward women. (p. 16)

Female Criminality and "Women's Lib"

The parallel between the rising incidence of crimes by women and the emergence of the contemporary women's movement has raised the issue of whether there is a causal connection between the two phenomena. While it is true that organizations like COYOTE have attracted national attention by their vigorous advocacy of the decriminalization of prostitution, Rita Simon (1975) questions whether women's lib has had any appreciable influence on women's involvement in crime. Noting the predominance of young, white, college educated, and professional women of middle and upper-middle class backgrounds in the women's movement, Simon sees a gulf between these types of women and the blue-collar female workers, high-school educated housewives, and black women who compose the bulk of female offenders that may be as great as that which separates men and women. Says Simon:

> *How likely it is, therefore, that the women's movement will significantly alter the behaviors, the perceptions, the beliefs, and the life styles of women already involved in criminal careers is still too early to say. But given the characteristics of the members of the women's movement, it is unlikely that it has had a significant impact, or that indeed it has made much of an impression on women already involved in crime. Indeed, most of these women have yet to hear of consciousness raising, and of sisterhood in a political sense; and those who have may well ridicule these sentiments or attack them as the empty mouthings of women whose lives have always been characterized by material comfort, stability, and secruity. (p. 18)*

Conclusion

There seems little doubt that the norm of chivalry toward women in the male-dominated criminal justice system has suffered considerable erosion in recent years, with the result that women are beginning to receive "more equal" treatment. But this is, at best, only a partial explanation for the rising crime rate among women. Of much greater importance is the fact that, as Freda Adler (1975) points out, our nation and society have been undergoing a "gradual but accelerating social revolution in which women are closing many of the gaps, social and criminal, that have separated them from men. The closer they get, the more alike they look and act" (p. 30). Women have no special endowment of morality. As their participation in an ever-widening range of work situations presents them with greater opportunities to commit crimes, women will encroach more and more on what were once the exclusive criminal domains of men: larceny, fraud, embezzlement, and other types of white-collar crimes. These trends are already apparent in the latest statistics on female criminality.

JUVENILE OFFENDERS

The rise in juvenile crime is one of the most serious aspects of the crime problem in the United States. In 1975, 30 per cent of all crimes cleared by arrest were committed by persons under 18 years of age; a total of 837,000 crimes were committed by youngsters under the age of 15. According to the *Uniform Crime Reports: 1976*, juveniles accounted for 34 per cent of the robberies, 53 percent of the burglaries, and 55 per cent of the automobile thefts committed in 1975. Both the frequency and the severity of crimes committed by juveniles have increased significantly in the past decade.

The Juvenile Justice System

As we noted previously, juveniles are handled differently and separately from adults in almost every part of the criminal justice system. Extensive use of differential treatment and the exercise of discretion at different stages of the criminal process cloud the juvenile crime picture.

Since most aspects of the American criminal justice system derive from the common law of England, so too does the foundation of our juvenile justice system. With respect to criminal responsibility, the English common law made three basic assumptions regarding age: First, a person under the age of 7 was presumed to be *incapable* of forming criminal intent. Second, an offender between 8 and 14 years of age was not held responsible for his criminal acts unless the *state* could prove that he could clearly distinguish between right and wrong. Finally, if the offender was over the age of 14, he was assumed to be responsible for his acts and could be punished. In this last case, the burden of proof was on the *defendant* to prove that he was not responsible.

The king was considered the father of his country (the doctrine of *parens patriae*) and assumed responsibility for the protection of any child who was in need of it. In England this was accomplished by the Chancery Courts, which made the needy child a ward of the state, under the protection of the king. The Chancery Court was designed to act with more flexibility than was possible under the more rigid standards of the criminal courts. The Chancery Court's main concern was for the welfare of the child, and procedures that might hamper the court in its beneficial actions were either circumvented or ignored. Thus, there were two concepts under the common law: (1) the presumption that children under certain ages are not responsible for criminal acts; and (2) a certain category of children were in need of protection by the state. It was not until the age for criminal responsibility was raised to 16, and in some jurisdictions 18, that these two ideas were merged in the concept of juvenile delinquency.

Despite concern for the welfare of their children, most communities have a tolerance point for behavior of juveniles. When this is reached or exceeded, the child can be taken into custody and recorded as a delinquent. The mixing of juvenile offenders with adult felons was a practice that had been in existence for centuries but was looked upon as repugnant in America's early history. It was not until 1899, however, that the delinquent juvenile began to receive differential attention in the courts. The first juvenile court was established in that year in Chicago. This was the first instance in which the delinquent joined the dependent and neglected child as a ward of the state. When the juvenile delinquent was thus placed under the general cloak of *parens patriae*, he was removed entirely from the formal criminal justice system.

Categories of Juveniles

There are essentially three kinds of children that come into contact with the juvenile court system. Children in two of these three categories have committed no offense but are either *dependent* (without family or support) or *neglected* (in a family situation that is harmful). The only category that involves offenses is that of the *delinquent* juvenile.

The *dependent* child has been recognized as needing the protection of the state to meet the basic requirements for life and comes to the state for a number of reasons, but most often owing to the death of the parents and the lack of other adult relatives who could take care of the child. In the early days of America, these unfortunates were taken in by other families. Later, as their numbers increased and these orphans and other dependent children gravitated to the growing cities, various types of institutions were developed to handle them. Orphanages, common in the 19th century, are seldom seen in America today. Some dependent children were kept in almshouses and other institutions, public and private, to provide them with food and shelter. Dependent children now are wards of the state and are subject to at least some control by the courts.

Neglected children are similar to dependent children, except that they are most often taken away from parents or relatives for their own protection or welfare. Many neglected children are "battered children." The neglected and abused child usually comes to the attention of the authorities through reports from neighbors, friends, or relatives, since even when badly abused, children are usually very loyal to their parents and seldom report the situation to the authorities.

There are two categories of *delinquent* juveniles. The first includes juveniles who have committed an *offense that would be a crime if it had been committed by an adult.* The second category of delinquent comprises individuals who have committed so-called *status offenses* — violations of statutes that are generally applied only to juveniles. Status offense legislation is often ambiguously worded. Phelps (1976) cites an example from the California Welfare and Institutions Code (Section 601):

> *Any person under the age of 18 years who persistently or habitually refuses to obey the reasonable and proper orders or directions of his parents, guardian, custodian or school authorities, or who is beyond the control of such person, or any person who is a habitual truant from school within the meaning of any law of this state, or who from any cause is in danger of leading an idle, dissolute, lewd, or immoral life, is within the jurisdiction of the juvenile court which may adjudge such a person to be a ward of the court.* (p. 37)

Phelps asks: How does a youngster prove he is not leading "an idle, dissolute, lewd, or immoral life"?

Juvenile justice authorities are sharply divided on the issue of jurisdiction over status offenses. Those who wish to retain jurisdiction argue that today's status offender is tomorrow's adult criminal and that further acts of delinquency cannot be prevented unless such juveniles are discovered. Opponents maintain that "the processing of juveniles in the formal authoritarian agencies is likely to reinforce the pattern of delinquency which the system proposes to eradicate" (Phelps, 1976, p. 38). These critics emphasize that the social services usually required to deal effectively with the problems of the status offender can be made available without formal adjudication.

In addition to the three major categories of juveniles, the court may also have to deal with other problems involving children, such as adoption, termination of parent's rights, appointment of a guardian, custody in divorce, and nonsupport. It is this broad over-reach of the juvenile court and the resultant conglomeration of children with widely different problems in juvenile detention and correctional facilities that has brought the most criticism to the system. Juvenile facilities, while generally of a much more humane quality than adult institutions, had and still have many serious drawbacks.

In re Gault: A Turning Point

In 1966, the case of *Miranda v. Arizona* produced turmoil in the criminal justice system. In 1967, the juvenile justice system also received a major jolt, again from the State of Arizona, in the most far-reaching case of that Supreme Court term: *In re Gault*. This case focused not on any single right but on a number of the rights incorporated into the Fourteenth Amendment's "due process" clause. Gerald Gault, a 15 year old, was sentenced to the "remainder of his minority" (6 years) for an offense for which the *maximum* penalty for an adult would have been only 2 months. During the course of his hearings, he was deprived of most of the privileges that had been granted to his adult counterparts. His appeal was heard by the United States Supreme Court on the issues of: notice of the charge, right to counsel, right to confrontation and cross-examination of witnesses, privilege against self-incrimination, right to a transcript of the proceedings, and right to appellate review. This case completely reshaped the direction of the juvenile justice system and replaced the concept of *parens patriae* with that of due process. As Justice Fortas pointed out, the informality and procedural laxity in the juvenile court were often followed by stern discipline in juvenile institutions, causing the juvenile to feel deceived.

With the assumption of due process as a right for juveniles in their proceedings, juvenile courts have been forced to act as courts first and as social control agencies second. The doctrine of *parens patriae* may continue to be followed, but in those cases in which the juvenile is threatened with criminal proceedings, the concept of due process will take precedence.

SUMMARY

The special category offenders with whom this chapter has dealt present problems for our criminal justice system, which is primarily structured for handling adult male offenders. Narcotics addicts, public inebriates, psychotic criminals, mentally retarded offenders, psychopaths, female offenders, and juvenile offenders are included within this designation. In each case, we have sought to describe the principal distinguishing characteristics and, within the limits of available information, the estimated number of these types of offenders within the population. Discussion was devoted to some of the factors that seem to be involved in the increase in female criminality over the past decade and a half. We also considered the impact on the juvenile justice system of the Supreme Court's decision in the landmark case *In re Gault*. The *Gault* decision seems to imply a fundamental change in the posture of the juvenile court, from implementing the doctrine of *parens patriae* to emphasizing due process — a change that tends to blur the distinction between the juvenile and adult criminal justice systems.

REVIEW

Find the answers to the following questions in the text:

1. Sketch the principal characteristics of the *dysfunctional drug user* (narcotics addict) that make him a poor risk for rehabilitation.

2. How important is the physiological addiction factor in narcotics addiction as a behavior pattern or life style?

3. What does the National Advisory Commission recommend under a multimodality treatment approach to narcotics addiction?

4. What is methadone? How does it operate as a narcotics antagonist in the treatment of heroin addiction?

5. What is a *civil detoxification center* and how does it function to change the "revolving door" syndrome in chronic alcoholism?

6. Who was Daniel M'Naghten? What significance does his case possess for the insanity defense?

7. How does the issue of insanity differ from that of incompetence? Which of these two accounts for the greater number of commitments in the United States?

8. Are there any differences in pattern for males and females with regard to the rising incidence of crimes during the past 10 to 15 years?

9. Has women's lib had any real impact on the female crime rate in this country?

10. Distinguish the categories of juveniles over whom the juvenile court has jurisdiction.

11. What are status offenses? What are some of the arguments, pro and con, for removing such offenses from the jurisdiction of the juvenile court?

12. Discuss the significance of the *Gault* case for the juvenile justice system.

TERMS TO IDENTIFY AND REMEMBER

special category offender
experimental drug user
dysfunctional drug user
"boss feeling"
methadone
detoxification center
antisocial (psychopathic) personality
parens patriae
In re Gault

Daniel M'Naghten
self-medicator
"mainlining"
withdrawal symptoms
"revolving door" syndrome
DWI offense
"masked criminality"
status offense

REFERENCES

Adler, F.: *Sisters in Crime*. New York: McGraw-Hill Book Co., 1975.
Allen, R. C. The law and the mentally retarded. *In* Menolascino, F. J., (ed.): *Psychiatric Approaches to Mental Retardation*. New York, Basic Books, 1970.
Brakel, S., and Rock, R.: *The Mentally Disabled and the Law*. Chicago, University of Chicago Press, 1971.
Brown, B. S., and Courtless, T. F.: *The Mentally Retarded Offender*. Rockville, Maryland, National Institute of Mental Health, Center for Studies of Crime and Delinquency, 1971.
Cleckley, H.: *The Mask of Sanity*. St. Louis, The C. V. Mosby Co., 1970.
Driver v. Hinnant, 356 F.2nd 761 (4th Cir. 1966).
Easter v. District of Columbia, 361 F.2nd 50 (D.C. Cir. 1966).
Federal Bureau of Investigation: *Uniform Crime Reports: 1975*. Washington, D. C., U. S. Government Printing Office, 1976.
Glueck, S.: *Mental Disorder and the Criminal Law*. Boston, Little, Brown & Co., 1962.

Goldfarb, R.: *Jails: The Ultimate Ghetto*. Garden City, New York, Anchor Press, 1975.

Haskell, M. R., and Yablonsky, L.: *Criminology: Crime and Criminality*. Chicago, Rand McNally, Inc., 1974.

In re Gault, 387 U.S. 1 (1967).

Kittrie, N.: *The Right To Be Different*. Baltimore, Johns Hopkins University Press, 1971.

Larner, J.: *The Addict in the Street*. New York, Grove Press, 1964.

Lombroso, C.: *The Female Offender*. New York, Appleton, 1903.

Menolascino, F. J.: A system of services for the mentally retarded offender. Crime and Delinquency *21*:57–64, 1975.

Miranda v. Arizona, 384 U.S. 436 (1966).

National Advisory Commission on Criminal Justice Standards and Goals: *Corrections*. Washington, D. C., U. S. Government Printing Office, 1973.

National Institute of Mental Health: *Directory of Institutions for Mentally Disordered Offenders*. Washington, D. C., U. S. Government Printing Office, 1972.

Nelkin, D.: *Methadone Maintenance: A Technological Fix*. New York, George Braziller, Inc., 1973.

Nimmer, R. T.: *Two Million Unnecessary Arrests*. Chicago, American Bar Association, 1971.

Phelps, T. R.: *Juvenile Delinquency: A Contemporary View*. Pacific Palisades, California, Goodyear Publishing Co., Inc., 1976.

Pittman, D. J., and Gordon, W. C.: *Revolving Door: A Study of the Chronic Police Case Inebriate*. New Brunswick, New Jersey, Rutgers Center of Alcoholism Studies, 1958.

Pollak, O.: *The Criminality of Women*. New York, A. S. Barnes, 1950.

Powell v. Texas, 392 U.S. 514 (1968).

President's Commission on Law Enforcement and Administration of Justice: *The Challenge of Crime in a Free Society*. Washington, D. C.: U. S. Government Printing Office, 1967.

Reckless, W. C., and Kay, B. A.: *The Female Offenders*. Report submitted to the President's Commission on Law Enforcement and Administration of Justice, 1967.

Robinson v. California, 370 U.S. 660 (1962).

Simon, R. J.: *Women and Crime*. Lexington, Massachusetts, D. C. Heath & Co., 1975.

Stone, A. A.: *Mental Health and Law: A System in Transition*. Washington, D. C., U. S. Government Printing Office, 1975.

Tampa Tribune. Drugs in prison. May 7, 1976, p. 3-A.

Thomas, W. I.: *The Unadjusted Girl*. New York, Harper and Sons, 1923.

Wolfgang, M. E., and Strohm, R. B.: The relationship between alcohol and criminal homicide. *Quarterly Journal of Studies on Alcoholism 17*: 411–426, 1956.

10 THEORIES OF CRIMINALITY

Theories of criminality have a twofold purpose: they help to organize existing information about criminal behavior into a coherent, systematic framework; and they serve to point the directions for further research by indicating potentially fruitful leads to be explored. For example, a proponent of the theory that criminality is a biological phenomenon would attempt to integrate the available knowledge about crime and delinquency with the findings of biological research and would direct the continuing quest for explanations of criminality toward structures and processes within the human organism. Similarly, a proponent of the theory that criminality is a sociological phenomenon would attempt to interpret the available information on criminal and delinquent behavior to square with the results of sociological research and would orient the search for causes of criminality toward social organizations, groups, and institutions to which the individual belongs. In addition, theories of criminality may aim at establishing some rational basis for programs designed to control, reduce, eliminate, or prevent crime and delinquency.

The formulation of comprehensive theories of the origins and determinants of criminality is fraught with difficulties, not the least of which is the problem of accurately defining criminality. As Shore (1971) has observed:

> Antisocial behavior is not a diagnostic category or unitary symptom, but a socially defined phenomenon closely tied to cultural values and often dependent upon the interpretation given a behavior pattern by those agencies responsible for the regula-

tion of social interaction. In certain communities, for example, the tolerance for deviance is lower and certain behavior may be labeled antisocial which, in another context, would not be considered deviant at all. (p. 456)

Nevertheless, Shore points out, there are some people who engage in violent, aggressive behavior despite the advantage of the best social opportunities, while others who have been subjected to extremely poor social conditions do not exhibit criminal or delinquent behavior. Thus, Shore concludes, "aside from the need to understand and explain the social and cultural forces that foster criminal behavior, *there is need for a theory of individual behavior that can account for individual differences and the ways in which individuals interpret and respond to social forces*" (p. 456) (italics added).

Research on the causes of criminal behavior has, for the most part, focused on four broad areas of inquiry:

1. Biological factors and genetic predispositions
2. Societal influences
3. Individual differences in the organization and functioning of hypothesized *intrapsychic* structures such as "personality," "attitudes," "self-concept," "motivation," etc.
4. Behavior differences which reflect the learning experiences and reinforcement history of the individual.

The biologist has sought explanations for criminality in the constitutional make-up of the individual; the sociologist has sought explanations for criminality in the processes that affect the behavior and experiences of people living in societal groups; the intrapsychically oriented psychiatrist and psychologist have sought explanations for criminality in the presumed personality configuration of the individual; and the behaviorally oriented investigator has sought explanations for criminality in the variables that affect the learning experiences of the individual. It must be noted also that neat categorizations of this kind do less than justice to criminological theorizing since many theorists have not hesitated to make use of concepts and methods taken from a variety of disciplines and approaches. Nor does this list provide room for theorists who have tried to fashion an integrative or eclectic approach to the understanding of criminality.

At the present time, there is no "grand theory" of criminality that encompasses all approaches to crime and organizes the empirical findings of many disciplines into some coherent, well integrated schema. For the time being, at least, we must be content with either theories of the "middle range," i.e., those that account for only a limited number of facts about crime and criminals, or "microtheories" that are even more restricted in their range of content and generality. Some of the biological, psychological, and psychiatric theories we shall shortly examine fall at the extremes of grand theory and microtheory, but most of the sociological theories are theories of the middle range.

Criminological theories do not merely stand on either side of clear lines drawn by professional specialization. In recent years, it has become increasingly evident that the position a criminological theorist takes on the origins of criminality and the policies he endorses with regard to the disposition of the criminal offender are much more than mere expressions of intellectual conviction; deeply involved are issues of value orientation and ideology.

The criminologist whose orientation might be called *humanistic* sees the offender as a victim of unfair societal arrangements and conceives of rehabilitation as a process of resocialization in which an effort is made to inculcate self-respect, dignity, and a sense of personal worth in the offender — qualities he was deprived of because of social injustice. At the risk of oversimplification, we could say that, according to this orientation, society owes a debt to the criminal, rather than the criminal owing a debt to society.

The criminologist with a *scientific/technological* orientation conceives of change in the criminal offender as *behavioral change*, the accomplishment of which is the end result of applying a behavorial technology based on principles that have been discovered and validated in the experimental laboratory. Humanists, however, insist upon voluntarism and freedom; they charge the scientific/technological group with exploiting conformity and determinism and employing coercive methodologies.

As Glock and Stark (1965) have observed, "The basic methodological assumption which has come to inform the social sciences is that man's behavior is determined in the same way that other natural phenomena are determined: that potentially every human act can be understood as a result of antecedent factors which operate to make the act inevitable" (p. 294). B. F. Skinner, in *Beyond Freedom and Dignity* (1971) has drawn from this deterministic assumption the behavioral conclusion that human beings are incapable of regulating their own behavior through the exercise of free will. Only by discarding completely our delusional belief in autonomous man, Skinner asserts, can we gain access to the true determinants of human behavior. "Skinnerian" has become a label for the group of scientists/technologists who advocate behavioral change methods.

This focus on behavioral science and the capacity for behavioral control that it has generated through technology leaves a bad taste in the mouth of the humanistically oriented criminologist, to whom it implies the loss of freedom at the hands of a bureaucratic elite who possess the power to exercise such control. Recently, an entire issue of the *American Criminal Law Bulletin*, with a lead article by Representative Charles B. Rangel (1975), was devoted to an examination of the legal issues raised by the employment of behavior modification programs within prisons.

An examination of the controversy between the humanistic and scientific/technological orientations is beyond both the scope and the appropriate concerns of this book. (The interested reader is directed to the first and second selections in the volume edited by Reasons (1974) for an illuminating and provocative discussion of some of the key issues in this controversy.) Our purpose in alerting the reader to the existence of this controversy is twofold: In the first place, it is one important reason why criminology has been unable to formulate anything approximating an integrative theory of criminality. Fundamentally involved are differences in philosophy that lie outside the limits of empirical verification — questions of free will versus determinism, of intuition versus scientific method, and so forth. Second, the presence of this divergence in viewpoint among criminologists helps to explain some basic contradictions in approach to the disposition of the criminal offender.

BIOLOGICAL THEORIES OF CRIMINALITY

In part because of the traditional American egalitarian social philosophy and in part because of the earlier excesses of criminological theorists, American criminological thought has been markedly inhospitable to the notion that organic factors may play an important role in the emergence of some forms of criminal behavior. As Allen (1970) has put it, "The extravagant claims, meager empirical evidence, naiveté, gross inadequacy, and stated or implied concepts of racial and ethnic inferiority" in the work of earlier theorists constitute a "disreputable history" that has thoroughly discredited the few important empirical findings of biological investigations of criminal behavior.

It is not our intention here to present a detailed description and critique of these earlier theories, since it is our belief that such material belongs more properly to a historical account of criminology than to a discussion of biological theories of criminality in the contemporary context. It is necessary, however, to provide a brief sketch of the forerunners of current biological theory and research with regard to criminality. As we shall see, most biological theorizing about the causes of criminal and delinquent behavior, past and present, has followed three broad, and not necessarily exclusive, lines of inquiry: (1) the anthropological or morphological approach; (2) the hereditary approach; and (3) the physiological approach.

The Anthropological/Morphological Approach

The foremost exponent of the anthropological approach in the latter half of the 19th century was Cesare Lombroso, an Italian army physician who sought to establish a relationship between certain physical characteristics and criminal behavior. Like many intellectuals of the time, Lombroso was heavily influenced by Darwin's writings on organic evolution. In Lombroso's view, the criminal offender could best be understood as a case of *atavism* — a throwback to some earlier, more primitive prototype of contemporary man. And the proof for this contention? Lombroso believed that those who were prone to criminality could be identified by certain "stigmata of degeneracy," such as a lantern jaw, pointed ears, sloping forehead, receding chin, and other anomalies or asymmetries of the body.

Since they were based largely on intuition and speculation, Lombroso's hypotheses failed to meet the test of empirical verification. Charles Goring, an English physician, obtained comparative anthropometric measurements on a large sample of British criminals and noncriminals. Goring (1913) concluded:

> *We have exhaustively compared . . . different kinds of criminals with each other, and criminals as a class with the law-abiding public. From these comparisons no evidence has emerged confirming the existence of a physical criminal type such as Lombroso and his disciples have described . . . . Our results nowhere confirm evidence nor justify the allegations of criminal anthropologists. They challenge their evidence at almost every point. In fact, both with regard to measurement and physical anomalies in criminals, our statistics present a startling conformity with similar statistics of the law-abiding classes. The final conclusion we are bound to accept . . . must be that there is no such thing as a physical criminal type.* (cited in Hardman, 1964, p. 202)

Lombroso's theory was later given new life by Ernest Hooton, an anthropologist. Hooton attempted to account for the failure to verify a relationship between physical features and criminality on the grounds that Lombroso had neglected to categorize criminals according to the type of offense they had committed. Said Hooton (1939):

> It is a remarkable fact that tall, thin men tend to murder and to rob, tall heavy men to kill and commit forgery and fraud, undersized thin men to steal and to burglarize, short heavy men to assault, to rape, and to commit other sex crimes, whereas men of mediocre body build tend to break the law without obvious discrimination or preference. (p. 376)

If Lombroso had incorporated these considerations, Hooton believed, his theory might have found confirmation. Unfortunately for Hooton, the critics failed to agree. They found nearly as much to object to in Hooton's own work as they had in Lombroso's, and they took Hooton to task for a variety of methodological flaws, ranging from ambiguous definitions of key concepts to systematic bias in his sampling procedures.

A more elaborate, and in some respects more sophisticated, effort was made by William Sheldon to relate delinquent behavior to physique, or *somatotype*. Sheldon (1949) postulated three basic somatotypes (body types): (1) the *endomorph* (rotund, with a predominance of visceral and fatty tissue); (2) the *mesomorph* (robust, with a predominance of muscle and bone tissue); and (3) the *ectomorph* (lean, with a predominance of skin and nervous tissue). Sheldon further postulated that each of these somatotypes is characterized by certain features of temperament and personality. Endomorphs are presumed to be affectionate, gregarious, fond of companionship and the creature comforts. By contrast, the ectomorph is seen as shy, retiring, and of a nervous disposition. The mesomorph is seen as delinquency prone as a consequence of his excessive energy, strength, and agility and his predilection toward physical activity as a release for his tensions. In an examination of delinquent boys in the city of Boston, Sheldon (1949) claimed to have found support for these contentions. He reported that delinquent boys tended to be stocky and physically strong, i.e., mesomorphs.

Like his morphological predecessors, Sheldon was sharply criticized for numerous methodological shortcomings in his work. His critics pointed out that, in contrast to Sheldon's premise, somatotypes are far from constant and are susceptible to variation with age and diet; that the statistical treatment of his data was riddled with errors; and that his system of somatotyping was contaminated, in that the same person who performed the classification of body types also carried out the personality typing. When objective tests were substituted for interviews, the correlations between personality and somatotype tended to disappear (Paterson, 1930).

The Gluecks (1950) conducted a large scale investigation that incorporated, among other variables, an assessment of Sheldon's somatotype. They found support for Sheldon's hypothesis that delinquent boys would show a statistical preponderance of mesomorphy. Hardman (1964) has this to say about their results:

> When we find a correlation between two variables, we are never justified in assuming that a cause-and-effect relationship exists — in this case, assuming that delinquency is causally related to body type. For instance, most crimes against persons — assault, bullying, strong-arm robbery, and rape — require better-than-average physique. The stringbean ectomorph and the roly-poly endomorph are not physically qualified for these offenses or for skylight burglary, which may require shinnying down a rope and up again, or for robbing boxcars on a moving train, or for removing a 500 pound safe. Further, social factors operate in selection of offenders. Recall your own childhood when you were choosing up sides for a game. Who was chosen first: the stringbeans, the roly-polies, or the muscle-and-blood boys? Since a sizable portion of our delinquency is gang delinquency, members may well be selected much the same way as play-group members. Social psychologists have demonstrated that strong, athletically inclined boys are given preferential group status and are selected as leaders. And finally we must take into account the cultural stereotypes that roly-poly people are jovial and jolly and big, burly, and bruisers go together like damn and Yankee. In short, because we expect people to behave in this manner . . . they tend to fulfill our expectations . . . . If we could accurately measure the effect of these three factors — the physical requirements of certain offenses, group selection of the more athletic, and our cultural expectations — I believe we could account for all of Glueck's correlations without assuming a direct causal relationship between body and behavior. (p. 205) (emphasis added)*

The Hereditary Approach

In Paris in 1968, a man named Daniel Hugon was brought to trial for murdering a prostitute. Later, Hugon attempted suicide

---

*Reprinted with permission of the National Council on Crime and Delinquency, from *Crime and Delinquency*, July 1964, p. 205.

and was given a thorough physical examination. A sample of his blood revealed that he was an XYY male, i.e., one of those presumably rare individuals born with an extra Y (male) chromosome instead of the normal complement of only one X (female) and one Y (male) chromosome. Hugon was given a reduced sentence as a consequence of this disclosure.

Since Hugon's trial, evidence of an XYY anomaly, coupled with mental retardation and neurological disorder, provided grounds for a plea of not guilty by reason of insanity for a man accused of murder in Australia. This defense has since been presented in several cases in the United States. The most notorious of these cases was that of Richard Speck, convicted in the brutal slayings of eight student nurses in Chicago in 1966. Speck, who is the clinical prototype of the XYY anomaly — tall, gangling, suffering from acne, and with a borderline IQ of 85 — was found to be without the XYY chromosomal abnormality.

The flurry of interest in the "genetics of abnormal behavior" aroused by media coverage of these cases — most of it poorly informed and provocatively handled — seems to have subsided as quickly as it arose, and public interest in the "born criminal" appears to have diminished considerably, which is probably as it should be. According to Dr. Digamber Borgaonkaar, the cytogeneticist who carried out the first XYY study in the United States (1969), there are at least two conditions that must be fulfilled before any significant conclusions can be reached with regard to the XYY male: First, large scale research must be conducted within the United States on both institutional and noninstitutional populations to determine the comparative incidence of the XYY chromosomal anomaly in the general population and among criminal offenders. Second, we will have to learn a great deal more than we know at present about the complex linkage between genetic abnormalities and adult behavior before we can begin to understand the operation of chromosomal anomalies like that of the XYY male. The first problem is essentially technical: to marshal enough people and resources to carry out a program of cytogenetic analysis of sufficient scope and magnitude to yield a representative sampling of male population of the United States. The second problem requires for its resolution some major advances in our knowledge of behavior genetics. It is impossible to predict whether such advances will be made in the foreseeable future, and it seems advisable, therefore, to reserve judgment on the role of hereditary factors in criminal behavior, at least for the time being.

The Physiological Approach

Clinical descriptions of the antisocial personality — the individual designated as "psychopathic" or "sociopathic" in earlier systems of nomenclature — have emphasized the centrality of certain behavioral features (e.g., impulsivity, lack of tolerance for sameness) to this personality configuration. As Quay (1965) has noted:

> The psychopath is almost universally characterized as highly impulsive, relatively refractory to the effects of experience in modifying his socially troublesome behavior, and lacking in the ability to delay gratification. His penchant for creating excitement for the moment without regard for later consequences seems almost unlimited. He is unable to tolerate routine and boredom. While he may engage in antisocial, even vicious behavior, his outbursts frequently appear to be motivated by little more than a need for thrills and excitement. (p. 181)

In seeking to account for these behavioral characteristics, Quay hypothesizes that the psychopath's "primary abnormality lies in the realm of basic reactivity and/or adaptation to sensory inputs of all types" (p. 181). Thus, according to the Quay theory, much of the behavior of the antisocial personality can be understood as *an extreme of stimulation-seeking behavior*.

Studies of sensory deprivation and perceptual isolation have been conducted in which subjects don blindfolds and padded clothing and lie on soft mattresses in darkened, sound-reduced chambers. These studies have affirmed that such experiences are affectively unpleasant and potentially motivating to the extent that the person will behave in such a way as to increase the level of intensity and variability of available stimulation. If one theorizes that the psychopath requires sensory inputs of greater intensity and variety than those of the average person, then much of the psychopathic individual's otherwise inexplicable thrill-seeking behavior and impulsivity becomes understandable.

Quay observes that there are two possible explanations for this condition: (1) lessened basal reactivity, and (2) increased adaptation rate. "The first [theory] is that basal reactivity to stimulation is lowered so that more sensory input is needed to produce efficient and subjectively pleasant cortical functioning. A second possibility is that there is a more rapid adaptation to stimulation which causes the need for stimulus variation to occur more rapidly and with greater intensity" (p. 181). Both these hypotheses have received limited support from empirical investigations.

Autonomic and Cardiovascular Research

In general, increased activity in the sympathetic division of the autonomic nervous system appears to have an excitatory or facilitative effect upon cortical activity in the brain. Lacey (1958), however, has suggested that this apparently does not hold true for increases in heart rate and blood pressure. Evidence is available that indicates that increased heart rate and blood pressure may actually lead to an inhibition of cortical activity.

Changes in heart rate or blood pressure become stimuli to internal receptors, whose activation may lead reflexly to changes in the relationship of the organism to the environment, in terms of the accessibility of the organism to environmental stimulus inputs. An individual with *cardiac lability* (a consistently exaggerated or hyperactive cardiovascular response pattern) might be described as a person who requires a higher level of intensity and a broader range of stimuli than the nonlabile individual in order to reach some response threshold. It is as though he is "several stimulus degrees under par."

In a series of studies beginning with the work of Funkenstein, Greenblatt, and Solomon (1949) and culminating in the Ohio Penitentiary study of Lindner and his associates (1970), the presence of such cardiac lability has been confirmed in a population of psychiatrically identified antisocial offenders. This research is in basic agreement with Quay's (1965) proposal that the antisocial (psychopathic) individual is characterized by pathological stimulation-seeking and that it is possible "to view much of the impulsivity of the psychopath, his need to create excitement and adventure, his thrill-seeking behavior, and his inability to tolerate routine and boredom as a manifestation of an inordinate need for increases or changes in the pattern of stimulation" (p. 182).

Support for the conclusions reached in this line of research was reported by Goldman, Dinitz, Lindner, Foster, and Allen (1974) in an investigation of the effects of various arousal drugs on the behavior of a small group of "simple" psychopaths. The study, which was conducted over a two year period at the Chillicothe Correctional Institution in Ohio, noted positive changes in the psychological status of the subjects. They reported themselves to be "more energetic, less anxious, having more restful sleep, better appetite, less impulsivity, decreased irritability and above all else, a markedly increased feeling of well-being" (p. 70).

These results suggest the possibility that for the small number of individuals who exhibit the characteristics identified with the so-called "simple" psychopath, there may be considerable promise in a program that combines parole and closely supervised medication. The authors rightly emphasize the serious moral, ethical, and legal implications of such a decision and acknowledge that the criminal justice system "will have to surround the treatment of this severe behavioral disorder with every possible legal safeguard to prevent encroachment on the civil liberties of this population" (p. 72).

SOCIOLOGICAL THEORIES OF CRIMINALITY

Sociological theories of criminality are directed toward finding answers to questions dealing with *collective* rather than individual behavior. The questions are likely to be similar to these: Why does Social Group A have a higher rate of crime than Social Group B? What factors are responsible for the increase in crimes against the person in the United States over the last 10 years? While sociological explanations do not deny the importance of motivation, they seek the locus for the determinants of motivation in societal arrangements that are external to the individual. Says Gwynn Nettler (1974):

> A strictly sociological explanation is concerned with how the structure *of a society or its* institutional practices *or its* persisting cultural themes *affect the conduct of its members. Individual differences are denied or ignored, and the explanation of collective behavior is sought in the patterning of social arrangements that is considered to be both "outside" the actor and "prior" to him. That is, the social patterns of power or of institutions which are held to be determinative of human action are also seen as having been in existence* before *any particular actor came on the scene. They are "external" to him in the sense that they will persist with or without him. In lay language,* sociological explanations of crime place the blame on something social that is prior to, external to, and compelling of a particular person. (p. 138)

Nettler identifies two types of sociological explanations of criminality: the *subcultural* variety and the *structural* variety. Both varieties assume that *culture conflict* is the principal source of crime; they differ, as Nettler indicates, in their evaluation of the conflict and, therefore, in their prescribed societal responses to crime.

The Structural Approach

The French sociologist Emile Durkheim (1858–1917) was one of the first writers to point out the "normality" of crime. Human behavior is not intrinsically either "normal" or "pathological": certain forms of conduct simply become labeled so by society. Thus, in a society of saints, singing too loud in church might be punished as severely as robbery would be in a prison society of thieves. In Durkheim's view, a society exempt from crime is impossible.

One of Durkheim's major contributions to our understanding of deviant behavior derives from his attempts to show how suicide is related to an individual's integration, or lack of integration, into stable social groups. He proposed that many suicides are the result of *anomie*, a societal condition of "normlessness" or "relative rulelessness," to use Nettler's (1957) definition, in which people experience a lack of meaningful rules and purpose in their lives.

The concept of anomie was extended by the American sociologist Robert K. Merton (1957) to explain the causes and nature of deviant behavior in modern Western societies. Merton is an analyst who considers socially deviant behavior to be just as much a product of the social structure as conformist behavior. He attempts to determine how the sociocultural structure exerts pressure toward deviation upon people variously located in that structure. He seeks an answer to the question: Why does the frequency of deviant behavior vary with social structure?

The structure of society is composed of a number of elements, but two are of essential importance to Merton's analysis: (1) culturally defined goals, those objectives defined as legitimate for all to strive toward, and (2) the regulatory norms that define and control the means of achieving the goals. It is Merton's central hypothesis that deviant behavior may be regarded sociologically as a symptom of dissociation between culturally prescribed aspirations and socially structured avenues for realizing those aspirations.

In American society, wealth is a basic symbol of success. Money obtained illegally can be spent just as easily as "hard earned" money and translated into the symbols of success. Merton sees American society as placing heavy emphasis upon wealth without a corresponding emphasis on the use of legitimate means for reaching this goal. Individual modes of adaptation to this situation may take one or a combination of several forms: *conformity, innovation, ritualism, retreatism,* and *rebellion.*

Merton points out that the greatest pressure toward deviant

behavior is experienced by people occupying positions in the lower class. Cloward and Ohlin, in a work entitled *Delinquency and Opportunity* (1960), employ this theory in explanation of urban gang delinquency. Their basic hypothesis is as follows:

> The disparity between what lower-class youth are led to want and what is actually available to them is the source of a major problem of adjustment. Adolescents who form delinquent sub-cultures, we suggest, have internalized an emphasis upon conventional goals. Faced with limitations on legitimate avenues of access to these goals, and unable to revise their aspirations downward, they experience intense frustrations; the exploration of nonconformist alternatives may be the result. (p. 86)

Nettler (1974) observes that this type of explanation views delinquency as *adaptive*, i.e., instrumental in the attainment of goals that are generally shared, and also as partly *reactive*, i.e., prompted by resentment on the part of delinquents at being deprived of things they believe should be theirs.

The Subcultural Approach

The term *culture* connotes a wide range of meanings: Coffey et al. (1974) claim to have turned up 160 meanings in their own search for a consensual definition. Much of this diversity in interpretation would appear to reflect variations in emphasis. Some social scientists stress the continuity of traditional values and their embodiment in distinctive artifacts and symbols as the essential core of culture. Others emphasize the importance of early learning experiences in shaping consistent patterns of human interaction and communication as the fundamental method for the transmission of culture. As Coffey et al. note, "Culture systems may on the one hand be considered as products of action, on the other hand as conditioning elements of further action" (p. 136).

Some cultural prescriptions are common to all members of a society, but there are differences of greater or lesser magnitude from one group or class to another within the society. "Subculture" is a term devised by social scientists to refer conveniently to variations within a society on its cultural themes, patterns, artifacts, and traditional ideas, as these are incorporated and expressed within various groups. Subcultures are presumed to have some stability and endurance. In addition, subcultures can vary widely in the magnitude and direction of their deviation from the larger culture. Under conditions in which the norms of the subculture impose different standards of conduct from those prescribed by the larger culture, the resulting normative conflict can become the source of criminal behavior.

A principal advocate of the "culture conflict" approach to delinquency is Walter B. Miller (1958). He does not go so far as to posit that the lower class in the United States is a criminal class, but he sees delinquency as the result of an "intensified response" of some boys to "focal areas of concern" found in the lower class culture. Lower class youth who conform to these values find themselves in inevitable conflict with the prevailing middle class mores and the law.

Miller uses the concept "focal concern" in preference to the concept "value," reasoning that it is more readily derivable from field observation, is descriptively neutral, and facilitates analysis of subcultural differences since it reflects actual behavior uncolored by an official "ideal." In specific terms, in the lower class culture concern over "trouble" means avoiding entanglements with official authorities or agencies of middle class society. "Toughness" (body tattooing, bravery, absence of sentimentality) is seen as related to being raised in a female dominated (matriarchal) home. There is an almost obsessive concern with masculinity and an antipathy toward homosexuality, which is expressed in baiting "queers." "Smartness" is defined as the ability to obtain the maximum amount of goods with a minimum of physical effort.

Traditionally, the deadening routine of lower class life has led people to seek relief in alcohol or evangelism; Miller's delinquents seek excitement in "booze, bands, and broads." Related to the belief among the lower class members that goal-directed efforts are futile is their concept of "fate." Many lower class persons view their lives as subject to a destiny over which they have no control. This attitude serves both as an inhibitor to initiative and as a compensation for failure. Miller sees the lower class emphasis upon "autonomy" as expressing itself in an ambivalent attitude toward authority, i.e., resenting external controls while actively seeking out restrictive environments (e.g., military enlistments). Their life style is summed up in the proverb: "Trouble is what life gets you into."

Cohen (1955, 1966) has tried to furnish an explanation for the development of a *delinquent subculture* — an antisocial way of life that has somehow become traditional in a society. According to Cohen, a subculture develops when a number of people with a common problem of adjustment are in effective interaction. The chief common problems around which the delinquent subculture revolves appear to be status problems. Certain children, particularly lower class children, are denied status in the middle class society because they cannot meet its criteria. The delinquent subculture deals with these problems by providing criteria of status that these children *are* able to meet. Specifically, the delinquent subculture functions simultaneously to combat internal forces in the individual, as represented by a "gnawing sense of inadequacy and low self-esteem," and to deal with external forces, the "hated agents of the middle-class." It does so by erecting a counter-culture that offers an alternative set of status criteria. The alternative status criteria offered by the delinquent subculture are in direct opposition to those of the middle class, to the point of rendering a "non-utilitarian, malicious, and negativistic" quality to the subculture.

The Radical Interpretation of Criminality

A number of criminologists, who are variously designated as "radical" or "new" criminologists, endorse a view of criminal behavior that is heavily influenced by Marxist theories. These writers see criminality as primarily an expression of class conflict. According to their interpretation, behavior designated as "criminal" by the ruling classes is the inevitable product of a fundamentally corrupt and unjust society; law enforcement agencies are the domestic military apparatus used by the ruling classes to maintain themselves in power; the causes of crime lie within society and its legal system, and therefore crime will persist until or unless both are made to change. The basic tenets of this position are outlined by Quinney (1974) in the following six propositions:

> 1. *American society is based on an advanced capitalist economy.*
> 2. *The state is organized to serve the interests of the dominant economic class, the capitalist ruling class.*
> 3. *Criminal law is an instrument of the state and ruling class to maintain and perpetuate the existing social and economic order.*
> 4. *Crime control in capitalist society is accomplished through a variety of institutions and agencies established and administered by a governmental elite, representing ruling class interests, for the purpose of establishing domestic order.*
> 5. *The contradictions of advanced capitalism — the disjunction between existence and essence — require that the subordinate classes remain oppressed by whatever means necessary, especially through the coercion and violence of the legal system.*
> 6. *Only with the collapse of capitalist society and the creation of a new society, based on socialist principles, will there be a solution to the crime problem.* (p. 16)

According to these criminologists, the fundamental inequities of the American criminal justice system can be divided into two principal categories: discriminatory treatment on the basis of class, and discriminatory treatment on the basis of race. While discrimination by race is fading to some degree in certain sectors of the system, it is clearly still a significant factor in the administration of justice. Discrimination by class is becoming more widespread than ever today, as the gap between classes widens with economic deterioration. Class and racial discrimination are not, of course, mutually exclusive, as is demonstrated by the position of poor blacks in relation to the process of justice.

Radical theoreticians reject the concept of individual guilt and responsibility for illegal acts committed by working class people against the persons and property of the bourgeoisie. They see these crimes as wholly justified acts of rebellion by slaves against masters. In their view, this makes the bulk of property crimes "political" crimes, morally acceptable and indeed almost mandatory in view of the criminal nature of society itself.

Assaults and property crimes by proletarian people against other proletarian people are not justified by radical theory but are understood as inevitable social distortions produced by capitalist society, which breeds racial distrust among the poor, protects the person and property of the bourgeoisie much more effectively than those of workers, and produces poverty and alienation.

Critics of the radical interpretation of criminality question whether class conflict can adequately account for a wide range of criminal behavior. McCaghy (1976) states:

> *The theory's application is actually limited to explaining legal reaction against behaviors threatening established economic interests. Thus there is no pretense at explaining such facets of the crime problem as a school janitor sexually molesting a ten-year-old student, parents brutally beating a baby because "it won't stop crying," or two friends trying to stab each other in a dispute over a fifty cent gambling debt.* (p. 96)

As McCaghy observes, the conflict perspective is not a statement of facts or of empirically verified relationships — it is a perspective that directs attention toward a *possible* interpretation of the facts.

THE INTRAPSYCHIC APPROACH TO CRIMINALITY

Responsibility for the management of a broad range of deviant behavior — behavior that is perceived by others as bizarre, threatening, or merely inexplicable — has been invested in the professional practitioner of psychiatry. Labeled "mental illness," such deviant behavior is ambiguously defined and may include anything from the "transient situational maladjustment" of an individual experiencing the pangs of bereavement to the strange grimaces and antic behavior of a person labeled "schizophrenic." The psychiatrist, as a member of the medical profession, employs a vocabulary and a set of concepts that constitute a series of elaborate metaphors and analogies that bear a tenuous — and at times even tortured — relationship to the physical disease models they emulate. Thus, the deviant individual becomes a "patient," his deviant behavior is referred to as "symptoms," the determinants of his behavior become the "underlying pathology," and so forth.

The conceptual underpinnings for psychiatry derive mainly from psychoanalysis, the system of thought created by Sigmund Freud. As Freud's ideas are sufficiently familiar to most readers, we shall confine ourselves in this account to a discussion of those aspects of psychoanalysis that bear more or less directly on the question of what consistutes the determinants of criminal behavior.

As viewed within the psychoanalytic framework, behavior is *functional* in a two-fold sense: (1) it operates to fulfill certain needs or drives, and (2) it has consequences for other aspects of behavior. But the importance that Freud attributed to *unconscious factors* adds further complexity to the interpretation of behavior, for it requires acceptance of the proposition that much, if not most, of the behavior exhibited by an individual possesses meaning that lies outside the range of awareness. Thus, neurotic behavior, for example, is construed as the outward *symbolic manifestation of dynamic dysfunction.* Such behavior represents, for the psychoanalyst, the unsuccessful attempt on the part of one component of personality (the ego) to exercise executive control over another component (the id).

The immediate and direct implication of this principle of motivational functionalism for understanding criminal behavior is that a focus on the criminal action itself (manifest function) will hinder any attempt to understand the causes of the crime. Says Feldman (1969):

> [L]ike any other behavior, criminal behavior is a form of self-expression, and what is intended to be expressed in the act of crime is not only observable in the act itself, but also may even be beyond the awareness of the criminal actor himself. So, for example, an overt criminal act of stealing may be undertaken for the attainment of purposes which are far removed from, and even contrary to, that of simple illegal aggrandizement; indeed, it may

even be ... that the criminal, in stealing, seeks not material gain
but self-punishment. The etiological basis of a criminal act can,
therefore, be understood only in terms of the functions, latent
as well as manifest, which the act was intended to accomplish.
(p. 434)

Although the specific functions of a given criminal act must be
sought in the life history of the individual offender, the general
etiological formula for psychoanalytic criminology asserts that
criminal behavior is an attempt at maintaining psychic balance or
restoring psychic balance which has been disrupted.

Despite a consensus of professional opinion among psychoanalytic criminologists concerning the general etiological ("psychic
balance") formula, considerably less unanimity is evident with
respect to the specific factors in the socialization of the individual
that dispose him toward criminality as a means of maintaining
psychic balance. Feldman (1969) identifies five variations on the
basic formula:

1. Criminality as neurosis
2. The antisocial individual as an instance of defective
socialization
3. Criminal behavior as compensation for frustration of
conventional psychic needs
4. Criminal behavior as a function of defective superego
5. Criminal behavior as anomie

As Feldman notes, the focus of these variant interpretations ranges
from a concentration on hypothesized internal factors to an
emphasis upon external conditions that may exert a decisive influence on the individual.

The weakness of this etiological formula is readily apparent. In
the case of the first interpretation, "criminality as neurosis,"
empirical data simply fail to support the contention that the
criminal is typically a neurotic individual who is compulsively
driven toward self-punishment. On the contrary, criminal offenders
appear to put forth every effort and use all their resources to elude
capture. Moreover, the empirical evidence we have been able to
gather suggests that "neurotic" personality characteristics are
distributed within the criminal population in approximately the
same proportion as that found in the noncriminal population.

Equally dubious is the view of the criminal as an antisocial character who seeks immediate gratification, lives entirely in the present, and is unable to withstand tedium and monotony. It is a criminological commonplace that many kinds of criminal behavior require extensive preparation by way of training in specific skills or systematic planning. Indeed, as Feldman observes, the areas of professional, organized, and white-collar crime seem to exemplify the operation of Freud's "reality principle."

In failing to give appropriate emphasis to the fact that patterned criminality is not the spontaneous creation of the individual offender, psychoanalytic criminology minimizes the crucial importance of social learning. According to Feldman (1969):

> [T]his learning process requires the individual's participation in the formation and maintenance of relationships with others who dispose of the necessary knowledge and put it to use. It is in the context of these relationships that the individual learns his criminality and adopts for himself distinctive criminalistic attitudes and precepts. Presumably, the experiences of such a learning process must have an effect on the personality of the individual undergoing them. Yet, this reciprocating influence of criminal experience on the personality of the criminal appears to have no consideration in psychoanalytic criminology. Indeed, all of the interpretations of the basic etiology formula share this common implicit assumption that the personality differentials to which causal status is attributed are temporally antecedent to the individual's participation in criminal activity. Nevertheless, it is at least a plausible alternative that such personality differentials are consequential precipitants of the individual's induction into criminality. And in failing to take this possibility into account, the entire structure of psychoanalytic criminology becomes vulnerable to the charge that it merely begs the question from the outset. (pp. 441–442)

Finally, in addition to these substantive criticisms, psychoanalytic criminology possesses some serious flaws when judged as a theory on formal grounds. Psychoanalytic constructs tend to be global and all-inclusive in nature and loaded with "surplus meaning"; rarely, if ever, are they anchored in explicit, observable events. Nevertheless, in time, such constructs become the "facts" of psychoanalysis, upon which even more speculatively elaborate concepts are based.

Most of the research generated by psychoanalytic theory seems to be directed not toward the subsequent modification of the theory in the light of newly acquired information but rather toward demonstrating the essential validity of the basic postulates and assumptions of the theory. Because of the ambiguity and lack of operational specificity of the constructs in the system, no hypothesis derived from psychoanalytic theory can be either clearly confirmed or clearly refuted. For these and other reasons, critics of psychoanalysis have charged that both the theory and its proponents are in conflict with the widely accepted canons of empirical verification and refutation implicit in the scientific method.

Reality Therapy

Glasser's (1965) "reality therapy" is a reaction to psychoanalysis and its emphasis upon unconscious motives and "psychic balance" in the genesis of criminality. Glasser sees criminal behavior as "irresponsibility." A youthful car thief, in his view, is not exhibiting "pathology" in traditional psychoanalytic terms; he is acting in an irresponsible manner — one that deprives others of the ability to fulfill *their* needs. Thus, the thief's desire to ride forces someone else to walk. Because it deals in the present and eschews the esoteric jargon of psychoanalysis, reality therapy has appealed to people who work in corrections, especially those who perceive the vigorous application of the "Protestant ethic" as the eventual solution to the crime problem. However, as a scientific explanation of criminal behavior, Glasser's concepts are untested — and perhaps are untestable.

Containment Theory

Containment theory (Reckless, 1962, 1967) is a sociopsychological theory that assigns a key role to the concept of "self." Whether this self will engage in criminal conduct is dependent upon the interrelationship between an "outer containment" system (the ability of society, groups, organizations, and the community to hold the individual within the bounds of accepted norms, rules, regulations, values, and expectations) and an "inner containment" system (the individual's ability to control and regulate his own behavior). Reckless hypothesizes that persons with poor self-concepts engage in more criminal behavior than do persons with good self-concepts. Critics of containment theory have pointed out that it is impossible to determine whether a poor self-concept emerges *before* or *after* delinquency and that not all persons with a poor self-concept engage in criminal activity. However, the most crucial question left unanswered by containment theory is why a poor self-concept should leave one vulnerable to delinquency?

SOCIAL LEARNING INTERPRETATIONS OF CRIMINALITY

In 1937, in a work entitled *The Professional Thief*, the criminologist Edwin H. Sutherland provided what has come to be regarded as the classic statement of a theory concerning the genesis of criminal behavior called *differential association*. What Sutherland attempted to do was account for the etiology of criminal behavior in the group-based learning experiences of the individual in terms of the following postulates:

1. Criminal behavior is learned.

2. Criminal behavior is learned in interaction with other persons in a process of communication.

3. The principal part of the learning of criminal behavior occurs within intimate personal groups.

4. When criminal behavior is learned, the learning includes: (a) techniques of committing the crime, which are sometimes very complicated, sometimes very simple; and (b) the specific direction of motives, drives, rationalizations, and attitudes.

5. The specific direction of motives and drives is learned from definitions of the legal codes as favorable or unfavorable.

6. A person becomes delinquent because of an excess of definitions favorable to violation of the law over definitions unfavorable to violation of the law.

7. Differential associations may vary in frequency, duration, priority, and intensity.

8. The process of learning criminal behavior by association with criminal and anticriminal patterns involves all the mechanisms that are involved in any other kind of learning.

9. While criminal behavior is an expression of general needs and values, it is not explained by those general needs and values since noncriminal behavior is an expression of the same needs and values.

In this form (i.e., as stated in these postulates), differential association remained untested, primarily as a consequence of difficulties involved in operationalizing the fundamental concepts on which the theory rested. Criminological investigators were unable to resolve the problems posed by mentalistic constructs such as "attitudes" and "motives." However, since Sutherland's time, considerable progress has been made in the understanding of the complex factors involved in learning. In particular, the work of B. F. Skinner and his followers in operant conditioning has increased our comprehension of the importance of *reinforcement* in the acquisition and maintenance of behavior. Given these advances, several theorists have felt that the theory of differential association needed to be updated in the light of contemporary knowledge of the learning process.

C. R. Jeffery (1965), a sociologist who studied under Sutherland, first attempted to modernize the theory of differential association by translating its language and concepts into those of operant conditioning. Jeffery stated that criminal or delinquent behavior is acquired through a process of *differential reinforcement*. Simply stated, a person is more likely to repeat behavior that has positive consequences (reward or removal of an aversive stimulus) than behavior culminating in negative conditioners (punishment or removal of a positive stimulus) or neutral consequences. Criminal behavior, like any other behavior, is maintained by its consequences. Thus, theft may result in the positive reinforcement elicited by the stolen item; murder and assault can produce positive reinforcement through biochemical change or, in the case of addiction, through removal of the aversive conditions of withdrawal.

According to Jeffery (1965), differential reinforcement theory makes several important assumptions:

> 1. The reinforcing quality of differential stimuli differs for different actors depending on the past conditioning history of each.
> 2. Some individuals have been reinforced for criminal behavior whereas other individuals have not been.
> 3. Some individuals have been punished for criminal behavior whereas other individuals have not been.
> 4. An individual will be intermittently reinforced and/or punished for criminal behavior, that is, he will not be reinforced every time he commits a criminal act. (pp. 295–296)

In other words, no two people are identical; everyone has a different history of conditioning. A given situation involving individuals with identical families, backgrounds, and associations in which only one steals can be explained by the fact that behavior is dependent upon:

1. The reinforcing quality of the stolen item
2. Past stealing responses that have been reinforced
3. Past stealing responses that have been punished

These three characteristics will differ in any pair of individuals despite any similarities in backgrounds or associations. Hence, Jeffery uses the term "differential reinforcement" because different conditioning histories exist for different individuals. Differential association theory cannot account for this phenomenon; thus, through Jeffery's application of reinforcement contingencies, a serious weakness in Sutherland's original theory is eliminated.

Of primary importance in Sutherland's theory is the proposition that social reinforcement is the mainstay of criminal behavior, or more simply, that other people serve as reinforcement through either verbal praise or active confederation in the behavior. People also serve as discriminative stimuli that provide valuable information to the individual concerning the potential for reward or punishment. For example, it is highly unlikely that deliquent behavior will occur in the presence of a uniformed officer. The officer indicates that the potential for reward is highly limited and that criminal behavior will, in all likelihood, result in punishment. Conversely, a juvenile in the presence of his peers is more likely to misbehave, as the potential for the rewards of social acceptance and praise is quite high. This phenomenon is demonstrated in the behavior patterns of the typical juvenile gang. People also can act as aversive stimuli through reprimanding, arresting, or even shooting the offender. All these behaviors represent Sutherland's concept of "attitudes" favorable or unfavorable to the criminal behavior.

Jeffery questions the exclusive importance of social reinforcement, pointing out that some criminal behavior is reinforcing in and of itself. For example, stolen goods serve as positive reinforcement whether or not anyone other than the thief is aware of them. Thus, Jeffery demonstrates a model of criminal behavior without social reinforcement, a concept that threatens the very foundation of the theory of differential association and current sociological ideas, all of which have emphasized the primary importance of social forces in the determination of behavior. This question of reinforcement contingencies must be empirically resolved and the theory restructured to account for results.

Robert Burgess and Ronald Akers (1966) presented a complete reformulation of Sutherland's differential association theory. They applied the principles of operant learning as outlined by Jeffery and verified their propriety through the presentation of experimental evidence. They reformed Sutherland's original nine proposals into a seven-statement presentation, incorporating modern learning theory into the original concepts. In 1973, Reed Adams, in an article entitled "Differential Association and Learning Principles Revisited," critically evaluated the Burgess and Akers propositions and reworked them into a cohesive, up-to-date theoretical presentation. In a later study, Adams (1974) contrasted the effects of social and nonsocial determinants of behavior. Results demonstrated that nonsocial factors *did* play a major role in the determination of misbehavior. Adams concluded that once acquired, criminal behavior is maintained by nonsocial reinforcers, with social factors involved to only a small extent. Thus, Adams has demonstrated the absolute necessity for the modernization of Sutherland's theory to include this concept.

The work of Jeffery, Burgess and Akers, and Adams has transformed differential association from a vague series of general statements into a theory that can be experimentally tested and supported. Through the absorption of relevant principles formulated since the theory was originally proposed, differential association has been revived in modern guise. This revision stands in sharp contrast to the obsolescent theories that persist in the social sciences in the absence of attempts at modernization.

SUMMARY

The theories of crime causation we have examined in this chapter have been an area of primary interest to criminologists for the past century. Origins of criminality have been sought in biological or physiological factors, psychological states or conditions, societal and group influences, and the effects of past learning. Although no "grand theory" of criminality has emerged that can account for all, or even a great deal of, criminal behavior, a number of theorists have contributed to our increasing understanding of criminality. More recently, the emphasis in criminology has moved away from *cause* and toward *process* as the focal point of criminological research. In addition, the "new," or "radical," criminologists have directed attention toward the criminal justice system itself as a possible major cause of continued and heightened criminality in our society.

REVIEW

Find the answers to the following questions in the text:

1. What are the two main purposes of theory?

2. Identify the four broad areas of inquiry toward which research on the causes of criminal behavior has been directed.

3. What are the two major orientations that can be discerned today among criminologists? How are these characterized, respectively?

4. What were some of the reasons for the lack of hospitality among American criminologists toward the notion that criminal behavior may be partially determined by biological factors? Has anything occurred in recent years to change this situation?

5. What is the XYY chromosomal anomaly? What is its significance for the criminal justice system?

6. How does Merton explain the relationship between social structure and deviant behavior?

7. How do the "focal areas of concern" of Miller's lower class youngsters compare and contrast with the areas of concern of middle class children?

8. Sketch the main features of the psychoanalytic approach to criminality. What are some of the chief criticisms that have been directed against this formulation?

9. What are some of the weaknesses of the Sutherland theory of differential association that later theorists (Jeffery, Burgess and Akers, and Adams) sought to remedy by "translating" the theory into concepts derived from operant conditioning?

TERMS TO IDENTIFY AND REMEMBER:

grand theory	microtheory
middle range theory	"stigmata of degeneracy"
somatotype	atavism
ectomorph	endomorph
mesomorph	XYY chromosomal anomaly
cardiac lability	antisocial personality
anomie	culture conflict
containment theory	psychoanalytic criminology
delinquent subculture	operant conditioning
focal concerns	differential association
reinforcement theory	reality therapy
radical criminology	

REFERENCES

Adams, R.: Differential association and learning principles revisited. Social Problems 20:458–470, 1973.

Adams, R.: The adequacy of differential association theory. Journal of Research in Crime and Delinquency 11:1–8, 1974.

Allen, H. E.: A biosocial model of antisocial personality. Paper presented at the Ohio Valley Sociological Society meeting, Akron, Ohio, May 1, 1970.

Borgaonkaar, D. S.: Personal communication, March 15, 1969.

Burgess, R. L., and Akers, R. A.: A differential association reinforcement theory of criminal behavior. Social Problems 14:128–147, 1966.

Cloward, R. A., and Ohlin, L. E.: Delinquency and Opportunity. Glencoe, Illinois, The Free Press, 1960.

Coffey, A., Eldefonso, E., and Hartinger, W.: An Introduction to the Criminal Justice System and Process. Englewood Cliffs, New Jersey, Prentice-Hall, Inc., 1974.

Cohen, A. K.: Delinquent Boys. Glencoe, Illinois, The Free Press, 1955.

Cohen, A. K.: The delinquency subculture. In Giallombardo, R. (ed.): Juvenile Delinquency: A Book of Readings. New York, John Wiley & Sons, Inc., 1966.

Feldman, D.: Psychoanalysis and crime. In Cressey, D. R., and Ward, D. (eds.): Delinquency, Crime, and Social Process. New York, Harper & Row, Publishers, 1969.

Funkenstein, D. H., Greenblatt, M., and Solomon, H. C.: Psychophysiological study of mentally ill patients. Part I: The status of the peripheral autonomic nervous system as determined by the reaction to epinephrine and Mecholyl. American Journal of Psychiatry 106:16–28, 1949.

Glasser, W.: Reality Therapy. New York, Harper & Row, Publishers, 1965.

Glock, C. Y., and Stark, R.: Religion and Society in Tension. Chicago, Rand McNally & Co., 1965.

Glueck, S., and Glueck, E.: Unraveling Juvenile Delinquency. New York, Commonwealth Fund, 1950.

Goldman, H., Dinitz, S., Lindner, L., Foster, T., and Allen, H.: A Designed Treatment Program of Sociopathy by Means of Drugs: A Summary Report. Columbus, Ohio, Program for the Study of Crime and Delinquency, 1974.

Goring, G.: The English Convict. London, H. M. Stationery Office, 1913.

Hardman, D. G.: The case for eclecticism. Crime and Delinquency 10:201–216, 1964.

Hooton, E. A.: Crime and the Man. Cambridge, Harvard University Press, 1939.

Jeffery, C. R.: Criminal behavior and learning theory. Journal of Criminal Law, Criminology and Police Science, 56:294–300, 1965.

Lacey, J. P., and Lacey, B. G.: Verification and extension of the principle of autonomic response stereotype. American Journal of Psychology 71:50–73, 1958.

Lindner, L., Dinitz, S., Allen, H., and Goldman, H.: An antisocial personality with cardiac lability. Archives of General Psychiatry 23:260–267, 1970.

McCaghy, C. H.: Deviant Behavior: Crime, Conflict and Interest Groups. New York, MacMillan, Inc., 1976.

Merton, R. K.: Social Theory and Social Structure. Glencoe, Illinois, The Free Press, 1957.

Miller, W. B.: Lower class culture as a generating milieu of gang delinquency. Journal of Social Issues 3:5–19, 1958.

Nettler, G.: A measure of alienation. American Sociological Review 22:670–788.1058

Nettler, G.: *Explaining Crime*. New York, McGraw-Hill Book Co., 1974.

Paterson, D. G.: *Physique and Intellect*. New York, Century, 1930.

Quay, H. C.: Psychopathic personality as pathological stimulation-seeking. American Journal of Psychiatry *122*:180–183, 1965.

Quinney, R.: *Critique of Legal Order: Crime Control in Capitalist Society*. Boston, Little, Brown and Co., 1974.

Rangel, C. B.: Introduction: behavior modification. American Criminal Law Review *13*:3–9, 1975.

Reasons, C. E. (ed.): *Criminology: Crime and Criminals*. Pacific Palisades, California, Goodyear Publishing Co., 1974.

Reckless, W. C.: A non-causal explanation: containment theory. Excerpta Criminologica *1*:131–135, 1962.

Reckless, W. C.: *The Crime Problem*. New York, Appleton-Century-Crofts, 1967.

Sheldon, W. H., et al.: *Varieties of Delinquent Youth*. New York, Harper & Brothers, 1949.

Shore, M. F.: Psychological theories of the causes of antisocial behavior. Crime and Delinquency *17*:456–468, 1971.

Skinner, B. F.: *The Behavior of Organisms*. New York, D. Appleton-Century, 1938.

Skinner, B. F.: *Beyond Freedom and Dignity*. New York, Alfred A. Knopf, Inc., 1971.

Sutherland, E. H.: *The Professional Thief*. Chicago, University of Chicago Press, 1937.

11 VICTIMS AND BYSTANDERS

Societal reactions to crime in the United States have traditionally focused upon the criminal offender — his detection, apprehension, prosecution, and rehabilitation. The criminologist has sought to account for crime causation in the societal arrangements that lead to a higher concentration of criminal offenses among certain groups or classes as well as in individual factors of personality, biology, and motivation. Until recently, however, the victim of criminal depredations has received comparatively little interest or attention from criminologists and even less from the criminal justice system itself. This is not to deny that some criminologists have taken an active interest in the victim; the term "victimology" denotes the specific study of criminal-victim relationships, a field in which criminologists have been involved for at least two centuries. Nevertheless, as Stephen Schafer (1968) has pointed out, the study of criminal-victim relationships "has always suffered from a lack of organized imagination." In Schafer's view:

> The subject was treated with only vague and oversimplified illusions. Such hints and implications by early criminologists have not shed any clear light upon the nature of the criminal-victim relationship . . . . Although the field of "victimology" has long been known, it has not been developed from its embryonic state and has not evolved its dynamic possibilities. (p. 4)

In the years since the publication of Schafer's book *The Victim and His Criminal* in 1968, significant efforts have been made to develop a theoretical base for organizing the results of research

332

on criminal-victim relationships, and we shall devote considerable space to a discussion of these developments in this chapter.

In recent years, criminological interest in victimology has been paralleled by a steadily growing concern for the victim of crime within the criminal justice system and agencies of local, state, and federal government. While the criminologist has addressed the criminal-victim relationship as a factor in crime causation, concern for the victim within the criminal justice system and the government has concentrated upon the issue of compensation and restitution for victims of crime. Efforts have been made to look closely at various groups within our society that are especially prone to victimization by criminal offenders (e.g., the elderly, children, the poor) and to develop models and programs for the delivery of services to victims who have suffered physical, psychological, or economic harm at the hands of criminal offenders.

No discussion of the nature of crime can be considered adequate if it fails to assign importance to the victim of criminal behavior. We shall begin this chapter with a brief historical sketch of the victim of crime and his treatment by society. We shall next consider the field of victimology and what Schafer (1968) identifies as two of its predominant concerns:

> 1. The need to recognize the role and responsibility of the victim
> 2. The offender's responsibility for the reparation of any harm, injury, or other disadvantage caused to his victim

We shall explore the topic of societal responsibility to the victim of crime and discuss some of the complex issues involved in compensation and restitution for victims of crime. This analysis requires that we examine persons and groups exhibiting victim proneness, including those just mentioned. Finally, we shall consider and evaluate a number of models that have been proposed for providing reparative services of various kinds for victims of criminal action.

Before leaving the subject of criminal-victim relationships, we shall deal briefly with a related matter: the bystander. The "Good Samaritan" who makes an effort to intervene to prevent harm to a potential victim by a criminal offender and the individual who watches impassively while criminal depredations are committed upon a hapless victim mark two extremes of participant-observer behavior that pose interesting and significant problems for society in general and for the criminologist in particular. The celebrated case of Catherine Genovese, who was murdered in front of her New York apartment while a number of people listened to her screams but made no effort to intervene, focused national attention on bystander behavior during violent criminal acts. Although comparatively little systematic research has been done in this important problem area, we will try to indicate what we consider to be some of the outstanding issues that require further examination.

THE VICTIM IN HISTORICAL PERSPECTIVE

In earliest times, redress of an injury or vengeful retaliation for a criminal action was the responsibility of the victim, his immediate family, or others who were bound to him by blood or by tribal loyalties. The beginnings of social control may thus be noted in the transition from the individual quest for retaliation to the identification of the injuries sustained by the victim with the interests of members of his family or social group. It is this notion of familial or "blood" relationships that is expressed in the concept of the "blood feud." Consanguinity implied a responsibility on the part of the individual's blood relatives to act on his behalf in seeking compensation or vengeance for injuries sustained as the result of a criminal action.

With the increase in population and the growth of the organs of social control, it became necessary for limits to be set by the rest of society with respect to the vendetta or blood feud. One obvious problem with the private vendetta was the lack of effective means for bringing a particular dispute to a conclusion. Once begun, the vendetta tended to become perpetual: each injury spawned a search for vengeance in the form of a counter-injury, and thus an endless cycle of retaliation and counter-retaliation was inflicted upon society. If one transfers this concept from the individual to the nation, and from one society to the international scene, it is possible to see in the mechanism of the vendetta a similarity to the modern arms race and the necessity for imposing stringent limitations upon weapons and armaments.

Talion law (*lex talionis*) represented an early effort on the part of society to impose constraints upon the potentially widening circle of damage caused by the vendetta. Central to this law was the concept of "an eye for an eye, a tooth for a tooth," that is, of appropriate or *justified retaliation*. According to this principle, an individual who has suffered the loss of an eye is not entitled to ask by way of retaliation that his aggressor suffer the loss of an eye plus a tooth. Therefore, talion law can be seen as an effort toward social defense, i.e., the imposition of curbs upon the parties to the vendetta to protect and maintain the social organization of the tribe or clan.

Additional efforts to mitigate the depredations of the blood feud resulted in the notion of compensation or the payment of damages to placate the victim and satisfy, at least partially, his desire for vengeance. Compensation was not always scaled in equal measure to the damage: Fry (1951) notes that the Law of Moses required four-fold restitution for stolen sheep and five-fold restitution for oxen; and Schafer (1968) observes that the Code of Hammurabi (circa 2200 B.C.), which was notorious for its deterrent cruelty, sometimes demanded as much as thirty times the value of the damage that was caused. Says Schafer, "The criminal's obligation to pay was enforced not in the interest of the victim, but rather for the purpose of increasing the severity of the criminal's punishment" (p. 12). With the passage of time, a system of tariff was introduced that established appropriate levels of recompense in relation to the type and extent of injuries inflicted upon an individual. These offenses generally did not include rape or murder, which were seen as too serious to be compensated except in terms of retaliation in kind. Even homicide, however, could be atoned for by a fine in livestock large enough to humiliate the offender and thus appease the desire of the victim's family for revenge.

In one form or another, the system of compensation or "composition"* has been employed in many of the cultures of the world. In the Germanic tribes most injuries were punishable by fines called *faida*, meaning "the feud commuted for money." In the development of Anglo-Saxon law, the *bot* or money payment used to atone for criminal action came into use, although some classes of particularly serious offenses had no bot, that is, they were "bot-less" or "boot-less." Paralleling the distinction between offenses for which there was and was not bot was the system of *wergilds*, which established a hierarchy among the injured parties. Thus a freeborn man was worth more than a slave, a man more than a woman, and an adult more than a child. Accordingly, the amount of restitution to be provided in the form of bot was determined by the nature of the crime and the age, sex, or rank of the injured party. Out of these types of distinctions

---

*According to *Black's Law Dictionary* (1968), composition "was the name given to a sum of money paid, as satisfaction for a wrong or personal injury, to the person harmed, or to his family if he died, by the aggressor. It was originally made by mutual agreement of the parties, but afterwards established by law, and took the place of private physical vengeance" (p. 358).

developed a complicated system of regulations that constituted the earliest codified law of the Anglo-Saxon people.

With the establishment of the king as a strong central authority, the conception of crime changed, as did the methods used in dealing with lawbreakers. Crimes became an offense against the king's peace and consequently a matter to be dealt with by public authority. Historically, the emphasis shifted away from compensation and restitution to various methods of corporal punishment and, in more recent times, to incarceration as the dominant way of handling offenders.

Decline in concern for the victim and for compensation or restitution seems to have been a widespread phenomenon in Western civilization. This trend was opposed by a number of individuals as well as by international prison congresses from the middle of the nineteenth century until well into the twentieth century. Schafer (1968) points out that at the International Prison Congress held in Stockholm, Sweden, in 1878, Sir George Arney, Chief Justice of New Zealand, and William Tallack proposed a general return to the ancient practice of making reparation to the injured. Rafaele Garofalo made the same proposal at a later International Prison Congress in Rome and wrote that reparation to the victim is a "matter of justice and social security." At the International Penal Association Congress held at Christiana, Sweden, in 1895, the following conclusions were agreed upon:

> 1. Modern law does not sufficiently consider the reparation due to injured parties.
> 2. In the case of petty offenses, time should be given for indemnification.
> 3. Prisoners' earnings in prison might be utilized for this end.

Four years later, the problem of victim compensation was extensively discussed at the International Prison Congress held in Paris in 1899. One of the principal questions on the agenda was "Is the victim of a delict sufficiently armed by modern law to enable him to obtain indemnity from the man who has injured him?" Despite such interest among criminologists, the victim's case at the turn of the century continued to be advanced without much success. It is Schafer's (1968) belief that:

[T]he victim is continuing to lose ground: if one examines the legal systems of different countries, one rarely finds an

instance in which the victim of a crime can be certain to expect full restitution. Similarly, hardly any legal systems take fully under consideration the victim's contribution to a crime. In those rare cases where there is state compensation, the system either is not fully effective or does not work at all. Where there is no system of state compensation, civil procedure and civil execution generally offer the victim insufficient compensation. While the punishment of crime is regarded as a concern of the state, the injurious result of the crime — that is to say, the wrong or damage to the victim — is regarded almost as a private matter. It recalls the lonely man of the early days of social development, who by himself had to find compensation, and who by himself had to take revenge against those who harmed or otherwise wronged him. Today's victim cannot seek satisfaction on his own, since his state forbids him to take the law into his own hands. At the same time, though, the state is not concerned with his precipitative or causative part in the criminal offense. (p. 26)

By the middle of the twentieth century, there was a renewal of interest in the idea of compensation to victims of crime. This rebirth of interest, which may be seen as part of a more general concern for civil rights and the rights of minorities, has led to renewed emphasis by criminolgists on the victim's role in the relationship between criminal and victim. In the following section, we shall consider the rise of "victimology," the systematic study of the criminal-victim relationship and the part that is played by the behavior of some persons in bringing about the occurrence of criminal actions which result in their being victimized.

THE CRIMINAL-VICTIM RELATIONSHIP AS A FACTOR IN CRIME

In 1948, Hans von Hentig published a book entitled *The Criminal and His Victim: Studies in the Sociology of Crime.* Hentig, who appears to have been impressed by Franz Werfel's novel *The Murdered One is Guilty*, advanced the hypothesis that the victim himself in a number of instances may be one of the causes of the crime committed against him. According to Schafer (1968), Hentig suggested that "in a sense, the victim shapes and molds the criminal in his crime and . . . the relationship between perpetrator and victim may be much more intricate than our criminal law, with its rough and mechanical definitions and distinctions, would suggest" (p. 40).

The relationship between criminal and victim, in Hentig's view, is one of reciprocity or mutuality, and a mutuality between "killer and killed, duper and dupe" raises serious questions about the distinctness of the categories of criminal and victim. As Hentig pointed out, although the "mechanical outcome [of a criminal action] may be profit to one party, harm to another, [the psychological interaction between the criminal and victim,] carefully observed, will not submit to this kindergarten label" (p. 4). In fact, there may be a possibility that the criminal himself is victimized. While Hentig failed to support his hypothesis by empirical research, his astute observations and imaginative ideas, such as the concept of the "activating sufferer," had a considerable impact on criminological thought.

Credit for the term "victimology" as the designation for an independent field of criminological study belongs to a French attorney of Rumanian birth named Mendelsohn, who published an article in 1937 in which he traced his views on the victim-criminal relationship more than a decade before the publication of Hentig's study. Findings from a questionnaire containing some 300 items that Mendelsohn had administered to his clients convinced him that a parallelism existed between the personality of the offender and that of the victim. He asked for the "divorce" of the "penal-couple" as the first step toward the development of a "new branch of science" called victimology.

Mendelsohn was quite thoroughgoing in his attempt to establish victimology as a new discipline. He proposed an entire terminology for victimology that included such new terms as "victimal" as the opposite of criminal, "victimity" as the opposite of criminality, and "potential of victimal receptivity" as meaning an unconscious aptitude on the part of the individual for being victimized. In Mendelsohn's view, victimology was not merely a branch of criminology but a "science parallel to it" or, better, "the reverse of criminology." Unfortunately, Mendelsohn's imaginative new terms never acquired much currency with either criminologists or other criminal justice professionals.

Victim Typologies

Having identified the victim as a potentially significant element of crime causation, it was natural and inevitable that both Hentig and Mendelsohn would attempt to develop a system for classifying victims according to type. The typologies they proposed were speculative, and even though neither author relied upon systematic empirical research, their proposals had value as guidelines for systematic inquiry.

Mendelsohn classified victims according to a single factor: the "correlation of culpability (imputability) between the victim and the delinquent." Mendelsohn's victims are grouped in the following categories according to the degree of their guilty contribution to the crime:

> 1. The "completely innocent victim." Mendelsohn regards them as the ideal victim as refers first of all to children and those who suffer crime while they are unconscious.
> 2. The "victim with minor guilt" and the "victim due to his ignorance." Mentioned as an example is the woman who "provokes" a miscarriage and as a result pays with her life.
> 3. The "victim guilty as the offender" and the "voluntary victim." In explanation Mendelsohn lists the following subtypes:
>   a. Suicide "by throwing a coin" if punishable by law
>   b. Suicide "by adhesion"
>   c. Euthanasia — "to be killed by one's own wish because of an incurable and painful disease"
>   d. Suicide committed by a couple (for example, "desperate lovers," healthy husband and sick wife)
> 4. The "victim more guilty than the offender." There are two subtypes:
>   a. The "provoker victim," who provokes someone to crime.
>   b. The "imprudent victim," who induces someone to commit a crime
> 5. The "most guilty victim" and the "victim who is guilty alone." These refer to the aggressive victim who is alone guilty of a crime (for example, the attacker who is killed by another in self defense).
> 6. The "simulating victim" and the "imaginary victim." Mendelsohn refers here to those who mislead the administration of justice in order to obtain a sentence of punishment against an accused person. This type includes paranoids, hysterical persons, senile persons, and children. (Schafer, 1968, pp. 42–43)

Hentig distinguished born victims from victims made by society. His typology, based upon psychological, social, and biological factors, contains 13 categories:

1. The young
2. Females
3. The old
4. The mentally defective and other mentally deranged persons
5. Immigrants
6. Minorities

7. Dull normals
8. The depressed
9. The acquisitive
10. The wanton
11. The lonesome and the heartbroken
12. Tormenters
13. The blocked, exempted, and fighting

In this typology, youth, old age, gender, and mental deficiency are all categories in which victim status is biologically determined, or at least this would appear to be the case upon cursory examination. A closer look, however, suggests that such categories as youth and old age are determined by more than biological factors alone; cultures differ widely with respect to the responsibilities, prerogatives, and shared expectations they ascribe to the young and elderly.

In the case of immigrants and minorities, social factors are seen as accounting for the proneness of the individual to victimization. The immigrant is especially vulnerable because immigration is not merely a change of residence, but "a temporary reduction to the extreme degree of helplessness in vital human relations." Stephen Schafer, who experienced the problems of the immigrant at first hand when he immigrated to the United States from Hungary, has this to say:

> Apart from linguistic and cultural difficulties, the immigrant often suffers from poverty, emotional disturbance, and rejection by certain groups in the new country. His competitive drive may evoke hostility. In these highly disturbing and conflict-producing situations the inexperienced, poor, and credulous immigrant, who desperately clutches at every straw, is exposed to various swindles. It takes many painful years for him to adjust to a new technique of living; only then can he escape from being victimized. It is amazing that while people in general cannot fully perceive the difficulties of the immigrant, one category of the population — its criminals — understands the immigrant's disturbed situation and takes advantage of it. (1968, p. 46)

Psychological factors are presumed to be predominately involved in the vulnerability to victimization of the depressed, the acquisitive, the wanton, the lonesome and the heartbroken, and the tormenter. In the case of the acquisitive, Hentig notes that "the greedy can be hooked by all sorts of devices which hold out a bait to their cupidity." Viewers of the movie "The Sting" and the television program "Switch" are familiar with the con man's fundamental belief that the likeliest potential "mark" (victim) is the individual with "larceny in his heart." The lonesome and heartbroken, who may be victims of crimes ranging from murder to fraud, lower their defenses while seeking companionship; and in the case of the depressed, Hentig believes that there is no malady graver or more dangerous than "a disturbance of the instinct of self-preservation."

Hentig's last category, the blocked, exempted, and fighting victims, includes the "individual who has [become so] enmeshed in a losing situation [that] defensive moves have become impossible or more injurious than the injury at criminal hands"; such is the position of the defaulting banker who has perpetrated a swindle in the hope of saving himself or the blackmail victim who is in a situation that precludes seeking the assistance of the police. It seems questionable to group the fighting victim with the others in this category, since fighting back is an act of resistance in crimes of violence. Consequently, the fighting victim is a "difficult victim," in contrast to the "easy victim" whose resistance is overcome by the superior strength of the criminal.

Hentig's typology can be criticized on several points: his categories are neither exhaustive nor mutually exclusive, with the result that there is considerable overlap among categories: for example, the elderly, depressed, lonesome, and heartbroken victim. It is difficult to correlate Hentig's psychological types with sociological data of the kind collected in most kinds of sociological research; we shall have something more to say about this later. In his critique of Mendelsohn's typology based on the amount of guilt attributable to victims and offenders, Silverman (1974) points out that "guilt is never defined to the point where researchers are given guidelines for placing events into categories. Further, this typology deals only with personal 'individual' victims, which indicates that it is not exhaustive of all victims" (p. 58).

Fattah (1967) proposed a rather complex typology with five major types of victims and 11 subgroups. The five major types include: (1) nonparticipating victims; (2) latent or predisposed victims; (3) provocative victims; (4) participating victims; and (5) false victims. These five groups are defined more specifically in terms of their subcategories; that is, the defining properties of the groups consist of psychological and sociological characteristics of the victims.

Sellin and Wolfgang (1964) offer a classification schema based primarily on victim-offender relationships that includes the following categories: (1) primary victimization; (2) secondary victimization; (3) tertiary victimization; (4) mutual victimization; and (5) no victimization. Using certain modifications and reformulations of this typology, Silverman (1974) carried out an empirical study that tested the accuracy and utility of the Sellin-Wolfgang typology. Silverman relates that the typology proved equal to the task of accommodating data derived from court and police records and goes on to state his belief that the typology is a "flexible instrument that may be molded to specific research needs" (p. 63).

The beginnings of almost any scientific endeavor are marked by a concern for *taxonomy*, or the classification of phenomena that the science endeavors to study. In addition to being comprehensive, mutually exclusive, and empirically useful, the classification scheme developed for categorizing phenomena should possess clarity and objectivity. Aside from these considerations, however, the question that is apt to be uppermost in the mind of the reader, after reviewing the attempts to form a victim typology, is "useful for what?" On the basis of the purposes they are intended to serve, Gibbons (1975) has identified two basic kinds of typologies that have been developed for the criminal offender: (1) *causal*, or ideological, typologies, which seek to identify patterns of criminal behavior presumed to develop from specific ideological backgrounds; and (2) *diagnostic* typologies, designed to provide the basis for treatment intervention. The typology is designed to do more than merely organize the existing information concerning a phenomenon; it should also help in orienting the search for new information. While it is doubtless premature to expect the relatively new field of victimology to have progressed very far in the attainment of these objectives, we would expect victim typologies to be of aid in the quest for a clearer understanding of the victim's role in the ideology, or causation, of various criminal offenses and also in the development of measures for treatment of the victims of crime, including compensation and restitution.

COMPENSATION AND RESTITUTION TO VICTIMS OF CRIME

Although the terms "compensation" and "restitution" are often used interchangeably, compensation and restitution represent two different points of view, as Schafer (1968) points out:

> Compensation, and criminal-victim relationships, concerns the counterbalancing of the victim's loss that results from the criminal attack. It means making amends to him; or, perhaps better

stated, it is compensation for the damage or injury caused by a crime against him. It is an indication of the responsibility of the society; it is a claim for compensating action by the society; it is civil in character and thus represents a non-criminal goal in a criminal case. As opposed to compensation, restitution in criminal-victim relationships concerns reparation of the victim's loss or, better, restoration of his position and rights that were damaged or destroyed by and during the criminal attack. It is an indication of the responsibility of the offender; it is a claim for restitutive action on the part of the offender; it is penal in character and thus represents a correctional goal in a criminal case. Compensation calls for action by society; restitution calls for a decision by a criminal court and payment by the offender. (p. 112)

MacNamara and Sullivan (1974) have noted that confusion of what is basically a punitive-corrective measure (offender restitution to the victim) with the doctrine of the state's responsibility for protecting its citizens when such restitution has proved inadequate (compensation) has characterized much of the discussion of proposed victim compensation laws in recent years and has created difficulties in interpreting and administering these laws.

Restitution includes the partial or complete restitution sometimes voluntarily offered by adult criminal offenders, particularly in white-collar crimes, to allay prosecution or to mitigate sentence. More commonly, however, restitution involves offender-restitution-to-the-victim proposals that aim at both punishment and offender rehabilitation. Such schemes have been adopted experimentally in the United States in recent years, principally by juvenile courts. MacNamara and Sullivan (1974) point out that offender-restitution-to-the-victim proposals have proved more popular in theory than feasible in practice for the following reasons:

1. Only a minority of offenders are apprehended and convicted. Who then would make restitution to victims whose attackers had not been brought to justice?

2. Offenders are generally of the lowest socio-economic stratum; hence they are devoid of assets or resources which could provide the basis for an equitable judgment.

3. The prison-earnings potential of offenders can scarcely be expected to meet a fraction of the costs of guarding, housing, clothing, and feeding them, to say nothing of the much greater cost of rehabilitating them.

4. The societal resistance to the re-employment of ex-convicts and their lack of vocational skills insure that their post-

prison employment will not prove sufficiently remunerative to permit any but token restitution payments.

5. The cost to the state of administering a system of offender restitution to the victims of his crimes would exceed the sums actually collected for reimbursing the victims for their injuries and losses. (p. 233)*

In addition, the damage done in many crimes, particularly crimes against the person that violate the victim's self-concept and dignity (e.g., forcible rape), would prove difficult if not impossible to quantify in monetary terms.

Restitution by adult offenders, either as a condition of probation or as a voluntary offer made in an effort to fend off anticipated prosecution or to mitigate sentence, has been largely limited to cases of fraud, embezzlement, forgery, and other white-collar offenses, and as MacNamara and Sullivan observe, "On more than one occasion such offers of restitution and their acceptance [have] come perilously close to the compounding of felonies" (p. 224). The authors also point out that in ordering restitution to be made by juvenile offenders or their parents, juvenile court judges have been less concerned with restoring the victim's loss than with teaching the offender that he must pay for his misdeeds. In cases of vandalism directed against schools, churches, and public property, there is usually little relationship between the amount of restitution ordered, usually in services rather than money, and the actual extent of the damage.

A noteworthy attempt at facilitating offender repayment to victims of crime is being made by the Minnesota Restitution Center, a community-based correctional program operated by the Minnesota Department of Corrections under a grant from the Governor's Crime Commission. This program is offered to selected property offenders who have been sentenced to the Minnesota State Prison, the State Reformatory for Men, or the Minnesota Institution for Women. The program focuses on the individual offender's gauging and making restitution to his victim. Eligibility for participation in the program is established by a thorough screening process that eliminates offenders with a history of drug dependency, severe psychiatric problems, or assaultive offenses, and intelligent individuals with adequate social skills who have chosen to earn their living outside the law with no demonstrated history of consistent attempts to make lawful employment their principal source of financial support. Once he has been selected

---

*Reprinted by permission of the publisher, from *Victimology* by Israel Drapkin and Emilio Viano (Lexington, Mass.: Lexington Books, D. C. Heath and Company, 1974).

for participation in the program, the offender works out a "restitution plan" with his victim. He becomes an inmate of Restitution House, where he resides until full restitution to his victim has been completed. During this period, he must pay for his room and board and also contribute to the support of his family (Minnesota Department of Corrections, 1976).

Victim Compensation Laws

We shall turn now to a consideration of victim compensation laws with the objective of identifying some of the major similarities and differences in the statutes, as well as some of the inadequacies and problems encountered in the interpretation and implementation of these laws. These statutes should not be confused with so-called "Good Samaritan statutes," which provide compensation for citizens killed or injured while attempting to prevent a crime, apprehend a criminal, or assist a police officer in controlling a breach of the peace.

Major similarities in the various compensation laws have been identified by MacNamara and Sullivan.*

> *1. Compensation for crimes against the person with demonstrable personal injury proximately resulting from the crime are compensable but crimes against property are not. This is largely a pragmatic distinction based on the anticipated difficulties of dealing with fraudulent or exaggerated claims (insurance companies have been plagued with such difficulties for decades); the astronomical cost of indemnifying even valid claimants with property losses (by far the highest incidence of crime in this category — burglary, larceny, auto theft, etc.) have inhibited legislative support; and the availability of both governmental and private insurance coverage for such property losses contributes to diminishing the urgency of support for such expanded coverage.*
>
> *2. Generally, no compensation can be claimed unless the injury results from an act specifically violative of the penal law (or as in the case of the Hawaiian legislation, a violation specifically set forth as compensable in the victim compensation act).*
>
> *3. Generally, injuries resulting from violations of the motor vehicle and traffic codes (including driving violations which are misdemeanors and felonies as for example, drunken driving) are not compensable except for criminal assaults in which the vehicle was utilized as the assaulting weapon.*
>
> *4. While some of the laws are somewhat unclear, or rather not sufficiently specific, the victims of intrafamilial crimes (wife-*

---

*Reprinted by permission of the publisher, from *Victimology* by Israel Drapkin and Emilo Viano (Lexington, Mass.: Lexington Books, D. C. Heath and Company, 1974).

beating, incestuous rape or sodomy, sibling assaults, etc.) are not compensated.

5. Victims who initiate or provide the criminal assault which results in their victimization are not compensable (but whether victims who ostentatiously display money or gems or who recklessly frequent areas of high crime incidence without good reason and are as a result assaulted and robbed should be compensated is left to the discretion of the board).

6. Offenders and their accomplices who may suffer injury to their involvement in illegal acts are not compensable.

7. The administrative boards and commissions set up to administer the victim compensation laws may be said to have limited discretion (England), moderate discretion (California), or broad discretion (New York) in determining to what extent a victim himself provoked or enticed his own victimization and adjusting their awards accordingly.

8. Trivial injuries are usually not compensable. Thus England requires three weeks loss of earnings; New York an out of pocket loss (e.g., for medical expenses) of not less than $100 or a two week loss of earnings; Maryland and Massachusetts a two week loss of earnings; California, Hawaii, and Nevada no minimum, with all three states discouraging trivial injury claims.

9. In England, Massachusetts, and Hawaii no showing of need is required in making a claim. But California, Maryland, Nevada, and New York direct that need be taken into account in determining both eligibility for an award and the extent of compensation awarded.

10. Maximum permissible compensation to a crime victim is difficult to determine in some jurisdictions, and in others it has already been increased by legislative actions since the original compensation laws went into effect. The Federal Victim Compensation Act ... sets the upper limit of compensation at $50,000 per victim, a far more generous maximum than is permitted by any of the other compensation laws; Nevada and California, for example, have $5,000 limits; New Jersey and Hawaii set the top payment at $10,000; New York allows up to $15,000 for loss of earnings but sets no limit for medical expenses (and has indeed made awards for medical expenses as high as $15,000 in at least one case); Maryland ties its allowances to the schedules in its state workmen's compensation law; England has no maximum in its law but in practice awards have been well below the more generous of the American maximum compensation payments.

11. Each of the laws set forth criteria for determining the amount of compensation, usually limiting repayment to actual out of pocket losses (including medical expenses, loss of earnings, loss of support for dependents of deceased victims). Hawaii permits consideration of "pain and suffering" but specifically excludes payment for "loss of happiness" and also for "punitive damages." (pp. 225–227)

Experience with the administration and implementation of victim compensation statutes over the past several years has revealed a number of problems inherent in such legislation and its effective implementation. Among the major difficulties encountered have been: fraudulent claims and attempts at multiple recoveries; questionable awards in some cases, which violate either the statute itself or the criteria for eligibility; inflated bills for medical expenses submitted by physicians, hospitals, and pharmacies; the failure of those who have submitted applications for compensation to receive any awards; and the tendency in nearly all jurisdictions for bureaucratic red tape and long delays to discourage applicants.

MacNamara and Sullivan feel that despite the difficulties encountered with victim compensation statutes there is "great potential in a *mandatory crime victims insurance scheme*, modeled perhaps on a combined social security-workman's compensation amalgam which would discharge the state's obligation to the victims of crime much more generously and much more generally" (p. 229) than can be expected under the systems we have mentioned.

Michael Fooner (1974) has sounded a note of caution with regard to victim compensation legislation. As the author of a previous paper (1962) on the kind of carelessness that invites crime — keeping cash, jewelry, and valuables at home or in hotel rooms to which burglars have easy access, leaving an automobile or its contents invitingly accessible to thieves — Fooner is concerned with the extent to which a particular proposal for victim compensation might contribute to a "temptation/opportunity pattern" in criminal behavior. Fooner states that when victim behavior follows a temptation/opportunity pattern, it: (1) contributes to a "climate of criminal inducements"; (2) adds to the economic resources available to criminal societies; and (3) detracts from the ability of law enforcement agencies to suppress the growth of crime. He maintains that if society is to assume responsibility for making the victim whole, it should also require victim behavior that will diminish temptation/opportunity situations for offenders. He suggests that legislative provisions might make victim compensation contingent upon actions not contributory to the crime; he also supports the use of educational programs on citizen defenses against criminality.

DELIVERY SYSTEMS FOR VICTIM SERVICES

In response to the growing public concern for the plight of the victims of criminal offenses, a variety of programs have been developed within recent years to provide victim services. Such programs are addressed to both immediate and long-term goals: They range from the use of crisis intervention techniques by police officers in the emergency treatment of victims of violent crime to the mobilization of community support for crime prevention activities. An extremely interesting proposal made by Dussich (1973) is to provide a community with an *ombudsman*, who would assist victims of crime by intervening in the crisis and acting as a community facilitator for directing the victim to the community's resources. These programs and proposals might be construed as examples of the general tendency toward institutionalizing and formalizing the kind of community support and ameliorative actions that were supplied informally by neighborhood residents at an earlier period in our history.

Dussich (1975) has conducted a thorough analysis of victim service models and their efficacy, and the following discussion draws heavily upon his account. In analyzing these programs, Dussich focuses upon the model or structure they employ and their various objectives or functions, which he categorizes as *primary* or *secondary*.

The primary function of most models is to deliver a broad range of services to crime victims on behalf of the respective agencies that operate as hosts for the programs. These services include the following:

> 1. Assuming immediate responsibility for the victim at the crime scene
> 2. Referring and/or transporting the victim to emergency medical or social service facilities
> 3. Providing the victim with a companion during the period immediately following the crime
> 4. Addressing the victim's family situation
> 5. Protecting the victim from unnecessary exploitation from the media, police, and courts
> 6. Thorough follow-up procedures and assurance of adequate delivery of public assistance services to victims
> 7. Assisting victims with their responsibilities to the court as key witnesses
> 8. Counseling the victims to prevent revictimization
> 9. Utilizing victim contact information in community crime prevention planning
> 10. Developing public awareness programs aimed at target-hardening, i.e., making more specific and concrete the goals to be sought in victim-oriented services.
> 11. Coordination of victim volunteer programs to supplement existing manpower needs

12. Assisting the families of victims with aftermath arrangements, e.g., insurance, funerals, compensations

13. Conducting victimization surveys to help pinpoint high victimization areas in need of attention

14. Providing the victim with information about the progress of the case and his role and responsibilities in that process

15. Institutionalizing community victim awareness

Secondary functions include a variety of objectives or services that are unique to various models. These include such objectives as encouraging victims to report crimes to the police and gathering information from victims that would assist in police crime prevention efforts — functions specific to the police model; as well as notifying victims who are witnesses as to when they must appear in court and help them to adjust their schedules to the court's schedule, in the case of the district attorney model. There are some secondary functions appropriate to all models, such as maintaining a hotline for crime victims who are in need of immediate help or providing victims with a community services directory listing key resources available.

Dussich notes that victim services programs may be located administratively within a police agency, the office of the public prosecutor, a hospital, or various other agencies, including the office of the county manager, a religious mission, a private agency, or a volunteer agency. The advantages of administrative placement of the victim services program are inseparable from the other characteristics and principal objectives of the agency. Says Dussich, "The phenomenon of manifest self-interest occurs in all models. The host agency, in large part, determines *what* the priorities are, and *how* they will be carried out" (p. 7). Thus, programs located within a police agency offer the advantages of quicker referral for victims, while they suffer from the fact that many victims shun anything associated with the police and are likely to refuse services from this source. Similarly, programs located within the office of the public prosecutor gain from identification with the prestige and authority of the judicial process; but on the other hand, the tendency of the prosecution to place greater stress on the victim as a witness rather than as a victim and the lack of operational closeness to immediate referral services that programs within police departments enjoy constitute definite disadvantages.

Among the other models identified by Dussich, the religious mission is a ready-made "caring agency, which is already staffed and funded, and offers distinct advantages with respect to the dedication of its personnel and acceptance within the community. Private agencies of various kinds usually enjoy greater flexibility in the delivery of services than do programs which are publicly funded. Unfortunately, such programs are apt to suffer from difficulties in obtaining access into the criminal justice system and process. Referrals to these programs . . . are made reluctantly and subsequent referrals made by the program to other community resources are given low priority" (p. 9). Despite community support, abundant manpower, and a high-level of motivation and enthusiasm among the volunteer participants, volunteer programs likewise suffer the disadvantage of being outside the formal criminal justice system. Like the private agency, they are extremely restricted in their ability to effect a lasting change within the system.

The value of any program, Dussich observes, is measured by its ability to deliver services to its clients. He identifies the two most relevant functions of a victim services program to be victim restoration and crime reduction. With respect to victim restoration, the three most obvious factors are physical recuperation from an assault, emotional readjustment from the trauma associated with the crime, and improvement of living conditions altered by the victimization. In terms of crime reduction, target areas include increased reporting of crime, increased offender conviction, increased offender responsibility, and crime prevention. Dussich remarks that the specialized handling of these services is developing into a new profession: victim advocacy. The main mission of the victim advocate is to "address the plight of victims locally and generate new techniques, strategies, and systems for humanizing the way victims are dealt with by the criminal justice system" (p. 1). His belief that the role of victim advocate must be legitimized and institutionalized is perhaps best exemplified by his proposal for the establishment of a victim ombudsman in the community. It is abundantly clear from Dussich's review of victim service models that the variety of services required by victims cannot be encompassed by the organizational structure and operations of any single public or private agency. We will probably witness a period of experimentation, of trial and error, during which victim service models and programs will be judged in terms of their efficacy and results. In any event, one might predict that the result will be a number of programs located in various host agencies within the public and private sectors, supported by both private and federal funding.

VICTIMIZATION SURVEYS

We pointed out earlier that nearly 40 years ago, Benjamin Mendelsohn constructed a questionnaire with more than 300 items, which he administered to his clients as a source of information about victims of crime. Subsequent research on the victim has made extensive use of interviews with *known* victims of crime, as well as police and court data when they are available. The problem with research on known victims is that much more crime is committed than is reported by victims and finally appears in official documentary sources. We have already mentioned (Chapter 2) the survey carried out by the National Opinion Research Center (NORC) for the President's Commission on Law Enforcement and Administration of Justice. A much-publicized finding of this survey was that more than twice as much major crime was reported by victims to the survey interviewers than had been reported to the police and tabulated in the *Uniform Crime Reports*.

Victim survey research was, and continues to be, considered an important supplement to the measurement of crime in a given area by tabulating the crimes reported to the police. According to Daniel Glaser (1970), this method of obtaining data, "by asking a representative sample of the population whether they had suffered from any of the various types of crimes in a recent period, provides a new type of evidence on the volume of crime" (p. 136). In addition to providing new ways of testing hypotheses derived from criminological theory, Glaser believes that victim survey research may be more important as a possible basis for theory and research on agencies of social control. Perhaps the best description of victim survey research is provided by the United States Department of Justice publication *Criminal Victimization Surveys in 13 American Cities* (1976):

> The National Crime Panel is a program designed to develop information not otherwise available on the nature of crime and its impact on society by means of victimization surveys of the general population. Within each locality surveyed, samplings are made of households and commercial establishments representative of the area in order to elicit information about experiences, if any, with selected crimes of violence and theft, including events that were reported to the police as well as those that were not. By focusing on the victim, the person likely to be most aware of details concerning criminal events, the surveys generate a variety of data, including information on the circumstances under which such acts occurred and on their effect. (p. 1)

Information gathered by this technique is expected to aid criminal justice authorities in their tasks of planning, analysis, and evaluation by supplying new insights into crime and its victims.

It is also expected to contribute to the achievement of the following goals:

> 1. To furnish a means for developing victim typologies
> 2. To provide data necessary to compute the relative risk of being victimized for identifiable sectors of society
> 3. To distinguish between stranger-to-stranger violence and domestic violence, and between armed and strong-arm assaults and robberies
> 4. To tally some of the costs of crime in terms of injury and/or economic loss sustained
> 5. To provide greater understanding of why certain criminal acts are not reported to the police

If victimization surveys are conducted periodically in the same area, they can supply information that can lead to the development of indicators sensitive to fluctuations in crime levels. And if they are carried out under the same procedures in different locales, they can provide the means for a comparison of the crime situation in two or more areas.

Victim surveys are not without their limitations. Not all types of crime can be satisfactorily investigated with this technique. As the United States Department of Justice publication *Crime and Victims* (1974) acknowledges:

> *Victimization surveys are most successful in measuring those crimes with specific victims who understand what happened to them and how it happened and who are willing to report what they know. This definition excludes so-called "victimless" crimes such as drunkenness, drug abuse, prostitution, and gambling. It also excludes crimes without specific victims, such as income tax evasion. Crimes of which the victim may not be aware also cannot be measured. Some attempted crimes fall into this category, as do some cases of fraud and embezzlement. Finally, crimes in which the victim himself has shown a willingness to participate in an illegal or questionable activity are not likely to be reported. Various types of swindles, con games, and blackmail are examples.* (p. 3)

Nevertheless, victimization surveys provide valuable information that is not available from any other source. Perhaps of greatest importance, they supply the means to study the victim himself:

> *Are some people more likely to become victims than others? Are persons who have once been victims of a crime more likely to*

*become victims again if they had never had the first experi-
ence? Do the victims of one type of crime differ from victims of
another type of crime? If so, how? Victimization surveys make it
possible to study the personal as well as the social and economic
characteristics of the victim.* (United States Department of
Justice, 1974, pp. 3–4)

Major Findings of Victimization Surveys

In addition to the NORC survey of 10,000 households, the
President's Commission's *Task Force Report: Crime and Its
Impact — An Assessment* (1967) contained the results of two
other victimization surveys. One of these was a pilot study of four
precincts in the District of Columbia; the other was an investigation of high and low crime rate areas in the cities of Chicago and
Boston.

The Washington, D.C., study covered only about 500 households and was chiefly concerned with problems of methodology.
As compared with an estimate of 10 per cent based on police
(*Uniform Crime Reports*) statistics, 38 per cent of the population surveyed had been victims of a serious crime within the year.
For every type of serious crime, the figure was considerably larger
in Washington, D.C., than in the United States as a hole. According to Hood and Sparks (1974):

> *This reflected the finding in the national survey that the rate
> of victimization was very much higher in the metropolitan cen-
> ters than in small cities and rural areas. In addition, there are
> good reasons for believing the methodology of the Washington
> study was better adapted for gaining reports of victimization.*
> (p. 164)*

Figure 11–1 shows that there was more than 5 times as much
serious crime in Washington, D.C., as was known to the police, and
in the case of serious larceny ($50 and over) the rate was 15 times
the *UCR* rate. Only about 7 per cent of the actual crime volume
was officially known.

It is difficult to make an accurate interpretation of the figures
given for Chicago because the survey happened to coincide with
the occurrence of a riot. In the two Boston precincts where respondents were asked about crimes committed against them in a

---

*Reprinted by permission of the publisher, from *Victimology* by Israel
Drapkin and Emilio Viano (Lexington, Mass.: Lexington Books, D. C. Heath
and Company, 1974).

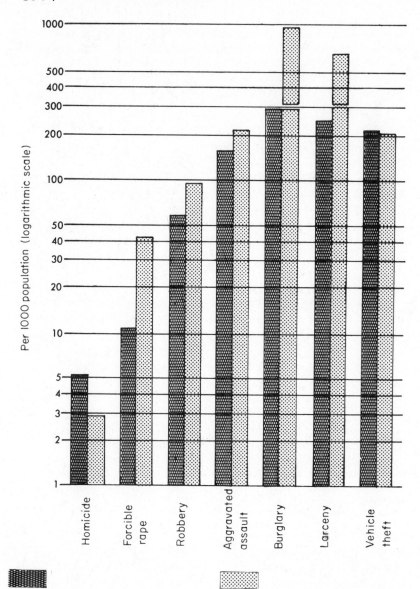

Per 1000 population (logarithmic scale)

Homicide — Forcible rape — Robbery — Aggravated assault — Burglary — Larceny — Vehicle theft

Official (Uniform) Crime Reports, calculated so as to be comparable with the survey data

Estimates derived from a survey of a national sample of households conducted for the President's Commission

Figure 11-1. Rates of serious crimes in the United States, 1965: comparison of official statistics and survey estimates. (From Hood, R., and Sparks, R., Citizens' attitudes and police practice in reporting offenses. Reprinted by permission of the publisher, from *Victimology* by Israel Drapkin and Emilio Viano (Lexington, Mass.: Lexington Books, D. C. Heath and Company, 1974, p. 165).

period of one year from July, 1965, to July 1966, results indicated there were five and three times as much crime, respectively.

A later victimization survey was carried out in the cities of Dayton, Ohio, and San Jose, California. According to the results of this study (United States Department of Justice, 1974) (Table 11-1), 16,000 persons 16 years of age or older in Dayton and 28,000 persons 16 or older in San Jose were victims of

TABLE 11-1. SELECTED CHARACTERISTICS OF PERSONS VICTIMIZED BY CRIME IN DAYTON, OHIO, AND SAN JOSE, CALIFORNIA (1970)*

	DAYTON	SAN JOSE
Total† number of persons victimized	16,310	28,290
Assault victims‡	12,230	22,190
Robbery victims	3,180	4,890
Personal larceny victims	1,690	2,330
Women as per cent of:		
Assault victims‡	31	34
Robbery victims	36	34
Personal larceny victims	49	30
Young men between 16 and 24 as a per cent of:		
Assault victims‡	40	32
Robbery victims	22	37
Personal larceny victims	19	33
Minority group members § as a per cent of:		
Assault victims	13	10
Robbery victims	27	12
Personal larceny victims	26	7
Low-income area residents as a per cent of:		
Assault victims‡	13	13
Robbery victims	38	21
Personal larceny victims	31	18

*From United States Department of Justice: *Crime and Victims: A Report on the Dayton-San Jose Pilot Survey of Victimization*. Washington, D.C., U. S. Government Printing Office, 1974, p. 19. Reproduced by permission of the United States Department of Justice.

†Numbers do not add to total because of persons who were victims of more than one type of crime.

‡Includes persons who reported they were victims of rape.

§Dayton figures are for black persons; San Jose figures are for persons of Spanish origin or descent.

assault, robbery, or personal larceny at least once during the year 1970. Roughly 75 per cent of the victimized people in both cities were victims of assault, more than 15 per cent were victims of robbery, and 10 per cent were victims of personal larceny. The crimes of robbery and personal larceny were nearly always carried out by strangers; the victims of assault were acquainted with their assailants in about half the cases. Approximately 70 per cent of victims in both cities were victimized by strangers.

The data collected in this victimization survey support the following conclusions about the characteristics of the victims:

> In both cities men were twice as likely to be victims of crime [as] women, and the very young were much more likely to be victims of crime than the very old. In both cities persons married and living with their spouses were much less likely to be victims of crime than the unmarried or the separated, divorced or widowed. The high rates for the unmarried are another manifestation of the rates for youth and young adults. In view of the extremely low rates for the elderly, the high victimization rates for the separated, divorced, or widowed probably reflect the situation for the separated and the divorced more than for the widowed. (United States Department of Justice, 1974, p. 21)

The high victimization rates for both young persons and males were seen as a reflection of the tendency for youths and young men to be victims of assault, especially attempted assault by strangers. The figures for robbery, on the other hand, show no substantial difference between the young and the elderly.

One of the more interesting findings of this study was that women and older persons are *less* likely to become victims of crime than are young men. This finding contrasts sharply with the widespread belief among both women and the elderly that they are especially vulnerable to crime. Such beliefs influence them to avoid places where there may be a high risk of crime (e.g., unlighted parking lots, deserted streets late at night). On the other hand, according to the authors of the report:

> [Y]ouths and young men may feel that any attempt to avoid potentially hazardous situations might appear to be an admission of lack of bravery. Furthermore, the behavior patterns and social habits of young men may produce a large number of situations especially conducive to the eruption of the assault incident. Whether some or all of these influences are at work, they indicate that the victimization rate for any segment of the population is the net effect of their vulnerability and the efforts they make to minimize that vulnerability. (p. 21)

A comprehensive victimization survey of 60,000 households and 15,000 businesses was reported in May, 1975, by the United States Department of Justice (1975a). This National Crime Panel publication incorporates data obtained in 1973 from 50 states and the District of Columbia and represents an effort to measure the extent of victimization among persons 12 years of age and over, households, and commercial establishments. It also attempts to study the nature and character of criminal incidents and their victims.

In 1973, selected crimes of violence and common theft in the United States resulted in 37 million victimizations (including attempts) involving individuals, households, and businesses. The victimizations were distributed according to the data in Table 11-2. Personal larceny was the most prevalent type of crime, while other crimes involving some type of violence or threat of violence accounted for about 15 per cent of the total.

An important aspect of personal crime is whether the victim and offender are acquainted. In a significant percentage of homicide cases, for example, the victim and perpetrator are well known or even related to one another. Less is known about victim-

TABLE 11-2. PER CENT DISTRIBUTION OF VICTIMIZATIONS
BY TYPE OF CRIME*

TYPE OF CRIME	PER CENT
All crimes	100.0
Crimes against persons	54.9
Rape	0.4
Robbery	3.0
Assault	11.2
Personal larceny†	40.3
Crimes against households	40.8
Burglary	17.1
Household larceny†	20.2
Motor vehicle theft	3.5
Crimes against businesses	4.4
Burglary	3.7
Robbery	0.7

*United States Department of Justice: *Criminal Victimization in the United States, 1973 Advance Report*. Washington, D.C., U. S. Government Printing Office, 1975, p. 1. Reproduced by permission of the United States Department of Justice.

†Personal larceny refers to the theft or attempted theft of property or cash with or without contact between victim and offender, but without force or the threat of force. Household larceny refers to theft or attempted theft of property or cash from the home (involving neither forcible nor unlawful entry) or its immediate vicinity.

TABLE 11-3. PROPORTION OF VIOLENT CRIMES INVOLVING
STRANGERS*

CRIME	PER CENT
All crimes	66
Rape	75
Robbery	86
Assault	60

*United States Department of Justice: *Criminal Victimization in the United States, 1973 Advance Report.* Washington, D.C., U. S. Government Printing Office, 1975, p. 3. Reproduced by permission of the United States Department of Justice.

offender relationships in the three crimes of violence (rape, robbery, and assault) measured by the National Crime Panel. Table 11-3 indicates that about two-thirds of all personal crimes of violence involved a confrontation between strangers. Lacking a previous data point as a basis for comparison, there is no way of gauging whether this finding represents a marked increase in victim risk involving strangers, but it certainly challenges the popular belief that crimes of violence are still essentially "crimes of intimacy."

An analysis of victimization rates from the National Crime Panel survey yielded significant differences with respect to certain selected personal characteristics:

1. Males were more likely than females to have been victimized by personal crimes
2. Black males had a higher victimization rate than white males
3. There were no significant differences between white and black females in overall personal victimization
4. Blacks were more likely to have been victims of rape, robbery, and assault, whereas whites were more likely to have been victims of personal larceny
5. Black males were more likely than white males to have been victims of aggravated assault, while white males had a higher victimization rate for simple assault.

With regard to age, the National Crime Panel data tended to support previous findings that place the highest victimization rates in the lowest age range. Twenty-five appears to mark a significant dividing line in crimes of violence: beyond this age, there is a sharp decrement in such crimes as assault.

Marital status and income level also affect victimization rates. Single persons and those who are separated or divorced had the highest rates of victimization, and lower-income blacks and whites were both highly vulnerable to victimization.

Critique

Before concluding this brief review of crime victimization surveys, we would like to make a few observations on the methods employed in such studies and the kinds of problems apt to be encountered by the researcher. As in the case of most field survey studies, many of the methodological problems in victimization research have centered on the matter of sampling. In the NORC survey and in the studies conducted in Washington, D.C., Boston, and Chicago, more than a quarter of those who were approached refused to be interviewed, thus introducing an immediate bias into the sample. The NORC survey questioned any adult over 18 in the household, asked first about offenses committed against him or her personally and then about those committed against others in the household. According to Hood and Sparks (1974):

> This method produced an over-representation of older persons and women in the sample (as they are more likely to be at home). The two other surveys therefore chose at random the adults to be interviewed so as to get a more representative sample of the household. But whichever method is used there is still the problem of estimating the accuracy of the information given by the respondent about other members of his household. In all three studies there was a suspiciously large difference between the number of incidences reported by the respondent about himself and those concerning others. In the national sample, it was estimated that the amount of crime committed against Negro families uncovered by the survey was only half of the actual amount of victimization. It was especially felt that reports would be less well known by respondents and therefore in the two city surveys all acts which had been committed against those under 18 years where not taken into consideration. (p. 167)*

An additional problem was the lack of comparability of survey data and police statistics. The limited range of offenses covered in

---

*Reprinted by permission of the publisher, from *Victimology* by Israel Drapkin and Emilio Viano (Lexington, Mass.: Lexington Books, D. C. Heath and Company, 1974).

the surveys, the age range of the respondents, and other differences meant that, at best, comparisons between survey findings and police data were in the nature of estimates, with an uncertain margin of error.

The reliability and validity of all survey data are, of course, contingent upon the truthfulness of the respondents. Deliberate falsification or fabrication of events is less of a problem in survey research than are problems involving the imperfect operation of memory. A good example of the extent to which forgetfulness on the part of the respondent can drastically affect victimization research is cited by Hood and Sparks (1974). In an effort to check the amount of under-reporting that occurred in Boston and Chicago, a record was made of all incidents in which citizens called the police over a specified period of time. Several months later, a sample of these citizens were interviewed. The authors note that more than a fifth of the respondents failed to mention the experience that had been recorded by the investigators! Hood and Sparks conclude that the most satisfactory victimization study would be one in which "a very large sample of the population was asked about incidents which occurred in a period of not more than three months before the interview date" (p. 170).

With all due regard for the importance of forgetfulness, the inadequacies of memory cannot account for the consistent finding from victimization studies that all crimes, including those considered to be the most serious (robbery, aggravated assault, forcible rape) are under-represented in police statistics to a substantial degree. In the studies we have reviewed here, respondents were asked whether the offense committed against them had been reported to the police, and if not, why not. The professional literature in criminology, as Hood and Sparks have noted, abounds with commonsense assumptions about factors that inhibit the reporting of crime:

> To begin with, behavior may not be perceived as "crime" by the victim or other witnesses. Where lies the difference between unsolicited sexual familiarity and indecent assault? When is a "lost wallet" assumed to be stolen? Is a stock shrinkage of 50 hair combs due to theft, and if so due to 50 thefts or one? Secondly, the victim may know that a crime has been committed, but still not report it. He may have sympathy for the offender — a relative for example; he may dislike or distrust the police and the courts; he may live in a community where it would be deviant to report a crime — where, for example, if one is hurt in a fight the consequence must be suffered in silence; he may fear reprisals or regard the harm done as too trivial in relation to the consequences for the offender of a conviction; he may fear that his own deviant

activity will be exposed (this, for example, is assumed to apply to the victims of theft by prostitutes and their pimps); and there are numerous other possibilities. Behavior regarded as criminal by the police may not be so regarded by those involved. This is especially thought to be true of offenses such as violence committed in working class areas and taking small amounts of material from work . . . . (pp. 170–171)*

The victimization studies cited shed further light on the reasons for not reporting crime. More than half of the respondents in these studies felt that nothing would be achieved by reporting the crime to the police. With the exception of criminal homicide, the only offense for which there was anything approaching reliable reports was automobile theft, presumably because of the possibility of claiming insurance benefits.

THE BYSTANDER

If it is fair to say that the victim of crime has been largely ignored in criminological research, it would be equally fair to say that the bystander has been totally ignored. Criminological interest in the bystander was dramatically aroused as a consequence of a tragedy that occurred in 1964. In the early morning hours of March 13, 1964, a young woman named Catherine Genovese was stabbed to death in front of her apartment in a middle class neighborhood in the Queens section of New York City. Thirty-eight of her neighbors admitted to having witnessed at least a part of the attack, but none of them went to her aid or even called the police until after she was dead. As Rosenthal (1964) observed, most of the witnesses were "neither defiant nor terribly embarrassed nor particularly ashamed. The underlying attitude, or explanation, seemed to be fear of involvement of any kind" (pp. 78–79). They responded with such statements as "I was tired," "We thought it was a lover's quarrel," "I didn't want my husband to get involved," and "I don't know."

The publicity surrounding the murder and the inaction of the witnesses provoked speculation, lay and professional, on the motives of the thirty-eight and the significance of the incident. The obvious question, "Why didn't someone help?" was asked repeatedly. Milgram and Hollander (1970) asked the more searching question: "Why should they?" Why should anyone have taken the trouble to go to the aid of the victim or even call the police?

---

*Reprinted by permission of the publisher, from *Victimology* by Israel Drapkin and Emilio Vanio (Lexington, Mass.: Lexington Books, D. C. Heath and Company, 1974).

A number of social conditions that characterize urban industrial life set up barriers to bystander action. First, most interaction
in modern society is on an impersonal rather than a personal level;
thus, for most people to respond positively to another's plight
requires an expression of care and concern that is atypical of the
way in which they respond in most situtations. In addition, the
middle class is not socialized to deal with or use violence, even
when it seems called for or justified by the circumstances. Furthermore, within a highly specialized society such as ours, extraordinary
situations are assumed to be the concern of specialists — in this
case the police. However, in many instances people even fail to
summon the police. This has been attributed to: (1) bystanders'
reluctance to get involved in situations in which they have no
personal responsibility or authority and which may cause them
embarrassment, resentment, delay, and possibly physical danger of
reprisal (McCall, 1975); (2) their belief that the police have already been notified; and (3) their feeling that the police would be
unable to do anything.

Latané and Darley (1970) have studied the circumstances
under which bystanders will take action to aid a victim. They indicate that the intervention process involves a sequence of five
decisions: (1) the bystander must notice that something is happen-
ing; (2) he must interpret the event as an emergency; (3) he must
assume some degree of personal responsibility for helping; (4) he
must decide on the appropriate form of assistance to be given; and
(5) he must implement the decision to intervene. McCall (1975)
maintains that the most critical factor in bystander response is
the assumption of some degree of personal responsibility for helping. Research has indicated that the assumption of such responsibility is inversely related to the number of persons present in the
situation (Latané and Darley, 1970). That is, the more persons
who witness a situation the less likely it is that any one of them
will act to assist a victim. Latané and Darley suggest four reasons
why this occurs:

*1. Others serve as an audience to one's action, inhibiting
[one] from doing foolish things*
*2. Others serve as guides to behavior and if they are inactive
they will lead the [bystander] to be inactive also*
*3. The interactive effect of these two processes will be much
greater than either alone; if each bystander sees other bystanders
momentarily frozen by audience inhibition, each may be misled
into thinking that the situation must not be serious*
*4. The presence of other people dilutes the responsibility
felt by any single bystander, making him feel that it is less necessary for himself to act (this has been referred to as diffusion of
blame or responsibility). (p. 125)*

Bystander Response and the Law

Conklin (1975) points out that our system of law in the United States does not generally require the witness to an emergency to help a victim whose predicament was not caused by the witness himself. In fact, says Conklin, "Anglo-American law warns witnesses that they face certain risks if they try to help a victim and fail; sometimes they may be sued for harming the victim as a result of errors they commit during their rescue attempt. Our legal system thus discourages bystander aid to victims" (p. 217).* In certain countries, such as France and Germany, affirmative action by witnesses is required by the law under certain conditions. Not only does American law fail to require assistance by witnesses in emergencies, but it also offers no incentives to help a victim, such as government compensation for injuries sustained in the rescue attempt. Moreover, in its failure to protect the well intentioned rescuer from a civil suit by a victim or his dependents, the law actually discourages altruistic behavior on the part of the prospective helper. Fear of possible legal repercussions can inhibit willingness to help even in situations in which there is no threat of physical injury.

Conklin points out some of the obstacles to enactment of Good Samaritan legislation, beginning with the lack of any organized interest group to lobby for passage of such a law. Part of the problem seems to involve the thorough acceptance by the public of the police as crime fighting specialists, and a massive selling job would be required for the public to accept the fact that, despite their status as specialists, the police require a great deal of public cooperation in order to function effectively. There is the additional problem that specialists — police, physicians, firefighters — tend to be critical of amateurish attempts by citizens to render aid in emergencies.

Despite these and other problems, Conklin places a great emphasis on the importance of Good Samaritan legislation:*

> Knowing that people are not legally obligated to help victims or to intervene in a crime may make potential offenders more likely to commit a crime. This will reinforce public fears and make Good Samaritan laws even more difficult to pass. Still, the absence of such laws is not the major reason that people do not respond to victims in distress, although such laws might occasionally influence behavior. The presence of a law, even if unenforced and lacking strong impact on behavior, might create confidence that others would help. This could increase social solidarity and make people more willing to walk the streets at night because the feeling that they could depend on others to

help in an emergency. This view might be inaccurate, but it still could be self-fulfilling if it led people to spend more time on the street, since potential criminals might be less willing to commit crimes in the sight of others. For such an effect to occur, a potential offender would have to feel that there was some chance of being interfered with or reported to the police by witnesses. (pp. 222–223)*

Until or unless the behavior of people in public places is supported by such legislation, the observation made by Alan Barth (Ratcliffe, 1966) seems especially appropriate:

> *Let us bear in mind . . . that the original Good Samaritan extolled by St. Luke was fortunate in not arriving on the scene until after the thieves had set upon the traveler, robbed him, and beaten him half to death. The Samaritan cared for him and showed him great kindness, but did not put himself in peril by doing so. Perhaps this is about as much as can be reasonably asked of the ordinary mortal man.* (p. 163)

SUMMARY

The victim of crime and his relationship with the criminal were briefly explored in this chapter. Beginning with an historical sketch of the ways in which various societies in the past have dealt with the victim of crime, the pioneering work of Hentig and Mendelsohn in the development of victim typologies was discussed and some consideration was given to the issue of victim compensation and restitution. Models for the delivery of victim services were also examined briefly. Victimization surveys and their significance for the assessment of crime were treated in some detail, and the chapter concluded with several observations on the bystander who remains a passive witness to someone else's victimization.

REVIEW

Find the answers to the following questions in the text:

1. What were some of the ways in which earlier societies attempted to provide compensation or restitution for victims of crime?

---

*Reprinted with permission of Macmillan Publishing Co., Inc., from *The Impact of Crime* by J. E. Conklin. Copyright © 1975 by John E. Conklin.

2. Discuss Hentig's contributions to victimology. How did he conceptualize the criminal-victim relationship?

3. What was the principal basis for Mendelsohn's classification of victims?

4. Discuss some of the advantages and disadvantages involved in attempting to develop a comprehensive victim typology.

5. How does compensation differ from restitution?

6. What are some of the factors identified by MacNamara and Sullivan that lessen the effectiveness of programs aimed at restitution?

7. Discuss the Minnesota Restitution Center and its approach to victim restitution.

8. What is a victim ombudsman? What are some of the functions such a person would be expected to perform?

9. Identify some of the services that a victim services delivery system might provide for crime victims.

10. How do victimization surveys help to augment our understanding of crime? What are some of the problems encountered in conducting such surveys?

11. Discuss the Catherine Genovese tragedy and identify some of the reasons why people failed to come to her aid.

12. Take a position (pro or con) with respect to Good Samaritan legislation and defend your position.

TERMS TO IDENTIFY AND REMEMBER:

victimology	*faida*	composition
compensation	restitution	*wergilds*
"penal-couple"	*bot*	Good Samaritan laws
typology	victim ombudsman	bystander

REFERENCES

Barth, A.: The Vanishing Samaritan. *In* Ratcliffe, J. M. (ed): *The Good Samaritan and the Law.* Garden City, N. Y., Doubleday & Company, 1966.

Conklin, J. E.: *The Impact of Crime.* New York, Macmillan, Inc., 1975.

Dussich, J. P. J.: The victim ombudsman: a proposal. Unpublished manuscript, Tallahassee, Florida, 1973.

Dussich, J. P. J.: Victim service models and the efficacy. A paper presented to the International Advanced Study Institute on Victimology and the Needs of Contemporary Society. Bellagio, Italy, July 1–12, 1975.

Fattah, E. A.: Toward a ciminological classification of victims. International Criminal Police Review, 1967.

Fooner, M.: The careless American: a study in adventitious criminality. A paper presented at the American Society of Criminology joint annual meeting with the American Association for the Advancement of Science,

Symposium on Psychiatry, Psychology, and Criminology. Philadelphia, December 29, 1962.

Fooner, M.: Victim-induced, victim-invited, and victim-precipitated criminality: some problems in evaluation of proposals for victim compensation. *In* Drapkin, I., and Viano, E. (eds.): *Victimology*. Lexington, Massachusetts, Lexington Books, 1974.

Fry, Margery: *The Arms of the Law*. London, Gollancz, 1951.

Gibbons, D. C.: Offender typologies — two decades later. Unpublished manuscript, Portland State University, 1975.

Glaser, D.: Victim survey research: theoretical implications. *In* Guenther, A. L. (ed.): *Criminal Behavior and Social Systems*. Chicago, Rand McNally & Company, 1970.

Hentig, H. von: *The Criminal and His Victim: Studies in the Sociology of Crime*. New Haven, Yale University Press, 1948.

Hood, R., and Sparks, R.: Citizens' attitudes and police practice in reporting offenses. *In* Drapkin, I., and Viano, E. (eds.): *Victimology*. Lexington, Massachusetts, Lexington Books, 1974.

Latané, B., and Darley, J.: *The Unresponsive Bystander: Why Doesn't He Help?* New York, Appleton-Century-Crofts, 1970.

MacNamara, D. E. J., and Sullivan, J. J.: Composition, restitution, compensation: making the victim whole. *In* Drapkin, I., and Viano, E. (eds.): *Victimology*. Lexington, Massachusetts, Lexington Books, 1974.

McCall, G. J.: *Observing the Law: Application of Field Methods to the Study of the Criminal Justice System*. Rockville, Maryland, National Institute of Mental Health, 1975.

Milgram, S., and Hollander, P.: The murder they heard. *In* Hartogs, R., and Artzt, E. (eds.): *Violence: Causes and Solutions*. New York, Dell Publishing Co., Inc., 1970.

Minnesota Department of Corrections. *The Minnesota Restitution Center*. Minneapolis, State of Minnesota, 1976.

President's Commission on Law Enforcement and Administration of Justice: *Task Force Report: Crime and Its Impact — An Assessment*. Washington, D. C., U. S. Government Printing Office, 1967.

Rosenthal, A. M.: *Thirty-eight Witnesses*. New York, McGraw-Hill Book Co., 1964.

Schafer, S.: *The Victim and His Criminal*. New York, Random House, 1968.

Sellin, T., and Wolfgang, M. E.: *The Measurement of Delinquency*. New York, John Wiley & Sons, Inc., 1964.

Silverman, R. A.: Victim typologies: overview, critique, and reformulation. *In* Drapkin, I., and Viano, E. (eds.): *Victimology*. Lexington, Massachusetts, Lexington Books, 1974.

United States Department of Justice: *Crime and Victims: A Report on the Dayton-San Jose Pilot Survey of Victimization*. Washington, D. C., U. S. Government Printing Office, 1974.

United States Department of Justice: *Criminal Victimization in the United States, 1973 Advance Report*. Washington, D. C., U. S. Government Printing Office, 1975a.

United States Department of Justice: *Criminal Victimization Surveys in 13 American Cities*. Washington, D. C., U. S. Government Printing Office, 1975b.

12 THE IMPACT OF CRIME ON U.S. SOCIETY

In this period of bicentennial celebration, public opinion polls continue to indicate that crime is second only to the state of the economy as a source of concern to a large number of Americans. During the recent past, it was difficult, if not impossible, to separate public anxiety over crime from apprehensions that were fueled by campus violence and urban rioting; but despite the fact that student protest activity and ghetto disturbances have subsided, there is abundant evidence that concern about crime in the United States has not significantly abated.

Is the public justified in its concern over crime? This is a simple question to ask, but it is one that is exceedingly difficult to answer. Social reality is largely what a society believes about itself. If the members of that society believe themselves to be unsafe in their homes, places of work and business, or in public areas, those feelings of insecurity become an essential part of the social reality that shapes people's perceptions. Nevertheless, as Gould (1971) points out, our political representatives and leaders bear the responsibility for helping to place the public's fear into proper perspective.

It was public concern for crime in 1966 and 1967 that helped to create an atmosphere of largely uncritical support for the passage of the Omnibus Crime Control and Safe Streets Act, landmark legislation that institutionalized federal support for the criminal justice system at the local and state levels. An important contribution to the passage of this bill was made by the publication in 1967 of the work of the President's Commission on Law

367

Enforcement and Administration of Justice in the form of a series of task force reports dealing with various aspects of the crime problem and the terminal report of the commission, *The Challenge of Crime in a Free Society*. The opening pages of this publication provided strong reinforcement for the prevalent feeling that the crime problem seemed to be getting completely out of hand. In other sections of the report, particularly in the task force report entitled *Crime and Its Impact — An Assessment* (1967), statements were made that indicated that the commission members felt that public concern about crime was misguided. For instance, the commission noted that "the public fears most the crimes that occur the least — crimes of violence. People are much more tolerant of crimes against property, which constitute most of the crimes that are committed against persons or households or businesses" (p. 88). The commission also stated that "the fear of crime may not be as strongly influenced by the actual instance of crime as it is by other experiences with the crime problem generally" (p. 89). Specifically, the commission was concerned about distorted crime reporting in the mass media.

Despite such reservations, the commission concluded that it was unable to say that "the public's fear of crime is exaggerated. It is not prepared to tell people how fearful they should be: that is something that each person must decide for himself. People's fears must be respected; certainly they cannot be legislated" (p. 88).

Although the commission was unwilling to say that Americans' fears about crime were unfounded, it reminded the readers of the report that the problem of crime is not new to the United States and may even have been worse in years past; and they might also have pointed out that crime is not unique to the United States. However, as Gould (1971) observes, "It is not crime in other nations that Americans are afraid of; they are afraid of crime in their own communities. And they are not concerned with whether crime is more or less prevalent today than it was a century ago; they are worried about whether it is more prevalent now than it was at some earlier point in their own lifetime" (p. 84). One simply has to believe that the members of the commission were aware of these concerns. In attempting to gauge the impact of crime on contemporary American society, it seems rather pointless, in our opinion, to search through history in order to show that the past decade was not the most lawless or violent in our national history or to provide historical documentation to show that crime waves are nothing new, that crime and violence, as well as public concern over crime and violence, rise and fall with regularity. Says Conklin (1975):

> *When there is a crime wave, people change their behavior to*
> *protect themselves, their families, and their property from the*
> *depredations of criminals. They feel like "hunted animals" and*
> *are "curfewed by their own fear." Sometimes, "in the daily*
> *lives of many citizens the fear of crime takes an even greater*
> *toll than crime itself." (p. 3)**

When communities respond to the crime threat by seeking refuge behind dead bolts, German Shepherds, electronic alarm systems, closed circuit television cameras, and security guards, these reactions constitute part of the indirect costs of crime. The direct costs of crime are measured in terms of dollars lost, injuries suffered, and lives taken. In the following pages, we will discuss the impact of crime on American society in terms of both direct and indirect costs. Our account will necessarily be impressionistic; no individual, professional group, or governmental body can provide exact figures on the toll exacted by the depredations of crime on our society. The best we can do is to try to make our estimates as realistic as possible.

THE ECONOMIC IMPACT OF CRIME

The most comprehensive and authoritative attempt to assess the economic impact of crime on our society was made by the President's Commission on Law Enforcement and the Administration of Justice in its *Task Force Report: Crime and Its Impact — An Assessment* (1967). In presenting its overall assessment, the commission was under no illusions concerning the accuracy of its figures. However, the members of the commission believed that whatever was lost in terms of absolute value was more than made up in the relative value of their estimates, as they expressed in the following rationale:

> *Risks and responses cannot be judged with maximum effec-*
> *tiveness until the full extent of economic loss has been ascer-*
> *tained. Researchers, policy makers, and operating agencies should*
> *know which crimes cause the greatest economic loss, which the*
> *least; on whom the costs of crime falls, and what the costs are to*
> *prevent or protect against it; whether a particular or general crime*
> *situation warrants further expenditures for control or prevention*
> *and, if so, what expenditures are likely to have the greatest im-*
> *pact. The number of policemen, the size of a plant security staff,*
> *or the amount of insurance an individual or business carries are*

*Reprinted with permission of Macmillan Publishing Co., Inc., from *The Impact of Crime* by J. E. Conklin. Copyright © 1975 by John E. Conklin.

controlled to some extent by economics — the balance of the value to be gained against the burden of additional expenditure. If the protection of property is the objective, the economic loss from crime must be weighted directly against the cost of better prevention or control. (p. 42)

In assembling its estimates, the commission made use of a variety of available information sources: police agencies, insurance companies, industrial security firms, trade associations, books, newspapers, and scholarly journals. It also relied upon the National Opinion Research Center (NORC) survey of 10,000 households, which reported sizable losses to individuals. The commission reported its conclusions in terms of six different categories of economic impact in both the private and public sector, as shown in Figure 12–1. The commission emphasizes that the totals given in Figure 12–1 should be taken to indicate "rough orders of magnitude rather than precise figures" (p. 43).

The total dollar figure for the six categories of economic impact in Figure 12–1 is $26,261,000,000. We might put this figure into perspective by noting that it exceeds by several billion dollars the total cost of the Apollo space program with its series of successful lunar flights; that it is roughly eight times the total foreign aid expenditure in any given year; and that it amounts to somewhere between a quarter and a fifth of our total defense budget for the year 1976.

Apart from their shock value in terms of sheer magnitude, these cost information figures are extremely interesting because they convey a picture of crime that is considerably different from that given by statistics on the number of offenses known to the police or the number of arrests:

1. Organized crime takes nearly twice as much income from gambling and other illegal goods and services as criminals derive from all other kinds of criminal activity combined.

2. Unreported commercial theft losses, including shoplifting and employee theft, are more than double those of all reported private and commercial thefts.

3. Of the reported crimes, willful homicide, though comparatively low in volume, yields the most costly estimates among those listed on the UCR Crime Index.

4. A list of the seven crimes with the greatest economic impact includes only two, willful homicide and larceny of $50 and over (reported and unreported), of the offenses included in the Crime Index.

5. Only a small proportion of the money expended for criminal justice agencies is allocated to rehabilitative programs for criminals or for research. (p. 43)

Economic Impact of Crimes and Related Expenditures
(Estimated in Millions of Dollars)

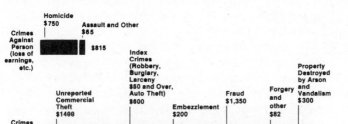

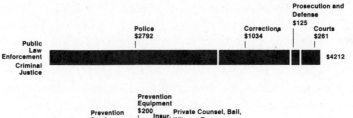

Figure 12–1. Economic Impact of Crimes and Related Expenditures (Estimated in Millions of Dollars). From President's Commission on Law Enforcement and Administration of Justice. *Task Force Report: Crime and Its Impact — An Assessment.* Washington, D. C.: U. S. Government Printing Office, 1967. Page 44, reproduced by permission of the U. S. Department of Justice.

Robbery, burglary, larceny, and auto theft figure prominently in police statistics, but these offenses account for less than one sixth of the total estimated dollar loss for all property crimes. By contrast, embezzlement, employee theft, and other forms of crimes involving business, which appear in relatively small numbers in the police statistics, bulk very large in dollar volume, accounting for most of the more than two billion dollars that businesses annually lose in crimes for which losses can be estimated. The commission estimates that in the grocery trade, shoplifting and employee theft almost equal the total amount of profit, yet fewer than one quarter of these and similar offenses are reported to the police.

Fraud is another offense that is seldom reported to the police. As the commission notes, "Expensive nostrums for incurable diseases, home improvement frauds, frauds involving the sale or repair of cars, and other criminal schemes create losses which are not only sizable in gross but also significant and possibly devastating for individual victims" (p. 43). The poor, the elderly, the infirm, and others living in straitened economic circumstances are among the likeliest victims of fraud.

Crimes Against the Person

The economic toll exacted by the crime of willful homicide is manifold. The victim's family or dependents lose a source of support; the community loses a productive worker; and the local, state, and federal governments are deprived of a source of tax revenue. The 1965 *Uniform Crime Reports* reported approximately 10,000 victims of murder and non-negligent manslaughter. On the basis of the average national wage at that time for persons of the same ages as the victims, the commission estimated the value of the victims' total future earning potential at the time of death as approximately 750 million dollars.*

Other index crimes against the person (assault, robbery, and rape) inflict personal injuries that may result in sizable losses to the individual victims for lost time at work, medical expenses, and other costs. Earning capacity may be permanently impaired in some cases. It has been estimated that some injury may occur in as many as two thirds of all reported index crimes against the

---

*The effects of inflation must be taken into account in considering these figures: Using 1967 as a base year, a 1965 dollar could buy $1.06 worth of goods, while a 1974 dollar could buy only $0.68 worth of goods. It is important to remember that, unless otherwise noted, the dollar estimates of the commission discussed in this chapter are based on 1965 dollars.

person. The commission estimates that if a loss of one week's wages of $100 and medical bills of $250 were assumed for each victim hospitalized and a total loss of $50 was assumed for victims injured but not hospitalized, the total loss for assault and other nonfatal crimes against the person in 1965 would have been approximately 65 million dollars.* It is noteworthy that this figure far exceeds the total amount paid to crime victims under all compensation laws presently in effect in the United States.

Crimes Against Property

When property is destroyed as a result of arson or vandalism, it is no longer part of the overall stock of goods and services available to society. Stolen property, on the other hand, is transferred by theft or other illegal means against the will of the owner to the criminal sector of society but it retains its utility. Thus, although the results may be the same from the victim's point of view, these losses are not alike.

The National Fire Protective Association estimated that arson losses accounted for approximately 74 million dollars out of a total fire property loss of approximately 1.5 million dollars in 1965. This figure excludes approximately 23 million dollars in losses attributable to incendiarism out of the 92 million dollars lost in forest fires in 1965. The United States Forest Service estimated that about one fourth of all forest fires in 1965 were incendiary in origin.

Vandalism, the willful or malicious destruction of property, is a widespread and costly offense for which only a small percentage of offenders are apprehended. Vandalism runs the gamut from offenses committed against individuals, such as breaking off a car aerial, to those directed against businesses and public service institutions. Public schools, transit systems, street lighting systems, and public housing projects all suffer significant losses from vandalism. Losses from glass breakage in public schools alone have been estimated at between four and five million dollars nationally, and vandalism can be so severe in high crime areas that windows are boarded up to prevent breakage. The commission notes that the average loss due to vandalism on housing and construction projects in the City of New York is nearly 30 per cent of construction costs.

Robbery is a confrontation crime that involves the taking of

---

*See footnote on opposite page.

property by force or the threat of force. Using the *Uniform Crime Report* estimates for 1965, the commission arrived at an adjusted figure of 27 million dollars; this figure represented a projected national loss of 30.3 million dollars minus the recovery rate of approximately 11.6 per cent for an average loss of $250 per robbery. The NORC survey of households, on the other hand, arrived at the substantially higher figure of 49.4 million dollars. Even this figure does not convey the full extent of loss from robbery, because 40 per cent of all robberies involved business establishments; since most of these would not have been covered by the survey, the total may have been as high as 60 to 65 million dollars.

Comparable discrepancies may be noted in the total estimates for the crime of burglary. While cost data based on *UCR* figures yielded an adjusted net reported loss of approximately 251 million dollars, the NORC household survey reported a loss of about 313 million dollars for individuals alone.

Larceny, excluding auto theft, is under-reported both for individuals and for businesses. The NORC survey yielded an estimate of 170 million dollars in individual losses alone. If we add to this figure 80 million dollars for business losses based on figures from the *UCR*, we arrive at a figure of 250 million dollars. Once again, this is a conservative estimate.

Business theft may be divided for purposes of convenience into thefts that occur in retail trade and those that involve nonretail business operations. In the case of retail trade, for example, it is difficult to distinguish losses due to shoplifting and losses due to employee dishonesty. As the commission notes:

> Retail firms commonly have a sizable amount of stock shortage or inventory shrinkage that cannot be accounted for by any known cause. Mark-downs, spoilage and other known causes of loss, such as burglary and robbery, are usually accounted for specifically and not included in the inventory shrinkage. The major part of the shrinkage is therefore due to record-keeping errors, shoplifting, employee theft, and embezzlement through stock record manipulation. While there is no reliable way to determine what losses are due to crime and what to error and other causes, the industry commonly estimates that as much as 75 to 80 per cent of all shrinkage is the result of some kind of dishonesty. (p. 48)

These losses are inevitably passed on to the consumer in the form of retail price increases in commodities. What this amounts to, as the commission points out, is in effect a crime tariff totaling more than 1.3 billion dollars annually or approximately 1 to 2 per cent of the value of all retail sales.

Outside the retail industry, the picture is even more obscure. Shrinkage figures for individual wholesale firms may go as high as 1/2 of 1 per cent of sales, with losses totaling in the millions even for a single firm. The transportation industry is especially susceptible to pilferage in the handling and transfer of merchandise. Losses may occur through pilferage at any point in the process, from the waterfront, through the trucking and railroad transfers, to the final destination.

Fraud is regarded by some criminological authorities (e.g., Sutherland and Cressey, 1974) as the most common of all criminal offenses. Although fraud encompasses any method of obtaining money or property through false pretenses (with the exception of forgery or counterfeiting), most of the arrests made for fraud involve the intentional passing of bad checks. Criminal fraud is distinguished from civil fraud on the basis of the extent and seriousness of the fraud, but in both cases, there is willful intent to deceive. Use of the mails for fraudulent purposes is a criminal offense; cheating a customer by delivering goods that are markedly inferior to those specified in a contract would be an example of civil fraud.

Whether or not one agrees with Sutherland and Cressey that fraud is the commonest of all criminal offenses, there can be little doubt that it is a pervasive offense. Fraud in the sale or promotion of securities has been calculated as being in the 75 to 100 million dollar range; the United States Postal Service estimates that mail fraud may run as high as 500 million dollars annually; the Food and Drug Administration reports that health frauds involving mislabeling and false claims concerning durgs and therapeutic devices may run to nearly 500 million dollars per year; on the basis of a survey, the Arthritis Foundation estimates that more than 250 million dollars is spent annually on worthless arthritis remedies alone; and recent studies of fraud involving automobiles indicate that consumers may be bilked of as much as 100 million dollars annually for expensive, unnecessary, or defective repairs. If we add to this list sizable losses to the public from fraudulent solicitations for charity, phoney land promotion schemes, worthless life insurance, fraudulent bankruptcies, improper debt consolidations, home study rackets, and frauds involving credit cards, it is difficult to escape the conclusion that fraud is probably the costliest, if not the commonest, of all crimes.

Other Crimes

Traffic Offenses. The commission cites the National Safety Council estimate that traffic offenses may be involved in as many as 90 per cent of all traffic accidents. Only a few traffic offenses, such as driving under the influence or hit-and-run, are regarded as criminal. While accurate estimate of the economic impact of hit-and-run driving has been made, the losses incurred by alcohol-involved accidents are known to be considerable. In 1965, during which there were 49,000 traffic fatalities and 13.2 million traffic accidents, the National Safety Council estimated that drinking may have been a factor in as many as half of all fatal accidents. The total cost of traffic fatalities and accidents attributed to driving under the influence was estimated by the commission at 1.8 billion dollars, as shown in Table 12–1.

Tax Fraud. Both the intentional failure to pay taxes that are due and the concealment of income for purposes of avoiding the payment of taxes constitute fraud. The President's Commission's *Task Force Report* (1974) states that whether the fraud is civil or criminal depends on the degree of willfulness involved. But as we noted previously with respect to fraud, this distinction is not adequate because willful intent is involved, or can be involved, in both civil and criminal fraud. As a practical matter, criminal prosecution is usually limited to the more serious (in terms of dollars) cases.

In 1965, 625 individuals were convicted of federal income tax fraud in cases involving between 70 and 100 million dollars in unpaid taxes. Civil fraud penalties of 35 to 45 million dollars were

TABLE 12–1. COST OF MOTOR VEHICLE ACCIDENTS (IN MILLIONS OF DOLLARS)*			
	ALL ACCIDENTS	DEATHS IN WHICH ALCOHOL MAY BE A FACTOR	TOTAL – DRIVING UNDER THE INFLUENCE
Property damage	3,100		442
Medical expenses	550		78
Wage loss	2,400	765	889
Insurance overhead	2,850		406
Total	8,900	765	1,816

*From President's Commission on Law Enforcement and Administration of Justice: *Task Force Report: Crime and Its Impact — An Assessment.* Washington, D. C., U. S. Government Printing Office, 1967, p. 51. Reproduced by permission of the United States Department of Justice.

also assessed in these cases. However, no estimate exists for tax fraud that goes undetected and unprosecuted; nor is there an estimate of unreported taxable income. According to the commission, on the basis of a survey of 1959 returns, the Treasury Department estimated unreported taxable income of 24.4 billion dollars or 7 per cent of the total reportable income.

Abortion. A cost figure of 120 million dollars is reported for the crime of abortion under this category of "other crimes" (Figure 12–1). The trend in the United States during the past decade has been toward the decriminalization of abortion, and the 1974 Supreme Court decisions on abortion did a great deal to hasten this process. Until or unless the status quo is changed, either by constitutional amendment or by a reversal on the part of the Supreme Court, criminal prosecution for abortion in most jurisdictions in the United States is highly unlikely.

Illegal Goods and Services

Organized crime in this country became a large scale enterprise in the 1920's as a supplier of illegal goods and services: booze, beer, broads, and bets. Although many things have changed in a half century — the repeal of Prohibition removed organized crime from the liquor and beer business — gambling continues to be the chief source of revenue for organized crime. A report to the commission put the total annual profits at 6 to 7 billion dollars, according to the following breakdown:

1. Bookmakers (horseracing, elections, prize fights, etc.): ten billion dollar turnover; 3 billion dollar plus profit.
2. Numbers, lotteries, punchboard: 5 billion dollar turnover; 1.5 billion dollar plus profit.
3. Illegal dice games: 3.5 billion dollar turnover; 1 billion dollar plus profit.
4. Illegal professional card games: 1 billion dollar turnover; 300 million dollar plus profit.
5. Illegal coin machines (all types): 500 billion dollar turnover; 150 million dollar plus profit.

The second largest revenue source for organized crime is loan sharking ("shylocking"), "an immensely profitable business where interest rates vary from one to 150 per cent per week with 20 per cent being common for small borrowers" (President's Commission, p. 53). Estimates place the annual toll for loan sharking operations in the 1 billion dollar plus category.

Drugs and vice also contribute to the yearly take of organized crime, perhaps to the extent of more than a half billion dollars. It is interesting to note that the commission failed to include in its estimates the costs of unorganized crime, the losses incurred through extortion, and the infiltration of organized labor. Although these costs may be only a fraction in dollar values of the losses incurred through gambling, their indirect effects upon American business and labor far exceed in importance those of gambling, which is a voluntary undertaking.

Public Expenditures for Criminal Justice

Until 1968, the costs of law enforcement and the administration of criminal justice in the United States were borne chiefly by local and state governments throughout the country. Federal expenditures for these services were largely restricted to the agencies of government responsible for the investigation and prosecution of federal crimes, such as the Office of the Attorney General, the federal court system, and the United States Department of Justice. This situation changed, however, with the passage in 1968 of the Omnibus Crime Control and Safe Streets Act. This legislation made available to states and local governments a large and steadily increasing amount of federal support for law enforcement and criminal justice-related activities.

The commission's figures on public expenditures for law enforcement and the criminal justice system are based on the situation as it existed in 1966; at that time, the estimate for the total cost of their operations was $4,212,000,000. The lion's share of this figure was the $2,792,000,000 in expenditures for law enforcement made by the nearly 40,000 law enforcement agencies throughout the country. Salaries and wages accounted for approximately 85 to 90 per cent of these costs.

The second largest expense in the administration of criminal justice was for corrections, including parole, probation, and other rehabilitation programs, in addition to incarceration. Approximately 80 per cent of all local and state expenditures in the correctional area were for institutional costs.

The remaining expenses for prosecution, defense, and the courts totaled $386,000,000. It should be kept in mind that the majority of courts at all levels exercise both civil and criminal jurisdiction. Moreover, these estimates were made before the impact of court decisions on the right to counsel had begun to be felt throughout the criminal justice system; estimates made at the present time would reflect substantial increases at every level in the judicial system.

Private Costs Related to Crime

This category spans a wide range of private costs related to crime, including the expenses involved in "employing equipment, services, or techniques to prevent its occurrence and reduce its impact; the cost of insuring against losses that crime might entail, the costs of being a party or witness in a criminal proceeding" (President's Commission, p. 56) and the earnings of criminals and offenders. Burglar alarms and security equipment have become a major industry in the United States, with total revenues that are expected to reach nearly a half billion dollars by 1980. The growth in the security equipment industry has been paralleled by rapid increases in the size and variety of private protective agencies, guards, and other special personnel. While the 1960 census indicated a total labor force of more than a quarter of a million persons employed in these capacities, 1970 census figures showed that this number had nearly doubled in the 10 year period from 1960 to 1970. The commission's estimate of approximately 1.35 billion dollars for the costs involved in security services as of 1966 would have to be substantially increased to accommodate both inflation and the large increase in the numbers of people employed in protective services.

Insurance costs related to crime include both the expenses involved in the purchase of insurance, particularly in high risk areas, and the losses paid out by insurance companies as a result of claims made by victims of crime. As the commission points out:

> If a crime occurs the insured suffers no further loss because he is indemnified by the insurance company. From the standpoint of all insured individuals as a group and of society as a whole, however, the fact of insurance does not alter the amount of loss due to criminal acts. It merely distributes the loss among a large number of insured persons rather than allowing it to fall solely on the victim. This service of distribution does not come free, and those who take advantage of it must pay for it. Collectively, the costs of doing so is the overhead cost of the insurance, that is, not the amount of the premiums paid but the amount of premiums paid less the amount of losses indemnified. (p. 58)

The annual figure for the overhead costs for insurance against theft, including embezzlement and auto theft, and vandalism was set by the commission at 300 million dollars.

The commission concludes its report by deploring the inadequacy of available figures and other information concerning the economic impact of crime. In the decade that has elapsed since the publication of this report, there have been some improvements in the various reporting systems that constitute the principal source of information on the economic impact of crime. The need for computing this grim arithmetic grows year by year with the increase in the rate of crime in this country. As the commission notes, we need more accurate up-to-date information, "not only to furnish a better basis for assessing the nature and amounts of the various kinds of losses but also as a means for developing new and improved measures of control" (p. 59).

PSYCHOLOGICAL AND SOCIAL IMPACT OF CRIME

Measuring the impact of crime in terms of economic factors is apt to impress most people as being somewhat analogous to trying to assess the seriousness of an accident by adding up the total medical expenses involved. Money and property are tangible possessions, so the argument runs, that can be replaced, even though their loss may impose a crushing burden on those who are living on the edge of poverty. An economic assessment of the impact of crime has the advantage, however, of providing some kind of objective dimension of measurement. In this section, we shall be concerned with both the psychological and the social effects of crime on contemporary American society. These forces, although they involve subjective factors and intangibles, constitute the most serious aspects of the crime problem in the view of many authorities.

Psychological Impact of Crime on the Victim

In reporting crime, it is customary to distinguish between crimes against property and crimes against the person. However, such distinctions tend to ignore or minimize the fact that property crimes inevitably involve adverse effects upon the victim that go beyond the *observable* losses of goods or money. Bard and Ellison (1974) have provided an insightful analysis of burglary, armed robbery, assault and robbery, and rape that emphasizes the psychological consequences of such crimes for the victims.

Burglary. The psychological impact of burglary on the individual is often disregarded because the only visible consequences to the victim are property losses, which are often covered by insurance. However, what is not recognized is that people regard their homes or apartments as extensions of themselves. Each home is unique in that it represents the personality of the occupants, and when a home is burglarized, the victim is often far more upset over the intrusion of the burglar into the home than the loss of property, because this represents a violation of a part of the individual's self.* The intrusion is also upsetting because in an urban-industrial society, in which privacy is at a premium, the home is the only place that offers the individual security and an escape from the pressures of everyday life.

Armed robbery constitutes an even greater "violation of self." Not only does the victim lose his personal property, but he also is deprived of his self determination while the crime is in progress. During the robbery the victim's fate rests in the unpredictable hands of the robber. This experience of powerlessness can have a profound psychological effect.

Assault and robbery represent a further violation of the self, for in addition to the loss of self determination and personal property, an injury is inflicted on the body, which can be regarded as "the envelope of self." This injury not only causes physical pain but also has a traumatic psychological effect. As Bard and Ellison suggest (1974), "victims are left with the physical evidence reminding them that they were forced to surrender their autonomy and also the fact that they have been made to feel like less than adequate people . . . a visible reminder of their helplessness to protect or defend themselves" (p. 71).

Forcible rape is the ultimate violation of self, short of homicide. The offender not only deprives the victim of self determination, and often inflicts physical injury, but he also intrudes internally into the victim's body. So far as the victim is concerned, it makes no difference which of the body orifices is breached, because it is the forceful entry into the body that traumatizes the victim. As Bard and Ellison (1974) emphasize, this kind of forceful intrusion would have to be one of the most telling crises that a victim can sustain, particularly in view of the moral taboos that surround the sexual act. Thus, in many cases, although the rape victim is not physically injured, the psychological injury may be catastrophic.

---

*"The self is an abstract concept: sometimes called ego. It is the sum of what and who a person feels he is. A large part of concept of self involves the body and the way in which one feels about the body, but it also includes such extensions of self as clothing, automobile, and home. For example, this may be expressed in such ways as: 'that's just the sort of home I expect him to have' " (Bard and Ellison, 1974, p. 70).

Fear and its Consequences

Basic to any psychological or social reaction to crime is fear — a gut level reaction that produces marked changes in individual behavior. The President's Commission notes that "the core of public anxiety about the crime problem involves a concern for personal safety" (1967, p. 87). The most intense fear is exhibited toward the crimes that are least likely to occur: murder, assault, and forcible rape. Ironically enough, the perpetrator in a large number of such crimes is likely to be a family member, close friend, or personal acquaintance. Nevertheless, what people fear most is violence at the hands of a stranger. Says Conklin (1975):

> Fear of crime is fear of the stranger, the unknown person who commits an unpredictable and violent attack on a vulnerable and innocent citizen who is merely going about his regular business. The stranger is seen as intending harm and is indiscriminate in his selection of a victim, making it difficult for the victim to avoid him. The popular view of the criminal is that he is a stranger or an outsider, someone different from those who fear crime.... [T]he common view of the criminal as an outsider has important effects. It enhances the fear of crime. It also makes the reintegration of the ex-convict into society difficult, pushing him back into a life of crime and increasing the threat to society. (p. 7)*

As we shall see, fear of the unknown assailant figures prominently in both individual and collective responses to crime. Fear of the stranger generalizes to fear of strange places, and eventually the public streets themselves are seen as unsafe. When fear of public places reaches a peak, people react by avoiding those areas that are perceived as potentially hazardous. Consequently, the interruption of normal traffic in various sections of the town or city removes one of the deterrents to criminal activity in such areas, which thus become increasingly frequented by persons bent upon crime.

Individual Defensive Reactions to Crime

People may react defensively to their fear of crime in a variety of ways: by arming themselves; by installing electric security systems and intruder detection devices; by reducing contact with

---

*Reprinted with permission of Macmillan Publishing Co., Inc., from *The Impact of Crime* by J. E. Conklin. Copyright © 1975 by John E. Conklin.

others; and by avoiding situations in which they may be exposed to danger. In addition to these individual defense reactions to crime, groups of people within the community may take various collective measures in response to the fear of crime.

Firearms

It has been estimated that there is approximately one privately owned firearm for every person in the United States, and many of these guns were originally purchased for protection against crime. In addition to firearms, Mace, tear gas guns, and other incapacitating substances and devices have become commercially available to the general public and enjoy brisk sales. There are wide differences in attitude among the population toward the ownership and potential use of firearms in defense of the home. In the South, and particularly the Southeast, ownership of firearms is supported by a cultural ethos according to which defense of the home is not merely a prerogative but also a cultural obligation. By contrast, in the Northeast, social control is viewed as the functional responsibility of law enforcement agencies; the cultural ethos provides relatively little support for the concept of home defense. Nevertheless, these generalizations leave a great deal of room for individual variation in attitudes and values, and national reports do not indicate any great shortage of customers for guns in the North and Northeast.

Security Systems

As we noted earlier, burglar alarms and security systems have become a big business in the United States. More than 5000 companies are competing to capture the market, and it is expected that the alarm business will be a 500 million dollar enterprise by 1980. It is possible to spend as little as a few hundred dollars for a relatively simple installation or as much as several thousand dollars for a comprehensive system with a number of sophisticated components. In either case, what the customer buys primarily is peace of mind — and this is heavily stressed in the sales approach of all companies.

Conklin (1975) identifies three types of alarm systems currently in use in residential settings:

> Perimeter systems protect points of entry to the house. Space or area systems guard the interior areas with photo-electric or ultrasonic devices. A third type involves listening devices that detect intruders in the home. All systems connect to an alarm,

with a noise producing signal in the home (which depends on actions by neighbors who hear the alarm) or an alarm connected directly to a police station or a central security office. Silent alarms which alert remote centers allow the police to surprise the intruder and make an arrest; they also do not require action by neighbors, which is wise in light of widespread unwillingness to report crime and get involved in crime. Alarm systems do not offer perfect protection, since they often fail to function properly and may be circumvented by burglars. They also create the problem that many false alarms are sounded. One study found that 94 per cent of the alarms that were sounded did not involve an illegal entry. Another study discovered that only two per cent of sounded alarms in a two week period were valid; many were set off because of poor installation, by mistake, or to see how quickly the police would respond. Some alarms are too sensitive to the movement of the occupants of the house. Others need to be turned on and off to prevent them from sounding when they should not; sometimes the alarm will have been left off when a burglary occurs. Because of the problem of false alarms some communities now charge for excessive alarms. (pp. 116–117)*

A local alarm is designed to perform several functions. First, it should operate as an effective deterrent to the intusion. Second, it should alert the occupants of the house to the presence of an emergency situation. Third, it may elicit a call to the police from a cooperative neighbor who hears it and is willing to respond.

Mr. Walter O'Brien (1976) of Dictograph Security Systems, a leading company in the security industry, noted that many alarm companies indicate to prospective customers that they can tie the residential security system directly in with the police. According to Mr. O'Brien, in most urban areas this is no longer possible because law enforcement agencies cannot accommodate the large and growing number of tie-ins. In most cases, the tie-in is effected through a central station operated by, or on behalf of, the alarm company. In many instances, small answering services are engaged to expand the alarm company's capacity to handle these tie-ins. Mr. O'Brien observed that the caliber of individuals employed by such firms — young, inexperienced people who generally receive low wages — is not consistent with the kind of capability for prompt, effective action that an emergency situation demands.

The earliest type of tie-in alarm system was the Modularm. This system involves leasing a pair of telephone wires from a tele-

---

phone company that run from the protected premises to either a central station or to a police station, sheriff's office, or an answering service working on behalf of the alarm company. In the event that the wires are disrupted, a trouble tone is emitted that serves the same purpose as an actual alarm.

The second type of tie-in employs a taperecorded message that triggers the transmission of a number of messages to up to three telephone numbers. The problem with this arrangement is that if someone answers the phone and puts it on hold, the tape recording spins off without an actual listener receiving the message.

The third and most modern type of equipment for tie-ins is the Electronic Digital Communicator. This piece of electronic dialing equipment employs the same technology that the large telephone companies incorporate in their complex systems with the capability of searching out a circuit that can reach the desired number. A call to Los Angeles at peak load time, for example, might reach the number via Portland or Seattle. The Electronic Digital Communicator provides this kind of versatility for the routing of security alarms.

The basic requirement for residential security is a system for the detection of perimeter intrusion, i.e., unauthorized entry through doors or windows. Many alarm companies have augmented protection of doors and windows by the utilization of interior devices — ultrasonic detectors, photoelectric beams, sound detection equipment — of a rather sophisticated type. Mr. O'Brien questions the wisdom of using such equipment in the average home. Apart from their expense, devices or systems that are extremely sensitive also tend to produce a high rate of false alarms. In their place, O'Brien recommends the use of relatively inexpensive interior traps — alarm devices that can be attached to interior doors, or pressure-sensitive units that can be placed under runners or carpeting on stairs.

For every innovation in security technology, there are attempts on the part of criminals to keep abreast of the advance — or surpass it, if possible. New tools can be put to uses that were not intended by the manufacturer. For example, the cordless battery-powered drill has not only proved a boon to the home handyman; it has also been adopted enthusiastically by burglars, who have discovered that even a sturdy door can be opened easily by drilling a series of holes in a square or rectangular pattern and kicking in the panel. In New York and New Jersey, entries have been made to both residential and commercial buildings through the roof; and in Washington, D. C., a number of successful burglaries were effected by chipping the mortar from between cinder blocks and removing the blocks.

Collective Reactions to Crime

Unless one is prepared to spend the rest of one's life in a steel vault, there are rapidly diminishing returns to an investment in even the most sophisticated alarm equipment. Given these and other considerations, many communities have chosen to take a *proactive* approach to the matter of self protection. While recognizing the value and importance of security measures such as those just mentioned, their efforts have emphasized organized, collective community activities in support of criminal justice agencies and operations.

Crime Reporting

It is assumed that the effectiveness of local law enforcement efforts can be increased to a significant degree by a citizenry alert to report: (1) crimes in the process of being committed; (2) information that might help in the solution of crimes; and (3) suspicious-looking persons and situations. This is an activity that lends itself to both individual and collective efforts. Operating under a variety of names such as Citizen Alert, Crime Alert, Crime Stop, Block Watch, and so on, citizen organizations have conducted campaigns to enlist volunteers in crime reporting.

In Buffalo, New York, a program called Community Radio Watch (CRW) is supported by the efforts of 46 area firms that employ over 2500 drivers. These companies operate vehicles with two-way radios. Drivers are instructed to report any kind of emergency (fire, accident, or crime) to their dispatchers, who transmit the messages to the appropriate authorities. CRW thus provides "a vast survelliance and communications network covering the entire county" (National Advisory Commission, 1974, p. 41).

In Battle Creek, Michigan, a citizen who reports a planned crime or who witnesses and reports a crime being committed may receive a cash award ranging from $50 to $1000. The Silent Observer Program, initiated in 1970 by the Battle Creek Area Chamber of Commerce, raises funds for the cash awards by the sale of posters that advertise the program and also from families of crime victims. In *CONtact* (1975) the program was described as follows:

> Any citizen witnessing a crime can call the police and have the reported information recorded on a two-part form. The individual is then assigned a code number. One form sheet is sent to the chamber and the other is filed. If the offender is found guilty, the prosecutor notifies the chamber. The chamber then

*notifies the local newspapers of the crime and the decision. The
reader then calls the chamber, tells that he was the silent observer
and gives his code number. He never needs to reveal his name.
Three non-law enforcement personnel determine if the silent
observer is eligible for the award.* (p. 1)

Within the first several weeks of its operation, the program produced five arrests. In subsequent years, many civic-minded people
refused to accept any reward for the information they were able
to supply to the police. TIP ("Turn in a Pusher") programs are
active in many major cities, and are aimed at identification of
drug dealers.

Property Identification

In many parts of the country, law enforcement agencies have
developed programs to encourage citizens to register personal
property with the police. Some agencies provide inscribing tools
for community residents to use in marking their personal belong-
ings with their social security number or operator's license number.
Each household is then supplied with a large display sticker, indicating that the residence is part of a theft-guard project, and a
master list of identification numbers is filed with the police department. One of the most successful programs of this kind was
carried out in Monterey Park, California. Property registration
produced a dramatic decrease in the burglaries that had plagued
area residents before the program was initiated.

Neighborhood Security

Volunteer safety patrols have been initiated by residents of
high-crime areas in a number of large cities. In New York, for
example, the city's Housing Authority Tenant Patrol program has
more than 11,000 members who provide security coverage for
hundreds of buildings. Equipped with phones or walkie-talkies,
local tenant patrols augment the regular police surveillance of large
housing projects. The Community Vigilance Program in Philadelphia supplies volunteer wardens who patrol designated areas in
two-man teams. The wardens are recruited and trained by the
police department, and they contribute a minimum of three hours
per week. Although they are not permitted to make arrests, they
patrol their assigned areas in automobiles and report all violations
to a base station, which relays the reports to the police.

Some idea of the range of surveillance provided by volunteer
safety patrols is conveyed by the National Advisory Commision's

(1974) description of the activities of CHEC (Citizens Helping Eliminate Crime), a group organized by the Sertoma Club of Lima, Ohio, in cooperation with local law enforcement authorities:

> Each participant is instructed to watch for a stranger entering a neighbor's house when it is unoccupied; a scream heard anywhere; strangers or strange cars in the neighborhood, school area, and parks; broken or open windows or doors; salesmen attempting to force entrance into a home; offers of merchandise at extremely low prices; anyone loitering in a parked car; persons leaving one car and driving off in another; anyone removing accessories, license plates, or gasoline from cars; anyone in a store concealing merchandise on their person; persons seen leaving or entering a business place after hours; the sound of breaking glass or other loud explosive noise; any vehicle parked with motor running; persons walking down the street peering into each parked car; persons involved in a fight; display of weapons, guns, and knives; strangers carrying appliances, household goods, luggage, or other bundles from a neighbor's home; persons loitering in secluded areas; and injured persons. (p. 41)

But security patrols do not confine their activities to observing illegal or suspicious behavior. They watch out for and report safety hazards, such as malfunctioning traffic signals and inadequate street lighting; they look in on community residents who are elderly or sick; and on occasion they even will shovel snow from sidewalks.

The efforts of volunteers in neighborhood security patrols are augmented by the contributions of citizens who have joined auxiliary or police reserve units. In New York City, each precinct has an auxiliary police unit composed of volunteers who serve without compensation. Applicants are selected on the basis of requirements that are not appreciably different from those used in the selection of academy recruits, and they undergo an intensive 10 week course of training. Auxiliary police members are supplied with uniforms and equipment but are usually not permitted to carry firearms. They have arrest powers and may use physical force when necessary. Members of the auxiliary units are on duty three nights per week and must average eight hours of duty per month.

CRIME AND THE PUBLIC

Criminologists, as we observed in Chapter 10, have attributed crime to a variety of causes, including biological predispositions, psychological factors, and societal arrangements. However, few criminologists, Conklin (1975) notes, have taken a systematic look at the contribution of the public itself to the crime problem in the United States. As we have already seen, people's reactions to crime can reinforce and aggravate this problem. Says Conklin:

> Crime generates suspicion and distrust, thereby weakening the social fabric of a community. Viewing ex-convicts as outsiders makes it difficult for them to become reintegrated into society, forcing them back to a life of crime and enhancing the crime problem. Crime leads people to avoid others and to take self-protective security measures, both of which actions erect barriers between the residents of a community. By diminishing social interaction and reducing natural surveillance of public areas, informal social control over potential criminals may be weakened and crime rates may increase. (p. 248)*

Faced with the inability of law enforcement agencies to curb the steady increase in crime, people accuse the police of ineffectiveness and become reluctant to involve themselves in crime prevention, even to the extent of reporting crimes to the police. Thus a vicious circle is initiated: retreatism and defensiveness on the part of the community lead to a decrease in the risk of apprehension for the offender, with the inevitable result that the offender is emboldened to commit more crimes.

Conklin acknowledges that a closely knit community can probably achieve a significant reduction in street crime. He believes that:

> [S]treet crime would decline if interpersonal relations were closer, if interaction among the residents of a community were more frequent, and if social bonds were stronger. A sense of responsibility for other citizens and for the community as a whole would increase individuals' willingness to report crime and the likelihood of their intervention in a crime in progress. Greater willingness of community residents to report crime to the police might also obviate the need for civilian police patrols. More interaction in public places and more traffic on the sidewalks would increase surveillance of the places where people now fear to go. More intense social ties would reinforce surveillance with a willingness to take action against offenders. (p. 249)*

But Conklin also recognizes that informal social control poses a definite threat to the "diversity of behavior that exists in a

---

*Reprinted with permission of Macmillan Publishing Co., Inc., from *The Impact of Crime* by J. E. Conklin. Copyright © 1975 by John E. Conklin.

pluralistic society" such as ours, despite its beneficial effects on the incidence of violent crime.

Most Americans view with abhorrence an anthill society like that of Communist China, where drab masses of boiler-suited citizens turn out with brooms and dustpans to sweep the streets, in response to a summons from the block leader, despite evidence that one's life and property are probably a great deal safer in Peking than in Chicago. In terms of these considerations, crime is part of the price we have to pay in exchange for enjoying our diversity of behavior and pluralistic society. Until or unless our tolerance level for crime is exceeded and we are willing to relinquish some of our cherished personal freedom in return for stricter forms of social control, we shall continue to have the kinds of crime and criminals for which we are willing to pay.

SUMMARY

In this chapter we have reviewed some of the attempts that have been made to assess the economic impact of crime in the United States. These crude estimates of what crime costs in dollars and cents are derived from a wide variety of sources and are subject to many shortcomings and weaknesses, but even by the most conservative criteria they convey a picture of staggering financial loss for the country as a whole. With regard to the social and psychological impact of crime, we have noted that fear of crime gives rise to individual defensive reactions, including a readiness to buy and keep firearms in one's residence and place of work or business and a growing receptivity toward electronic security devices. Collective reactions to the threat of crime have taken the form of volunteer activity in support of law enforcement agencies, but such activity is largely restricted to a minority of persons in any given community. For most Americans, the principal mode of response to the crime problem is to avoid areas that are perceived as high in potential risk.

REVIEW

Find the answers to the following questions in the text:

1. What was the major contribution of the Omnibus Crime Control and Safe Streets Act to the improvement of the criminal justice system in the United States?

2. Which type of crime(s) are most feared by the American people?

3. How are direct and indirect costs of crime distinguished?

4. What category of crime is identified by some criminologists as most frequently committed?

5. Who are the likeliest victims of fraud?

6. Describe some of the alarm systems currently used in residential settings?

7. Why do the authors maintain that security systems for the home are subject to diminishing returns with respect to the size of the investments?

8. What are three important things that citizens can do to assist the police? Why don't they do them more often?

9. What are the major differences between security patrols and auxiliary police units?

10. Why does inscribing property help to deter thieves from stealing it? What should be done in connection with inscribing?

TERMS TO IDENTIFY AND REMEMBER:

fraud	Omnibus Crime Control and Safe Streets Act
business theft	Electronic Digital Communicator
perimeter alarm systems	Silent Observer Program
area alarm system	CHEC
Modularm	TIP

REFERENCES

Bard, M., and Ellison, K.: Crisis intervention and investigation of forcible rape. Police Chief, May, 1974, pp. 68–74.

Conklin, J. E.: *The Impact of Crime.* New York, Macmillan, Inc., 1975.

Federal Bureau of Investigation: *Uniform Crime Reports: 1964.* Washington, D. C., U. S. Government Printing Office, 1965.

Gould, L. C.: Crime and its impact in an affluent society. *In* Douglas, J. D. (ed.): *Crime and Justice in American Society.* Indianapolis, The Bobbs-Merrill Co., Inc., 1971.

National Advisory Commission on Criminal Justice Standards and Goals: *A Call for Citizen Action.* Washington, D. C., U. S. Government Printing Office, 1974.

O'Brien, W. E.: Residential burglar alarms and security systems. Personal interview, Rockville, Maryland, February, 1976.

President's Commission on Law Enforcement and Administration of Justice: *The Challenge of Crime in a Free Society.* Washington, D. C., U. S. Government Printing Office, 1967.

President's Commission on Law Enforcement and Administration of Justice: *Task Force Report: Crime and Its Impact — An Assessement.* Washington, D. C., U. S. Government Printing Office, 1967.

Sutherland, E. H., and Cressey, D. R.: *Introduction to Criminology.* Philadelphia, J. B. Lippincott, Inc., 1974.

The Silent Observer program. *CONtact 12*:1, 1975.

NAME INDEX

SUBJECT INDEX